Creating Safe and Supp
Learning Environments

The importance of creating safe spaces for lesbian, gay, bisexual, transgender, and questioning (LGBTQ) students in the school environment cannot be overstated. It is one of the most prominent issues facing school professionals today, and its success has lasting, positive effects on the entire student body. Drawing on the expertise of researchers and practitioners, *Creating Safe and Supportive Learning Environments* provides a comprehensive examination of the topics most relevant for school professionals. The first section lays out the theoretical foundation and background school professionals need to understand the social and political trends that impact LGBTQ individuals, the development of sexual orientation and gender identity, risk and resilience factors, and the intersection of LGBTQ identity with other aspects of diversity. The second section explores topics critical for the development of safe, supportive school environments, including understanding legal and ethical mandates, training school personnel, addressing bullying and harassment, and developing inclusive classrooms. Special topics related to counseling LGBTQ students, supporting families of LGBTQ students, becoming an ally and advocate in the schools, and connecting with community resources are also covered.

Emily S. Fisher, PhD, is an associate professor in the school psychology program at Loyola Marymount University in Los Angeles, California.

Karen Komosa-Hawkins, PhD, is an assistant professor in the counseling program at Loyola Marymount University in Los Angeles, California.

Creating Safe and Supportive Learning Environments

A Guide for Working with Lesbian, Gay, Bisexual, Transgender, and Questioning Youth and Families

Edited by
Emily S. Fisher and
Karen Komosa-Hawkins

Routledge
Taylor & Francis Group

NEW YORK AND LONDON

First published 2013
by Routledge
711 Third Avenue, New York, NY 10017

Simultaneously published in the UK
by Routledge
27 Church Road, Hove, East Sussex BN3 2FA

Library of Congress Cataloging in Publication Data
Creating safe and supportive learning environments : a guide for working with lesbian, gay, bisexual, transgender, and questioning youth, and families / edited by Emily S. Fisher and Karen Komosa-Hawkins.
    p. cm.
    Includes bibliographical references and index.
    1. Homophobia in schools—Prevention.   2. Sexual minority students.
    3. Sexual minority parents.   I. Fisher, Emily S., 1974-editor of
    compilation.   II. Chiasson, Judy. Putting sexual orientation and gender
    identity in context.
    LC212.8.C74 2013
    370.86'64—dc23
                                                            2012040267

ISBN: 978-0-415-89611-5 (hbk)
ISBN: 978-0-415-81917-6 (pbk)
ISBN: 978-0-203-80763-7 (ebk)

Typeset in Minion
by RefineCatch Limited, Bungay, Suffolk

Contents

About the Contributors

Melanie Elyse Brewster, PhD, is an assistant professor of psychology and education at Columbia University and earned her doctorate from the University of Florida. She teaches courses on psychotherapy, vocational theories and career counseling, and diversity/social justice. Her research focuses on the experiences of marginalized groups and examines how experiences of discrimination, prejudice, and stigma may shape the mental health of minority group members. Dr. Brewster also examines potential resilience factors that may promote the mental health of marginalized individuals.

Douglas Bruce, PhD, MSW, is an assistant professor in the department of health sciences at DePaul University. He has extensive experience in mixed methods behavioral research and evaluation of HIV education, prevention, and treatment programs in the US, the Caribbean, and India. His research investigates how identity development and social processes such as stigma, marginalization, and migration function as determinants of health behavior among young gay and bisexual men. His work also focuses on the secondary prevention needs of young men living with HIV/AIDS.

Ashley Candelaria, MS, is a doctoral student in the school psychology program at the University of Kentucky. Her research interests include fostering positive mental health outcomes through school-based intervention, with an emphasis on strengthening school-based interventions for grieving youth.

Stuart F. Chen-Hayes, PhD, is associate professor and program coordinator for counselor education/school counseling at Lehman College of the City University of New York. His research interests are LGBTQ issues in schools and families, transforming school counseling, and college access/readiness/success counseling. He has written 50 refereed articles and book chapters and given 225 professional presentations. He is co-author of the forthcoming *101 Solutions for School Counselors and Leaders in Challenging Times* (Corwin Press). He is a consultant with the National Center for Transforming School Counseling and the National Association for College Admission Counseling.

Judy Chiasson, PhD, is a member of the Human Relations, Diversity and Equity Office of the Los Angeles Unified School District. She advocates for safe and affirming campuses for lesbian, gay, bisexual and transgender students, staff, and families by creating inclusive policies, practices, and curriculum designed to reduce bias, bullying, hazing, and intergroup bias. She believes that social justice is integral to education and partners with local and national organizations to build social competency in school communities.

Cirleen DeBlaere, PhD, is an assistant professor of counseling psychology at Lehigh University. She currently teaches courses on research methodology and writing, counseling skills, and professional ethics. Dr. DeBlaere's research examines the experiences of individuals with multiple and intersecting marginalized identities. To date, her research has focused on the links of multiple discrimination experiences to mental health. She also investigates potential moderating and mediating variables in the discrimination–mental health relation to identify points of intervention and inform the development of mental health-promoting strategies for multiple marginalized individuals.

Dennis M. Emano, PhD, is an associate professor and mental health counselor at the College of DuPage. Dr. Emano has extensive clinical experience working with diverse populations, including LGBTQ individuals, in elementary schools, university counseling centers, community mental health centers, and hospitals. In addition to working with the LGBTQ Advocacy Team on campus, Dr. Emano helps conduct Safe Zone trainings for staff and faculty. His research focuses on LGBTQ communities and communities of color.

Dorothy L. Espelage, PhD, is a professor in the department of educational psychology at the University of Illinois, Urbana-Champaign. Dr. Espelage has conducted research on bullying, homophobic teasing, sexual harassment, and dating violence for the last 20 years. She has over 100 research publications and four books. She is Associate Editor of the *Journal of Counseling Psychology*, Vice-President of Division E of the American Educational Research Association, and co-Chair of the *National Partnership to End Interpersonal Violence*. She is PI on a CDC-funded randomized clinical trial of a prevention program in 36 middle schools to reduce bullying and sexual violence.

Alicia L. Fedewa, PhD, is an assistant professor in the school psychology program at the University of Kentucky. Her research interests include the relationship between curricular physical activity and children's academic, behavioral, and mental health outcomes; teacher training programs for implementing physical activity in classrooms; and effects of systems-wide diversity training programs for Lesbian, Gay, and Bisexual (LGB) youth and children with LGB parents.

Emily S. Fisher, PhD, is an associate professor in the School Psychology Program at Loyola Marymount University. She received her doctorate in Counseling/Clinical/School Psychology from the University of California, Santa Barbara. Dr. Fisher's research focuses on supporting students' social and emotional development, working with teachers to promote inclusive and culturally responsive classroom practices, and helping school personnel work effectively with LGBTQ students and families. Dr. Fisher co-authored the book *Responsive School Practices to Support Lesbian, Gay, Bisexual, Transgender, and Questioning Students and Families* as part of Routledge's School-Based Practice in Action Series. Dr. Fisher provides consultation and trainings for schools, districts, and professional organizations.

Grady L. Garner, Jr., PhD, is core faculty in the clinical PsyD program in military psychology at the Adler School of Professional Psychology. Dr. Garner's clinical and research efforts focus on improving mental health outcomes for socially marginalized individuals (youth and adults) and LGBTQ uniformed military service members. Dr. Garner co-chairs APA's Division 44 Committee on Bisexual Issues, which is dedicated to deepening the understanding of and advocacy for bisexual individuals.

Emily A. Greytak, PhD, is a senior research associate at the Gay, Lesbian & Straight Education Network (GLSEN), a national non-profit organization focusing on LGBT issues in K-12 education. Her research interests include the experiences of transgender and gender nonconforming youth, the capacity of school personnel to address LGBT issues, and the evaluation of training programs. Prior to working at GLSEN, she conducted research for a variety of non-profit and educational institutions, such as the Anti-Defamation League, the National Sexual Violence Resource Center, and the School District of Philadelphia. She also currently serves on the Board of Directors for SAFER (Students Active For Ending Rape).

Gary W. Harper, PhD, MPH, is a professor in the department of health behavior and health education at the University of Michigan's School of Public Health. Dr. Harper's research and community intervention work focus on the HIV prevention and sexual health promotion needs of gay/bisexual male adolescents of color. He is a former chair of the American Psychological Association's Committee on Lesbian, Gay, and Bisexual Concerns, and has published findings from his federally funded LGBT research in multiple peer-reviewed journals. Dr. Harper also has received several awards for his commitment to ethnic minority concerns in LGBT research, practice, and training.

Omar B. Jamil, PhD, is a researcher at the University of Michigan and a lecturer at the University of Illinois at Chicago. His research interests focus on the sexual and ethnic identity development and integration processes among gay/bisexual/questioning male ethnic minority adolescents. His research also examines the link between identity development and HIV risk behaviors. He is currently working with Dr. Gary Harper at the University of Michigan to develop a culturally and developmentally specific HIV prevention intervention for young black gay/bisexual/questioning men.

Kelly S. Kennedy, PhD, is an assistant professor in the school psychology and school counseling programs at Chapman University in Orange, California. Her research focuses on improving school-based practices in multicultural competence, counseling, and data-based decision making. Dr. Kennedy is a member of the Consortium for the Advancement of School Psychology in Vietnam (CASP-V), is the editor for the *Trainer's Forum* and an associate editor of *Contemporary School Psychology*. She is co-author of *Responsive School Practices to Support Lesbian, Gay, Bisexual, Transgender, and Questioning Students and Families*.

Karen Komosa-Hawkins, PhD, is an assistant professor in Loyola Marymount University's Counseling Program. She received her doctorate in School Psychology from Loyola University Chicago. Dr. Komosa-Hawkins is a credentialed school psychologist and licensed educational psychologist. She has worked within school and community settings serving primarily underprivileged and marginalized children, adolescents, and families. Dr. Komosa-Hawkins teaches courses on prevention and intervention and legal and ethical issues. Her research interests include social-emotional learning, culturally competent practices, prevention, mentoring, and resilience. Dr. Komosa-Hawkins also provides training to school-based professionals on how to create safe and supportive school environments for LGBTQ youth and families.

Joseph G. Kosciw, PhD, is the Gay, Lesbian & Straight Education Network's (GLSEN) senior director of research and strategic initiatives. He trained as a family therapist and has worked as a school counselor and psychoeducational consultant in K-12 schools. Dr. Kosciw has been conducting community-based research for over 15 years, program evaluations for non-profit social service organizations and for local and state government, including Gay Men's Health Crisis, Safe Horizons, the New York City Mayor's Office for AIDS Policy Coordination and the New York State Department of Health. He serves on the editorial boards of the *Journal of LGBT Youth* and the *Journal of Youth and Adolescence*.

Robert A. McGarry, EdD, is the director of education for GLSEN. Dr. McGarry is a former school district administrator with experience leading curriculum development on both the local and state level. His professional and academic passions, exemplified by his doctoral thesis: *Troubling Teachable Moments: Initiating Teacher Discourse on Homophobic Speech*, brought him to GLSEN where he guides the development of evidence-based educator resources and serves as a spokesperson on LGBT issues in K-12 schools.

Asaf Orr is a staff attorney at the National Center for Lesbian Rights and works on issues related to families and youth. He began his career as a Tom Steel Fellow at a non-profit legal services organization, where he directed a project that represents youth in education-related matters who are denied an education on the basis of their sexual orientation or gender identity. In addition to representing clients, Mr. Orr also provides trainings to students, parents, educators, health care providers, and lawyers on the rights of LGBTQ youth in schools. He has provided those trainings in California and around the country.

Mrinalini A. Rao is a doctoral candidate of counseling psychology in the department of educational psychology at the University of Illinois, Urbana-Champaign. Her research interests include assessing the impact of peer victimization on psychological outcomes among early adolescents through rigorous longitudinal modeling.

Caitlin Ryan, PhD, is a clinical social worker who has worked on LGBT health and mental health for nearly 40 years. She is practitioner (school and community settings), educator and researcher whose work on LGBT health has shaped policy and practice for LGBT youth and adults. She directs the Family Acceptance Project at San Francisco State University—the first research, education, intervention, and policy project—to help ethnically and religiously diverse families support their LGBT children. She and her team are developing a new family model of wellness, prevention and care for LGBT children and adolescents, based on this research.

Ronni Sanlo, EdD, is a retired professor in higher education/director emeritus of the UCLA LGBT Center. Her consultation, research, and many publications focus on sexual-orientation issues in higher education. Dr. Sanlo was the founding chair of the Consortium of Higher Education LGBT Resource Professionals, and is the originator of the award-winning Lavender Graduation, a commencement event that celebrates the lives and achievements of graduating LGBT college students. Dr. Sanlo lives in Palm Desert, CA, where she directs her company, Purple Books Publishing, and plays rotten but passionate golf.

G. Thomas Schanding, Jr., PhD, is a licensed specialist in school psychology with Sheldon Independent School District and licensed psychologist in Houston, Texas. Dr. Schanding has taught at the University of Houston and worked in early childhood programs and medical settings. His research interests center around applied behavior analysis, assessment and intervention of childhood emotional/behavioral disorders, universal screening procedures, and multicultural issues, with a focus on LGBTQ youth. Dr. Schanding previously served as the chair of the National Association of School Psychologists' LGBTQ Committee and currently volunteers with the Gay Lesbian Straight Education Network-Houston Chapter to end anti-LGBTQ harassment in schools.

Anneliese A. Singh, PhD, is an associate professor in the department of counseling and human development services at the University of Georgia. Her research, advocacy, and clinical practice focus on the resilience of historically marginalized groups, such as transgender youth and adults, South Asian women survivors of child sexual abuse, and queer people of color. Dr. Singh is the past president of the Association of LGBT Issues in Counseling. Dr. Singh is also a safe schools activist and co-founded the Georgia Safe Schools Coalition, where she works with LGBTQ youth at the intersection of race/ethnicity, social class, and disability amongst others. She is the recipient of over 11 awards for her integration of research, practice, and social justice change.

Joy S. Whitman, PhD, is an associate professor in the counseling program at DePaul University. She received her doctorate in counseling psychology from West Virginia University. She currently serves as the chair in the department of counseling and special education and teaches introductory and theories courses in counseling. Dr. Whitman is the governing council representative for the Association for Lesbian, Gay, Bisexual, and Transgender Issues in Counseling. Her research is focused on training counselors to provide affirmative therapeutic treatment to lesbian, gay, bisexual, and transgender clients and students. She also maintains a small private practice, serving lesbian, bisexual, and gay clients.

Part I
Theoretical Foundations and Background

1 Supporting Lesbian, Gay, Bisexual, Transgender, and Questioning Students and Families

Emily S. Fisher

Today's schools are faced with many responsibilities that are above and beyond, yet related to, academics; they also must address students' social, emotional, and behavioral development. School professionals are expected to support all of these aspects of students' development, whether in the classroom, cafeteria, or counselor's office. Few topics in the school system elicit as strong a response from individuals in the school community as discussions related to sex, sexuality, and gender nonconformity. Feelings about these topics draw on people's family background and upbringing, personal experiences, religious beliefs, political orientation, and myriad other factors that shape one's morals and values. Some may think that these conversations have no place in the schools, but students who identify as or are identified by others as lesbian, gay, bisexual, transgender, or questioning (LGBTQ) are at a significantly increased risk for academic, social, and emotional problems related to experiences of bullying, harassment, and discrimination at school. Similarly, parents who identify as lesbian, gay, bisexual, or transgender (LGBT) and their children report high levels of harassment and discrimination in the school system. Engaging in conversations about the topics of sex, sexuality, and gender nonconformity may cause discomfort and disagreement for some members of the school community, but these discussions are necessary first steps in making schools safe places where all students can learn, grow, develop, and maximize their potential.

Given that 10–20% of teenagers report engaging in some type of same-gender sexual experience (Eisenberg & Resnick, 2006; McFarland & Dupuis, 2003), it is highly likely that there are students in every secondary school who identify as lesbian, gay, bisexual, or questioning (LGBQ). Additionally, at some schools, there will be students who identify as transgender or engage in gender nonconforming behaviors. LGBTQ students report high levels of physical harassment, verbal harassment, and feelings of being unsafe at school because of their sexual orientation (Kosciw, Diaz, & Greytak, 2008). These experiences of discrimination at school, along with potentially negative experiences in family and community contexts, interact with the normal tumultuousness and stress of adolescence to place LGBTQ students at increased risk for substance abuse, encounters with law enforcement, depression, and suicide (Crothers, 2007; Eisenberg & Resnick, 2006; Espelage et al., 2008; Savin-Williams, 1994, 2001).

Families headed by LGBT parents also should be given consideration by the school community, as it is estimated that there are more than seven million children being raised in LGBT-headed households (Kosciw & Diaz, 2008). Given that it is commonly accepted that parental involvement in children's schooling is beneficial, and that it has been found that LGBT parents are highly involved in their children's education (Kosciw & Diaz, 2008), it is important for schools to implement processes that help all families feel welcome. Additionally, children from households headed by LGBT parents often experience feelings of invisibility, bullying, and harassment similar to that of students who identify as LGBTQ, and these students often are targeted because of their perceived sexual orientation and the sexual orientation of their parents (Fox, 2007; Kosciw & Diaz, 2008).

The experts who have contributed to this book make a strong case for all students to have their right to an educational environment free of harassment, bullying, and violence protected. Furthermore, it is the legal, ethical, and moral responsibility of every member of the school community to contribute to the education, growth, and development of all students. This book provides information for school professionals to help them create positive school environments that are supportive and inclusive of LGBTQ students and families.

Intended Audience

Every member of the school community must be held to the standard of equitable and ethical treatment of students. In a time when information is widely available, school professionals will find high quality resources to educate themselves and to address overt and covert forms of discrimination and prejudice within the school system. It is the responsibility of school professionals to be fully informed and equipped to not only prevent problems whenever possible, but also to respond appropriately when problems arise.

Administrators

In public schools, educators do not get to choose who they teach, and they must provide equal access to all aspects of the educational program for all students regardless of the educators' personal beliefs. School administrators are critical in guiding efforts to make schools safe, responsive, and inclusive for LGBTQ students and families. As the leaders of schools, administrators are charged with the task of implementing state and local laws and policies (and in the absence of such, creating site-level policies to address important issues). Additionally, administrators set the tone for the school community when it comes to communicating expectations for the treatment of LGBTQ students and families. Without support from administrators and other key stakeholders, school-wide efforts to ensure safe educational environments and inclusive practices will be met with limited success (Ervin & Schaughency, 2008). It has been suggested that school administrators take a proactive role in ensuring that schools are meeting the needs of LGBTQ students (Szalacha, 2003), as "good schools make deliberate attempts to shape school culture in positive directions" (Goodenow, Szalacha, & Westheimer, 2006, p. 575). Additionally, administrators may be found legally liable in instances when they do not act to ensure that LGBTQ students are granted equal access to safe schools (McFarland & Dupuis, 2003).

There are several key considerations for administrators in creating school environments to support LGBTQ students and families. First, administrators need to familiarize themselves with federal, state, and local policies related to the protection of LGBTQ students and families (Young & Mendez, 2003). Next, administrators should interpret these policies and create guidelines for how school personnel are expected to respond to bullying and harassment targeting LGBTQ students and the disciplinary action to be taken (Kosciw, Diaz, & Greytak, 2008; McFarland & Dupuis, 2003). Third, administrators can ensure that all school personnel receive professional development to create a common understanding of the needs of LGBTQ students and families and to teach them about school policies and expectations (Young & Mendez, 2003). Finally, administrators can enlist school psychologists, school counselors, and other school-based mental health professionals to help develop appropriate prevention and intervention programming to support LGBTQ students and students with LGBT family members (Crothers, 2007; Young & Mendez, 2003).

Teachers and Teaching Assistants

As the school professionals who spend the most time in direct contact with students, teachers and teaching assistants play a critical role in the experiences that LGBTQ students have in school. When LGBTQ students experience higher levels of supportiveness from teachers, they are more likely to have positive attitudes towards school and experience an overall greater sense of well being (Murdock & Bolch, 2005). Because teachers and teaching assistants are on the "front line" in the school (in classrooms, hallways, lunchroom, yard, etc.), they are most likely to hear derogatory comments being made, witness acts of harassment or bullying, and be approached by students who are victims or witnesses of bullying. At the same time, teachers and assistants are in the best position to intervene immediately when harassment and bullying occur and to refer victims and perpetrators to administrators for disciplinary action and to school-based mental health professionals for counseling, as appropriate.

Along with administrators, teachers work within district guidelines to plan and implement curriculum in all academic areas. Although there has been much attention paid to the importance of making curriculum more inclusive and responsive to learners from diverse backgrounds, the "lives, stories, contributions, and existence" (Chan, 1996, p. 22) of LGBTQ students and families typically are excluded from curriculum. Teachers, who are knowledgeable about students' developmental levels, can work to integrate images of LGBTQ individuals into the classroom curriculum through books and activities and, related to this, can create an atmosphere that is welcoming and inclusive of LGBT-headed families.

School-Based Mental Health Professionals

School psychologists, school counselors, and other mental health professionals working in the schools are in a unique position to promote school success for all students, particularly those at risk for academic, social, and emotional difficulties, including those who identify as LGBTQ. These school professionals can provide indirect support to LGBTQ students and families by working with school professionals, such as advising administrators in the development of policies and procedures, providing training and staff development activities for teachers and other stakeholders within the school community, and consulting with teachers to establish inclusive and responsive classrooms and curriculum (Crothers, 2007; DePaul, Walsh, & Dam, 2009; Fisher & Kennedy,

2012; Fisher et al., 2008). School-based mental health professionals also can directly support LGBTQ students by providing prevention, intervention, and counseling services for those students at risk for and already experiencing difficulties at school, as well as working with students who perpetrate bullying and harassment (Crothers, 2007; DePaul, et al., 2009; Fisher & Kennedy, 2012; Fisher et al., 2008; Whitman, Horn, & Boyd, 2007).

Scope of the Book

Drawing on the expertise of researchers and practitioners, this book provides a comprehensive examination of topics most relevant for school professionals related to LGBTQ students and LGBT-headed families. The book is divided into two sections. The first section provides the theoretical foundation and background school professionals need to work effectively with LGBTQ students and families. In Chapter 2, Judy Chiasson and Ronni Sanlo review historical and contemporary social and political trends impacting LGBTQ individuals. In Chapter 3, Omar B. Jamil, Gary W. Harper, and Douglas Bruce explore the development of sexual orientation and gender identity. Next, from a strengths perspective, Karen Komosa-Hawkins and G. Thomas Schanding Jr. offer an in depth review of risk and protective factors for LGBTQ individuals across contexts in Chapter 4, and Anneliese A. Singh discusses the unique experiences and needs of transgender and intersex students in Chapter 5. In the final chapter in this section, Chapter 6, Cirleen DeBlaere and Melanie Brewster examine the intersection of LGBTQ identity and other aspects of diversity.

   With this deeper understanding of the background and context, the second section of this book then explores topics critical for the development of safe, supportive school environments for LGBTQ individuals. In Chapter 7, Asaf Orr and Karen Komosa-Hawkins provide a comprehensive examination of legal and ethical mandates impacting schools and school personnel. In Chapter 8, Joy S. Whitman addresses the current state of pre-service training programs and identifies strategies for providing professional development for school personnel. Dorothy L. Espelage and Mrinalini A. Rao review research and strategies to address harassment and bullying in Chapter 9, and Emily A. Greytak and Joseph G. Kosciw provide concrete methods of developing classroom curriculum that is representative of and responsive to LGBTQ students in Chapter 10. In Chapter 11, Alicia L. Fedewa and Ashley Candelaria explore issues related to making schools and classrooms more inclusive of LGBT-headed families. Grady L. Garner Jr. and Dennis M. Emano address affirmative counseling for LGBTQ students in Chapter 12, and Caitlin Ryan and Stuart F. Chen-Hayes review research and strategies to best work with diverse families of LGBTQ students in Chapter 13. In Chapter 14, Robert A. McGarry discusses how school professionals can be allies and advocates for LGBTQ students. Finally, in Chapter 15, Kelly S. Kennedy provides information about developing Gay-Straight Alliances and accessing community resources to provide support for all students and families.

Terminology

Throughout this book, common terminology will be used. This terminology is what is currently viewed as acceptable and respectful within the community of individuals who identify as lesbian, gay, bisexual, transgender, and questioning. It is important for school professionals to become familiar with and comfortable using this terminology, as this is an important first step in facilitating open communication and creating supportive, inclusive school environments.

Sex generally refers to the biological characteristics that make an individual male or female. *Gender* refers to the expression of masculinity or femininity. Related to this, *gender identity* refers to how an individual chooses to express gender and can be thought of on a continuum from highly masculine to highly feminine. Gender identity can be expressed through clothing, hair style, facial hair, and so on. Gender expression is considered flexible as styles change and an individual chooses to express different aspects of himself or herself. These terms are extensively covered in Chapter 5.

Sexual orientation is a broad term used to identify an individual's sexual and emotional attractions. Individuals who identify as lesbian or gay are considered to have a homosexual orientation. Individuals who are attracted to those from the opposite sex are considered to have a heterosexual orientation. In this book, the term *heterosexual* is used instead of the term *straight*, as the term straight may imply that other orientations are crooked or wrong.

Lesbian refers to a girl or woman who is sexually and emotionally attracted to another girl or woman. Similarly, *gay* refers to a boy or man who is sexually and emotionally attracted to another boy or man, although at times, *gay* might refer to any person who is not heterosexual. *Bisexual* refers to an individual who is attracted to both girls or women and boys or men. Bisexual individuals may be in a heterosexual or same-sex relationship.

Transgender refers to an individual who is born with the sexual characteristics of either a boy or girl, but very strongly identifies as an individual of the opposite sex. Transgender individuals often feel as if they were born in the wrong body. For example, a teenager who was born with biological characteristics of a girl, but whose gender identity is that of a boy and assumes the gender characteristics of a boy is transgender. This person may or may not have sex reassignment surgery, which is the process of changing the identifiable characteristics of an individual's sex of birth. In this example, the person may have breast removal surgery to help the outside appearance match the internal experience of being a boy. For more information on these topics, see Chapter 5.

Often a "Q" is added to the acronym LGBT making it LGBTQ. For the purpose of this book, the Q refers to *questioning*. The term questioning is used to describe individuals who are in the process of better understanding their sexual orientation. Individuals who are questioning may not yet have determined if they identify as heterosexual, homosexual, or bisexual. Questioning most likely occurs during adolescence, but can happen at any time in a person's life. Individuals themselves may not identify as questioning; rather, it is a term that may be applied by others to someone who seems uncertain of his or her sexual orientation. Within the LGBTQ community, Q can sometimes refer to *queer*. While this is a term that has been embraced by some people within the LGBTQ community, it may be offensive to other individuals within the community and is generally considered inappropriate for use by those outside of the community.

Sexual minority is an inclusive term that refers to lesbian, gay, bisexual, transgender, and questioning individuals. These individuals often experience discrimination, marginalization, and invisibility similar to individuals from other minority groups (e.g., ethnic minority groups).

Though the aforementioned terms are generally accepted, it is important to note that there likely will be variability in terminology used among different communities in different parts of the country. Similarly, many individuals will have their own terminology to define their sexual orientation or gender identity. It is appropriate for school professionals to ask questions such as, "What terminology do you prefer?" or "How do you identify yourself?". These questions indicate an openness to learn about and a willingness to accept the individual, just as the use of acceptable terminology suggests a sensitivity to an individual's experiences. Additionally, avoiding making assumptions (e.g., assuming heterosexuality) and using gender-neutral terms (e.g., romantic interest or partner) is a way school professionals can communicate openness and inclusivity.

All school professionals have a role and responsibility in providing a safe learning environment for all students, and students who are at risk for experiencing harassment, bullying, and discrimination at school may need professionals to take extra steps to ensure their school success. With a better understanding of the unique challenges and experiences of LGBTQ students and LGBT-headed families in the school system; knowledge of appropriate prevention and intervention efforts to eradicate bullying, harassment, and discrimination; and strategies to promote academic, social, and emotional growth, educators can make a difference in the lives of all of the students they serve. These steps will go a long way in creating school climates in which all students feel safe and supported and can reach their potential.

References

Chan, C. S. (1996). Combating heterosexism in educational institutions: Structural changes and strategies. In E. D. Rothblum & L. A. Bond (Eds.), *Preventing heterosexism and homophobia* (pp. 20–35). Thousand Oaks, CA: Sage Publications.

Crothers, L. (2007). Bullying of sexually diverse children and adolescents. *NASP Communiqué, 35*, 28–30. Retrieved from http://www.nasponline.org/publications/cq/mocq355bullying.aspx

DePaul, J., Walsh, M. E., & Dam, U. C. (2009). The role of school counselors in addressing sexual orientation in schools. *Professional School Counselor, 12*, 300–308. doi:10.5330/PSC.n.2010-12.300

Eisenberg, M. E., & Resnick, M. D. (2006). Suicidality among gay, lesbian and bisexual youth: The role of protective factors. *Journal of Adolescent Health, 39*, 662–668. doi:10.1016/j.jadohealth.2006.04.024

Ervin, R. A., & Schaughency, E. (2008). Best practices in accessing the systems change literature. In A. Thomas & J. Grimes (Eds.), *Best practices in school psychology* (5th ed., pp. 853–873). Bethesda, MD: The National Association of School Psychologists.

Espelage, D. L., Aragon, S. R., Birkett, M., & Koenig, B. W. (2008). Homophobic teasing, psychological outcomes, and sexual orientation among high school students: What influence do parents and schools have? *School Psychology Review, 37*, 202–216. Retrieved from http://www.nasponline.org/publications/spr/index.aspx?vol=37&issue=2

Fisher, E. S., & Kennedy, K. S. (2012). *Responsive school practices to support lesbian, gay, bisexual, transgender, and questioning students and families.* New York: Routledge.

Fisher, E. S., Komosa-Hawkins, K., Saldana, E., Hsiao, C., Miller, D., Rauld, M., & Thomas, G. M. (2008). Promoting school success for lesbian, gay, bisexual, transgendered, and questioning students: Primary, secondary, and tertiary prevention and intervention strategies. *California School Psychologist, 13*, 79–91. Retrieved from http://www.caspsurveys.org/NEW/pdfs/journal08.pdf#page=79

Fox, B. (2007). One of the hidden diversities in schools: Families with parents who are lesbian or gay. *Childhood Education, 85,* 277–282. doi:10.1080/00094056.2007.10522932

Goodenow, C., Szalacha, L., & Westheimer, K. (2006). School support groups, other school factors, and the safety of sexual minority adolescents. *Psychology in the Schools, 43,* 573–589. doi:10.1002/pits.20173

Kosciw, J. G., & Diaz, E. M. (2008). Involved, invisible, ignored: The experiences of lesbian, gay, bisexual and transgender parents and their children in our nation's K-12 schools. New York: GLSEN. Retrieved from http://www.familyequality.org/_asset/5n43xf/familiesandschools.pdf

Kosciw, J. G., Diaz, E. M., & Greytak, E. A. (2008). The 2007 National School Climate Survey: The experiences of lesbian, gay, bisexual and transgender youth in our nation's schools. New York: GLSEN. Retrieved from http://www.lgbt.ucla.edu/documents/2007NationalScoolClimate Survey.pdf

McFarland, W. P., & Dupuis, M. (2003). The legal duty to protect gay and lesbian students from violence in schools. In T. P. Remley, M. A. Hermann, & W. C. Huey (Eds.), *Ethical and legal issues in school counseling* (2nd ed., pp. 341–357). Alexandria, VA: American School Counselor Association.

Murdock, T. B., & Bolch, M. B. (2005). Risk and protective factors for poor school adjustment in lesbian, gay, and bisexual (LGB) high school youth: Variable and person-centered analyses. *Psychology in the Schools, 42,* 159–172. doi:10.1002/pits.20054

Savin-Williams, R. C. (1994). Verbal and physical abuse as stressors in the lives of lesbian, gay male, and bisexual youths: Associations with school problems, running away, substance abuse, prostitution, and suicide. *Journal of Consulting and Clinical Psychology, 62,* 261–269. doi:10.1037/0022-006X.62.2.261

Savin-Williams, R. C. (2001). A critique of research on sexual-minority youths. *Journal of Adolescence, 21,* 5–13. doi:10.1006/jado.2000.0369

Szalacha, L. A. (2003). Safer sexual diversity climates: Lessons learned from an evaluation of Massachusetts' Safe Schools Program for Gay and Lesbian Students. *American Journal of Education, 110,* 58–88. doi:10.1086/377673

Whitman, J. S., Horn, S. S., & Boyd, C. J. (2007). Activism in the schools: Providing LGBTQ affirmative training to school counselors. *Journal of Gay & Lesbian Psychotherapy, 11,* 143–154. doi:10.1300/J236v11n03_08

Young, E. L., & Mendez, L. M. R. (2003). The mental health professional's role in understanding, preventing, and responding to student sexual harassment. In M. J. Elias & J. E. Zins (Eds.), *Bullying, peer harassment, and victimization in the schools: The next generation of prevention* (pp. 7–23). New York: Haworth Press.

2 Putting Sexual Orientation and Gender Identity in Context

Historical Influences and Social Trends

Judy Chiasson and Ronni Sanlo

"The most certain test by which we judge whether a country is really free is the amount of security enjoyed by minorities."

John E. E. Dalberg, Lord Acton, *The History of Freedom in Antiquity*, 1877

The quest for freedom and equity was the driving force of the United States' (U.S.) first settlers, and U.S. history has been shaped by the call for social equality. Though racial, ethnic, and cultural prejudices persist, there is a general consensus that bigotry is inherently wrong. However, prejudice toward sexual minority people remains endorsed in many social institutions and communities that otherwise decry prejudice and discrimination. In order to understand the current social and political climates for lesbian, gay, bisexual, transgender, and queer/questioning (LGBTQ) students and families, it is necessary to examine the history of oppression, stigmatization, and marginalization encountered by this population across time.

LGBTQ as a Social Group

There is a reciprocal process by which individuals form or are assigned a group identity. A social identity is an individual's self-concept within the context of membership in a social group (Turner & Oakes, 1986). It is formed both by the ways that members feel similar to each other (in-group identity) and the ways they differ from members of other groups (out-group identity). This act of expanding one's personal identity to include (or exclude) a given group identity is at the basis of ethnocentrism and social stereotyping (Turner & Oakes, 1986).

The act of othering creates a structure wherein the parties who hold privilege and power can affect practices that benefit some groups, sometimes at a cost to other groups (Johnson, 2006). LGBTQ individuals are a unique social group in that they have intersecting identities. Most LGBTQ persons are born to heterosexual parents. Unlike other identities that have a familial lineage (e.g., race, religion, culture), homosexuality individuates LGBTQ persons from their family and community of origin. Some are actually expelled from their families and communities as a result of coming out (Ryan, 2009). Sexual orientation and gender identity also are relatively invisible. Consequently, LGBTQ people may simultaneously suffer the effects of social inequities with respect to LGBTQ concerns while being protected from them on an individual level if they are not recognized as LGBTQ.

Loden and Rosener created a "diversity wheel" to visually represent the core identities of sexual orientation, age, race, ethnicity, and gender at the wheel's hub with less fixed influences such as education, income, geographic location, and religion on the outer ring (as cited in Johnson, 2006). This imagery represents how the bestowed privilege associated with being an able-bodied white man, for example, could be offset by being gay in a conservative religious community. Furthermore, there exists a paradox of shifting and situational patterns of privilege and marginalization (Johnson, 2006). This chapter timelines the historical perspectives that supported the identification and marginalization of homosexuals and sexual minorities to the current trends that suggest a brighter, more affirming future for LGBTQ concerns.

Overview of LGBTQ Historical Influences

The invisibility of and silence about LGBTQ individuals obscure their presence throughout history. Nonetheless, there are historical accounts of same-sex love in the 2400 B.C. tomb of the male couple Niankhkhnum and Khnumhotep (Reeder, 2000), in the poetry of the 630 B.C. lyrist Sappho (Rutledge, 1992), and in the two-spirited indigenous people of America (Jacobs, Thomas, & Lang, 1997). Yet, homosexuality only came to the attention of social scientists in the Victorian era. Krafft-Ebing's (1888) famously titled book *Psychopathia Sexualis* labeled people whose sexual behavior, emotions, or attractions varied from the normative male/female paradigm as "perverts" or "inverts." The term "homosexual," as referring to persons with erotic feelings for the same sex, entered the literature in the 1890s (Katz, 1983). It would be another 50 years before discrimination based on sexual orientation received scholarly attention.

Divergent Views of Homosexuality

Until the nineteenth century, same-sex activity was pathologized and criminalized. Homosexuality as a course of scientific study began in Europe in the mid-nineteenth century. In 1864, German lawyer Karl Ulrichs argued against the criminalization of homosexuals, asserting that same-sex attraction was congenital based on his theory that gay men were responding to their innate female "souls" (Katz, 1983).

Berlin was considered to be the most welcoming city in the world for gays and lesbians in the 1920s (Ginn, 1995). Magnus Hirschfeld of the Institute for Sexual Science in Berlin conducted the earliest sex survey at the turn of the twentieth century (Ginn, 1995). Based on his survey of over 6000 students and factory workers, Hirschfeld concluded that 2.2% of the population was homosexual. This "intersex," as gays and lesbians were called, was considered to be a harmless biological anomaly like color blindness. Researchers at the time argued for merciful tolerance for the plight of these "inverts." The Scientific Humanitarian Committee, founded in Germany, traveled to the U.S. to preach tolerance toward homosexuals. However, their work and the relative comfort that gays and lesbians felt came to an abrupt demise with the rise of Hitler in the mid-1930s (Coyle & Kitzinger, 2002).

Openly gay Ernst Roehm held an influential position in the Nazi Party as the head of the Stormtroopers (Giles, 2002). Political rivals fueled the notion that homosexuality was a threat to racial purity. Hitler ordered that his ranks be purged (Giles, 2002), and on

June 30, 1934, Roehm and 1000 other people deemed to be a threat to Hitler were killed in the Night of the Long Knives (Austin, 2011). Shortly thereafter, Paragraph 175 of the German Criminal Code was revised to criminalize homosexuality, sending gay and lesbian people to concentration camps (Austin, 2011). Gay men were forced to wear a pink triangle which marked them for particularly brutal treatment. An estimated 10,000 to 15,000 homosexual men ("175ers") died in the camps, most within a few short months of their arrival. Lesbians wore black triangles to designate them as political prisoners and were sent to the Spring of Life homes for impregnation (Heger, 1980).

Gay Rights Movement in the United States

The first sustained effort in the U.S. for gay and lesbian rights began after World War II, when relocations to large cities such as Miami Beach, New York, Chicago, San Francisco, and Los Angeles provided many gays and lesbians with their first opportunity to meet one another and to break through the stifling curtain of invisibility. In the 1950s, gays and lesbians were branded as Communists and subversives. Those suspected of being gay or lesbian were harassed in bars, parks, or any gathering spot. They often were entrapped by undercover police into revealing their sexual orientation and purged from military and governmental jobs (Katz, 1983; Marcus, 1992). Thus, living a double life that concealed one's sexual orientation was a critical survival skill.

Throughout the 1950s and 1960s the gay rights movement quietly brewed under the mentorship of such leaders as Morris Knight, Harry Hays, Ivy Bottini, and Reverend Troy Perry. The most explosive and significant moment in the U.S. gay rights movement was the 1969 Stonewall Rebellion (Carter, 2004). Often considered the flashpoint of the gay rights movement, the Stonewall Rebellion occurred when the gay, lesbian, and transgender patrons' resistance to a police raid at the Stonewall Inn escalated into three days and nights of rioting (Carter, 2004). While the Stonewall Rebellion was the catalyst for the rise of the Gay Liberation Front movement on college campuses (Herdt, 1989), it would be over 20 years before the movement extended to gay youth with the establishment of the first high school-based support group (Jennings, 2006).

Over the decades, the gay rights community has expanded to include the broad spectrum of persons who are marginalized because of their actual or perceived sexual orientation or gender identity, as well as those who are associated with the community. Similarly, the terms "biphobia" and "transphobia" raise awareness of the many faces of bias, including those based on gender, sex, and sexual orientation (Eliason, 1997; Gerhardstein & Anderson, 2010). A gay pride parade (of which there are hundreds around the world) may include bisexual, transgender, and heterosexual allies who are joined in both the experience of shared oppression and their desire to promote a more inclusive and affirming society.

Recognizing Homophobia and Depathologizing Homosexuality

Around the same time as Stonewall, prejudice based on sexual orientation emerged as a field of study. The term *homophobia* was coined in the 1960s to describe the fear of being in the presence of homosexuals (Herek, 2004). The term homophobia is broadly used to describe the continuum from discomfort and awkwardness to extreme hatred of what may be interpreted or perceived as homosexual. Blumenfeld (1992) asserted that homophobia still permeates U.S. culture; its political, educational, and religious institutions; and even our private relationships.

Many early scholars of non-normative sexuality and gender identity approached their work through a binary lens of homosexual versus heterosexual and male versus female. That dichotomized perspective is slowly being replaced by one that is more nuanced and contextualized and recognizes a continuum of sexual orientation and gender identity (Hammack, Thompson, & Pilecki, 2009).

In 1973, the American Psychiatric Association depathologized homosexuality by revising the diagnosis of homosexuality in the Diagnostic and Statistical Manual of Mental Disorders, second edition (DSM-II) (Kleinplatz, 2001). Homosexuality remained in the DSM under the category of ego-dystonic (feeling anxiety and a desire to change one's orientation) until 1987 when it was removed from the DSM's third edition revised (DSM-III-R) (Kleinplatz, 2001). Two years after the American Psychiatric Association's revision, the American Psychological Association (APA) issued this affirming recommendation:

> Homosexuality per se implies no impairment in judgment, stability, reliability, or general social and vocational capabilities; further, the American Psychological Association urges all mental health professionals to take the lead in removing the stigma of mental illness that has long been associated with homosexual orientations.
>
> (Conger, 1975, p. 633)

Despite the professional associations' calls for acceptance, there was and still is a formidable body of professionals who have built their practices around trying to repair homosexuality (Green, 1987; Nicolosi, 1991; Rekers, 1977). The APA conducted a systemic review of these sexual orientation change efforts (also known as *reparative therapy*) and reported that any supposed evidence of their effectiveness has "serious methodological problems" (APA, 2009, p. 2). APA concluded that "efforts to change sexual orientation are unlikely to be successful and involve some risk of harm, contrary to the claims of SOCE [sexual orientation change effort] practitioners and advocates" (APA, 2009, p. v).

Social and Political Trends

Akin to the civil rights movement, the gay rights movement has sought social equity on various fronts, including same-sex marriage, military service, anti-discrimination laws, and hate crimes. In fact, legal precedent related to racial equality often serves to guide contemporary social issues surrounding LGBTQ rights.

Same-Sex Marriage

Marriage as a romantic commitment between two people is a relatively new social development. For most of history (and still a practice in some countries) marriage was a brokered business agreement between two families (Haeberle, 1983). Love and romance had little place. The Protestant Reformation of the sixteenth century introduced the concept of marriage as a civil matter under the jurisdiction of the government

(Haeberle, 1983). By the nineteenth century all marriages needed to be officiated by the state. Religious marriages were permitted only after the civil marriage (Haeberle, 1983).

Every state has its own eligibility requirements for heterosexual couples who wish to marry. The restrictions primarily address the age of consent, residency, waiting periods, and familial relationships (see http://www.usmarriagelaws.com). Once married, the marriage is recognized in every state and by the federal government.

The right to marry has been challenged in two landmark incidents, one having to do with interracial unions and the other nearly 40 years later having to do with same-sex marriage. In 1958 Mildred Jeter (an African American woman) and Richard Loving (a Caucasian man) were married in the District of Columbia, but when they returned home to Virginia, they were arrested for violating Virginia's Racial Integrity Act, which banned marriage between any white and non-white person (*Loving v. Virginia*, 1967). The Lovings plead guilty and were given the choice of one year of prison or 25 years of exile from the state of Virginia (*Loving v. Virginia*, 1967). They chose to leave the state. The Lovings contested the ruling, asserting that Virginia's decision violated the Fourteenth Amendment (*Loving v. Virginia*, 1967). Their case was ultimately heard by the U.S. Supreme Court, which ruled:

> The freedom to marry has long been recognized as one of the vital personal rights essential to the orderly pursuit of happiness by free men. Marriage is one of the "basic civil rights of man," fundamental to our very existence and survival. . . . To deny this fundamental freedom on so unsupportable a basis as the racial classifications embodied in these statutes, classifications so directly subversive of the principle of equality at the heart of the Fourteenth Amendment, is surely to deprive all the State's citizens of liberty without due process of law. The Fourteenth Amendment requires that the freedom of choice to marry not be restricted by invidious racial discriminations. Under our Constitution, the freedom to marry, or not marry, a person of another race resides with the individual and cannot be infringed by the State.
>
> (*Loving v. Virginia*, 1967, Section II, para. 1–2)

The Supreme Court's designation of marriage as a "basic civil right of man" was a major step toward equal rights, but it did not extend to same-sex couples. As a result, same-sex couples across the country who applied for marriage certificates were routinely denied.

The path toward marriage equality for same-sex couples has been fraught with many wins and losses. *Baehr v. Lewin* is another landmark case that was argued in the state of Hawai'i. Hawai'i stands as an example of the seesaw of legislations and rulings that have occurred throughout the country. In 1990, three same-sex couples in Hawai'i applied for and were denied marriage licenses. The couples sued the State Health Director John C. Lewin whose denial of the applications was upheld by the Hawai'i Attorney General's office (Chang, 1996). The case was appealed to the Supreme Court of Hawai'i (where it was retitled from *Baehr v. Lewin* to *Baehr v. Miike*), which ruled that the decision to bar the couples from marriage was unconstitutional. The State Legislature responded by passing Act 217 in 1994, redefining marriage to include only mixed-sex couples and offering comprehensive domestic partnership to same-sex couples. The couples persisted and, in 1996, appeared before Judge Chang who ruled that the state did not have any compelling interest in denying same-sex couples the ability to marry (Chang, 1996). In

1998, however, Hawai'i voters approved an amendment to their state constitution restricting marriage to mixed-sex couples (State of Hawai'i, 1998).

People on all sides of the issue carefully watched Hawai'i's proceedings, wondering how the country would be affected if Hawai'i approved same-sex marriage (Coolridge, 1998). In response to the pending ruling in Hawai'i, the U.S. federal government scrambled to pass the Defense of Marriage Act (DOMA), citing compelling federal consequences. "H.R. 3396 is a response to a very particular development in the State of Hawaii ... The prospect of permitting homosexual couples to 'marry' in Hawai'i threatens to have very real consequences both on federal law and on the laws (especially the marriage laws) of the various States" (Defense of Marriage Act [DOMA], 1996, p. 2). In its definition of marriage as a legal union between one man and one woman, the Subcommittee on the Constitution referenced Judeo-Christian morality cited fiscal impacts and stated that the purpose of marriage is "begetting children" (DOMA, 1996, p. 14).

In the years since DOMA passed, civil unions and domestic partnerships have been enacted across the country, granting same-sex couples a patchwork of rights and responsibilities (Freedom to Marry, 2012). At the time of this writing (2012), six states allow same-sex marriages, and another three have non-discrimination clauses against same-sex couples from other states (Freedom to Marry, 2012). Thirty-one states have constitutional amendments prohibiting same-sex marriages and/or civil unions (Freedom to Marry, 2012).

Proponents of marriage equality hope to follow in the footsteps of *Loving v. Virginia*. Several states have questioned the ethics and constitutionality of banning same-sex marriage and of putting a civil rights issue up to popular vote, such as with California's Proposition 8, which gave voters the choice of whether to recognize same-sex marriage (Dolan & Williams, 2010). Massachusetts recognized same-sex marriages in 2003 (Massachusetts Trial Court Law Libraries, n.d.). The First U.S. Circuit Court of Appeals in Massachusetts heard two related cases wherein the plaintiffs, same-sex couples who were legally married in Massachusetts, asserted that DOMA was discriminatory because it did not recognize the validity of their marriages under federal law. In their unanimous 2012 ruling on behalf of the plaintiffs, Federal Judge Michael Boudin wrote, "Under current Supreme Court authority, Congress' denial of federal benefits to same-sex couples lawfully married in Massachusetts has not been adequately supported by any permissible federal interest" (Ellement, Finucane, & Valencia, 2012, para. 10). The next step in such a case would be the United States Supreme Court. The Obama administration, however, announced that it would not defend the constitutionality of the DOMA (Montopoll, 2011). Furthermore, should the Supreme Court refuse to hear the case, the ruling of the lower court would probably stand.

Don't Ask, Don't Tell

Similar to marriage, the government has always had the right to determine eligibility for military service. When the Civil War broke in 1861, the military sought to revisit the 1792 federal law that banned Negroes from bearing arms (Freeman, Schamel & West, 1992), due to the desire of free Blacks to serve their country coupled with the need for able-bodied enlistees. Frederick Douglass saw military service as a "golden opportunity" for Blacks to prove their loyalty and win the full rights of citizenship (Douglass, 1863).

It took many decades for the military to become integrated. During World War II, the National Association for the Advancement of Colored People (NAACP) tirelessly advocated for full integration of troops (MacGregor, 1979). The Army resisted, citing deference to prevailing social attitudes. At the time, the majority of Caucasian and almost half of African American soldiers preferred segregated units; many were adamantly opposed to integration. However, the constant pressure from civil rights activists ultimately broke these barriers (MacGregor, 1979).

The military's efforts to increase inclusion of African Americans were coupled by a parallel effort to increase exclusion of homosexuals. Whereas homosexual activity had always been barred, new screening protocols shifted to exclude homosexual persons based on identity, not just behavior (Bérubé, 1990). However, the scrutiny with which these protocols were followed correlated with the need for personnel, such that many gays and lesbians enlisted, only to be dishonorably discharged when the pressing need for their services abated (Bérubé, 1990).

As the gay civil rights movement gained momentum, it looked as if the ban on homosexuals might be lifted. President Clinton's 1993 attempt to lift the ban completely was met with extreme opposition. After much debate, a compromise was reached. The ban on same-sex sexual activity remained, but service members and recruits would no longer be questioned about their orientation. *Don't Ask, Don't Tell* (DADT) allowed lesbian and gay service members to continue serving *if* they remained completely closeted (Service Members Legal Defense Network, n.d.).

Activists noted many parallels between the military's racial segregation and its ban on gays and lesbians. Both practices cited prevailing social attitudes, security risks, competency, and potential cost to the morale of the troops as justification (Quindlen, 2009). In the 18 years that DADT was in effect, 14,500 service members were fired under its provisions (Service Members Legal Defense Network, n.d.).

President Obama signed legislation to repeal DADT in December 2010. Upon the bill's repeal in September 2011, the military halted all suspensions and investigations related to DADT and invited service members who had been discharged under it to reapply for military service. The repeal directed all service members to work respectfully with those who may hold different views and beliefs (Memorandum for Secretaries of the Military Departments, 2011).

Anti-Discrimination Laws

The inconsistent application of equal rights and opportunities extends to anti-discrimination protections related to employment and housing.

Employment. Title VII of the Civil Rights Act of 1964 makes it unlawful for an employer to refuse to hire, to fire, or to otherwise discriminate against a person on the basis of race, color, religion, sex, or national origin (U.S. Equal Employment Opportunity Commission, n.d.). Congress revisited Title VII in 1967 and 1990 to add discrimination based on age and on disability (Vagins, 2007). However, there are no federal protections to cover employment discrimination based on sexual orientation or gender identity. The proposed Employment Non-Discrimination Act (ENDA) would add sexual orientation and gender identity to federal non-discrimination regulations. The Act has been introduced to every Congress (except for the 109th Congress) since 1993. ENDA has yet to receive sufficient votes to pass the Senate and the House of Representatives.

The lack of federal legislation on employment discrimination protection for LGBTQ workers has created a patchwork of policies that vary by state and by employer. An estimated 85% of Fortune 500 companies include sexual orientation in their non-discrimination policies; 33% also include gender identity. Sixteen states ban discrimination based on sexual orientation; another five also include gender identity (Human Rights Campaign [HRC], 2011). Nevertheless, LGBTQ individuals consistently report sexual orientation-based bias and discrimination in the workplace, with 37% reporting harassment and 12% reporting having lost their job (Pizer, Mallory, Sears & Hunter, 2012; Sears & Mallory, 2011). The incidents for transgender persons are even higher, with 90% reporting harassment and 47% reporting differential treatment in hiring, promotion, or retention (Pizer et al., 2012; Sears & Mallory, 2011).

Housing. Title VIII of the Civil Rights Act of 1968 (Fair Housing Act) prohibits housing discrimination based on race, color, national origin, religion, sex, familial status, and disability. Sexual orientation and gender identity are not protected under federal housing discrimination regulations. The federal government extends to heterosexual married couples 1138 benefits that are not available to same-sex couples (HRC, 2011). These rights run the gamut from taxes, insurance, and inheritance to medical decisions and hospital visitations. Marriage establishes a couple as kin, with associated rights and responsibilities. Without the right to marry, same-sex couples are considered unrelated individuals under the eyes of the law.

In January 2012, the federal Department of Housing and Urban Development (HUD) released new regulations that would address discrimination based on sexual orientation and gender identity in federal housing programs. The regulation recognizes same-sex couples and their children as families and prohibits housing providers who receive HUD-funding from asking or considering sexual orientation and gender identity in securing HUD-assisted housing or mortgage loans (Department of Housing and Urban Development, 2012). On the state level, 16 states prohibit housing discrimination based on sexual orientation. Another four states also prohibit discrimination based on gender identity (HRC, 2011).

Hate Crimes

Despite the strides the civil rights movement has made toward equality, LGBTQ individuals continue to be frequent targets of discrimination, prejudice, and hate crimes. Hate crimes and incidents are motivated by bias based on race, religion, sexual orientation, ethnicity/national origin, and disability and often are institutionalized. The victim of a hate crime may be an individual, a business, an institution, or society as a whole (Federal Bureau of Investigation [FBI], n.d.). Victims can be targeted based on their actual or perceived association with the identified group.

The Federal Bureau of Investigation (FBI) began to formally collect and analyze data on hate crimes in compliance with the Hate Crime Statistics Act of 1990 (FBI, n.d.). In 2010, almost 20% (1470 incidents) of hate crimes reported to the FBI were based on sexual orientation. The majority of these (57%) were attributed to bias against gay males.

The Shepard/Byrd Law of 2009 expanded the hate-crime legislation to include crimes based on gender, gender identity, and juvenile status as protected categories, but the data are not yet available. Forty-five states have hate crime laws. Of these, 17 states include hate crimes attributed to sexual orientation-bias; another 13 states also include crimes attributed to gender identity-bias (National Gay and Lesbian Task Force, 2012). It should be noted that many counties and municipalities have their own hate crime laws that are not mirrored at the state level.

It is critical for students, families, and educators to stay abreast of state and national laws and local policies related to equity, opportunity, and civil rights; these regulations are continuously evolving. Having a clear sense of the rights and protections afforded LGBTQ individuals will help to create and sustain a safe and supportive learning environment and allow for advocacy efforts on behalf of LGBTQ youth and families within the context of schools and beyond.

School Contexts: Past to Present

Education, as the microcosm of society, has served as a proxy battlefield for social conflicts about issues as varied as religious expression, freedom of speech, gender equality, and LGBTQ recognition and rights. Consequently, education has served as the staging ground for a number of landmark court decisions. The 1925 Scopes Monkey trial debated the right to teach evolution (Jurist Legal Intelligence, n.d.), while *Mendez v. Westminster* (1946) and *Brown v. Board of Education* (1954) confronted racial segregation. The *Tinker v. Des Moines* (1969) ruling on freedom of speech held that "students do not lose their constitutional rights at the schoolhouse gate" (United States Courts, n.d.). The civil unrest that persists today directly impacts both LGBT educators and LGBTQ students alike.

LGBT Educators

On March 17, 1964, the Florida Legislative Investigative (sometimes interchanged with Investigation) Committee, called the Johns Committee after its chair, Senator Charley E. Johns, published a report entitled *Homosexuality and Citizenship in Florida*. The purpose of the Johns Committee was to identify methods to detect and remove lesbian or gay individuals from Florida's schools and other state-funded agencies (Harbeck, 1997; Sanlo, 1999; Sears, 1997). Public school teachers, primarily in the Tampa area, and college professors and students at the University of Florida and Florida State University were the main targets of this investigation (Sanlo, 1999). Many teachers—some of whom were gay and some of whom were *perceived* to be gay—were publicly named and forced to resign. As Pendleton (1993) and Sears (1997) noted, the Johns Committee's campaign ruined careers and destroyed families. Some teachers committed suicide due to the shame and humiliation they felt.

Sears (1997) documented the voices of those who survived the Johns Committee rampage. One educator said, "Tenure didn't mean a goddam thing. If they wanted to get rid of you they would find a way. And they did" (Sears, 1997, p. 81). A female educator added, "People were told that they were under suspicion because of their [single] marital status" (Sears, 1997, p. 81).

When the Johns Committee report was presented to the Florida legislature in March of 1964, it was perceived to be pornographic and deeply disturbing (Sears, 1997). The legislature, though it continued to be repressive toward lesbian and gay people, discontinued funding for the Johns Committee (Sears, 1997). John Evans, the day-to-day director of the now disbanded Johns Committee, spoke to the Florida Federation of Women's Clubs in Jacksonville in mid-1964. He warned that "Homosexuality was still flourishing in Florida educational institutions, with allegations of homosexuality and references to 123 individuals then, and presumably now, teaching in Florida schools" (Sears, 1997, p. 998).

In 1977, popular singer and Florida Orange Juice Queen Anita Bryant fronted the fundamentalist Christian-supported "Save Our Children" campaign which banned gays and lesbians from teaching in Miami, Florida (Sanlo, 1999). Her campaign was successful and led to the overturning of the local gay rights ordinance (Sanlo, 1999). The Florida legislature responded by introducing its first anti-gay laws that prohibited adoption by gays and lesbians (Sanlo, 1999). In 1978, the California Briggs Initiative attempted to ban not only gays and lesbians from working in public schools but also anyone who supported gay rights (Lipkin, 1999). Both campaigns effectively instilled fear among LGBT teachers and allies that persists to this day.

As employees, teachers and administrators in public education have fewer rights than do their students. Federal mandates guarantee that children are entitled to a free and appropriate public school education. Compulsory education laws vary from state to state, but generally require that all children attend school until graduation or the age at which their state allows dropping out (between 14 and 17) (National Conference of State Legislatures, 2011). Hence, legal pressures keep public schools and students intertwined regardless of a potentially conflictual relationship. By contrast, teachers do not have such obligations; they are free to resign at any time. LGBT school staff may hide their identities for a variety of reasons, most often due to a fear of backlash. Within the structure of school districts, substantial decision-making authority is granted to a single person, the on-site principal, who may not be supportive of LGBT individuals. Untenured teachers and most administrators are at-will employees with contracts that expire at the end of the academic year. Certainly, schools are obligated to adhere to state and federal labor laws of non-discrimination, but no explanation or justification is required when choosing whether to renew the contract of a non-tenured employee or to reassign an administrator. Consequently, it is very common for LGBTQ students to take a more visible and vocal role in advocating for equity at the school site than LGBT school staff.

Even parents who espouse positive attitudes toward gays and lesbians often draw the line at their child having an openly gay or lesbian teacher (Chiasson, 2006). It is not uncommon for a school to transfer an employee about whom the community complains. Additionally, there are countless stories of teachers and administrators whose performance evaluations plunged once their LGBT identity was revealed. For example, in deciding whether he should come out at his school, one elementary teacher wrote "I saw street signs of my two paths. Along the 'No Way' [route] I saw lots of notoriety and praise. Along 'Yes Blvd.' I came across ridicule, harassment, discrimination, [and] possible job loss" (Burgess, 1993, p. 28). Judy Chiasson, an openly gay high school teacher and co-author of this chapter, shared a personal experience:

I feel that LGBT teachers have a unique obligation and opportunity to educate their school community about LGBT concerns. One day my principal and I met with my student and her mother to discuss the student's chronic truancy. The mother countered with an assertion that the *real problem* was that I, the lesbian teacher, had an inappropriate interest in her daughter and had been stalking her. There was a deafening silence as the principal paused, took a breath, and then confronted the parent on her diversionary tactic and slanderous accusation. I was immensely grateful for the principal's response. In another school or in another era, that conversation could have likely ended my career.

Many LGBT administrators fear that revealing their identity will lose them the respect of their colleagues and thwart their careers. In addition, employees hesitate to advocate on behalf of the LGBTQ students for fear that their identities and intentions will be questioned (Sanlo, 1999).

Children mimic the prejudices of their parents and the communities in which they live. Adolescents are most likely to share homophobic attitudes with their parents yet least likely to share racist ones (O'Bryan, Fishbein, & Ritchey, 2004). Adolescents may be particularly vicious toward teachers whom they perceive to be LGBT, yet many teachers do not report the abuse to administration for fear of being seen as incapable of managing their classrooms. Nonetheless, there is an increasing visibility among LGBT teachers and administrators. Unlike their veteran counterparts, younger teachers are unlikely to have been traumatized by anti-gay fear mongering incited by such measures as the Save the Children campaign and the Briggs Initiative. Many young teachers participated in Gay-Straight Alliances (GSAs) themselves and cannot imagine going into the closet now that they are professionals.

LGBTQ Students

Society's discomfort with sexuality, particularly within the context of schools, certainly extends to youth and often marginalizes LGBTQ youth. For example, not so long ago (and sometimes currently) students who became pregnant quietly withdrew from school. The federal government began funding abstinence-only education in 1981 to address a host of economic and health concerns that were attributed to [heterosexual] youth sexual activity (Perrin & DeJoy, 2003). Nonetheless, the heterosexism of most health classes completely neglects the needs of LGBTQ students (Mayo, 2007).

LGBTQ school activism became visible in the 1980s in major cities across the country. In 1984, Virginia Uribe, a teacher at Fairfax High School in Los Angeles, was disturbed to learn that one of her 14 year old students had been kicked out of his home and was attending his third high school because of chronic anti-gay harassment (Uribe, 1994). Seeing an unmet need, Uribe founded Project 10, the first school-based outreach initiative for gay and lesbian youth (Uribe, 1994). Project 10 continues as a thriving voice for LGBTQ students and staff in the Los Angeles Unified School District, working directly with schools to ensure safe and affirming campuses, investigating allegations of bias, orienting new employees about LGBTQ concerns, writing inclusive policies and curriculum, and making recommendations regarding legislation. At one time, schools felt the need to be protected from their gay and lesbian students; now there is a growing attitude that LGBTQ students need to be protected from their schools (Griffin & Ouellett, 2003).

In the mid-1980s several LGBTQ youth support networks were founded across the country including the Sexual Minority Youth Assistance League (SMYAL; http://www. smyal.org) in Washington, DC and the Boston Alliance of Gay, Lesbian, Bisexual, and Transgender Youth (BAGLY; http://www.bagly.org). The Jacksonville Area Sexual Minority Youth Network (JASMYN) was founded in 1993 by a gay teen who responded to his own sense of isolation and suicidal thoughts by reaching out for support (http://www.jasmyn.org).

The first GSA was reluctantly started in 1990 by high school teacher Kevin Jennings (Jennings, 2006). Jennings was unsure of what consequences he would incur at his New England boarding school for supporting his gay and lesbian students (Jennings, 2006). He later founded the Gay and Lesbian Independent School Teachers Network, which ultimately grew to become the Gay, Lesbian, and Straight Education Network (GLSEN), a leading national organization devoted to building safe schools (Jennings, 2006). Jennings was hired as assistant deputy secretary over the Office of Safe and Drug-Free Schools under President Obama, and the Gay-Straight Alliance became a national network, the GSA Network (GSA Network, 2009), with over 850 student clubs serving over 1 million students across the nation.

Nonetheless, there are numerous examples of public school districts and school boards bowing to community opposition to GSAs. Legal action was necessary in West Bend, Wisconsin (Weisberg, 2011); Flour Bluff, Texas (Quinto-Pozos, 2011); Nassau County, Florida (American Civil Liberties Union, 2009); Orange, California (Lambda Legal, n.d.); and Salt Lake City, Utah (Lambda Legal, 2000) for students to be able to exercise their federally guaranteed Equal Access Right to establish GSAs. See Chapter 7 of this volume for more information on legal issues regarding GSAs and equal access.

In Los Angeles, a small group of teachers and activists decided that the best way to combat homophobia would be to work directly with the very students, teachers, and community members who perpetrated the bias. They realized that prejudice thrives in the silence of invisibility, so, in 1991, they turned their passions and skills to establishing a discretely named Speakers Bureau (M. L. Eselun, personal communication, May 28, 2012). That first year, the Speakers Bureau facilitated 51 homophobia-reduction workshops to some very hostile audiences in schools, churches, businesses, and organizations in Los Angeles (M. L. Eselun, personal communication, May 28, 2012). Undaunted, the Speakers Bureau continued to grow. Renamed as Gays and Lesbians Initiating Dialogue for Equality (GLIDE) in 1994, they now conduct hundreds of LGBTQ-diversity workshops in the greater Los Angeles area every year and are a standard part of many schools' curricula (http://www.socal-glide.org).

Schools as Danger Zones. LGBTQ students are often targets of bullying and harassment, which has received widespread media attention following a spate of suicides linked to anti-gay bullying (Mellin & Hinojosa, 2011). In 2001, the American Association of University Women (AAUW) found sexualized bullying to be pervasive in schools, with 83% of girls and 79% of boys reporting school-based sexual harassment (e.g., making sexual comments and jokes or calling others gay or lesbian). According to their findings, "Students ranked being called gay or lesbian more upsetting than being forced to do something sexual other than kissing" (American Association of University Women, 2001, p. 10).

In the same year, the Human Rights Watch (2001), an independent organization dedicated to defending and protecting human rights, found that LGBT students endured oppressive levels of verbal and physical assaults from peers and that the teachers and administrators who were entrusted to preserve student safety tacitly or overtly encouraged the abuse. The Human Rights Watch's scathing condemnation should have been a wakeup call for schools across the country:

> In violation of its obligations under international law to provide protection from discrimination, the federal government has failed to enact measures that would explicitly provide protection from violence and discrimination based on sexual orientation and gender identity [and] the problem is not that these youth are gay, lesbian, bisexual or transgender. The problem is the impunity of school officials who, through acts of commission and omission, violate these students' right to be free from persecution and discrimination.
>
> (Human Rights Watch, 2001, pp. 3–4)

More recent research reveals that LGBTQ students continue to experience high levels of victimization at school. The Gay, Lesbian, and Straight Education Network (GLSEN) has been collecting data on LGBT youth since 1999 and has found consistently high levels of bullying and harassment over a 10 year period (Kosciw, Greytak, Diaz, & Bartkiewicz, 2010). More on harassment, bullying, and related outcomes can be found in Chapter 9 of this volume.

Schools as Safe Zones. Despite the substantial victimization and staggering risk factors, many LGBTQ youth are thriving. Advocacy efforts exist at the local, state, and national levels. For instance, the number of registered GSAs in the U.S. has grown from 40 clubs in the San Francisco Bay area in 1988 to over 850 clubs in 2011 in high schools and middle schools across the country (GSA Network, 2009). GSAs work to end isolation, develop leaders, empower youth, and make school safer through their alliances (GSA Network, 2009). As one youth leader said:

> I think a large part of empowerment is not only experience but also knowledge, and I know that a lot of us here, who, from GSAs, have a lot of experience and knowledge around GLBTQ issues, so that I think by running GSAs, you take part in the GLBTQ movement that it really empowers all of us.
>
> (Russell, Muraco, Subramaniam, & Laub, 2009, p. 896)

Friends and social networks are powerful protective factors against peer victimization and aggression (Erath, Flanagan, & Bierman, 2008), though more so for boys than for girls (Besag, 2006). While LGBTQ students consistently experience more bullying than do their heterosexual peers, the act of coming out actually seems to increase resilience. Birkett, Espelage, and Koenig (2009) found that questioning youth had higher levels of depression, substance abuse, and truancy than did lesbian, gay and bisexual-identified youth. Similarly, Greytak, Kosciw, and Diaz (2009) found that "transgender youth who were open about their identities had overall lower risk factors than did their closeted peers" (p. 13).

Parents are advocating for their LGBTQ children as well. Parents and Friends of Lesbians and Gays (PFLAG) was started by one lone mother marching in the 1972 New York Gay Pride Parade to support her son (Parents and Friends of Lesbians and Gays

[PFLAG], 2012). Now PFLAG has more than 500 chapters nationwide (PFLAG, 2012). These proud parents speak not only for their own children but for all LGBTQ persons.

School personnel are arguably the most critical agents for LGBTQ youth in building communities where students feel safe, secure, and accepted. There are numerous ways that schools create and support safe and affirming environments. Kosciw, et al. (2010) found that GSA and LGBTQ youth community program attendance was significantly related to how open students were about their sexual orientation. In this same study, students who were out reported better psychological well-being and school belongingness. The presence of supportive school personnel is core to school safety. The more supportive staff are, safer LGBTQ students feel. Students who observe staff intervening to address anti-gay comments feel safer, are less likely to miss school, and have higher academic achievement and educational aspirations (Kosciw et al., 2010). Progressive school districts make extra efforts to ensure that their non-discrimination policies are followed with fidelity on their school campuses. They realize the power of positive role models and encourage inclusion of LGBTQ topics in the curriculum and LGBTQ visibility on campus.

Numerous professional organizations promote safe and inclusive campuses for LGBTQ youth, such as the National Education Association (NEA):

> NEA believes that a great public school is a fundamental right of every child—free from intimidation and harassment, and safe for all students, including those who identify as gay, lesbian, bisexual, and transgendered. There is only one real issue for educators: We are responsible for our students' safety and education. We must ensure that everyone is given the opportunity to achieve and thrive.
>
> (National Education Association, 2011)

Likewise, the National Association of School Psychologists ([NASP], 2011) affirms that all youth have equal opportunities to participate in and benefit from educational and mental health services within schools regardless of sexual orientation, gender identity, or gender expression. Harassment, inequitable support, and other discriminatory practices toward LGBTQ youth violate their rights to receive equal educational opportunities, regardless of whether the discrimination and hostile comments are directed at individuals or the entire group. Failure to address discriminatory actions in the school setting compromises student development and achievement (NASP, 2011).

In addition to the endorsements of professional organizations, legislation in support of inclusive educational practices has been passed in some jurisdictions. For example, the California Senate passed SB 48 on July 14, 2011. The Fair, Accurate, Inclusive, and Respectful (FAIR) Education Act calls for schools to include the contributions of LGBT Americans in social studies curricula, expanding upon existing mandates to include the contributions of persons with disabilities and members of other cultural groups (e.g., women, Native Americans, African Americans, Mexican Americans, Asian Americans, and European Americans) (California Senate Bill 48, 2011). Yet, there was a flurry of negative responses to the FAIR Education Act, including efforts to overturn the ruling (Watanabe, 2011). Opponents asserted that inclusive education is one of the "immoral laws forced on children, teachers and school districts" (RescueYourChild. com, 2012).

All schools and school districts have the ethical and moral obligation to create learning environments where all students are included and engaged in a community that supports optimal personal, social, and academic growth. Schools must be safe for all students to learn and for all faculty to teach. As Biegel (2010) states, "The right to be out has emerged today as a strong and multifaceted legal imperative" (p. 3). Updating school policies, embracing social justice, and committing to make schools safe for every student to succeed are critical to this end.

Society is a complex mechanism. As a social group, the LGBTQ community has a history that is scarred with maltreatment and injustice. Some of these injustices were born in malice, others were born in ignorance. But through it all, there have been, and continue to be, leaders, heroes, and allies who dare to challenge the status quo and fight for social justice. In spite of the strides that the LGBTQ movement has made, heterosexism and homophobia not only persist but also pervade our society and culture. The more resilient and fortunate few may experience heterosexism and homophobia as a persistent and inevitable bias; others experience them as an oppressive and stifling force that undermines their well being. Though attitudes, mores, and laws have certainly changed, there is substantial room for growth. Looking at our past can help us understand our present and enable us to build a future where all people are affirmed and recognized.

References

Allport, G. (1954). *The nature of prejudice.* Boston: Addison-Wesley Publishing, Inc.

American Association of University Women. (2001). *Hostile hallways: Bullying, teasing, and sexual harassment in school.* United States: Association of University Women Educational Fund.

American Civil Liberties Union. (2009, February 10). ACLU sues Nassau County Schools to enforce right of Gay Straight Alliance to meet at Yulee High School and Yulee Middle School. Retrieved from http://www.aclu.org/lgbt-rights_hiv-aids/aclu-sues-nassau-county-schools-enforce-right-gay-straight-alliance-meet-yulee-

APA Task Force on Appropriate Therapeutic Responses to Sexual Orientation. (2009). *Report of the task force on appropriate therapeutic responses to sexual orientation.* Washington, DC: American Psychological Association.

Austin, B. (2011). Homosexuals and the holocaust. Retrieved from http://frank.mtsu.edu/~baustin/homobg.html

Bérubé, A. (1990). *Coming out under fire: The history of gay men and women in World War II.* New York: Free Press. Retrieved from http://psychology.ucdavis.edu/rainbow/html/military_history.html

Besag, V. E. (2006). Bullying among girls: Friends or foes? *School Psychology International, 27,* 535–551. doi:10.1177/0143034306073401

Biegel, S. (2010). *The right to be out: Sexual orientation and gender identity in America's public schools.* Minneapolis, MN: University of Minnesota Press.

Birkett, M., Espelage, D., & Koenig, B. (2009). LGB and questioning students in schools: The moderating effects of homophobic bullying and school climate on negative outcomes. *Journal of Youth Adolescence, 38,* 989–1000. doi:10.1007/s10964-008-9389-1

Blumenfeld, W. (Ed.) (1992). *Homophobia: We all pay the price.* Boston, MA: Beacon.

Burgess, G. (1993). Crossroads: Turning point for a fourth grade teacher. In S. McDonnell-Celi (Ed.), *Twenty-first century challenge: Lesbians and gays in education: Bridging the gap* (pp. 27–29). NJ: Lavender Crystal Press.

California Senate Bill 48. (2010). Retrieved from http://info.sen.ca.gov/pub/11-12/bill/sen/sb_0001-0050/sb_48_bill_20110714_chaptered.html

Carter, D. (2004). *Stonewall: The riots that sparked the gay revolution.* New York, NY: St. Martin's Press.

Chang, K. (1996). The Baehr vs. Miike decision: Why gays should be allowed to marry. Retrieved from http://www.bidstrup.com/hawaii.htm

Chiasson, J. (2006). Lifting the veil of heterosexism: Effecting attitudinal change towards sexual minorities (Unpublished doctoral dissertation). The Claremont Graduate University, California.

Conger, J. J. (1975). Proceedings of the American Psychological Association, Incorporated, for the year 1974: Minutes of the annual meeting of the Council of Representatives. *American Psychologist, 30,* 620–651. doi:10.1037/h0078455

Coolridge, D. (1998, November 2). Voters finally get a say on same-sex marriage. *Wall Street Journal.* Retrieved from http://www.wallstreetjournal.com

Coyle, A., & Kitzinger, C. (2002). *Lesbian and gay psychology: New perspectives.* Oxford: Blackwell Publishers, Ltd.

Defense of Marriage Act. (1996), P. L. No. 104-199, 110 Stat. 2419 (1997). Retrieved from http://www.gpo.gov

Department of Housing and Urban Development. (2012). *Equal access to housing in HUD programs regardless of sexual orientation or gender identity.* Federal Register, 77(23). (February 3), 5662-5676. Retrieved from http://hud.gov

Dolan, M., & Willams, C. (2010, August 5). Appeal promised after federal judge finds state's Prop. 8 unconstitutional. *The Los Angeles Times.* Retrieved from http://articles.latimes.com/2010/aug/05/local/la-me-gay-marriage-california-20100805

Douglass, F. (1863). Men of color, to arms! Retrieved from http://teachingamericanhistory.org/library/index.asp?document=440

Eliason, M. J. (1997). The prevalence and nature of biphobia in heterosexual undergraduate students. *Archives of Sexual Behavior, 26*(3), 317–326. doi:10.1023/A:1024527032040

Ellement, J., Finucane, M., & Valencia M. (2012, May 31). Federal appeals court in Boston rules defense of marriage act unconstitutional. *The Boston Globe.* Retrieved from http://www.boston.com/metrodesk/2012/05/31/federal-appeals-court-boston-rules-defense-marriage-act-unconstitutional/cAEWI0tDSz8m1lsLN5fwAN/story.html

Erath, S. A., Flanagan, K. S., & Bierman, K. L. (2008). Early adolescents school adjustment: Associations with friendship and peer victimization. *Social Development, 17,* 853–870. doi:10.1111/j.1467-9507.2008.00458.x

Federal Bureau of Investigation. (n.d.). *Hate crimes.* Retrieved from http://www.fbi.gov/about-us/investigate/civilrights/hate_crimes

Freedom to Marry. (2012). *States.* Retrieved from http://www.freedomtomarry.org/states

Freeman, E., Schamel, W. B., & West, J. (1992). The fight for equal rights: A recruiting poster for Black soldiers in the Civil War. *Social Education, 56*(2), 118–120.

Gay-Straight Alliance Network. (2009). *History and accomplishments.* Retrieved from http://www.gsanetwork.org/about-us/history

Gerhardstein, K. R., & Anderson, V. N. (2010). There's more than meets the eye: Facial appearance and evaluations of transsexual people. *Sex Roles, 62*(5/6), 361–373. doi:10.1007/s11199-010-9746-x

Giles, G. J. (2002). The denial of homosexuality: Same-sex incidents in Himmler's SS and police. *Journal of the History of Sexuality, 11*(1/2), 256–290.

Ginn, H. L. (1995). Gay culture flourished in pre-Nazi Germany. *Update: Southern California's Gay & Lesbian Weekly Newspaper.* Retrieved from http://www.qrd.org/qrd/usa/california/update/gay.culture.flourished.prenazi.germany-10.95

Green, R. (1987). *The "sissy boy" syndrome and the development of homosexuality.* New Haven, CT: Yale University Press.

Greytak, E. A., Kosciw, J. G., & Diaz, E. M. (2009). *Harsh realities: The experiences of transgender youth in our nation's schools.* New York, NY: GLSEN.

Griffin, P., & Ouellett, M. (2003). From silence to safety and beyond: Historical trends in addressing lesbian, gay, bisexual and transgender issues in K-12 schools. *Equity & Excellence in Education, 36,* 106–114.

Haeberle, E. (1983). *The sex atlas.* New York, NY: The Continuum Publishing Company.

Hammack, P. L., Thompson, E., & Pilecki, A. (2009). Configurations of identity among sexual minority youth: Context, desire, and narrative. *Journal of Youth and Adolescence, 38*(7), 867–883. doi:10.1007/s10964-008-9342-3

Harbeck, K. (1997). *Gay and lesbian educators: Personal freedoms, public constraints.* Malden, MA: Amethyst Press.

Heger, H. (1980). *The men with the pink triangle.* Boston, MA: Alyson Publications, Inc.

Herdt, G. (1989). Gay and lesbian youth: Emergent identities and cultural scenes at home and abroad. In Gilbert Herdt (Ed.), *Gay and lesbian youth* (pp. 1–42). New York, NY: Harrington Park Press.

Herek, G. M. (April 2004). "Beyond 'homophobia': Thinking about sexual prejudice and stigma in the twenty-first century". *Sexuality Research & Social Policy, 1*(2), 6–24. doi:10.1525/srsp.2004.1.2.6

Human Rights Campaign. (2011). *Statewide laws & housing policies.* Retrieved from http://www.hrc.org/state_laws

Human Rights Watch. (2001). *Hatred in the hallways: Violence and discrimination against lesbian, gay, bisexual, and transgender students in U.S. schools.* New York, NY: Human Rights Watch.

Jacobs, S., Thomas, W., & Lang, S. (Eds.) (1997). *Two-spirit people: Native American gender identity, sexuality, and spirituality.* Champaign, IL: University of Illinois Press.

Jennings, K. (2006). *Mama's boy, preacher's son.* Boston, MA: Beacon Press.

Johnson, A. (2006). *Privilege, power and difference.* Boston, MA: McGraw Hill.

Jung, P., & Smith, R. (1993). *Heterosexism: An ethical challenge.* Albany, NY: State University of New York Press.

Jurist Legal Intelligence. (n.d.). *Famous trials.* Retrieved from http://jurist.lwaw.pitt.edu /trials

Katz, J. N. (1983). *Gay/lesbian almanac: A new documentary.* New York, NY: Harper.

Kleinplatz, P. J. (2001). *New directions in sex therapy: Innovations and alternatives.* London, England: Psychology Press.

Kosciw, J., Greytak, E., Diaz, E., & Bartkiewicz, M. (2010). *The 2009 National School Climate Survey: The experiences of lesbian, gay, bisexual and transgender youth in our nation's schools.* New York, NY: GLSEN.

Krafft-Ebing, R. F. (1888). *Psychopathia Sexualis: A clinical-forensic study.* Stuttgart, Germany: Self-published.

Lambda Legal. (2000). *Salt Lake School district official sued for nixing yet another student club.* Retrieved from http://www.lambdalegal.org/news/ny_20000411_salt-lake-school-district-official-sued

Lambda Legal. (n.d.). *Colín v. Orange Unified School District.* Retrieved from http://www.lambdalegal.org/in-court/cases/colin-v-orange-unified-school-district

Lipkin, A. (1999). *Understanding homosexuality, changing schools.* Boulder, CO: Westview Press.

Loving v. Virginia, 388 U.S. 1 (1967). Retrieved from http://caselaw.lp.findlaw.com/scripts/getcase.pl?court=us&vol=388&invol=1

MacGregor, M. J. (1979). Integration of the armed forces 1940–1965. Washington DC: Center of Military History United States Army. Retrieved from http://www.history.army.mil/books/integration/IAF-FM.htm

Marcus, E. (1992). *Making history: The struggle for gay and lesbian equal rights.* New York, NY: Harper Perennial.

Massachusetts trial court law libraries. (n.d.). *Massachusetts Law about same-sex marriage.* Retrieved from http://www.lawlib.state.ma.us/subject/about/gaymarriage.html

Mayo, C. (2007). *Disputing the subject of sex: Sexuality and public school controversies.* New York, NY: Rowman & Littlefield Publishers, Inc.

Mellin, E., & Hinojosa, T. (2011). Anti-gay bullying and suicide: Implications and resources for counselors. *Penn State: The Counselor Education Newsletter, 5*(2). Retrieved from http://www.ed.psu.ed/educ/epcse/counselor-education/newsletters

Memorandum for Secretaries of the Military Departments. (2011). Repeal of "don't ask, don't tell" (DADT): Quick reference guide. Retrieved from http://www.defense.gov/home/features/2010/0610_dadt/Quick_Reference_Guide_Repeal of DADT_APPROVED.pdf

Montopoll, B. (2011, February 23). Obama administration will no longer defend DOMA. *CBS News.* Retrieved from http://www.cbsnews.com/8301-503544_162-20035398-503544.html

National Association of School Psychologists. (2011). Lesbian, gay, bisexual, transgender, and questioning youth (Position Statement). Retrieved from: http://www.nasponline.org/about_nasp/positionpapers/LGBTQ_Youth.pdf

National Conference of State Legislatures. (2011). Retrieved from http://www.ncsl.org/default.aspx?tabid=12943

National Education Association. (2011). LGBT adolescent school victimization. Retrieved from http://www.nea.org/home/42485.htm

National Gay and Lesbian Task Force. (2012). Hate crimes laws map. Retrieved from http://thetaskforce.org/reports_and_research/hate_crimes_laws

Nicolosi, J. (1991). *Reparative therapy of male homosexuality.* Northvale, NJ: Jason Aronson, Inc.

O'Bryan, M., Fishbein, H., & Ritchey, P. (2004). Intergenerational transmission of prejudice, sex role stereotyping, and intolerance. *Adolescence, 39*(155), 407–426.

Parents and Friends of Lesbians and Gays. (2012). PFLAG's history. Retrieved from http://community.pflag.org/page.aspx?pid=267

Pendleton, R. (1993, July 5). The Johns Report identifies teachers. *Florida Times-Union,* p. 1.

Perrin, K., & DeJoy, S. (2003). Abstinence only education: How we got here and where we're going. *Journal of Public Health Policy, 24*(3/4), 445–459.

Pizer, J., Mallory, C., Sears, B., & Hunter, N. (2012). Evidence of persistent and pervasive workplace discrimination against LGBT people: The need for Federal legislation prohibiting discrimination and providing for equal employment benefits. *Loyola of Los Angeles Law Review, 45,* 715–779. Retrieved from http://williaminstitute.law.ucla.edu

Quindlen, A. (2009, April 3). The end of an error. *Newsweek Magazine.* Retrieved from http://www.thedailybeast.com/newsweek/2009/04/03/the-end-of-an-error.html

Quinto-Pozos, M. (2011). Texas community turns out to support Gay-Straight Alliance. *American Civil Liberties Union.* Retrieved from http://www.aclu.org

Reeder, G. (2000). Same-sex desire, conjugal constructs, and the tomb of Niankhkhnum and Khnumhotep. *World Archaeology 32*(2), 193–208. doi:10.1080/00438240050131180

Rekers, G. (1977). Atypical gender development and psychosocial adjustment. *Journal of Applied Behavioral Analysis. 10*(3), 559–571. doi:10.1901/jaba.1977.10-559

RescueYourChild.com. (2012). *About us.* Retrieved from http://rescueyourchild.com/About_Us.html

Russell, S. T., Clarke, T. J., & Clary, J. (2009). Are teens "post-gay"? Contemporary adolescents' sexual identity labels. *Journal of Youth and Adolescence, 38*(7), 884–890. doi:10.1007/s10964-008-9388-2

Russell, S., Muraco, A., Subramaniam, A., & Laub, C. (2009). Youth empowerment and high school gay-straight alliances. *Journal of Youth Adolescence, 38,* 891–903. doi:10.1007/s10964-9382-8

Rutledge, L. W. (1992). *The gay decades.* New York, NY: Plume Publishing.

Ryan, C. (2009). Family rejection as a predictor of negative health outcomes in white and Latino lesbian, gay, and bisexual young adults. *Pediatrics, 123*(1), 346–352. doi:10.1542/peds. 2007-3524

Saillant, C. (2011, December 19). Teen gets 21 years in prison for killing gay classmate. *The Los Angeles Times.* Retrieved from http://latimesblogs.latimes.com/lanow/2011/12/teen-gets-21-years-in-prison-for-killing-gay-classmate.html

Sanlo, R. (1999). *Unheard voices: The effects of silence on lesbian and gay teachers.* Westport, CT: Greenwood Press.

Sears, B., & Mallory, C. (2011). *Documented evidence of employment discrimination and its effect on LGBT people.* The Williams Institute. Retrieved from http://williamsinstitute.law.ucla.edu/research/workplace/documented-evidence-of-employment-discrimination-its-effects-on-lgbt-people/

Sears, J. T. (1997). *Lonely hunters: An oral history of lesbian and gay Southern life, 1948–1968.* University of Virginia, VA: Westview Press.

Servicemembers Legal Defense Network. (n.d.) *About "Don't Ask, Don't Tell."* Retrieved from www.sldn.org/pages/about-dadt

State of Hawai'i. (1998). 1998 General Elections Precinct Report. Retrieved from http://hawaii.gov/elections/results/1998/general/98swgen.htm

Turner, J., & Oakes, P. (1986). The significance of the social identity concept for social psychology with reference to individualism, interactionism and social influence. *British Journal of Social Psychology, 25*(3), 237–252. doi:10.1111/j.2044-8309.1986.tb00732.x

United States Courts. (n.d.). Retrieved from http://uscourts.gov

U.S. Equal Employment Opportunity Commission. (n.d.). *Laws enforced by EEOC.* Retrieved from http://www.eeoc.gov/laws/statutes/

U.S. Marriage Laws. (2012). Retrieved from http://www.usmarriagelaws.com

Uribe, V. (1994). Project 10: A school based outreach to gay and lesbian youth. *The High School Journal, 77*(1/2), 109–112.

Vagins, D. (2007). *Working in the shadows: Ending employment discrimination for LGBT Americans.* Washington, DC: ACLU Public Counsel for Civil Rights and Civil Liberties. Retrieved from http://www.aclu.org

Watanabe, T. (2011, October 11). California schools scrambling to add lessons on LGBT Americans. *The Los Angeles Times.* Retrieved from http://www.latimes.com/news/local/la-me-gay-schools-20111016,0,6753592.story

Weisberg, L. (2011, May 21). West Bend school sued for refusing Gay-Straight Alliance. *Wisconsin Gazette.* Retrieved from http://www.wisconsingazette.com/breaking-news/west-bend-school-sued-for-refusing-gay-straight-alliance.html

3 Adolescent Development
Identity, Intimacy, and Exploration

Omar B. Jamil, Gary W. Harper, and Douglas Bruce

Adolescence is generally understood as a time of great personal growth and development in the lifespan of an individual. Though the specific years when adolescence begins and ends has been the subject of debate among many researchers (e.g., Arnett, 2004; Erikson, 1980; Steinberg, 2008), overall it is generally accepted to occur within the second decade of one's life. For many adolescents, the true period of growth is made apparent through the physical changes of puberty. However, these changes also occur with vast development of the brain, namely in the development of the frontal lobe and prefrontal cortex (Casey, Tottenham, Liston, & Durston, 2005; Myers, 2007). This increased brain development leads to advances in an adolescent's cognitive abilities. Many scholars have described these specific changes in the adolescent brain according to a variety of models and theories (e.g., Demetriou, Cristou, Spanoudis, & Platsidou, 2002; Keating, 2004; Piaget, 1963), but one significant outcome reflected in the consensus of these cognitive development frameworks is the ability of the adolescent to engage in abstract thinking.

According to Piaget (1963), abstract reasoning is developed during the Formal Operations stage of cognitive development and forms the basis for full formal adult thinking. Though hypothetical/abstract thinking may be helpful for understanding external concepts and engaging in problem-solving, hypothetical thinking also can be beneficial in more internal or introspective cognitive processes (Piaget, 1963). It is through this process of internal abstract thinking, among other cognitive changes, that adolescents begin to question and have a deeper understanding of their self-concept. During this process adolescents become keenly aware and hypercritical of their external presentation to others and consequently to other people's perceptions of them. As a result, during adolescence, young people gradually develop a greater understanding of their sense of self and/or their own identity (Erikson, 1980), including their sexuality.

Ego Identity Development

Our current understanding of identity development has been greatly influenced by the seminal work of Erikson (1980) and his stage theory of identity development, which emphasizes the growth of the individual throughout the lifespan. Consisting of eight stages, Erikson's stages are generally bound by age, beginning in childhood with a stage involving basic trust and autonomy issues and progressing to ego integrity in late adulthood until death. Each specific stage is marked with a specific conflict of identity for the individual. If the individual undergoes the necessary experiences in order to resolve the conflict, his/her sense of identity is strengthened. On the other hand, if a conflict is not resolved at the age defined by the stages, the individual will carry the conflict into later stages of life.

Of particular importance for this chapter is stage five, *adolescence*, where Erikson (1980) asserts that the individual is faced with the important challenge of developing a sense of identity in her/his occupation, sex roles, politics, and religion. Though Erikson's theory did not specifically address sexual orientation, he did discuss the importance of identifying with one's masculinity/femininity through the clarification of one's "sex roles" (Erikson, 1980). Development of an identity involves creating a self-image which is meaningful to oneself and to significant individuals within one's community. This conflict of determining one's identity, conceptualized by Erikson (1980) as one's ego identity, is termed *ego identity vs. identity diffusion*. If an adolescent does not attain a sense of identity at the end of this stage, she/he will lack clarity regarding who she/he is and what her/his role is in life (*identity diffusion*).

Expanding on the initial work by Erikson, specifically the concept of *ego identity vs. identity diffusion*, Marcia (1966) identified four ego identity statuses to which individuals may belong depending on (a) the degree that the individual has explored the various aspects of his/her identity, and (b) the commitment to identity based on the exploration process. Exploration is marked by confusion or uncertainty regarding one's identity which leads to an explorative process (i.e., "Who am I?"), while commitment is characterized by a decisive statement regarding one's identity (i.e., "I am . . ."). However, both crisis/exploration and commitment may occur singularly, concurrently, or both may be absent in the individual, with varying combinations of these processes leading to four potential identity statuses. Those who have engaged in crisis/exploration and who have made a commitment have attained *identity-achievement*, which is considered the strongest sense of ego identity. Youth who have an incomplete sense of identity without either engaging in crisis/exploration or making a commitment (or both) are in a status of (a) *foreclosure*: acceptance without questioning of an identity imposed by family or significant others, (b) *moratorium*: where exploration may have occurred with no clear commitment, or (c) *identity-diffusion*: where neither exploration nor commitment to an identity has occurred. In addition to developing a sense of one's occupational aspirations, as well as religious, political, and moral ideologies, Marcia (1980) noted that a component of ego identity also involved an understanding of one's sexual orientation. The emergence of sexual desires in adolescence, and the implications on developmental milestones such as dating and intimacy, has promoted a field of research concerning the processes of sexual orientation identity development.

Sexual Orientation Identity Development

Initial theorists of sexual orientation identity development (Cass, 1979; Coleman, 1982; Troiden, 1989) suggest that this type of identity development begins with a stage where the individual is unaware of same-sex attractions, but still experiences a generalized sense of marginalization marked by feelings of being different in some way from peers. This sense of being different later progresses to an awareness of personal same-sex attractions, and subsequent exploration of sexual orientation identity through same-sex sexual experiences and/or exploration of a "gay community" through participation in lesbian, gay, or bisexual (LGB)-oriented activities. This process may be inhibited if the individual incorporates negative attitudes and beliefs about homosexuality into her/his self-concept, termed "internalized homophobia" (Maylon, 1981–1982). For those who overcome negative self-bias, the process of exploration entails the individual gradually accepting a personally appropriate label to describe her/his sexual orientation identity. Similar to the process of ethnic identity development, an LGB person's identity may fluctuate from valuing her/his sexual orientation community as better than heterosexuals, to later identifying the "gay community" and LGB identity as being equal to those within the larger heterosexual community. The initial theories of sexual orientation identity development suggest that development occurs in a linear progression.

D'Augelli's (1994) model of LGB identity development presents a different perspective than prior models, as it is based in a social constructivist view of sexual orientation and takes a more fluid lifespan development approach to sexual identity. This model presents sexual identity development in terms of six interactive processes or steps, as opposed to rigid progressive stages, emphasizing an individual's ability to move forward and backward between steps based on interactions and experiences. By being fluid, this model attends to individual differences and trajectories in sexual orientation identity development. The processes involve (a) exiting a heterosexual identity, (b) developing a personal LGB identity status, (c) creating an LGB social identity, (d) becoming an LGB offspring, (e) developing an LGB intimacy status, and (f) entering an LGB community.

Though previous theories have examined sexual identity development from both a male and female perspective, Diamond's (2005) research suggests that sexual orientation identity development may entail a very different process for girls and women. Through her research following the patterns of attractions toward men and women over an eight-year period, Diamond (2005) identified a variety of lesbian subtypes, termed "stable" and "fluid" to represent the stability or fluidity, respectively, of women's sexual attractions toward men and women. She suggests that fluidity in sexual orientation among women is impacted by social pressures to be in heterosexual relationships, which are promoted early in a young girl's development (Diamond, 2004). Diamond's research highlights the complexities of desire and the challenges in determining labels for one's sexual orientation.

Savin-Williams (2005) stated that there are many trajectories to identity development among gay and lesbian youth, and that previous models of understanding identity development through a progression of phases or stages does not address the diversity of such a complicated process. He identified several themes which are important in understanding identity development among gay and lesbian youth, including (a) feeling different, (b) same-sex attractions, (c) doubting one's heterosexuality, (d) same-sex behavior, (e) self-identification, (f) disclosure, and (g) acceptance. Though many of these themes were identified in previous sexual orientation identity development theories (Cass, 1979; Coleman, 1982; Troiden, 1989), Savin-Williams (2005) stated that these are a general framework for identity development, which may include some of the above themes but may include additional ones as well.

Recent research by Harper and colleagues (2010) suggests that for gay, bisexual, and questioning (GBQ) male youth, their conceptualizations of sexual orientation identity are in constant evolution based on cognitive evaluative processes and life experiences. Harper et al.'s (2010) empirically based model of same-sex sexual orientation identity suggests that sexual orientation identity development is a reciprocal, transactional process whereby a young man evaluates his (a) awareness of same-sex attraction and (b) participation in sexual orientation identity-related explorative experiences, all occurring within the context of proximal and distal influences. Proximal sources of influence include family, peers, and influential others, while distal influences include the perceived roles and responsibilities of what it means to be same-sex attracted, as well as social/cultural pressures and religion. Although the model presents temporal ordering of processes, these may occur in a cyclical fashion and do not necessarily result in one definitive moment where sexual orientation identity is fully achieved. Instead, these processes may occur and change over time, with new experiences resulting in changes in proximal and distal influences.

Harper et al.'s (2010) model proposes that there is first an *awareness of same-sex attraction*. This awareness may occur through various live or cyber-reality experiences, resulting in an individual's realization that he finds members of the same sex attractive or desirous. This awareness then leads to a *cognitive evaluation* of same-sex attraction influenced by both proximal and distal socio-cultural forces. Following this awareness and subsequent evaluation, the individual may engage in *sexual orientation identity related explorative experiences*. As with the initial same-sex attraction awareness, these experiences may occur either live or within an Internet setting and may range from learning more about the "gay community" by attending an LGB event or organization, to experiencing same-sex physical or emotional sexual/pre-sexual contact. Participation in sexual orientation identity explorative experiences and subsequent evaluation of these experiences is an ongoing reciprocal transactional process of influence. As the youth participates in these experiences there is an evaluative process regarding the fit of these experiences vis-à-vis his emerging sense of self. The evaluative process occurs in three realms: (a) affect, (b) cognitions, and (c) behavior. As with the cognitive evaluation process, the evaluative process is impacted by proximal and distal influences.

Though Harper et al.'s (2010) model is derived from research on gay, bisexual, and questioning young males, similar elements such as awareness of sexual attractions and sexual identity exploration, among others, have been observed in previous identity theories (Cass, 1979; Coleman, 1982; Troiden, 1989; Savin-Williams, 2005) which apply to both men and women. Additionally, Diamond's (2008) discussion of sexual orientation among women also addresses the role of contextual factors, as well as cognitive evaluation of experiences and orientation, in the development of sexual orientation identity for women.

Transgender Identity Development

While sexual orientation identity refers to the patterns of romantic and sexual attractions towards members of the same and/or other sex, gender identity describes an individual's sense of being male, female, or androgynous. Though all individuals undergo some development of gender identity, recent research has examined how gender identity develops among individuals who are transgender. Factor and Rothblum (2008) suggested that within the past 15 years, transgender individuals have increased in visibility to the extent that those who are identifying as transgender in contemporary society may have a significantly different experience than those who came to accept their gender identity during a time when transgender individuals were less visible. This assertion is based on an examination of data regarding the average age of transgender identity disclosure, which revealed that disclosure previously occurred in later adulthood but now is occurring much earlier.

Morgan and Stevens (2008) examined some of the developmental factors which impacted transgender identity development among a group of female-to-male transgender adults. Though these were retrospective accounts, they identified several key factors which can be further expounded in research. First, the participants indicated a strong sense of disconnection between their biological sex and their personal sense of gender. This disconnect manifested in discomfort with those activities and dress imposed by others because of their biological gender and preference for identifying with the other gender. During puberty, the participants recalled experiencing great discomfort resulting from the development of their secondary sexual characteristics, such as breasts, and engaged in compensatory behaviors, such as binding, to minimize their appearance. They also were resistive to imposed standards of dress, and conflicts in the home were common. Compensatory behaviors often would continue until individuals "reached the breaking point" whereupon they made decisions to transition to the other gender. Typically this decision was made in early adulthood, though primarily done when outside of their parents' household (Morgan & Stevens, 2008). More in-depth information on transgender individuals can be found in Chapter 5 of this volume.

Multiple Identity Development among LGBTQ Youth

The diversity of lesbian, gay, bisexual, transgender, and questioning (LGBTQ) persons within the United States, and the lack of research on LGBTQ persons of color in general, has led some researchers to focus on the intersection of ethnic and sexual orientation identities among LGBTQ people of color (e.g., Dube & Savin-Williams, 1999; McCready, 2004; Wilson & Harper, 2012). When exploring the influence of possessing multiple minority statuses on health and development, some researchers have proposed utilizing an intersectional framework which recognizes the importance of exploring the complex interplay between oppressed and privileged identities and statuses related to factors such as sexual orientation, gender, race/ethnicity, social class, and (dis)ability (Bowleg, Burkholder, Teti, & Craig, 2008; Price, 2011; Wilson & Harper, in press). It is understood that these social identities are not merely additive, but instead create an intricate interaction that can be influenced by the composition and visibility of an individual's oppressed and privileged statuses (Bowleg et al., 2008; Croteau, Talbot, Lance, & Evans, 2002; Szymanski & Meyer, 2008).

Although much of the multiple identities research for LGBTQ people of color has focused on adult populations, some studies have explored these phenomena among youth. Jamil, Harper, Fernandez, and the Adolescent Medicine Trials Network for HIV/ AIDS Interventions' (2009) study of ethnic minority GBQ male youth found that ethnic identity and sexual orientation identity formation occur concurrently during adolescence, but the two appear to be unique processes that are influenced by different factors. Ethnic identity development was informed by growing awareness of one's own ethnic and cultural heritage, and supported by peers, family members, and forms of cultural expression such as food, music, and holidays. In contrast, sexual orientation identity development was supported by community-based organizations, peers, and information gathered via the Internet. The process of sexual orientation identity development was described as a private process, whereas ethnic identity development was a public process (Jamil et al., 2009).

Another study conducted a comparison of same-sex sexual orientation milestones in adolescents from different ethnic/racial groups (Rosario, Schrimshaw, & Hunter, 2004). Although they found no differences among Latino, African American, and White youth in terms of the timing of these developmental milestones, there were differences with regard to connection to the LGB community and sexual orientation disclosure. Black youths were found to take part in fewer social activities within the LGB community than those from other ethnic/racial groups, and Black and Latino youths tended to disclose their sexual orientation to fewer persons than their White counterparts (Rosario et al., 2004). Chapter 6 of this volume addresses the diversity of LGBTQ individuals in greater depth.

Identity Exploration, Acceptance, and Disclosure

In light of the changing attitudes and increasing acceptability of sexual and gender diversity, recently, researchers (e.g., Harper, Bruce, Serrano, & Jamil, 2008; Kubicek, Carpineto, McDavitt, Weiss, & Kipke, 2011; Mustanski, Lyons, & Garcia 2011) have examined how identity development may occur for contemporary adolescents and young adults, many of whom choose to disclose their identities much earlier than those individuals who were participants in early sexual orientation and gender identity research (e.g., Cass, 1979; Coleman, 1982; Troiden, 1989). More current research has highlighted the importance of technology in sexual orientation identity exploration, the fluidity of sexual orientation identity, and the process of disclosing same-sex sexual attractions to others (Harper et al., 2008; Kubicek et al., 2011; Mustanski et al., 2011). Given the paucity of research and theory on transgender adolescents, the following section will focus only on sexual orientation identity. Chapter 5 of this volume expands on transgender identity development and experiences.

Sexual Orientation Identity Exploration

Due to its widespread acceptability and use among LGBTQ youth, the Internet has become a facilitative tool in the sexual orientation development of young people. Qualitative studies conducted by Harper et al. (2008) and Mustanski et al. (2011) have revealed that gay, bisexual, questioning, and queer identified male youth reported using the Internet to assist them in their sexual orientation identity development process. Harper et al. (2008) revealed that the Internet facilitated the development of sexual orientation identity by: (a) increasing self-awareness of youth's sexual orientation identity; (b) learning about sexual orientation identity and gay culture; (c) connecting with other gay/bisexual youth; (d) finding support and acceptance for their sexual orientation identity; (e) increasing comfort with their sexual orientation identity; and (f) facilitating their coming out process. Similarly, Mustanski et al.'s (2011) data revealed three primary themes related to the Internet's role in sexual orientation identity development, including (a) connecting to the gay community, (b) accessing information about coming out, and (c) viewing online same-sex erotica. Additionally, Kubicek and colleagues (2011) emphasized the importance of the Internet in providing youth with a place to learn about their same-sex desires and attractions early in their sexual orientation identity exploration (Kubicek et al., 2011).

The participants in Harper et al.'s (2008) study noted that the Internet provided access to an array of resources where they could safely explore their sexual orientation and learn about their sexual orientation identity. The youth stated that they used Internet message boards and chat rooms where they could connect with and find support from other individuals. These forms of connection allowed for varying levels of anonymity, whereby youth could connect without a username and converse anonymously, or choose to selectively disclose varying degrees of information. By managing their level of privacy, the participants could connect safely without fear of reprisal or unwanted disclosure to those in their family or immediate peer groups. Ethnic minority GBQ youth also identified message boards and chatrooms which were specifically oriented to African American or Latino LGBTQ people as a means to not only connect with ethnically similar GBQ young men, but also find mentorship and support among other ethnic minority LGBTQ people.

In addition to the Internet, Vargas and colleagues (2007) discussed the roles that schools and community agencies have in the maintenance of a supportive climate for gay, lesbian, and questioning youth in urban settings. Through their interviews with youth and school educators and administrators, they found that school staff often support sexuality-related bullying and create an overall hostile environment for sexual minority youth, who are often still struggling with their own identity. Despite the many institutional barriers to creating a positive and supportive climate, they identified that school-based organizations such as Gay-Straight Alliances (GSAs) provide a safe environment for students who are exploring and accepting their sexual orientation identity. In addition to GSAs, one participant noted that incorporating sexuality-related bullying into the general bullying prevention curriculum not only contributed to decreasing rates of sexuality-related bullying, but also improved the environment of sexual minority youth in schools. Finally, Vargas et al. (2007) noted that community organizations outside of the school setting also were identified as having a positive role in the development and support of gay, lesbian, and questioning youth.

Sexual Orientation Identity Acceptance

Acceptance of one's identity as an LGB person is typically a part of the sexual orientation development process but may fluctuate as individuals continue to explore and expand their sense of self and identity. Although sexual orientation acceptance was once marked by a definitive label as lesbian, gay or bisexual, contemporary youth are choosing alternative identity labels when they confirm their same-sex sexual attractions. Savin-Williams (2005) noted that an increasing number of youth are refusing to attach a sexual orientation label to describe their sexual orientation identity for a variety of reasons:

- Youth may choose to avoid identifying as "gay" to preserve their physical safety if they live in a potentially hostile environment toward lesbian and gay individuals;

- Refusing to identify with a non-heterosexual sexual orientation label may reflect a sense of internalized homophobia, where society's negative messages against homosexuality are accepted and have a negative impact on the self;
- The terms under the "LGBTQ" umbrella do not fully represent the fluidity in sexual orientation that youth experience;
- Youth may fully embrace their sexual orientation but oppose the philosophy behind relegating their identity to a specific label;
- Youth may not see a fit between themselves and the stereotypes of gay and lesbian individuals portrayed in the media; and
- Youth may abandon sexual orientation identity labels for political reasons, either to make a political statement against labeling or as part of a larger struggle against racism, classism, or sexism.

In addition to selecting an identity label as a sign of sexual orientation acceptance, dating and public acknowledgments of same-sex romantic relationships are other signs of acceptance and comfort with same-sex attraction. Finding potential dating partners may present a challenge though for LGB youth, as Glover, Galliher, and Lamere (2009) reported that adolescents and young adults with same-sex attractions typically have fewer opportunities for sexual experiences compared to their heterosexual peers. When opportunities do exist and LGB adolescents engage in dating and romantic relationships, there are multiple psychological benefits that can result, including higher self-esteem and lower rates of depression.

Sexual Orientation Identity Disclosure

During the identity development processes of self-exploration and self-acceptance, LGB youth typically disclose their emerging sexual orientation identity to others. Recent research by Grov, Bimbi, Nanin, and Parsons (2006) indicates that lesbian and gay youth are disclosing their same-sex attractions to others, including their parents, at a significantly younger age than in past generations. They also noted that though the timing of awareness of same-sex sexual attractions did not differ among ethnic groups, White lesbian and gay youth had disclosed their sexual orientation to others at significantly higher rates than Latino/a, African American, and Asian youth. This racial difference also was identified by research conducted by Rosario and colleagues (2004), who found that compared to their White counterparts, Latino/a and African American youth disclosed their sexual orientation to fewer individuals. Further, Rosario and colleagues (2004) noted that African American youth participated in gay-related social and recreational activities less often than White youths. In examining the disclosure process specifically towards parents, Savin-Williams and Ream (2003) found that common reactions were positive, including support and acceptance, while others were slightly negative, which commonly manifested in fears for their child's safety. A minority of the participants expressed being rejected, which included verbal or physical harassment by their parents. Recent research demonstrates the critical importance of parental acceptance once a youth discloses her/his LGB sexual orientation to a parent, as higher levels of parental rejection have been associated with increased rates of suicide attempts, depression, illegal drug use, and unprotected sexual intercourse compared with peers from families with low to no levels of family rejection (Ryan, Huebner, Diaz, & Sanchez, 2009). Heatherington and Lavner (2008) emphasize the importance of also exploring the more long-term process of family acceptance after an adolescent discloses her/his sexual orientation and have created a conceptual model of positive family acceptance that presents both individual-level and relational-level variables associated with positive outcomes using a family-systems approach.

Implications for School Professionals

It is important for all members of the school community (e.g., teachers, administrators, counselors, psychologists, social workers) to keep in mind that while the students served in an educational setting are learning academic content in the classroom, they also are continually learning about themselves while they attempt to form an integrated identity. To best assist students in the process of sexual orientation identity development, the provision of a range of resources, as indicated in the research reviewed in this chapter, is paramount. Developing and providing a range of culturally and developmentally appropriate materials in a variety of settings within academic institutions, both in physical (e.g., books, movies, etc.) and virtual (e.g., websites, Internet chat rooms) formats, ensures that youth will have access to vital resources when they are most needed. Having such resources easily accessible in a safe space is preferable, such as LGBTQ-focused handouts placed with other resource materials throughout the institution, so that young people can access materials without fear of being "outed." Being able to access information without unwanted disclosure of one's sexual identity is very important for many students including those who are still living in their parents' home, since parents may remove financial and emotional support if a child discloses her/his sexual orientation (Rivers & D'Augelli, 2001).

Given the amount of time that adolescents spend in school, schools are ideal places to have open and honest conversations about same-sex sexuality, which could assist in the sexual orientation identity development of LGB adolescents. Unfortunately, recent data demonstrate that gay/bisexual male youth did not learn about same-sex sexual activity from school, family, or friends (the typical sources for heterosexual youth), and instead learned about it from Internet websites (usually pornography) or from their first sexual experience with a man (Kubicek, Beyer, Weiss, Iverson, & Kipke, 2010). One reason for this lack of focus on LGB sexuality in schools may be widespread heterosexism and homophobic victimization in schools, which may create unsafe environments for open discussion of same-sex sexuality. This is supported by the Gay, Lesbian, and Straight Education Network (GLSEN)'s 2009 National School Climate Survey of 7,261 middle and high school students, which found that 90% of lesbian, gay, bisexual, and transgender (LGBT) students experienced harassment at school in the prior year, almost two-thirds felt unsafe because of their sexual orientation, and nearly one third of LGBT students skipped at least one day of school in the prior month because they felt unsafe (Kosciw, Greytak, Diaz, & Bartkiewicz, 2010).

Including same-sex sexual desire and activity as part of normative sexual expression in comprehensive sexuality education programs could also create opportunities for discussions regarding sexual diversity that may impact the way heterosexual youth view their same-sex attracted peers, thus increasing the likelihood of acceptance. Teachers will need to work to create more accepting classroom environments prior to such discussions (Davidson, 2006; Jamil & Harper, 2010; McCready, 2004) in order to ensure the safety of LGBTQ students and to avoid the occurrence of negative physical and mental health effects. School-based comprehensive sexuality education interventions also would provide an opportunity to address LGB youth either prior to their sexual debut or early in their sexual lives, and assist in creating a healthier sexual orientation identity development process.

Though the processes of sexual orientation identity development for LGBTQ youth cannot be succinctly encapsulated into one specific trajectory, it is clear that the processes are intense and very complex, and thus involve maneuvering, flexibility, and effort in order to develop a positive sense of self. In order to best serve these young people, school professionals must be committed and creative when accessing and assisting these young people to assure that they develop into integrated and well-adjusted members of society.

References

Arnett, J. (2004). *Emerging adulthood: The winding road from the late teens through the twenties.* New York, NY: Oxford University Press.

Bowleg, L., Burkholder, G., Teti, M., & Craig, M. L. (2008). The complexities of outness: Psychosocial predictors of coming out to others among Black lesbian and bisexual women. *Journal of LGBT Health Research, 4*(4), 153–166.

Casey, B. J., Tottenham, N., Liston, C., & Durston, S. (2005). Imaging the developing brain: What have we learned about cognitive development? *Trends in Cognitive Science, 9*, 104–110.

Cass, V. C. (1979). Homosexual identity formation: A theoretical model. *Journal of Homosexuality, 4*, 219–235.

Coleman, E. (1982). Developmental stages of the coming out process. *Journal of Homosexuality, 9*, 105–126.

Croteau, J., Talbot, D., Lance, T., & Evans, N. (2002). A qualitative study of the interplay between privilege and oppression. *Journal of Multicultural Counseling & Development, 30*(4), 239–258.

D'Augelli, A. R. (1994). Identity development and sexual orientation: Toward a model of lesbian, gay, and bisexual development. In E. J. Trickett & R. J. Watts (Eds.), *Human diversity: Perspectives on people in context.* (pp. 312–333). San Francisco, CA: Jossey-Bass.

Davidson, S. M. (2006). Exploring sociocultural borderlands: Journeying, navigating, and embodying a queer identity. *Journal of Men's Studies 14*(1), 13–26.

Demetriou, A., Cristou, C., Spanoudis, G., & Platsidou, M. (2002). The development of mental processing: Efficiency, working memory, and thinking. *Monographs of the Society for Research in Child Development, 67*(1), Serial No. 268.

Diamond, L. M. (2004). Emerging perspectives on distinctions between romantic love and sexual desire. *Current Directions in Psychological Science, 13*, 116–119.

Diamond, L. M. (2005). A new view of lesbian subtypes: Stable versus fluid identity trajectories over an 8-year period. *Psychology of Women Quarterly, 29*, 119–128.

Diamond, L. M. (2008). *Sexual fluidity: Understanding women's love and desire.* Cambridge, MA: Harvard University Press.

Dube, E. M., & Savin-Williams, R. C. (1999). Sexual identity development among ethnic sexual-minority male youths. *Developmental Psychology, 35*(6), 1389–1398.

Erikson, E. (1980). *Identity and the life cycle.* New York, NY: Norton.

Factor, R., & Rothblum, E. (2008). Exploring gender identity and community among three groups of transgender individuals in the United States: MTFs, FTMs, and genderqueers. *Health Sociology Review, 17*, 235–253.

Glover, J. A., Galliher, R. V., & Lamere, T. G. (2009). Identity development and exploration among sexual minority adolescents: Examination of a multidimensional model. *Journal of Homosexuality, 56*, 77–101.

Grov, C., Bimbi, D. S., Nanin, J. E., & Parsons, J. T. (2006). Race, ethnicity, gender, and generational factors associated with the coming-out process among lesbian and bisexual individuals. *Journal of Sex Research, 43*(2), 115–121.

Harper, G. W., Bruce, D., Serrano, P., & Jamil, O. B. (2008). The role of the Internet in the sexual identity development of gay and bisexual male adolescents. In P. L. Hammack & B. J. Cohler (Eds.), *The story of sexual identity: Narrative perspective on the gay and lesbian life course* (pp. 297–326). New York, NY: Oxford University Press.

Harper, G. W., Fernandez, M. I., Jamil, O. B., Hidalgo, M. A., Torres, R. S., Bruce, D., & The Adolescent Trials Network for HIV/AIDS Interventions. (2010, August). *An empirically-based transactional model of same-sex sexual orientation identity development.* Poster session presented at the Annual Meeting of the American Psychological Association, San Diego, California.

Heatherington, L., & Lavner, J. (2008). Coming to terms with coming out: A review and recommendations for family system-focused research. *Journal of Family Psychology, 22*, 329–343.

Jamil, O.B., & Harper, G. W. (2010). School for the self: Examining the role of educational settings for identity development among gay/bisexual/questioning male youth of color. In C. Bertram, M.S. Crowley, & S. Massey (Eds.), *LGBTQ youth in their educational contexts* (pp. 175–202). New York, NY: Peter Lang Publishers.

Jamil, O. B., Harper, G. W., & Fernandez, M. I., & The Adolescent Trials Network for HIV/AIDS Interventions. (2009). Sexual and ethnic identity development among gay-bisexual-questioning (GBQ) male ethnic minority adolescents. *Cultural Diversity and Ethnic Minority Psychology, 15*(3), 203–214.

Keating, D. (2004). Cognitive and brain development. In R. Lerner & L. Steinberg (Eds.), *Handbook of adolescent psychology* (2nd ed., pp. 45–84). New York, NY: Wiley.

Kosciw, J., Greytak, E., Diaz, E., & Bartkiewicz, M. (2010). *The 2009 National School Climate Survey: The experiences of lesbian, gay, bisexual and transgender youth in our nation's schools.* New York, NY: GLSEN.

Kubicek, K., Beyer, W. J., Weiss, G., Iverson, E., & Kipke, M. D. (2010). In the dark: Young men's stories of sexual initiation in the absence of relevant sexual health information. *Health Education and Behavior, 37*(2), 243–263.

Kubicek, K., Carpineto, J., McDavitt, B., Weiss, G., & Kipke, M. D. (2011). Use and perceptions of the Internet for sexual information and partners: A study of young men who have sex with men. *Archives of Sexual Behavior, 40*(4), 803–816.

Marcia, J. E. (1966). Development and validation of ego-identity status. *Journal of Personality and Social Psychology, 3*, 551–558.

Marcia, J. E. (1980). Identity in adolescence. In J. Adelson (Ed.), *Handbook of adolescent psychology.* New York, NY: Wiley.

Maylon, A. K. (1981–1982). Psychotherapeutic implications of internalized homophobia in gay men. *Journal of Homosexuality 7*(2–3), 59–69.

McCready, L. (2004). Understanding the marginalization of gay and gender non-conforming black male students. *Theory Into Practice, 43*(2), 136–143.

Morgan, S. W., & Stevens, P. E. (2008). Transgender identity development as represented by a group of female-to-male transgendered adults. *Issues in Mental Health Nursing, 29*, 585–599.

Mustanski, B., Newcomb, M., Du Bois, S., Garcia, S., & Grov, C. (2011). HIV in young men who have sex with men: a review of epidemiology, risk and protective factors, and interventions. *Journal of Sex Research, 48*(2–3), 218–253.

Myers, D. G. (2007). *Psychology* (8th ed.). New York, NY: Worth Publishers.

Piaget, J. (1963). *The origins of intelligence in children.* New York, NY: W.W. Norton & Company, Inc.

Price, K. (2011). It's not just about abortion: Incorporating intersectionality in research about women of color and reproduction. *Women's Health Issues, 21*(3, Suppl), S55–S57.

Rivers, I., & D'Augelli, A. R. (2001). The victimization of lesbian, gay, and bisexual youths. In A. R. D'Augelli & C. J. Patterson (Eds.), *Lesbian, gay and bisexual identities and youth: Psychological perspectives* (pp. 199–223). New York, NY: Oxford University Press.

Rosario, M., Schrimshaw, E. W., & Hunter, J. (2004). Ethnic/racial differences in the coming-out process of lesbian, gay, and bisexual youths: A comparison of sexual identity development over time. *Cultural Diversity & Ethnic Minority Psychology, 10*(3), 215–228.

Ryan, C., Huebner, D., Diaz, R. M., & Sanchez, J. (2009). Family rejection as a predictor of negative health outcomes in White and Latino lesbian, gay and bisexual young adults. *Pediatrics,123*(1), 346–352.

Savin-Williams, R. C. (2005). *The new gay teenager.* Cambridge, MA: Harvard University Press.

Savin-Williams, R. C., & Ream, G. L. (2003). Sex variations in the disclosure to parents of same-sex attractions. *Journal of Family Psychology, 17*(3), 429–438.

Steinberg, L. (2008). *Adolescence* (8th ed.). New York, NY: McGraw-Hill.

Szymanski, D., & Meyer, D. (2008). Racism and heterosexism as correlates of psychological distress in African American sexual minority women. *Journal of LGBT Issues in Counseling, 2*(2), 94–108.

Troiden, R. R. (1989). The formation of homosexual identities. *Journal of Homosexuality, 17,* 43–73.

Vargas, K., Graybill, E., Mahan, W., Meyers, J., Dew, B., Marshall, M., . . . Birckbichler, L. (2007). Urban service providers' perspectives on school responses to gay, lesbian, and questioning students: An exploratory study. *Professional School Counseling, 11*(2), 113–119.

Wilson, B. D. M., & Harper, G. W. (2012). Race and ethnicity in lesbian, gay and bisexual communities. In C. J. Patterson & A. R. D'Augelli (Eds.), *Handbook of psychology and sexual orientation.* New York, NY: Oxford University Press.

4 Promoting Resilience in Lesbian, Gay, Bisexual, Transgender, and Questioning Youth

Karen Komosa-Hawkins and
G. Thomas Schanding, Jr.

Much of the existing literature on lesbian, gay, bisexual, transgender, and questioning (LGBTQ) youth has focused on the various risks and corresponding negative outcomes associated with an LGBTQ identity and has underemphasized the extent to which LGBTQ individuals evidence positive outcomes or resilience (Savin-Williams, 2005). A resilience or health/wellness framework rejects a traditional pathological or deficit model, which assumes a negative developmental trajectory (Savin-Williams, 2005). Instead, it takes a more balanced and strengths-based approach, emphasizing the strengths/assets that contribute to positive adjustment and development despite potential vulnerability due to heightened risks associated with LGBTQ status. The aim of this chapter is to identify factors that place LGBTQ individuals at risk for maladjustment, as well as factors (protective processes) that moderate/mediate these risks or serve to buffer individuals from negative outcomes so as to understand how to effectively promote well-being through prevention or appropriately intervene if and when risks outweigh protections.

A first step in addressing the challenges/stressors of this population is to minimize the amount of environmental risk associated with an identity of LGBTQ. Research suggests that when these environmental risks are minimized and protective factors are optimized, youth will experience better social-emotional, academic, and career outcomes, with the majority of LGBTQ youth developing into happy and healthy adults (Eisenberg & Resnick, 2006; Savin-Williams, 2005; Williams, Connolly, Pepler, & Craig, 2005). Professionals cannot begin to make positive changes without fully understanding both risks and protections. Understanding risks and negative outcomes provides impetus for taking action to eliminate or minimize risks. On the other hand, a focus on protections not only informs prevention, but also gives us hope and expectations for more positive outcomes. This chapter will address resilience as it relates to the unique assets and needs of LGBTQ youth. First, the spectrum of resilience within the LGBTQ population will be touched upon, followed by an exploration of resilience, and, lastly, an examination of individual, family, and community risks and protections specific to the LGBTQ population as a whole will be addressed.

Spectrum of Resilience

It is important to recognize the vast heterogeneity of the LGBTQ population in terms of the spectrum of risk and protection (Eisenberg & Resnick, 2006; Savin-Williams, 2005;

Williams et al., 2005). When risks outweigh protections, individuals are more vulnerable to experiencing internalizing symptoms (e.g., anxiety, depression) and/or externalizing symptoms (e.g., health-compromising or behavior problems), which also may contribute to negative school-related outcomes (e.g., poor attendance/truancy, academic failure, dropout) amongst other problems (e.g., self-harm, homelessness; Williams et al., 2005). On the other hand, environmental factors contribute to significant variability in terms of risks and protections encountered. Furthermore, there is a need to understand each unique and whole person within his/her context and according to his/her worldview so that preventions and interventions are appropriate and effective (Condly, 2006; Murdock & Bolch, 2005; Sameroff, Gutman, & Peck, 2003; Savin-Williams, 2005).

For purposes of this chapter, LGBTQ is discussed as a population; however, variations exist within this group based on whether an individual identifies as L, G, B, T, or Q, and due to cultural and individual differences (Busseri, Willoughby, Chalmers, & Bogaert, 2006; Savin-Williams, 2005). The heterogeneity found within the LGBTQ population will be further explored in Chapter 6 of this volume. Given the diversity that exists, an ecological framework is recommended for understanding the multiple contexts and factors that interact and are at play in healthy and successful child/adolescent adjustment, whereby positive developmental outcomes and potential are optimized despite any adversity encountered (Elias, Parker, & Rosenblatt, 2006; Horn, Kosciw, & Russell, 2009; Sameroff et al., 2003; Savin-Williams, 2005). It is this coexistence of positive adaptation and adversity that contributes to resilience (Luthar, Cicchetti, & Bronwyn, 2000).

Understanding Resilience

Resilience[1] is a complex, multidimensional construct representing the interplay of risk and protective factors and/or processes (Condly, 2006; Luthar et al., 2000). Resilience is broadly defined as the successful achievement of developmental tasks and/or demonstration of positive adaptation or adjustment in one or more domains of functioning despite adversity, challenges, stress, trauma, or toxic environments (Condly, 2006; Luthar et al., 2000, Masten, 2001; Masten, Herbers, Cutuli, & Lafavor, 2008). Adversity can be conceptualized as a threat to basic needs being met or an impediment to accomplishing developmental tasks/goals (Winslow, Sandler, & Wolchik, 2006). It is well established that the greater the risk or adversity, the *more likely* an individual's mental health will be compromised, *potentially* resulting in poor outcomes, while at the same time, the greater number of protections are thought to increase the likelihood of more favorable outcomes (e.g., social-emotional competence, academic achievement, mental health; Sameroff et al., 2003; Winslow et al., 2006). In fact, every context has the potential to serve as a source of protection or risk. For example, if youth experience a safe/secure, nonjudgmental, and supportive environment, they are more likely to optimize their development and adjustment; whereas, if youth experience a toxic, unsafe, and unsupportive environment, they are predisposed for challenges or difficult transitions and thus, more likely to experience maladjustment (Tharinger & Wells, 2000).

Resilience is regarded as more than merely an absence of psychopathology or impairment; it also is evidence of the competencies necessary to negotiate the demands of life's various contexts (Masten, 2001; Masten et al., 2008). Examples of external adaptation consist of academic achievement or absence of delinquency, while examples of internal adaptation are psychological well-being or low levels of distress (Masten, 2001). The three established domains of resilience for children are educational, social-emotional, and behavioral (Condly, 2006; Luthar et al., 2000), and Condly (2006) suggests that there are two additional domains for adolescents: romantic and occupational. It is recognized that individuals may appear resilient in one or more domain and not another (Condly, 2006).

Distinguished from resiliency, which denotes an unchangeable trait, resilience is viewed as a context-dependent dynamic process that can be altered through intervention (Condly, 2006; Luthar et al., 2000). In other words, resilience is not a fixed state, but rather the result of continuously evolving risks and protections that interact with an individual as he/she progresses through various developmental stages (Luthar et al., 2000). There is no one single type of risk or protection that predicts a certain outcome, nor a universal risk/protective factor for all children/adolescents, but rather a complex and individualized constellation of risks and protections (Condly, 2006; Sameroff et al., 2003). Furthermore, the best predictor of adjustment is arguably an individual's unique cumulative *risk profile* (or as we prefer to call it, *resilience profile*), which is the ratio of cumulative risks and protections at any given time based on an individual's ecological context (e.g., family, peer group, school, neighborhood) and internal capacities (e.g., intellect, coping skills, temperament; Sameroff et al., 2003). To effectively solve multifaceted problems, a transactional-ecological model of resilience is recommended (Condly, 2006; Elias et al., 2006; Masten, 2001; Sameroff et al., 2003). A transactional-ecological model takes into account the complex and reciprocal interrelations that occur among the various environments with which an individual interacts.

Assessing the individual, family, and community risk and protective factors that interact for a particular individual will help to determine his/her level of resilience, which informs an individual's resilience profile and dictates how best to support LGBTQ individuals in general. The *individual domain* characterizes intrapersonal traits (e.g., temperament and personality) and cognitive/intellectual, emotional, and behavioral capacities, including emotional regulation, coping skills, and self worth (Condly, 2006; Luthar et al., 2000; Sameroff et al., 2003; Winslow et al., 2006). The *family domain* is conceptualized by various family characteristics (e.g., structure, dynamics, cohesion, warmth, responsivity, stability, support, involvement, and connectedness), as well as parenting style and parent–child relationships/attachments (Condly, 2006; Luthar et al., 2000; Sameroff et al., 2003; Tharinger & Wells, 2000; Winslow et al., 2006). The *community domain* consists of social environment factors found within a child/adolescent's school and/or neighborhood, including the availability of extrafamilial supports and resources found within both informal and formal networks (e.g., religious affiliations, extracurricular activities, or community agencies; Condly, 2006; Luthar et al., 2000; Sameroff et al., 2003; Winslow et al., 2006).

The complex interactions of individual, family, and community factors cannot be overstated. For example, if a child has formed secure attachments with his/her primary caregivers (family domain), the child will tend to develop more flexible and resourceful coping/problem-solving styles (individual domain) and will be more likely to seek out (and less resistant to) support from sources outside of the family (community domain) (Tharinger & Wells, 2000). The next section of this chapter will examine the risks and protections within each of these domains.

Individual Domain

Risks/Challenges

The research related to the individual-level risks of LGBTQ individuals has been mixed. Based on the findings of several studies, LGBTQ individuals exhibit increased depression, anxiety, hopelessness, and suicidality relative to heterosexual individuals (Espelage, Aragon, Birkett, & Koenig, 2008; Fergusson, Horwood, & Beautrais, 1999; Goodenow, Szalacha, & Westheimer, 2006; Safren & Heimberg, 1999). However, much of the research examining risk has relied on small samples of LGBTQ individuals (Fergusson et al., 1999). Nonetheless, in a report released by the Centers for Disease Control and Prevention (CDC, 2011), gay and lesbian youth were more likely to seriously consider attempting suicide compared to heterosexual youth (29.6% versus 11.7%, respectively), while 26.7% of students questioning their sexual orientation reported attempting suicide, and bisexual students were reportedly most at-risk of suicidal ideation (40.3%). In examining those who *actually attempted* suicide, the CDC found that gay, lesbian, and bisexual students were more likely to attempt suicide (25.8–28%) compared to heterosexual youth (6.4%).

Less research has focused on overall mental health issues for LGBTQ youth. In one of the first studies in this area, Mustanski, Garofalo, and Emerson (2010) found that LGBT youth had a higher prevalence of mental health disorders compared to a national sample of youth; the rates for LGBT youth were comparable to prevalence rates for urban and ethnically/racially diverse youth. According to minority stress theory, environmental stressors related to sexual orientation, such as higher incidences of discrimination, stigmatization, oppression, victimization, and harassment, likely contribute to poorer mental health consequences (Matthews & Adams, 2009). These events may threaten an individual's sense of safety and security, resulting in a greater risk for psychological or emotional distress and increased vulnerability for mental health problems (Herek, 2009; Kenny & Hage, 2009; Matthews & Adams, 2009). LGBTQ individuals are further at risk due to internalized homophobia/biphobia/transphobia, heterosexism, and social isolation, all of which contribute to and are exacerbated by decreased feelings of school belongingness, poorer attendance, increased truancy, and higher school dropout rates (Matthews & Adams, 2009; Murdock & Bolch, 2005; Tharinger & Wells, 2000). LGBTQ individuals also may experience social pressure to hide their identities and conform to heterosexual behaviors or activities, which may increase social anxiety and further limit access to social supports and resources (Safren & Pantalone, 2006). Additionally, those individuals who have been psychologically or physically victimized are at greatest risk for mental health problems and suicide (Rivers & D'Augelli, 2001).

Another area of risk for LGBTQ youth is substance abuse. Several studies have documented increased substance use and earlier onset of substance use for LGBTQ youth (Corliss et al., 2010; Marshal, Friedman, Stall, & Thompson, 2009). This includes smoking cigarettes (Easton, Jackson, Mowery, Comeau, & Sell, 2008), alcohol use (Ziyadeh et al., 2007), and nonprescription drug use (e.g., marijuana, crack/cocaine, heroin, etc.; Orenstein, 2001). Substance use, in turn, is correlated with risky sexual behaviors (Garofalo, Mustanski, McKirnan, Herrick, & Donenberg, 2007). Less is known regarding transgender youth and substance abuse; however, Garofalo and colleagues

(2007) indicated that 65% of male-to-female transgender youth reported alcohol use in the past year. Numerous environmental factors contribute to substance use and abuse in LGBTQ youth such as rejection, beliefs supporting drugs, parental approval of substance use, exposure to peers who use substances, and mental health problems (Tucker, Ellickson, & Klein, 2008). Despite these individual-level risks and challenges, which leave LGBTQ individuals more vulnerable, there are a number of protections that may buffer the existing risks/stressors.

Protections

A variety of intrapersonal strengths have been identified in the literature as necessary (though not always sufficient) precursors to positive adjustment or what Sameroff and colleagues (2003) call *stress resistance*. Intrapersonal strengths believed to serve as a source of protection are innate traits, such as a positive temperament and disposition (e.g., easy-going, sociable, etc.) and high intellect (Tharinger & Wells, 2000). Additionally, an individual with higher self-esteem is regarded as having a propensity toward resilience, suggesting a need for bolstering students' sense of self. In fact, self-acceptance, which is a positive view of oneself, including one's sexual orientation and/or gender identity, is believed to contribute to increased self-esteem (DePaul, Walsh, & Dam, 2009; Friedman & Morgan, 2009; Tharinger & Wells, 2000) and was found in one study to predict positive mental health for LGBTQ youth (Hershberger & D'Augelli, 1995). It also has been suggested that ethnic minority status, once thought to heighten risk, may actually buffer the stress related to experiences of heterosexism, due to an individual's capacity for coping with racism and the disadvantages associated with minority status (Meyer, 2010).

Other intrapersonal qualities purported to strengthen an individual's resilience include self-efficacy, self-confidence, self-worth, empathy, hope, planfulness, talents, and faith (Tharinger & Wells, 2000). On the other hand, one's faith might be a source of risk if it is at odds with one's sexual or gender identity. Yet other intrapersonal strengths believed to protect LGBTQ youth include social-emotional competencies,[2] such as problem-solving and conflict resolution skills (Masten et al., 2008).

One coping skill thought to be protective, particularly for LGBTQ individuals, is *adaptive distancing*, whereby an individual distances him or herself from destructive relationships in order to protect him/her self from being hurt (Tharinger & Wells, 2000, p. 162). Similarly, Condly (2006) and Elias et al. (2006) refer to the reciprocal nature of interactions between an individual and his/her environment such that positive responses from others contribute to an individual's self-worth, while at the same time an individual's qualities elicit certain responses (negative or positive) from others. This interaction between individual qualities and interpersonal relationships alludes to the complexity of risks and protections and relates to the family domain.

Family Domain

Risks/Challenges

For the majority of youth, families constitute a supportive, nurturing, accepting environment that promotes healthy development. For LGBTQ youth, however, the family unit may pose certain risks to physical, social, and emotional growth. Disclosing his/her sexual orientation or gender identity may place the adolescent at risk of being rejected by the family, which may lead to isolation and/or contribute to conflicted relationships (Rivers & D'Augelli, 2001). In fact, the mere anticipation of a negative response to disclosure causes significant stress for an individual (Hershberger & D'Augelli, 1995; Rivers & D'Augelli, 2001). For those rejected by their family, there is an increased risk of poor self-esteem/ worth, attempted suicide, depression, illegal drug use, and risky sexual behaviors (Rivers & D'Augelli, 2001; Ryan, Huebner, Diaz, & Sanchez, 2009). Furthermore, LGBTQ youth may become homeless due to their family's rejection as a result of their sexual orientation disclosure or gender expression, with recent research estimating that 20–35% of homeless youth identify as LGBTQ (Cochran, Stewart, Ginzler, & Cauce, 2002; Van Leeuwen et al., 2006). LGBTQ homeless youth are at increased risk of discrimination (Milburn, Ayala, Rice, Betterham, & Rotheram-Borus, 2006), risky sexual behaviors and sexually transmitted diseases (Kipke et al., 2007), and compromised mental health (Cochran et al., 2002).

Even when youth remain at home, there is an increased risk of discrimination and emotional and physical abuse from their family due to a sexual minority or gender variant status (Rivers & D'Augelli, 2001). Saewyc and colleagues (2006) found that LGB youth consistently reported a higher prevalence of physical and sexual abuse by family members as compared to their heterosexual counterparts. While one in eight heterosexual boys reported physical abuse, as many as one in three gay or bisexual boys reported physical abuse. Similarly, lesbian and bisexual girls reported more physical abuse than heterosexual girls, being twice as likely to be abused. While rates of sexual abuse amongst females are nearly equivalent, regardless of sexual orientation, with one in four females reporting a history of sexual abuse, one in four bisexual boys and one in five gay boys indicated sexual abuse compared to less than one in ten heterosexual boys. No data were reported for transgender youth in this study.

Protections

As referenced earlier in this chapter, quality and secure attachments[3] contribute to an internalized working model of one's self and others that leads to healthy development, relationships, and adaptive skills (Tharinger & Wells, 2000). Furthermore, strong attachments, a close and/or positive relationship to a caring parental figure, family connectedness, and authoritative parenting (i.e., warmth, structure, and high expectations) are well established sources of protection for children and adolescents, including LGBTQ youth (Tharinger & Wells, 2000). Additionally, parental acceptance and support is linked to higher self-esteem and well-being for LGBTQ youth (Friedman & Morgan, 2009). In fact, supportive and cohesive families contribute to positive outcomes related to coming out/disclosure, as opposed to the increased risks (e.g., emotional disturbance, internalized homophobia, low self-esteem, depression, substance use, and increased risk behaviors and suicidality) associated with little or no familial support or rejection (Eisenberg & Resnick, 2006; Rivers & Noret, 2008; Ryan et al., 2009). Thus, a supportive family has implications for not only improving mental health, but also preventing homelessness and family violence for LGB youth (Ryan et al., 2009).

It is important to note, however, that sexual minority and gender variant youth differ from other oppressed groups since family members typically do not share their sexual/

gender minority status, which potentially eliminates a buffer or resource that is often in place for other minorities (Matthews & Adams, 2009). Alternatively, Matthews and Adams (2009) contend that the LGBTQ community may serve as a surrogate family of sorts in terms of supporting, socializing, and contributing to a positive self worth and sense of identity, once again highlighting the transactional nature of resilience domains.

While the family domain may serve a protective function, its protective capacity appears to operate when combined with protections found within the community domain (e.g., positive/supportive school climate and supportive peers), as well as when community-level risks (e.g., exclusion, discrimination, and/or bullying) are minimized (Espelage et al., 2008; Hershberger & D'Augelli, 1995; Murdock & Bolch, 2005). For instance, supportive families may be able to moderate the negative mental health effects of being the victim of bullying when the victimization is low grade (e.g., verbal comments), but not for more severe bullying (e.g., property destruction or physical harm; Hershberger & D'Augelli, 1995). Still other research has demonstrated that family support in combination with support from friends and a supportive school climate led to better school adjustment for LGBTQ youth in terms of grades, school belongingness, and school behavior (Murdock & Bolch, 2005). Thus, an examination of community-level risks and protections is warranted.

Community/School Domain

Risks/Challenges

In examining all of the ecological systems in which LGBTQ youth navigate, the community certainly influences the trajectory of developmental outcomes. Institutions such as neighborhoods, community centers, parks and recreation, judicial bodies, social services, religious facilities, and schools constitute a social world that can either facilitate or hinder the development of children and adolescents. Critical risk factors in these areas, particularly schools, focus around experiences of exclusion, discrimination, harassment, victimization, and bullying/violence.

LGBTQ youth are at greater risk of experiencing bullying, sexual harassment, and physical abuse compared to their heterosexual peers (Berlan, Corliss, Field, Goodman, & Austin, 2010; Williams, Connolly, Pepler, & Craig, 2003). According to the latest National School Climate Survey conducted by the Gay, Lesbian, Straight Education Network (GLSEN; Kosciw, Greytak, Diaz, & Bartkiewicz, 2010), schools appear to be a hostile environment for many LGBTQ youth. Based on youth report, approximately 84% of students were verbally harassed due to their sexual orientation, with 63% harassed because of their gender expression. Beyond that, reports of physical harassment (e.g., pushing or shoving) and assault (e.g., punched or injured with a weapon) ranged from 12% to 40%. Over half of all LGBTQ youth experienced cyberbullying. Furthermore, experiences of discrimination and victimization contribute to stress, anxiety, and low self-esteem for LGBTQ youth who may experience angst about future exposures and/or exclusion from particular school events, such as prom (Murdock & Bolch, 2005; Szalacha et al., 2003).

Over the past 10 years, homophobic remarks in schools have decreased; however, experiences of harassment and assault have remained steady (Kosciw et al., 2010). School climate (e.g., lack of anti-bullying policies, non-inclusive curriculum, and unavailability of support groups) has been found to be related to negative outcomes such as depression/suicidality, alcohol/marijuana use, and truancy (Birkett, Espelage, & Koenig, 2009). LGBTQ youth also are at risk for lower educational achievement due to experiences of harassment and victimization at school (Kosciw et al., 2010; O'Shaughnessy, Russell, Heck, Calhoun, & Laub, 2004). Lower academic achievement may have a longer-term impact by affecting LGBTQ students' access to post-secondary education and merit-based financial aid (e.g., scholarships, grants).

Much less research exists regarding other community institutions; however, Himmelstein and Bruckner (2010) investigated school and criminal punishments given to LGB youth. Even when taking into account the offense, LGB youth were up to three times more likely to receive punishment from schools or other authorities (i.e., police, court system) than their heterosexual peers. Regarding health care, Ussher (2009) outlines the implications of health care and mental health research developed from a heterocentric view, leading to the marginalization and invisibility of LGBTQ individuals. Those practitioners who are insensitive to issues of sexuality and gender may fail to screen, evaluate, or treat LGBTQ youth in the most appropriate manner.

Protections

Because schools represent a significant developmental context for LGBTQ students, many community-level supports/resources involve the school context and/or school-based professionals. Moreover, resilience is contingent on the complex interplay of various school-related factors (e.g., positive school climate, teacher and peer support, less victimization, and school belongingness) and social support outside of school, all of which contribute to school adjustment levels (Murdock & Bolch, 2005). These interconnected school/community-level protections take the form of social support from a peer and/or an adult outside of the family; a safe, supportive, and inclusive school environment; and school-wide preventions aimed at fostering resilience.

Social support. There is an extensive body of literature related to the positive effects of social support, which may be informal (e.g., support from peers/friends or an adult outside of the family, such as a teacher, coach, mentor, or family friend) or formal (e.g., Gay-Straight Alliances [GSAs], support groups, community agencies, or mentoring programs). Social support has been linked to better mental health outcomes for LGBTQ youth, including fewer somatic complaints, anxiety, depression, interpersonal problems, suicidality, and substance abuse, as well as a greater sense of self-esteem, self-efficacy, stability, and security (Davidson & Demaray, 2007; Eisenberg & Resnick, 2006; Espelage et al., 2008; Friedman & Morgan, 2009; Goodenow et al., 2006; Williams et al., 2005). Not only does social support have the capacity to improve students' overall well-being, it has been shown to help ameliorate the negative experiences often encountered by LGBTQ youth or moderate/mediate the poor outcomes that might result from such negative experiences (Davidson & Demaray, 2007; Goodenow et al., 2006; Ross, 2005; Williams et al., 2005).

Given the typical risk profiles of LGBTQ youth, it is that much more critical to provide social support to sexual minority and gender variant youth both in general and related to sexual health (Friedman & Morgan, 2009). In doing so, it is important to recognize the complexity of social support for LGBTQ youth. In fact, sexual minority youth report fewer social supports and less satisfaction with social support provided as compared to non-minorities (Safren & Pantalone, 2006). However, individuals with more integrated sexual/gender identities report greater perceived support relative to their peers who have not yet disclosed their identity or come out (Friedman & Morgan, 2009). In fact, as was found in one recent study, questioning students, particularly those who had experienced homophobic teasing, are at greater risk for depression, substance use, and suicide relative to both heterosexual and LGB students (Espelage et al., 2008). Thus, questioning students have unique experiences and needs related to social support that may differ from the needs of LGBT students who may find more support because of their fully integrated sexual/gender identities. This notion points to the need for school personnel to not only be supportive, but also to be visible and accessible advocates and mentors for LGBTQ students (Murdock & Bolch, 2005).

In some instances, it may be enough to have supportive school personnel (Graybill, Varjas, Meyers, & Watson, 2009); support from teachers and staff contributes to a greater sense of safety, academic success, and an increased likelihood of attaining higher education (DePaul et al., 2009). However, who or what serves as a source of support will vary from person to person, as will the type of support needed (i.e., emotional versus instrumental; Davidson & Demaray, 2007). Just because social support is provided does not mean that students will always perceive the presence, availability, or accessibility of support or deem the available resources as supportive. Students may require assistance with finding supportive individuals in their lives (Matthews & Adams, 2009), may need to be equipped with the social skills necessary to access the existing support (Davidson & Demaray, 2007), or may need counseling to overcome any social anxiety that might be interfering with their capacity to elicit the necessary support (Safren & Pantalone, 2006). On the other hand, it may be necessary to teach others, particularly heterosexual individuals, how to be supportive allies, including countering myths and promoting supportive/affirmative beliefs and behaviors (Friedman & Morgan, 2009; Matthews & Adams, 2009).

The perceived presence or availability of existing support, including supportive adults and personal/social counseling, has contributed to significantly lowering stress and suicide risk for LGBTQ youth (Davidson & Demaray, 2007; Goodenow et al., 2006). Additionally, Ross (2005) found that formal and informal mentoring provided by gay adult mentors assisted gay college students with achieving a more integrated sexual identity, increasing cultural awareness, and achieving a greater sense of community, while also contributing to their academic and social success in college and overall well-being. Furthermore, mentors may serve as role models and assist with acculturation and identity development by providing advice, challenging misconceptions, and dispelling heterosexism (Ross, 2005). To date, there are no known research studies of mentoring lesbian, bisexual, questioning, or transgender youth; however, it is likely that similar positive outcomes would result if such mentoring were provided. Since youth are self-identifying as LGBTQ much earlier than in the past, it is crucial to provide this type of support earlier in their development and schooling in an effort to promote their health and wellness.

Often times, it is a school counselor or school psychologist who is the primary resource of support for LGBTQ youth; however, Weiler (2003) suggests identifying a school-based professional other than a counselor or psychologist who can act as the LGBTQ resource or point person in an effort to normalize (or to avoid pathologizing) sexual minority and gender variant individuals. More formalized support networks (e.g., GSAs/support groups) provide opportunities to build students' assets and social-emotional competence, which serve to protect students from any risks encountered, while also keeping students engaged in school and thereby preventing truancy and/or dropout (Masten et al., 2008). School-based support groups and GSAs also have been found to predict significantly safer and more supportive school climates (Goodenow et al., 2006).

Affirmative school environments. In addition to social support, an affirmative and positive school climate is yet another community-level protection that is deemed necessary to render positive outcomes (or moderate negative outcomes), particularly for LGBTQ youth (Espelage et al., 2008; Tharinger & Wells, 2000). Schools need to create a culture that promotes acceptance, sensitivity, and awareness and provide a *safe space* that is supportive of sexual minority and gender variant youth and their allies. It is imperative for sexual/gender minority students to view school authorities as sympathetic, approachable, and both willing and prepared to intervene in instances of bullying/harassment so that students do not feel isolated, unprotected, or unsupported (Goodenow et al., 2006). Experiences of supportive teachers and positive school environments contribute to a heightened sense of school belongingness. When students feel that they are valued members of the school community, they are protected against school adjustment problems (Murdock & Bolch, 2005). Feeling safe at school also has been found to protect against suicide risk in LGB adolescents (Eisenberg & Resnick, 2006).

A safe space is contingent on updating policies and procedures to eliminate discrimination, bullying, harassment, and hate as well as educating all stakeholders, which includes training school-based professionals to be culturally competent, particularly with regard to LGBTQ-specific knowledge and skills (DePaul et al., 2009; Goodenow et al., 2006; Graybill et al., 2009; Henning-Stout, James, & Macintosh, 2000; Matthews & Adams, 2009; McCabe & Rubinson, 2008; Rivers & D'Augelli, 2001; Weiler, 2003; Whitman, Horn, & Boyd, 2007). Furthermore, it is important for all stakeholders to understand that an individual's interactions with a hostile environment are what contribute to increased risk for poor outcomes, as opposed to the problem being internal to the student. To this end, partnering with national, state, or local professional organizations and community agencies has proven to be helpful in creating affirmative and supportive school climates (Matthews & Adams, 2009; Whitman et al., 2007). Moreover, providing a supportive and inclusive school climate is a prerequisite for LGBTQ students to feel safe and is done through primary prevention wherein the problem is tackled proactively, systemically, collaboratively, and systematically (DePaul et al., 2009; Graybill et al., 2009; Matthews & Adams, 2009; Rivers & D'Augelli, 2001; Whitman et al., 2007). Chapter 8 of this volume provides in-depth coverage of the training of school professionals, while Chapter 9 covers bullying prevention and Chapter 10 addresses how to create inclusive school curriculum.

Prevention. Prevention/intervention programs focused on LGBTQ youth also have been effective in improving the school climate, but the extent to which programs are implemented is dependent on the political climate of the school, district, local community, and region (Horn & Nucci, 2006). As with any prevention programming, strategic planning is crucial and involves formulating realistic action plans informed by the local culture/climate and needs (Henning-Stout et al., 2000). Thus, it is recommended that primary prevention efforts aimed at changing negative biases (beliefs/attitudes) and behavior be integrated into more generalized primary prevention approaches involving character/moral development, social-emotional learning, diversity training, or violence/bullying prevention (Henning-Stout et al., 2000; Horn & Nucci, 2006).

While there is a need to be proactive as opposed to reactive, there is certainly a place for primary, secondary, and tertiary level responses to support LGBTQ students, where all students are supported through universal prevention (school-wide), students identified as at-risk are supported by selective preventions, and students experiencing significant needs/symptoms are served by intensive interventions (DePaul et al., 2009; Fisher et al., 2008; Henning-Stout et al., 2000; Winslow et al., 2006). This public health approach to prevention takes into account the varying levels of risk and protection, which dictate the level of prevention or intervention that is warranted for a particular student. Since risks tend to have a cumulative effect, prevention and early intervention are recommended in order to avoid the need for more costly compensatory approaches wherein resources must be spent on both reversing maladaptation and fostering healthy adaptation (Masten et al., 2008). A risk protective model of resilience is much more cost-effective, such that resources are expended on social-emotional health within primary and secondary preventions that yield positive outcomes and minimize maladjustment, and thus, require less intensive interventions (Kenny & Hage, 2009; Masten et al., 2008). Furthermore, tertiary interventions, such as psychotherapy, are reactive and generally only deal with the individual level to the neglect of systemic variables, proving to be an insufficient and much more costly approach (Kenny & Hage, 2009; Masten et al., 2008; Matthews & Adams, 2009).

Schools are well positioned to bolster protection by fostering the development of adaptive systems known to reduce risk and promote the social-emotional competence that leads to healthy development and adjustment (Masten et al., 2008). Not only can universal prevention programs counter homophobia and heterosexism; but also such programs can equip all students with the social-emotional competencies necessary to navigate the demands of child and adolescent development, including the skill of resource/support seeking indicative of individual-level protection (Davidson & Demaray, 2007; Elias et al., 2006). Given the empirical support for social-emotional competencies contributing to reduced maladaptation, particularly in terms of educational resilience, it is recommended that these skills (e.g., awareness of self and others, self-management, interpersonal, and decision-making) be explicitly taught in order to equip all students with effective coping strategies (Davidson & Demaray, 2007; Elias et al., 2006).

Additionally, it may be necessary to educate parents about the critical need for support and how to be supportive, which speaks to the necessity of fostering effective school–family–community partnerships in order to ensure academic and social-emotional success of LGBTQ students in particular (Ryan & Martin, 2000). Prevention/intervention efforts will be most successful when focused not only on preventing negative outcomes (reducing risk), but also on fostering the protective processes known to be associated with adaptive or positive outcomes (Elias et al., 2006; Winslow et al., 2006). School-based preventions/interventions that are grounded in resilience theory and are comprehensive, coordinated/integrated, multifaceted, and developmental in scope have been well supported in the literature to successfully promote positive outcomes, both at the individual and systemic level (Elias et al., 2006; Winslow et al., 2006).

Notes

1 A thorough review of resilience and its complexities is well beyond the scope of this chapter. For additional background, readers are directed to the work of authors such as Garmezy, Rutter, Luthar, Masten, and Sameroff.
2 For more information on social-emotional learning preventions/interventions, readers are encouraged to visit http://www.casel.org.
3 For more information on Attachment Theory, readers are directed to Bowlby's work (1969, 1973, and 1980).

References

Berlan, E. D., Corliss, H. L., Field, A. E., Goodman, E., & Austin, S. B. (2010). Sexual orientation and bullying among adolescents in the growing up today study. *Journal of Adolescent Health, 46*(4), 366–371. doi:10.1016/j.jadohealth.2009.10.015

Birkett, M., Espelage, D. L., & Koenig, B. (2009). LGB and questioning students in schools: The moderating effects of homophobic bullying and school climate on negative outcomes. *Journal of Youth & Adolescence, 38*(7), 989–1000. doi:10.1007/s10964-008-9389-1

Busseri, M. A., Willoughby, T., Chalmers, H., & Bogaert, A. R. (2006). Same-sex attraction and successful adolescent development. *Journal of Youth and Adolescents, 35*(4), 563–575. doi:10.1007/s10964-006-9071-4

Centers for Disease Control and Prevention. (2011). Sexual identity, sex of sexual contacts, and health-risk behaviors among students in grades 9–12—youth risk behavior surveillance, selected sites, United States, 2001–2009. *Morbidity and Mortality Weekly Report, 60*(7), 1–133. Retrieved from http://www.cdc.gov/mmwr/pdf/ss/ss6007.pdf

Cochran, B. N., Stewart, A. J., Ginzler, J. A., & Cauce, A. (2002). Challenges faced by homeless sexual minorities: Comparison of gay, lesbian, bisexual, and transgender homeless adolescents with their heterosexual counterparts. *American Journal of Public Health, 92*(5), 773–777. doi:10.2105/AJPH.92.5.773

Condly, S. J. (2006). Resilience in children: A review of literature with implications for education. *Urban Education, 41*(3), 211–236. doi:10.1177/0042085906287902

Corliss, H. L., Rosario, M., Wypij, D., Wylie, S. A., Frazier, A. L., & Austin, S. B. (2010). Sexual orientation and drug use in a longitudinal cohort study of U.S. adolescents. *Addictive Behaviors, 35*(5), 517–521. doi:10.1016/j.addbeh.2009.12.019

Davidson, L. M., & Demaray, M. K. (2007). Social support as a moderator between victimization and internalizing-externalizing distress from bullying. *School Psychology Review, 36*(3), 383–405. Retrieved from http://www.nasponline.org/publications/spr/pdf/spr363davidson.pdf

DePaul, J., Walsh, M. E., & Dam, U. C. (2009). The role of school counselors in addressing sexual orientation in schools. *Professional School Counseling, 12*(4), 300–308. doi:10.5330/PSC.n.2010-12.300

Easton, A., Jackson, K., Mowery, P., Comeau, D., & Sell, R. (2008). Adolescent same-sex and both-sex romantic attractions and relationships: Implications for smoking. *American Journal of Public Health, 98*(3), 462–467. doi:10.2105/AJPH.2006.097980

Eisenberg, M. E., & Resnick, M. D. (2006). Suicidality among gay, lesbian, and bisexual youth: The role of protective factors. *Journal of Adolescent Health, 39*(5), 662–668. doi:10.1016/j.jadohealth.2006.04.024

Elias, M. J., Parker, S., & Rosenblatt, J. L. (2006). Building educational opportunity. In S. Goldstein & R. B. Brooks (Eds.), *Handbook of resilience in children* (pp. 315–336). New York, NY: Springer Science+Business Media, Inc.

Espelage, D. L., Aragon, S. R., Birkett, M., & Koenig, B. W. (2008). Homophobic teasing, psychological outcomes, and sexual orientation among high school students: What influence do parents and schools have? *School Psychology Review, 37*(2), 202–216. Retrieved from http://www.nasponline.org/publications/spr/pdf/spr372espelage.pdf

Fergusson, D. M., Horwood, L. J., & Beautrais, A. L. (1999). Is sexual orientation related to mental health problems and suicidality in young people? *Archives of General Psychiatry, 56*(10), 876–880. doi:10.001/archpsyc.56.10.876

Fisher, E. S., Komosa-Hawkins, K., Saldaña, E., Thomas, G. M., Hsiao, C., Rauld, M., & Miller, D. (2008). Promoting school success for lesbian, gay, bisexual, transgendered, and questioning students: Primary, secondary, and tertiary prevention and intervention strategies. *The California School Psychologist, 13*, 79–91. Retrieved from http://www.eric.ed.gov/PDFS/EJ878353.pdf

Freedner, N., Freed, L. H., Yang, Y. W., & Austin, S. B. (2002). Dating violence among gay, lesbian, and bisexual adolescents: Results from a community survey. *Journal of Adolescent Health, 31*(6), 469–474. doi:10.1016/S1054-139X(02)00407-X

Friedman, C. K., & Morgan, E. M. (2009). Comparing sexual-minority and heterosexual young women's friends and parents as sources of support for sexual issues. *Journal of Youth and Adolescence, 38*, 920–936. doi:10.1007/s10964-9361-0

Garofalo, R., Mustanski, B. S., McKirnan, D. J., Herrick, A., & Donenberg, G. F. (2007). Methamphetamine and young men who have sex with men: Understanding patterns and correlates of use and the association with HIV-related sexual risk. *Archives of Pediatrics & Adolescent Medicine, 161*(6), 591–596. doi:10.1001/archpedi.161.6.591

Goodenow, C., Szalacha, L., & Westheimer, K. (2006). School support groups, other school factors, and the safety of sexual minority adolescents. *Psychology in the Schools, 43*(5), 573–589. doi:10.1002/pits.20173

Graybill, E. C., Varjas, K., Meyers, J., & Watson, L. B. (2009). Content-specific strategies to advocate for lesbian, gay, bisexual, and transgender youth: An exploratory study. *School Psychology Review, 38*(4), 570–584. Retrieved from http://www.nasponline.org/publications/spr/pdf/spr384graybill.pdf

Henning-Stout, M., James, S., & Macintosh, S. (2000). Reducing harassment of lesbian, gay, bisexual, transgender, and questioning youth in schools. *School Psychology Review, 29*(2), 180–191. Retrieved from http://www.nasponline.org/publications/spr/pdf/spr292harassment.pdf

Herek, G. M. (2009). Hate crimes and stigma-related experiences among sexual minority adults in the United States: Prevalence estimates from a national probability sample. *Journal of Interpersonal Violence, 24*(1), 54–74. doi:10.1177/088626050831647

Hershberger, S. L., & D'Augelli, A. R. (1995). The impact of victimization on the mental health and suicidality of lesbian, gay, and bisexual youths. *Developmental Psychology, 31*(1), 65–74. doi:10.1037/0012-1649.31.1.65

Himmelstein, K. E. W., & Bruckner, H. (2010). Criminal-justice and school sanctions against nonheterosexual youth: A national longitudinal study. *Pediatrics, 127*(1), 2009–2306. doi:10.1542/peds.2009-2306

Horn, S. S., Kosciw, J. G., & Russell, S. T. (2009). Special issue introduction: New research on lesbian, gay, bisexual, and transgender youth: Studying lives in context. *Journal of Youth and Adolescence, 38*(7), 863–866. doi:10.1007/s10964-009-9420-1

Horn, S. S., & Nucci, L. (2006). Harassment of gay and lesbian youth and school violence in America: An analysis and directions for intervention. In C. Daiute, Z. Beykont,

C. Higson-Smith, & L. Nucci (Eds.), *International perspectives on youth conflict and development* (pp. 139–155). New York, NY: Oxford University Press, Inc.

Kenny, M. E., & Hage, S. M. (2009). The next frontier: Prevention as an instrument of social justice. *Journal of Primary Prevention, 30*(1), 1–10. doi:10.1007/s10935-008-0163-7

Kipke, M. D., Kubicek, K., Weiss, G., Wong, C., Lopez, D., Iverson, E., & Ford, W. (2007). The health and health behaviors of young men who have sex with men. *Journal of Adolescent Health, 40*, 342–350. doi:10.1016/j.jadohealth.2006.10.019

Kosciw, J. G., Greytak, E. A., Diaz, E. M., & Bartkiewicz, M. J. (2010). *The 2009 National School Climate Survey: The experiences of lesbian, gay, bisexual, and transgender youth in our nation's schools.* New York, NY: GLSEN.

Luthar, S. S., Cicchetti, D., & Bronwyn, B. (2000). The construct of resilience: A critical evaluation and guidelines for future work. *Child Development, 71*(3), 543–562. doi:10.1111/1467-8624.00164

Marshal, M. P., Friedman, M. S., Stall, R., & Thompson, A. L. (2009). Individual trajectories of substance use in lesbian, gay, and bisexual youth and heterosexual youth. *Addiction, 104*(6), 974–981. doi:10.1111/j.1360-0443.2009.02531.x

Masten, A. S. (2001). Ordinary magic: Resilience processes in development. *American Psychologist, 56*(3), 227–238. doi:10.1037//0003-066X.56.3.227

Masten, A. S., Herbers, J. E., Cutuli, J. J., & Lafavor, T. L. (2008). Promoting competence and resilience in the school context. *Professional School Counseling, 12*(2), 76–84. Retrieved from http://schoolcounselor.metapress.com/content/rp3rv814qjh1m878/fulltext.pdf

Matthews, C. R., & Adams, E. M. (2009). Using a social justice approach to prevent the mental health consequences of heterosexism. *Journal of Primary Prevention, 30*(1), 11–26. doi:10.1007/s10935-008-0166-4

McCabe, P. C., & Rubinson, F. (2008). Committing to social justice: The behavioral intention of school psychology and education trainees to advocate for lesbian, gay, bisexual, and transgendered youth. *School Psychology Review, 37*(4), 469–486. Retrieved from http://www.nasponline.org/publications/spr/pdf/spr374mccabe.pdf

Meyer, I. H. (2010). Identity, stress, and resilience in lesbians, gay men, and bisexuals of color. *The Counseling Psychologist, 38*(3), 442–454. doi:10.1177/0011000009351601

Milburn, N. G., Ayala, G., Rice, E., Betterham, P., & Rotheram-Borus, M. J. (2006). Discrimination and exiting homelessness among homeless adolescents. *Cultural Diversity and Ethnic Minority Psychology, 12*(4), 658–672. doi:10.1037/1099-9809.12.4.658

Murdock, T. B., & Bolch, M. B. (2005). Risk and protective factors for poor school adjustment in lesbian, gay, and bisexual (LGB) high school youth: Variable and person-centered analyses. *Psychology in the Schools, 42*(2), 159–171. doi:10.1002/pits.20054

Mustanski, B. S., Garofalo, R., & Emerson, E. M. (2010). Mental health disorders, psychological distress, and suicidality in a diverse sample of lesbian, gay, bisexual, and transgender youths. *American Journal of Public Health, 100*(12), 2426–2432. doi:10.2105/AJPH.2009.178319

Orenstein, A. (2001). Substance use among gay and lesbian adolescents. *Journal of Homosexuality, 41*(2), 1–15. doi:10.1300/J082v41n03_01

O'Shaughnessy, M., Russell, S., Heck, K., Calhoun, C., & Laub, C. (2004). *Safe place to learn: Consequences of harassment based on actual or perceived sexual orientation and gender non-conformity and steps for making schools safer.* San Francisco, CA: California Safe Schools Coalition.

Rivers, I., & D'Augelli, A. (2001). The victimization of lesbian, gay, and bisexual youths. In A. D'Augelli & A. C. Patterson (Eds.), *Lesbian, gay, and bisexual identities and youth: Psychological perspectives* (pp. 199–223). New York, NY: Oxford University Press.

Rivers, I., & Noret, N. (2008). Well-being among same-sex- and opposite-sex- attracted youth at school. *School Psychology Review, 37*(2), 174–187. Retrieved from http://www.nasponline.org/publications/spr/pdf/spr372rivers.pdf

Ross, F. E. (2005). *Achieving cultural competence: The role of mentoring in sexual minority identity development* (Doctoral dissertation). Retrieved from Dissertations & Theses: Full Text - ProQuest (Publication No. AAT 3178476).

Ryan, C., Huebner, D., Diaz, R. M., & Sanchez, J. (2009). Family rejection as a predictor of negative health outcomes in White and Latino lesbian, gay, and bisexual young adults. *Pediatrics, 123*(1), 346–352. doi:10.1542/peds.2007-3524

Ryan, D., & Martin, A. (2000). Lesbian, gay, bisexual, and transgender parents in the school systems. *School Psychology Review, 29*(2), 207–216. Retrieved from http://www.nasponline.org/publications/spr/pdf/spr292parents.pdf

Saewyc, E. W., Skay, C. L., Pettingell, S. L., Reis, E. A., Bearinger, L., Resnick, M., . . . Combs, L. (2006). Hazards of stigma: The sexual and physical abuse of gay, lesbian, and bisexual adolescents in the United States and Canada. *Child Welfare, 85*(2), 195–213.

Safren, S. A., & Heimberg, R. G. (1999). Depression, hopelessness, suicidality, and related factors in sexual minority and heterosexual adolescents. *Journal of Consulting and Clinical Psychology, 67*(6), 859–866. doi:10.1037/0022-006X.67.6.859

Safren, S. A., & Pantalone, D. W. (2006). Social anxiety and barriers to resilience among lesbian, gay, and bisexual adolescents. In A. M. Omoto & H. S. Kurtzman (Eds.), *Sexual orientation and mental health: Examining identity and development in lesbian, gay, and bisexual people* (pp. 55–71). Washington, DC: American Psychological Association.

Sameroff, A., Gutman, L. M., & Peck, S. C. (2003). Adaption among youth facing multiple risks: Prospective research findings. In S. S. Luthar (Ed.), *Resilience and vulnerability: Adaption in the context of childhood adversities* (pp. 365–391). New York, NY: The Press Syndicate of the University of Cambridge.

Savin-Williams, R. C. (2005). Resilience and diversity. In R. C. Savin-Williams (Ed.), *The new gay teenager* (pp. 178–193). Cambridge, MA: Harvard University Press.

Szalacha, L. A., Erkut, S., Coll, C. G., Fields, J. P., Alarcon, O., & Ceder, I. (2003). Perceived discrimination and resilience. In S. S. Luthar (Ed.), *Resilience and vulnerability: Adaption in the context of childhood adversities* (pp. 415–435). New York, NY: The Press Syndicate of the University of Cambridge.

Tharinger, D., & Wells, G. (2000). An attachment perspective on the developmental challenges of gay and lesbian adolescents: The need for continuity of caregiving from family and schools. *School Psychology Review, 29*(2), 158–172. Retrieved from http://www.nasponline.org/publications/spr/pdf/spr292attach.pdf

Tucker, J. S., Ellickson, P. L., & Klein, D. J. (2008). Understanding differences in substance use among bisexual and heterosexual young women. *Women's Health Issues, 18*(5), 387–398. doi:10.1016/j.whi.2008.04.004

Ussher, J. M. (2009). Heterocentric practices in health research and health care: Implications for mental health and subjectivity of LGBTQ individuals. *Feminism & Psychology, 19*, 561–567. doi:10.1177/0959353509342933

Van Leeuwen, J. M., Boyle, S., Salomonsen-Sautel, S., Baker, D., Garcia, J., Hoffman, A., & Hopfer, C. J. (2006). Lesbian, gay, and bisexual homeless youth: An eight-city public health perspective. *Child Welfare Journal, 83*(2), 151–170. doi:10.1037/a0020705

Weiler, E. M. (2003, December). Making school safe for sexual minority students. *Principal Leadership Magazine, 4*(4), 10–13. Retrieved from http://www.nasponline.org/resources/principals/nassp_glbqt.aspx

Whitman, J. S., Horn, S. S., & Boyd, C. J. (2007). Activism in the schools: Providing LGBTQ affirmative training to school counselors. *Journal of Gay & Lesbian Psychotherapy, 3*(4), 143–154. doi:10.1300/J236v11n03_08

Williams, T., Connolly, J., Pepler, D., & Craig, W. (2003). Questioning and sexual minority adolescents: High school experiences of bullying, sexual harassment, and physical abuse. *Canadian Journal of Community Mental Health, 22*(2), 47–58.

Williams, T., Connolly, J., Pepler, D., & Craig, W. (2005). Peer victimization, social support, and psychosocial adjustment of sexual minority adolescents. *Journal of Youth and Adolescents, 34*(5), 471–482. doi:10.1007/s10964-005-7264-x

Winslow, E. B., Sandler, I. N., & Wolchik, S. A. (2006). Building resilience in all children. In S. Goldstein & R. B. Brooks (Eds.), *Handbook of resilience in children* (pp. 337–356). New York, NY: Springer Science+Business Media, Inc.

Ziyadeh, M. J., Prokop, L. A., Fisher, L. B., Rosario, M., Field, A. E., Camargo, C. A., & Austin, S.B. (2007). Sexual orientation, gender, and alcohol use in a cohort study of U.S. adolescent girls and boys. *Drug & Alcohol Dependence 87*(2–3), 119–130. doi:10.1016/j.drugalcdep.2006.08.004

5 Transgender and Intersex Students
Supporting Resilience and Empowerment

Anneliese A. Singh

Transgender and intersex youth are very distinct groups from one another (and from lesbian, gay, and bisexual youth), yet many of their concerns in schools may be overlapping. This chapter focuses on how school professionals may support transgender and intersex students in their academic and personal success. The chapter first reviews the defining concepts and theoretical lenses helpful in understanding transgender and intersex students. Then, an overview of the needs of each group is discussed in more depth. Building on this foundational information, an empowerment and resilience model is proposed for working with transgender and intersex youth across multiple concerns—from the family and social services to healthcare and legal and/or ethical issues. Finally, the importance of collaborative advocacy and social justice issues that school professionals must attend to in developing transgender and intersex-affirmative environments in school settings are discussed.

Let's "Not" Talk about Gender, Sex, and Sexual Orientation in Schools

School systems in the United States (U.S.) largely avoid the topics of gender, sex, and sexual orientation all together (Singh & Burnes, 2009; Child Welfare League, 2006). This avoidance of constructs that influence virtually every aspect of students' lives is generally rooted in a struggle of values, parental involvement, religious dogma, and often sheer ignorance (Gay, Lesbian, and Straight Education Network [GLSEN], 2009). In other words, school educators themselves lacked important training on these topics during their own studies, and thus feel ill-prepared to engage parents, students, and other educators in these discussions. Fortunately, there is a movement towards a more affirmative approach to educator training with regard to the constructs of gender, sex, and sexual orientation. For instance, Vavrus (2008) engaged in an innovative study of 38 pre-service teachers and used an autoethnographic method to develop a space in which pre-service teachers could explore their own gender and sexuality, in order to inform their future K-12 teaching practices. Participants shared that experiences of their own gender identity, heteronormative and patriarchal norms, education about sexuality, school experiences, and identities as teachers influenced their conceptions of normative gender education and sexuality. This type of educator training is vitally important in order to develop awareness that every person in the school system has a gender identity and expression that needs to be valued and supported.

Definitions

The word *transgender* refers to individuals whose sex assigned at birth does not align with their gender identity and expression. The term *intersex* is used to refer to individuals whose chromosomal make-up or biological characteristics do not align with those defined as male or female. Both of these terms will be explored in more depth later in this chapter. In order to ensure a clear understanding of the definitions of *gender, sex,* and *sexual orientation,* one must first acknowledge that these are each socially constructed and shaped by cultural perspective. The definitions offered here certainly emerge from a predominantly White, western context, and should be challenged, expanded, and stretched to fit other perspectives (Singh & Burnes, 2009). Gender is typically a word linked to an identity, yet it is rarely understood in this manner. *Gender identity,* for instance, is our sense of what our internal gender "feels like" to us. The words typically associated with gender identity are "woman" and "man" or "boy" and "girl;" yet, there are many other definitions and constructions of gender identities that go beyond this gender binary. For students, their gender identity is internal; yet, this gender identity also has a gender expression. This gender expression is often defined as *feminine* or *masculine,* again reinforcing and reifying the idea of the gender binary.

Transgender and intersex people, who have existed across time and cultures around the globe, often defy the idea of the gender binary (Peletz, 2006). For instance, transgender students may be assigned a *sex* at birth (with sex also defined along a binary as "male" or "female"), yet they may not associate with the gender identity and gender expression society expects of them according to the sex they were assigned at birth. Therefore, a critical starting point for educators is to understand that sex and gender norms in society have reinforced a binary construct (male versus female, boy versus girl); however, these binaries are inaccurate because of the incidences of multiple gender identities, gender expressions, and chromosomal make-ups that exist. Many people, not just educators, will experience confusion about the complexities of gender, sex, and (as will be discussed) sexual orientation because of the many ways the three constructs overlap. However, in order to be more helpful, responsive, ethical, and meaningful educators, it is better to shift away from rigid notions of gender, sex, and sexual orientation and away from the idea that adults "should know" better than students. Instead, educators are encouraged to embrace the complexity, intricacies, and positive exploration that is involved in building supportive environments for their students to define their multiple identities, including these three areas.

Sexual orientation is a term that describes the attractions a student may have to other people. Sexual orientations, similar to gender identities and gender expressions, are numerous, evolving, and changing, often according to societal norms. For instance, a *straight* or *heterosexual* sexual orientation may be discussed as an attraction one has to the "opposite sex." However, based on our earlier discussion of gender and sex, we know that sex might not be the most helpful word to use and that there is no such thing as "opposite" when it comes to gender because of the fluidity of gender. Therefore, it can be more helpful to discuss a straight sexual orientation as a student who has attractions to a person with a gender identity that they do not share and a lesbian or gay student as one who has attractions to others who predominantly share a similar gender identity. Once we have unpacked the false gender binary, it becomes less meaningful to define *bisexual* as one who has attractions to "both sexes," when we know there are multiple genders.

Again, these definitions of sexual orientation are woefully incomplete, while simultaneously very complex (Butler, 1990). Thus, the reason that young people may prefer to use broader umbrella terms, such as *queer*, is to more fully capture the range of their attractions (or a multitude of other terms that are self-generated and more reflective of their actual and potential attractions). Also important is for educators to recognize that sexual orientation, gender identity, and gender expression often intersect with one another, again defying binary and rigid definitions. For instance, a transgender girl who was assigned male at birth, yet defines herself as a young woman also may have a queer identity—where she has attractions to primarily other girls or may be open to attractions to multiple gender identities and gender expressions (Burnes & Chen, 2012).

Statistics

Many people working in schools want to know how many transgender and intersex students there are. Sometimes wanting this knowledge has good intention, such as to show the importance and existence of these groups. Other times, the intention is less clear—such as wanting to know whether the number of transgender and intersex young people warrants attention to their specific concerns. Despite the reason for wanting this information, the reality is that the statistics about transgender and intersex youth are not well documented. Statistics on the prevalence of transgender individuals is a controversial topic. Although there are no accurate estimates of transgender youth, the American Psychiatric Association (2000) reports studies estimating the numbers of transgender adults seeking *sex reassignment* (a less pathological term is *gender affirmation*) surgeries at 1 in 100,000 men and 1 in 30,000 women. However, these estimates are based on dated (and often methodologically unsound) studies. In addition, these estimates use gender-affirmation surgery as a marker to count from (excluding transgender people who do not want to have surgeries) and do not take into account the hostile or non-responsive environments transgender individuals live in that may preclude them from self-identifying to others. Similarly, the Intersex Initiative estimated the prevalence of intersex births as ranging from 1 in 1,666 to 1 in 150,000 depending on the chromosomal variation (Blackless, Charuvastra, Derryck, Fausto-Sterling, Lauzanne, & Lee, 2000). Yet, in addition to less than affirmative societal environments, it can be difficult to assess intersex status, both of which may explain the wide range of estimates and why these numbers are likely low estimates.

Many of the statistics that are more widely circulated or known entail transgender youth's experiences of societal hostility—in schools, in families, and in communities at large. The Gay, Lesbian, and Straight Education Network (GLSEN, 2009) surveyed 295 transgender youth, between 13 and 20 years old, across the United States. Although a predominantly White, financially resourced, urban, and educated sample, the survey is one of the first to document statistics concerning transgender young people's lives. About 90% of the sample shared that they experienced verbal harassment about their own or others' gender identity, gender expression, and/or sexual orientation. Also concerning was that these researchers found that between 32% to 39% of the transgender youth surveyed heard school staff engage in sexist, homophobic, or non-affirmative comments about other people on a "frequent" or "often" basis. Unfortunately, there are no known studies of the experiences of intersex young people in a similar manner.

Feminist, Multicultural and Social Justice Considerations of Gender and Sex

Because of the very real safety concerns that exist for students who are transgender or intersex in schools, it is imperative for educators to understand feminist, multicultural, and social justice considerations of gender and sex. As previously discussed, rigid and binary notions of gender exist in schools and society at large. These restricted understandings not only contribute to misunderstandings, but also to gaps in service provision for transgender and intersex youth.

Feminist Perspective

A feminist view of gender and sex requires that an educator question societal assumptions and traditions about these constructs, and seek to develop a school climate that empowers students concerning these constructs and identities (Gonzalez & McNulty, 2010; Singh & Burnes, 2009). Using a feminist lens in schools also allows educators to identify the power differentials that limit the ways that transgender and intersex youth can maximize their potential and have their unique points of view valued. Educators also can understand that "the personal is political" (Worrel & Remer, 2003, p. 76) in terms of how societal discrimination may influence individual students' lives (Brown, 2004).

Multicultural Perspective

Similarly, multiculturalism allows educators to understand that transgender and intersex students have multiple identities (Gonzalez & McNulty, 2010). As such, a transgender person who is a person of color may have a very different experience due to experiences of racism than a transgender student who is White (Singh & Jackson, 2012). In another instance, an intersex person who does not have access to financial resources and healthcare may have distinctly different needs than an intersex student who can access these resources (Burnes & Richmond, 2012). In addition, worldviews frame how transgender and intersex students may experience family, religious and/or spiritual affiliation, and community groups, amongst many other institutions (Roberts & Singh, in press). Depending on the worldviews and values related to transgender and intersex identities within these institutions, transgender and intersex students may have positive support in their lives, lack affirmative contexts, or have a mixture of both positive and non-affirming environments (Burnes & Richmond; 2012; Singh & Burnes, 2009).

Social Justice Perspective

Finally, a social justice perspective is critical for educators aiming to understand and support transgender and intersex students. Social justice is a value educators may hold that readily translates into efforts to improve access, equity, and participation for all students within and outside of their school lives, including those who are typically marginalized, such as transgender and intersex students (Crethar, Rivera, & Nash, 2008; Roysircar, 2006). For instance, transgender and intersex students do not only experience discrimination related to gender (sexism), but also conflation of gender and sexual orientation (heterosexism)—in addition to many other systems of oppression that may affect their lives (e.g., classism, ableism, nationalism). A combination of feminist, multicultural, and social justice frameworks guide educators to expand choices, protections, and access for transgender and intersex youth, in addition to understanding their cultural worldviews and the related societal oppressions that may operate in their lives.

Transgender Students 101

History, Culture, and Presence of Transgender People across the World

One of the first places for educators to look in order to develop awareness, knowledge, and skills in working with transgender students is in history books. For so many people in society—from parents, family, friends, and others in the lives of transgender students—there is an assumption that being transgender is a new fad or an issue that has more recently gained attention. This framing of transgender concerns reflects a myth that masks the significant and meaningful his-tories, her-stories, and "t-stories" transgender people have had across time and place. The word *transgender* emerged from a western context in the 1970s and was used more commonly in the 1980s as a term used to describe gender variant people (Feinberg, 1996). However, there have been words to denote a transgender identity in existence for many centuries.

Although a full exploration of the many cultural expressions of transgender people in the world is outside of the scope of this chapter, educators should be aware of a few key examples in order to help transgender students know that they are not "freaks" or "weird;" rather, transgender students are a natural expression of humanity and worthy of being valued. Although colonization histories have had a devastating impact on transgender people in countries outside of and within the U.S., transgender communities continue to persist (Peletz, 2006). Within indigenous/First Nations peoples, transgender tribe members are called *two-spirit* or *inter-spirit*, referring to the existence of both masculine and feminine qualities in one person (Balsalm, Huang, Fieland, Simoni, & Walters, 2004). In India, transgender people are called *Hijras*, or the *third sex*, and historically played important roles in birth and wedding rituals by offering blessings and sacred rites (Sulekha, 2008). *Kathoey* is the name for transgender people in Thailand (Sanders, 2008), and in Hawaii transgender people are called *Mahu* (Shallcross, 2006). The various words that exist to describe transgender people across cultures signify the value and worth of transgender individuals.

It is helpful for educators to have knowledge of the important roles that transgender people have played across many cultures in the past and present in order to provide this information to transgender students, their families, and other educators. Transgender people are elected officials in many counties and also work in all of the major professions in society (Roberts & Singh, in press). It also is important to recognize the history of discrimination, misunderstanding, and decimation of transgender people post-colonization. Therefore, it is additionally important to end discrimination, prejudice, and harm directed towards transgender students, as well as to help transgender students see themselves within the legacy of transgender communities and contributions across cultures.

History of Deficit-Oriented Diagnosis and Treatment

Another foundational understanding of transgender people that is important for educators supporting transgender students is an awareness of the pathological approach to diagnosis and treatment of transgender people. For instance, the *Diagnostic Statistical Manual-IV-TR* (DSM-IV-TR; APA, 2000) includes Gender Identity Disorder (GID, 302.85) as a mental disorder. There remains tension in the transgender health provider community, and within the transgender community itself, about the definition of GID. Those who support the diagnostic inclusion of GID in the DSM-IV-TR, cite the importance of the diagnosis for healthcare coverage and consistent definitions for psychological treatment. Those who question GID's inclusion in the DSM-IV-TR may prefer a medical understanding of transgender identities or question the very nature of defining transgender identities apart from other natural expressions of gender within society. In other words, critics of GID as a DSM diagnosis argue that a natural expression of gender does not denote pathology.

As the DSM-IV-TR is revised and reexamines the criteria for GID, there are likely to be some major changes in future editions. The DSM-IV-TR criteria for GID currently include a "cross-gender identification" and "play with toys of the opposite sex." Critics of this definition take issue with the definitions of gender and sex (as discussed earlier in this chapter: how can an "opposite" sex exist when there are in reality multiple gender identities and gender expressions, and what constitutes "cross-gender" considering this?). Amongst many other critiques of the current GID criteria, two major identified problems are (a) the idea that the disorder persists even when a student may not experience dysphoria (or distress) and (b) the separation of diagnoses for children, adolescents, and adults. The Professionals Concerned with Gender Diagnosis in the DSM (2010) have suggested the following statement on diagnosis for adolescents (and also have issued statements on the child and adult diagnoses) that may influence the definition of Gender Identity Disorder in the fifth revision of the DSM:

> We believe the focus of this diagnosis should be on dysphoria (defined as distress, extreme discomfort, or an emotional state of disease), because it is discomfort, not a particular gender identity or expression, that is the psychological issue. It is essential that the diagnostic criteria focus on anatomical distress or distress with current assigned gender role, with explicit verbalization from the youth that his or her current gender role or anatomical sex does not match his or her internal sense of gender. Gender dysphoria may also be manifested by distress or discomfort with deprivation . . . of social role or anatomy that is congruent with experienced gender identity. Experienced gender is not limited to fixed binary roles, but may encompass fluidity, masculinity, femininity, both, or neither.

Because there has been much debate and controversy about the revision of the diagnostic categories related to gender, educators will need to be aware of these debates and advise students and families to educate themselves on both the current and proposed revisions.

Competencies for Working with Transgender Students

Due to the history of colonization and denigration of transgender people, in addition to the deficit-based definition of GID, educators are in need of strength-based competencies for working with transgender students in schools. Although there are few guidelines for these competencies, there are some significant transgender-positive documents and resources that may guide educators' work with transgender students. The American Counseling Association's (ACA) *Competencies for Counseling with Transgender Clients* (2010) outlines specific competencies within eight domains of training for counselors, in addition to discussing the sociopolitical context of transgender people. Although geared toward transgender people's needs in counseling, all educators will find this document helpful as it highlights the many assumptions, stereotypes, discriminations, and prejudices they face in addition to describing strength-based, feminist, multicultural, and social justice strategies for supporting transgender people's resilience.

There are also Standards of Care for medical and psychological professionals who work with transgender people that were developed by the World Professional Association of Transgender Health (WPATH) in 1979 with the most recent revisions released in 2011. The goal of the Standards of Care is to create a common language for medical and psychological professions to communicate with one another and coordinate treatment with transgender clients. The Standards of Care have been criticized for positioning medical and psychological professionals as gatekeepers holding significant power in transgender people's lives. In the revised version (WPATH, 2011), the authors emphasize the flexible nature of the standards. Educators should be aware that these standards exist to help service providers support, and not pathologize, transgender youth.

The revised standards emphasize the role of diverse identities (e.g., culture, race/ ethnicity, etc.) in the lives of transgender people. Also significant is the acknowledgment that the revision of the standards is "not intended to limit efforts to provide the best available care to all individuals" (WPATH, 2011, p. 3). This is especially significant as many transgender people experience medical and psychological professionals as gatekeepers who hold an undue amount of power over the decisions they make about their lives and bodies related to their gender identity and expression (ACA, 2010). Finally, educators can refer transgender students and their families to the Standards of Care online so that they can become informed, as well as be able to advocate on behalf of the student during medical and psychological appontments. See Appendix A for an awareness activity and Appendix B for a case study of a transgender middle school student.

Intersex Students 101

History, Culture, and Presence of Intersex People around the World

As discussed earlier, accurate statistics of intersex people are a challenge to identify, including intersex youth. The words *intersex* and *intersexuality* have been used over the last two decades for "various forms of atypical somatosexual develoment" (Schweizer, Brunner, Schutzmann, Schonbucher, & Richter-Appelt, 2009, p. 189). Recently, some have called for a shift from using the umbrella term of intersex to "disorders of sex development" (DSD); at the same time, there are those who critique the use of such language due to the emphasis on "disorder" rather than using words that are more affirming of the multitude of gender expressions and gender identities (e.g., "variation") (Schweitzer et al., 2009). It is important for educators to know that much debate exists within and outside of intersex communities regarding the history of deficit frameworks that have existed in medical and psychological treatment. For instance, there was consensus within the medical community that an "optimal gender policy" should guide intervention with intersex infants, and the word optimal was used to describe primarily anatomical functioning aligning most closely with an XX or XY chromosomal expression of anatomy (Schweitzer et al., 2009).

It also is important to know that some people will want to use the word *ambiguous* to describe the anatomies of intersex infants and children. However, the term ambiguous indicates that there is a "normal" expression of sex—either male or female—and everything else that does not fit this binary is "different." Therefore, it is best to refrain from using this term and instead endeavor to use the words that describe specific psychosexual expressions included within the intersex umbrella (e.g., Klinefelter Syndrome, Turner Syndrome, etc.), and, most importantly, use the words with which a student identifies.

History of Deficit-Oriented Diagnosis and Treatment

Similar to the treatment of transgender youth, intersex youth have had complicated, and often negative, interactions with the medical and psychological communities. Within the U.S., medical professionals have poorly understood intersex youth. For instance, for many years, physicians would direct parents in making surgical decisions about intersex youth's genital anatomies during infancy or childhood. The result of these early medical interventions for many intersex people was a sense of their sex and gender identities and gender expressions not being in alignment and/or feeling there was "missing" information about their bodies (Barnes & Richmond, 2012; Diamond & Sigmundson, 1997).

Currently, more attention has been given to questioning the utility of early surgical treatments and, instead, working with intersex youth and their families to make more collaborative decisions later in life (De Silva, 2007). The Accord Alliance (formerly called the Intersex Society of America; http://www.accordalliance.org/) was established to educate intersex people, their families, and healthcare providers about their needs in treatment. This organization designed a *Quality Care Indicator Checklist* (2011) in order to help individuals and families understand important components involved in selecting quality healthcare provider treatment for intersex people. This is an important resource that educators can refer students and families to so they may ensure their child's needs are being met.

Competencies for Working with Intersex Students

Although there is some ongoing work within the American Counseling Association on competencies for working with intersex people, and many national organizations may include intersex within their statements on LGBTQ youth, a major document guiding healthcare professionals' work with intersex youth is the *Clinical Guidelines for the Management of Disorders of Sex Development in Childhood* (CMDSD, 2008). The goal of this document is to lessen the harm to intersex people and their loved ones as they engage with the healthcare system and are presented with major decisions ranging from surgeries and hormone treatment to support groups and educational information.

A major competency outlined in these guidelines includes "telling the truth" to families of intersex youth so they can understand the potential consequences and implications for various medical interventions. Additional guidelines include discussions of gender assignment, psychosocial support, timing of medical interventions (e.g., surgeries, hormone therapy), sexual well-being, and reducing the harm of stigma for intersex children and their families with regard to medical care. Within the guidelines, there are also scripts healthcare professionals may use in speaking with families and a list of articles, books, DVDs, and other informational material sources on intersex concerns—all of which may be helpful for educators. See Appendix C for a case study of an intersex high school student and Appendix D for an activity examining issues affecting transgender and intersex students in schools.

Developing Empowerment and Resilience in Transgender and Intersex Students

There are numerous dimensions of transgender and intersex students' lives in which educators can support the development of personal empowerment and resilience. Three major dimensions are reviewed: (a) family education and support, (b) social support, and (c) healthcare access. Each section will begin with a discussion of transgender students' needs and end with intersex students' needs.

Family Education and Support

For transgender students, families may be a source of support or a challenge to their resilience (Singh & Burnes, 2009). For many transgender students, their families may not understand that a variety of gender activities, norms, and identities are natural for their children (Cooper, 2009). Families also may see their transgender children experience bullying based on their gender variance; or transgender students may experience abuse within their families as family members attempt to force their children to conform to societal gender norms and expectations (Grossman & D'Augelli, 2006). Additionally, many families simply lack information about transgender identities. Therefore, the role of educators in transgender students' lives is to make a clear assessment about the extent to which families are educated about transgender individuals/experiences, understand and have resources for supporting their transgender children, and ensure the safety of transgender children within and outside of family systems.

In a similar regard, intersex students may or may not have families who have education and support about intersex issues (Lev, 2006). Especially because intersex students vary in the extent to which they have information about being intersex, in addition to possibly not having information that they are intersex, it becomes important for educators to be able to validate and affirm multiple expressions of gender within their schools instead of assigning these behaviors solely to sex (Burnes & Richmond, 2012). In this manner, educators also can encourage the families of intersex students to develop nurturing family environments that do not just tolerate gender variance in behaviors and expressions, but also support gender identity exploration (Varjas et al., 2008). Families may struggle with the "normality" of this approach; however, providing them with good information about gender variance being natural can be very affirming for families and their intersex children (Lev, 2006).

Social Support

As the GLSEN (2009) survey of transgender youth in U.S. schools points out, transgender students may experience physical harassment (in addition to the verbal harassment discussed earlier in the chapter) based on their gender identity (27.2%) and/or sexual orientation (40.1%). These statistics are concerning and contribute to transgender students missing school due to safety concerns (46%). Although surveys of the experiences of intersex students are rare, school systems typically are not structured to be sites of empowerment and resilience for youth who do not conform to a gender binary (Singh & Burnes, 2009; Varjas et al., 2008).

Considering the barriers that exist within school systems, where transgender and intersex students spend the majority of their day, the social supports in their lives warrant focused attention. In a large focus group study of service providers who work with LGBTQ youth, helping professionals identified deficits in meeting the needs of transgender youth. These deficits were especially related to HIV/AIDS risks and the invisibility of transgender youth who were straight-identified and may not access LGBTQ youth serving organizations (Travers et al., 2010).

Healthcare Access

Although many transgender and intersex students may not seek, want, or desire medical interventions (e.g., surgeries, hormone therapy) or counseling, there are many who do, and yet, there are significant healthcare barriers for them. Traditionally there may be a concern about the age of children and an uncertainty about the degree to which children are "sure" about their identities. It is important to remember, though, that gender fluidity is a natural aspect of most people's lives, and it is the self-identification of a gender variant identity and expression over time that is most critical. To be able to understand how transgender or intersex students identify over time, they should have access to healthcare, both physical and psychological supports that feel good to them and are affirmative to their identities. In addition, these same youth will certainly seek healthcare for other considerations than their gender identity (Weber, 2010). Therefore, it is important for educators to understand the importance of healthcare access, especially for students who may be unable to afford treatment or to find an affirmative provider, and how this access may influence students' experiences within school settings.

Social Justice and Advocacy Strategies with Transgender and Intersex Students

Despite laws that protect transgender and intersex students (see Chapter 7 of this volume), transgender and intersex students who do not fit the more rigid notions of gender binary are not guaranteed a positive, affirming school climate in U.S. educational systems. Therefore, in addition to addressing the family and social supports, healthcare access, and legal and ethical protections they need, educators will need to be prepared to take ongoing, proactive action in school and community settings to support youth activism and use of media/social networking as tools for socially just change on behalf of transgender and intersex students.

School Settings

Recent research has investigated the important prevention science necessary to develop positive and affirming environments for LGBTQ youth. In terms of school settings, Heck, Flentje, and Cochran (2011) sampled 145 LGBTQ youth and found that the students who attended school with a Gay-Straight Alliance (GSA) experienced more positive school experiences, less substance use, and lower psychological stressors than those attending a school without a GSA.

For transgender and intersex children, safe and supportive environments may be developed by: providing the option of using the bathroom of the gender a student feels comfortable in and/or a gender-neutral bathroom; addressing transgender and intersex children with the name and pronouns they select for themselves; ensuring the classroom and school environment is free of any bullying directed at transgender and intersex children; and responding to the needs of transgender and intersex students and their families in a positive and affirming manner (GLSEN, 2009; Gonzalez & McNulty, 2010; Singh & Burnes, 2009).

Singh and Jackson (2012) identified several ongoing and proactive advocacy strategies educators may engage in within school systems for LGBTQ youth that also can be applied to intersex students:

- Ensure that the categories of gender identity, gender expression, and sexual orientation are enumerated—or listed—as protected categories within a school's non-discrimination and anti-bullying policies.
- Collaborate with administration to conduct school-wide assessments of the climate for LGBTQI students within schools.
- Organize professional development trainings on LGBTQI student issues within schools.
- Intervene immediately when LGBTQI bullying arises.
- Seek to integrate transgender and intersex concerns throughout school decisions (e.g., paperwork revisions, policy changes, family meetings, PTA meetings).
- Advocate for the school curriculum and libraries to have information included on intersex and transgender people.
- Engage in outreach to parents about transgender and intersex students at school.
- Collaborate with transgender and intersex youth serving community organizations.
- Integrate LGBTQI youth issues into the diversity training within disciplines and units represented within a school.

Fostering Youth Activism and Use of Media/Social Networking

Despite the fact that school environments are often unsafe places for transgender and intersex students, their resilience often has taken the form of activism, and more recently, the form of media/social networking. For instance, whether students begin GSAs or whether they advocate on behalf of themselves for their rights to be respected in schools, transgender and intersex student voices can be some of the most powerful motivators for educators to make positive changes in improving school climates (Gonzalez & McNulty, 2010). Yet, despite the fact that transgender and intersex students are attending schools that are reflective of common discriminations and prejudices based on gender and sexual orientation, they have the capacity for resilience, which may assist them both in and out of schools (Burnes & Chen, 2012; Singh & Jackson, 2012).

Transgender and intersex youth generally have more access to the Internet than ever before, and there are numerous opportunities for them to access information that affirms their identities, connects them with other transgender and intersex youth, and provides them with information about their rights that should be protected at school through affirmative school policies. Because transgender and intersex youth are at risk to experience multiple stressors related to their minority identity status (Kelleher, 2009), and because their gender identities also may intersect with other minority statuses (e.g., class, race/ethnicity, ability, etc.), media and social networking may affirm their lived experiences beyond their gender identity and any resources that might be available in their local community.

At the same time, it is important for educators to take the lead in activism and advocacy, and to not place the sole burden of these activities on transgender and intersex students. For instance, educators may advocate on behalf of transgender and intersex students by initiating policy changes, lobbying legislators, and engaging in community-building with other advocates committed to making schools safer for transgender and intersex students. In doing so, it may be most helpful for educators to use a combination of recent statistics and research studies, in addition to highlighting youth stories and/or voices.

Educators may also support transgender and intersex youth (and allies) activism by brainstorming the positive and negative uses of media and social networking when advocating for their rights in schools (Singh, 2010). Additionally, because cyber-bullying through social networking activities may be used in ways that have the potential to harm others, educators should be able to not only intervene in these areas, but also be able to teach appropriate social networking and other technology skills related to advocacy. Although there are certainly challenges in teaching and developing these skills, the positive potential of using these media makes it worth having these conversations with youth and other educators to bring attention to how to create better environments for transgender and intersex students. Also, there are many schools where the words transgender, intersex, and other terms related to safe schools advocacy may not be searchable on school computers. The American Civil Liberties Union (ACLU) has an important project helping educate LGBTQI students on their rights to be able to search these websites on their school computers called "Don't Filter Me," and educators can help connect transgender and intersex students with the resources related to this project (http://www.aclu.org/dont-filter-me-web-content-filtering-schools).

Conclusion

This chapter has discussed an overview of the most significant knowledge and skills of which educators need to be aware in order to support transgender and intersex students in school settings. Developing competencies in working with transgender and intersex students and implementing affirmative interventions with fellow educators, students, parents, family members, and friends is a critical goal in order to develop positive environments for these youth. A major aspect of developing these competencies includes educators' understanding of the social justice issues (e.g., healthcare access, financial barriers, transphobia, etc.) that impact the lives of transgender and intersex students. These social justice issues become exacerbated when educators are not well trained to support or to be responsive to the needs of transgender and intersex students. With good training and information on transgender and intersex students, however, educators can advocate for the issues that impact these youth in schools. In doing so, educators will develop more positive and safe environments for all students.

References

Accord Alliance. (2011). Quality care indicator checklist. Retrieved from http://www.accordalliance. org/dsd-guidelines.html.

American Counseling Association. (2010). Competencies for counseling with transgender clients. *Journal of LGBT Issues in Counseling, 4*(3), 135–159. doi: 10.1030/15538605.2010.524839

American Psychiatric Association (APA). (2000). *The diagnostic and statistical manual of mental disorders* (Revised 4th ed.). Washington, DC: Author.

Balsalm, K. F., Huang, B., Fieland, K. C., Simoni, J. M., & Walters, K. L. (2004). Culture, trauma, and wellness: A comparison of heterosexual and lesbian, gay, bisexual, and two-spirit Native Americans. *Cultural Diversity and Ethnic Minority Psychology, 10*(3), 287–301. doi: 10.1037/1099-9809.10.3.287

Blackless, M., Charuvastra, A., Derryck, A., Fausto-Sterling, A., Lauzanne, K., & Lee, E. (2000). How sexually dimorphic are we? Review and synthesis. *American Journal of Human Biology, 12*, 151–166. doi: 10.1177/0193723511426293

Brown, L. (2004). *Subversive dialogues: Theory in feminist therapy.* New York, NY: Basic Books.

Burnes, T. R., & Chen, M. (2012). Multiple identities of transgender individuals: Incorporating a framework of intersectionality to gender crossing. In M. Harway & R. Josselin (Eds.), *Multiple Identities.* New York, NY: Oxford University Press.

Burnes, T. R., & Richmond, K. (2012). Counseling strategies with intersex clients: A process-based approach. In M. Pope & S. Dworkin (Eds.), *Counseling lesbian, gay, bisexual, and transgender persons and their families* (pp. 35–44). Alexandria, VA: American Counseling Association.

Butler, J. (1990). *Gender trouble: Feminism and the subversion of identity.* New York, NY: Routledge.

Child Welfare League of America, Inc. (2006). *Out of the margins: A report on regional listening forums highlighting the experiences of lesbian, gay, bisexual, transgender, and questioning youth in care.* Lambda Legal Defense and Education Fund: Washington, DC. Retrieved from www. cwla.org/programs/culture/outofthemargins.pdf

Consortium of the Management of Disorders of Sex Development (CMDSD). (2008). *Clinical Guidelines for the Management of Disorders of Sex Development in Childhood.* Retrieved from http://www.accordalliance.org/dsdguidelines/htdocs/clinical/index.html

Cooper, K. (2009). Social work practice with transgender and gender variant youth and their families. In G. P. Mallon (Ed.), *Social work practice with transgender and gender variant youth* (2nd ed., pp. 128–131). New York, NY: Routledge/Taylor & Francis Group.

Crethar, H. C., Rivera, E. T., & Nash, S. (2008). In search of common threads: Linking multicultural, feminist, and social justice counseling paradigms. *Journal of Counseling and Development, 86*(3), 269–278. doi:10.1002/j.1556-6678.2008.tb00509.x

De Silva, A. (2007). Physical integrity and self-determination: A critique of medical guidelines on intersexuality. *Zeitschrift für Sexualforschung, 20,* 176–185. doi:10.1080/10538720802235310

Diamond, M., & Sigmundson, H. K. (1997). Management of intersexuality: Guidelines for dealing with individuals with ambiguous genitalia. *Archives of Pediatrics and Adolescent Medicine, 151,* 1046–1050.

Feinberg, L. (1996). *Transgender warriors: Making history from Joan of Arc to Dennis Rodman.* Boston, MA: Beacon Press.

GLSEN (2009). Harsh realities: The experiences of transgender youth in our nation's schools. Washington, DC: Author. Retrieved from http://www.glsen.org/cgi-bin/iowa/all/news/record/2388.html

Gonzalez, M., & McNulty, J. (2010). Achieving competency with transgender youth: School counselors as collaborative advocates. *Journal of LGBT Issues in Counseling, 4*(3–4), 176–186. doi:10.1080/15538605.2010.524841

Grossman, A. H., & D'Augelli, A. R. (2006). Transgender youth: Invisible and vulnerable. *Journal of Homosexuality, 51*(1), 111–128. doi:10.1300/J082v51n01_06

Heck, N.C., Flentje, A., & Cochran, B.N. (2011). Offsetting risks: High school gay-straight alliances and lesbian, gay, bisexual, and transgender (LGBT) youth. *School Psychology Quarterly, 26*(2), 161–174. doi:10.1037/a0023226

Kelleher, C. (2009). Minority stress and health: Implications for lesbian, gay, bisexual, transgender, and questioning (LGBTQ) young people. *Counselling Psychology Quarterly, 22*(4), 373–379. doi:10.1080/09515070903334995

Lev, A. (2006). Intersexuality in the family: An unacknowledged trauma. *Journal of Gay & Lesbian Psychotherapy, 10*(2), 27–56. doi:10.1300/J236v10n02_03

Peletz, M. G. (2006). Transgenderism and gender pluralism in Southeast Asia since early modern times. *Current Anthropology, 47*(2), 309–325. doi:10.1086/498947

Professionals Concerned with Gender Diagnoses in the DSM. (2010). Statement on gender incongruence in adolescents in the DSM-5. Retrieved from http://gidconcern.wordpress.com/statement-on-gender-incongruence-in-adescents-in-the-dsm-5/

Roberts, J., & Singh, A. A. (in progress). Fear of a trans planet: Gender around the world. In L. Erickson-Schroth (Ed.), *Trans bodies, trans selves.*

Roysircar, G. (2006). Prevention work in schools and with youth: Promoting competencies and reducing risks. In R. L. Toporek, L. Gerstein, N. Fouad, G. Roysircar, & T. Israel (Eds.), *Handbook for social justice in counseling psychology: Leadership, vision, and action* (pp. 130–145). Thousand Oaks, CA: Sage.

Sanders, D. (2008). Sexual and gender diversity. In D. P. Forsythe (Ed.), *Oxford Encyclopedia of Human Rights* (pp. 443–442). New York, NY: Oxford University Press.

Schweizer, K., Brunner, F., Schutzmann, K., Schonbucher, V., & Richter-Appelt, H. (2009). Gender identity and coping in female 46, XY adults with androgen biosynthesis deficiency (intersexuality/DSD). *Journal of Counseling Psychology, 56*(1), 189–201. doi:10.1037/a0013575

Shallcross, D.M. (2006). A 'ole kane a 'ole wahine: Māhūs' experiences of gender and intimacy. (Unpublished doctoral dissertation). Argosy University/Hawaii, Honolulu, Hawaii.

Singh, A. A. (2010). It takes more than a rainbow sticker! Using the ACA Advocacy Competencies with queer clients. In M. Ratts, J. Lewis, & R. Toporek (Eds.), *Using the ACA Advocacy Competencies in counseling* (pp. 29–41). Alexandria, VA: American Counseling Association.

Singh, A. A., & Burnes, T. R. (2009). Creating developmentally-appropriate, safe counseling environments for transgender youth: The critical role of school counselors. *Journal of LGBT Issues in Counseling, 3*(3–4), 215–234. doi:10.1080/15538600903379457

Singh, A. A., & Jackson, K. (2012). Queer and transgender youth: Education and liberation in our schools. In T. Quinn & E. R. Meiners (Eds.), *Sexualities in education: A reader*. New York, NY: Peter Lang Publishing.

Sulekha. (2008). First transgender or Hijra to be elected to office. Retrieved from http://forums.sulekha.com/forums/coffeehouse/first-transgender-Indian-or-hijra-to-be-elected-to-public-office-895354.htm

Travers, R., Guta, A., Flicker, S., Larkin, J., Lo, C., McCardell, S., & van der Meulen, E. (2010). Service provider views on issues and needs for lesbian, gay, bisexual, and transgender youth. *Canadian Journal of Human Sexuality, 19*(4), 191–198.

Varjas, K., Dew, B., Marshall, M., Graybill, E., Singh, A., & Meyers, J. (2008). Bullying in schools towards sexual minority youth. *Journal of School Violence, 7*(2), 59–86. doi:10.1300/J202v07n02_05

Vavrus, M. (2008) Sexuality, schooling, and identity formation: A critical pedagogy for teacher education. *Teaching and Teacher Education, 25*(3), 383–390. doi:10.1016/j.tate.2008.09.002

Weber, S. (2010). Nursing care of families with parents who are lesbian, gay, bisexual, or transgender. *Journal of Child and Adolescent Psychiatric Nursing, 23*(1), 11–16. doi:10.1111/j.1744-6171.2009.00211.x

Worell, J., & Remer, P. (2003). *Feminist perspectives in therapy: Empowering diverse women* (2nd ed.). Hoboken, NJ: John Wiley & Sons.

World Professional Health Association of Transgender Health. (2011). Standards of care for the health of transsexual, transgender, and gender non-conforming people, version 7. Retrieved from http://www.wpath.org/publications_standards.cfm

APPENDIX A

Awareness Activity 1: The Ian Benson Project

In October of 2007, Ian Benson, a transgender boy in high school, committed suicide. His mother established the Amethyst Ribbon Campaign to help bring awareness to the important needs of transgender youth in schools, families, and communities. Visit the website of Transgender Youth Family Allies (http://www.imatyfa.org) to learn about this campaign and transgender youth-supporting organization. Identify five specific ways you as an educator might use the web resources of this organization to support transgender students in your school setting.

APPENDIX B

Case Study 1: Transgender Middle School Student—Brooke

There is a student in your history class who, after class, asks you to begin using female pronouns ("her") and a feminine name (Brooke). Brooke was assigned *male* at birth, and has been in your class for three months. Brooke tells you she is a girl and wants to be recognized as her identified gender. Using a combined feminist, multicultural, and social justice framework, list at least 10 considerations for your interactions with Brooke.

APPENDIX C

Case Study 2: Intersex High School Student—Elijah

You are a high school math teacher and one of your most outstanding students is named Elijah. You have had Elijah in two classes, and he is also in the student math club for which you are an advisor. You know his parents and the group of friends with whom he hangs out. One day after class, Elijah shares with you that he is intersex. Using a feminist, multicultural, and social justice framework, identify at least 10 important considerations for responding to Elijah's disclosure to you.

APPENDIX D

Activity 2: Gathering Knowledge About Transgender and Intersex Students

Consider the typical levels of school—elementary, middle, and high school. For each level, list the important considerations based on the developmental needs of transgender and intersex students at that school level. What are the differences and similarities for transgender and intersex students at each of these levels?

6 Diversity across the Lesbian, Gay, Bisexual, Transgender, and Questioning Community

Cirleen DeBlaere and Melanie Brewster

Increasingly, the need to attend to the diversity within the lesbian, gay, bisexual, transgender, and queer/questioning (LGBTQ) community is being recognized (e.g., Beckstead & Israel, 2007; Moradi, DeBlaere, & Huang, 2010). The intersection of sexual orientation/gender identities with other important social identity variables is essential to acknowledge if we are to develop effective and culturally appropriate interventions and prevention programs aimed at promoting the mental and physical health of LGBTQ youth. As Garnets (2002) noted, "no single element of identity, be it class, race, gender, disability, or sexual orientation can truly be understood except in relation to the others" (p. 123). Furthermore, the confluence of community, family, and cultural factors as well as the impact of oppression can affect the development and salience of various identities (Fukuyama & Ferguson, 2000). Thus, the current chapter presents theoretical and empirical literature on the intersection of important identity and social factors with sexual orientation/gender identity for LGBTQ youth. These factors include race/ ethnicity, religion, socioeconomic status, and urban density (e.g., rural, suburban, urban). To provide a context for this discussion, we first define important terminology, including privilege, prejudice, stigmatization, and discrimination, and present models of intersectionality. Finally, because family and community aspects are often critical to the development and manifested experience of all the identity and social factors presented, discussion of family and community is integrated throughout the chapter.

Concepts of Privilege, Oppression, and Intersectionality

Multiple social identities are often discussed in terms of societal status with certain social identities recognized as privileged and others as oppressed (e.g., Croteau, Talbot, Lance, & Evans, 2002). *Privilege* is defined as unearned "entitlements, advantages, and dominance conferred upon them [a specific group] by society" (Black & Stone, 2005, p. 243). The United States (U.S.) culture has been described as heterocentric, ethnocentric, and androcentric with heterosexual persons, White individuals, and men identified as the privileged or "prototypical" groups (Purdie-Vaughns & Eibach, 2008). Particularly relevant to the discussion of LGBTQ youth is the concept of heterosexual privilege. Heterosexual privilege is based on the societal belief that heterosexuality is the normative expression of sexual orientation (i.e., heteronormative) and confers advantages to heterosexual individuals. Examples of heterosexual privilege include institutional acknowledgment (e.g., marriage rights), cultural substantiation of one's sexual orientation (e.g., depiction of predominately heterosexual romantic relationships in the media), and personal safety (e.g., less threat of anti-LGBTQ hate crime victimization; Black & Stone, 2005). Alternatively, non-prototypical members of identity groups – LGBTQ persons, racial/ethnic minority individuals, and women – experience oppression in the forms of prejudice, stigmatization, and discrimination (Purdie-Vaughns & Eibach, 2008). Non-prototypical identities refer to the subordinate-group identities of social identity groups (Purdie-Vaughns & Eibach, 2008).

Prejudice has been defined as an attitude about a group based on negative or stigmatizing beliefs (Dovidio, Bringham, Johnson, & Gaertner, 1996; Kwok et al., 2011); *stigmatization* represents the devaluation of a social identity by others (Crocker, 1999). The related concepts of prejudice and stigmatization are thought to lead to discrimination or unfair treatment, and research generally supports this assertion (Dovidio et al., 1996). Another term that is increasingly utilized in literature on diverse youth is marginalization. *Marginalization* describes the multitude of ways in which diverse youth "are isolated, excluded, or opt out from resources they need to succeed" (Venzant Chambers & McCready, 2011, p. 1354). Thus, discrimination and marginalization represent behaviors or actions while prejudice and stigmatization correspond to more attitudinal and/or belief dimensions of oppression. An important extension of our understanding of the behavioral and attitudinal mechanisms of privilege and oppression is the recognition of multiple non-prototypical social identities. The term *double jeopardy* frequently has been used to represent the idea of cumulative disadvantage relative to possessing multiple minority identities (Reid, 1984). In particular, double jeopardy was initially intended to represent the multiple forms of discrimination (i.e., racism and sexism) experienced by racial/ethnic minority women (Purdie-Vaughns & Eibach, 2008). Since that time, terms such as *triple jeopardy* and *multiple jeopardy* also have been utilized to represent the inclusion of discrimination experiences related to additional minority identities such as sexual orientation and social class (Purdie-Vaughns & Eibach, 2008). For instance, an Asian American bisexual young woman would be hypothesized to be the target of racism, heterosexism, and sexism.

However, there are different views about how these mechanisms of oppression operate for individuals with multiple minority identities. These conceptualizations have been termed *the additive model* and *the interactive model* (Purdie-Vaughns & Eibach, 2008). The additive model argues that a person experiences a distinct form of discrimination for each minority identity she/he possesses and that those multiple discrimination experiences are aggregated (Purdie-Vaughns & Eibach, 2008). Thus, the more minority or non-prototypical identities a person possesses, the greater the cumulative effect of her/his discrimination experiences. On the other hand, the interactive model, also termed *the intersectionality model* (Cole, 2009), purports that identification with more than one minority group constructs a novel experience, including discrimination experiences, that are inimitable, non-additive, and not divisible into the individual identities that originally comprised them. Thus, the outcome experience is distinct from the simple sum impact of each minority identity alone. Furthermore, within this conceptualization, each identity's meaning and associated experience can only be fully understood within the context of the other social identities with which it coexists (Diamond & Butterworth, 2008). For instance, in some studies with African American women, researchers have noted the challenge for participants to determine the social identity that elicited the discrimination experiences they described (e.g., Yoder & McDonald, 1998). Rather than attributing their discrimination experiences to being a *woman* or *African American*, they stated that their experiences were due to their being an *African American woman*, a unique social identity intersection not reducible to either identity alone. One Black queer youth put it this way, "You got bashed because you're queer. No, no, no; it happened because I'm Black . . . it's never that clear" (Daley, Solomon, Newman, & Mishna, 2007, p. 19). Cole (2009) argues that, although scholars have often distinguished the additive and intersectional approaches, each offers plausible assertions about the ways in which multiple minority identities may be concurrently experienced. In the sections that follow, we discuss the intersections of several important identity and social variables with LGBTQ identity.

LGBTQ Youth and Racial/Ethnic Minority Communities

An area of social privilege that has received arguably the most attention across diverse disciplines is race/ethnicity (Black & Stone, 2005). However, several authors have lamented the lack of attention to racial/ethnic minority LGBTQ populations in both research and practice with LGBTQ youth (e.g., Barney, 2003; Travers et al., 2010). In addition, when reviewing literature about racial/ethnic LGBTQ youth, it is important to highlight limitations of extant research with racial/ethnic minority LGBTQ individuals (DeBlaere, Brewster, Sarkees, & Moradi, 2010). For instance, the use of culturally aware and inclusive terminology in research continues to be problematic as many sexual minority people of color do not identify as LGBTQ; terms such as *same-gender loving*, *down low*, or *Fa'fafine* may be used commonly within cultural communities, but be unknown to researchers (DeBlaere et al., 2010; Parks, 2001; Wolitski, Jones, Wasserman, & Smith, 2006). Similarly, others have discussed that much of the research investigating the experiences of LGBTQ persons have included few (if any) transgender participants (e.g., Moradi & DeBlaere, 2010). Thus, it is important to consider that the present summary of available literature may not represent the experiences of all racial/ethnic LGBTQ youth.

Racially/Ethnically Diverse LGBTQ Youth

As was previously stated, the intersection of a racial/ethnic identity with LGBTQ identity represents a unique interaction. Consequently, the experience of a Native American LGBTQ youth is likely to vary from the experience of a Latina LGBTQ youth. Furthermore, the experience of a Latina lesbian youth will vary from the experience of a Latina bisexual youth. Although it is critically important to acknowledge these uniquenesses and within-group variability, it is also important to identify some of the potential overlaps in experience that have been discussed in prior theoretical and empirical literature. These commonalities can provide a foundation from which to develop more nuanced understandings of the experiences of specific racial/ethnic minority LGBTQ youth.

The shared experiences of racially/ethnically diverse LGBTQ persons often have been discussed within a risk/resilience framework. With regard to risk, several authors have discussed the belief that racial/ethnic minority LGBTQ persons experience their sexual orientation identity to be in tension with their cultural communities (e.g., Moradi et al., 2010). More specifically, LGBTQ youth and adults may experience racism from the LGBTQ community and heterosexism from their respective racial/ethnic communities (Travers et al., 2010). In addition, some have argued that heterosexual privilege is the only form of privilege that certain racial/ethnic minority groups possess (Fukuyama & Ferguson, 2000). Consequently, LGBTQ individuals may face a difficult dilemma. Coming out as LGBTQ could translate into the loss of belonging in their respective racial/ethnic communities; these communities provide important familial and social connections and protection from racism as well as the benefits associated with heterosexual privilege (Fukuyama & Ferguson, 2000). Furthermore, proponents of the risk perspective argue that racial/ethnic minority LGBTQ individuals may experience more heterosexist stigma and discrimination than their White LGBTQ counterparts at least partly because heterosexism is argued to be more prevalent in racial/ethnic minority communities than White communities (Daley et al., 2007; Moradi et al., 2010). For all of these reasons, racial/ethnic minority LGBTQ persons may be more likely to conceal their sexual orientation, and extant research seems to support this assertion (e.g., Moradi et al., 2010). In a qualitative study of LGBTQ youth service providers and advocates, participants stated that racial/ethnic minority LGBTQ youth experienced more bullying and were more likely to conceal their sexual orientation than White LGBTQ youth (Daley et al., 2007). However, it is important to note that research comparing heterosexist beliefs between racial/ethnic minority and White communities has been inconsistent, with some studies finding that racial/ethnic minority communities espouse more heterosexist beliefs and other studies reporting no difference (e.g., Moradi et al., 2010).

Alternatively, the resilience perspective argues that the multiple minority identities of racial/ethnic LGBTQ persons facilitate the development of certain unique compensatory and/or protective factors that actually promote their well-being in comparison to White LGBTQ individuals (Moradi et al., 2010). For instance, racial/ethnic minority LGBTQ persons may utilize coping strategies developed to address racism to combat other forms of discrimination like heterosexism (Moradi et al., 2010). Another strategy discussed in the literature is role-flexing, which refers to an individual's ability to orient her/himself to a more valued identity in a particular milieu. With role-flexing, racial/ethnic minority LGBTQ persons may avoid direct stigmatization by reorienting themselves to an identity (race/ethnicity or sexual orientation) that will be more valued and supported in a given environment (Bowleg, Huang, Brooks, Black, & Burkholder, 2003). Indeed, racial/ethnic minority persons are thought to develop bicultural competencies that allow them to function in both minority and majority contexts (Constantine & Sue, 2006). However, Fukuyama and Ferguson (2000) warn that there may be costs associated with being biculturally adept. They discuss the potential experience of "cultural strain" (p. 100) associated with attempting to manage two intensely conflictual identities or the splitting off of identities that are inconsistent with a particular cultural context.

Taken together, the literature discussed suggests that possessing both a racial/ethnic and sexual orientation/gender minority identity can be associated with potential costs and benefits. Although these general conceptualizations of risk and resilience provide an important foundational framework to begin to understand the lived experience of racial/ethnic LGBTQ youth, examination of particular racial/ethnic minority groups within the LGBTQ community is also important to better elucidate cultural values and circumstances unique to a given racial/ethnic group. Thus, we next discuss the experiences of African American/Black, Asian American, Latina(o)/Hispanic, and Native American/Indigenous LGBTQ youth in particular.[1] However, we caution that the information provided is general and overarching and that school professionals should attend to and acknowledge the diversity within and among the racial/ethnic groups presented.

African American/Black LGBTQ Youth

Interdependence among family and community members as well as the role of churches have been discussed as important in the development of African American/Black LGBTQ youth (Greene & Boyd-Franklin, 1996; Parks, 2001). However, these connections are presented as both potentially supportive and marginalizing. For example, African American/Black churches may be a source of support, providing an important protective factor for race-related stressors like racism, while also routinely espousing heterosexist ideals of gender roles and negating the sexual orientation/gender identity of African American/Black LGBTQ youth (Parks, 2001). As discussed previously, many African American/Black sexual/gender minority youth may not self-label as LGBTQ or follow the same "coming out" trajectories as youth of White descent. Parks (2001) noted that a lack of self-labeling is related to experiences of prejudice and discrimination (resulting in high unemployment and incarceration rates), as many African American/Black LGBTQ youth feel disempowered in society. Consequently, they may embrace a façade of heightened masculinity or femininity to avoid being labeled as a sexual/gender minority person. Additional potential risk factors such as poverty, family conflicts, and participation in risky behaviors (e.g., unsafe sex) also may increase the susceptibility of African American/Black LGBTQ youth to psychological distress, substance use, problems in school, and delinquency (Garbarino, 1995; Parks, 2001; Rotheram-Borus, Rosario, Van-Rossem, Reid, & Gillis, 1995; Savin-Williams, 1994).

Asian American LGBTQ Youth

Given the significant immigration histories of Asian American populations, levels of acculturation (i.e., socialization to the dominant cultural group) and enculturation (i.e., socialization to the individual's indigenous culture; Kim & Abreu, 2001) and associated traditionality of family values are important to consider when conceptualizing the identity development and experience of Asian American LGBTQ youth. Lower levels of acculturation and more traditional family values have been linked to lower tolerance toward LGBTQ people (Greene, 1994; Newman & Muzzonigro, 1993). In addition, values common among many Asian cultures such as deference to elders, conformity, interdependence, respect, *ishin-denshin* (communicating without words), and maintenance of traditional gender roles may make explicitly coming out as LGBTQ a threatening, disrespectful, and/or disobedient act toward the family (Akerlund & Cheung, 2000; Chan, 1989; Ho, 1995). It also may be viewed as a rejection of traditional cultural values (Chan, 1989). Consequently, Asian American LGBTQ youth may decide against coming out to their families because they believe that they will bring shame to their parents, be disowned, or have their identity negated/denied (Choi, Yep, & Kumekawa, 1998). Similar to African American/Black LGBTQ youth, Asian American

LGBTQ youth may experience psychological symptoms such as low self-esteem and internalized hatred (Choi et al., 1998). Beyond psychological distress, LGBTQ issues and sex more generally can be considered taboo topics in Asian cultures often resulting in a lack of formal sex education for Asian American LGBTQ youth (Poon & Ho, 2002). Indeed, some research suggests that Asian American LGBTQ youth report less knowledge of sexually transmitted diseases than other youth (Poon & Ho, 2002). Thus, social stigma surrounding sexual/gender minority issues in Asian American communities may put Asian American LGBTQ youth at an elevated risk for HIV and other sexually transmitted infections (STIs).

Latina(o)/Hispanic American LGBTQ Youth

Analogous to Asian American LGBTQ youth, Latina/o LGBTQ youth represent a diverse racial group with a significant immigration history (Zamora-Hernandez & Patterson, 1996). Also similar, attitudes toward Latina/o LGBTQ youth are linked strongly to levels of acculturation and traditional family values such that less acculturation and greater adherence to traditional family values are associated with more negative attitudes toward Latina/o LGBTQ persons (Akerlund & Cheung, 2000). *Familism* is considered the key cultural value among Latina/o persons; closeness within the family, including open and candid communication, is expected (Bernal, Cumba-Avilés, & Sáez Santiago, 2006). Religion also has been identified as an important variable to consider in the experience of Latina/o LGBTQ youth. Religion may create a conflict for Latina/o LGBTQ youth as Christian value systems (particularly Catholicism) often strongly denounce LGBTQ identities and prescribe distinct gender role expectations (Carballo-Dieguez, 1989; Duarte-Velez, Bernal, & Bonilla, 2010). For instance, men are expected to provide for and protect family members with loyalty (i.e., *machismo*), whereas women are expected to be submissive, caring, and modest (Carballo-Dieguez, 1989). LGBTQ identification may be seen as a direct affront to these prescriptions. Similarly, while closeness of family can provide a source of support for Latina/o LGBTQ youth, it also may foster a need to remain secretive about sexual orientation/gender identity if youth believe that their identity will not be accepted. For example, a Latino gay youth from one case study stated "I feel bad, I feel false because they believe things about me that I am not. They have expectations of me that I cannot fill" regarding his sexual identity (Duarte-Velez et al., 2010, p. 900). Further, close-knit family structures in Latina/o cultures often come with the expectation that youth will live with their parents until they are married, an arrangement that is understandably problematic for an LGBTQ person who is not out to her/his family (Akerlund & Cheung, 2000). To evade heterosexist stigma and in-group discrimination, some Latina/o LGBTQ youth may engage in unsafe same-gender sex on the "down low"—a practice that is linked with increased STIs (Wolitski et al., 2006).

Native American/Indigenous LGBTQ Youth

Native American people in the U.S. come from culturally heterogeneous groups comprised of hundreds of distinct tribes. Today, more than 50% of Native Americans live in urban regions (Forquera, 2001). In general, Native American youth report higher levels of poverty, psychological symptomatology, substance use, and suicidal ideation while attaining lower levels of education compared to their White counterparts (Barney, 2003). In past tribal histories, the terms *two spirit* or *berdache* referred to Native American individuals who engaged in same-gender sexual behavior or followed non-traditional gender roles (Adams & Phillips, 2006). Within many traditional indigenous cultures, sexuality and gender identity were viewed as fluid, and LGBTQ individuals were seen as different, but not deviant, from heterosexual and gender conforming individuals (Bridges, Selvidge, & Matthews, 2003). As Native tribes became increasingly colonized, attitudes about sexual orientation shifted and evolved to reflect more Western hetero-sexist views and a rejection of historical LGBTQ-affirming aspects of tribal life (Allen, 1986; Walters, 1997). However, more recently, there has been a return to affirming and celebrating *two-spirit* identity among some Native groups (Lang, 1998). Despite this support across several different tribes, accumulating research suggests that Indigenous and Native American LGBTQ youth constitute a vulnerable population with an elevated risk for physical and sexual abuse compared to indigenous and Native American heterosexual youth (Barney, 2003). It may be that cultural affirmation of *two-spiritedness* is less likely to be exhibited with more acculturated Native American youth.

Religiosity

In the previous section, religion was identified as an important variable for certain racial/ethnic minority communities. Religious affiliations can provide social, community, and familial support systems for youth, and for many, strong faith is linked to psycho-logical well-being and physical health (for a review, see Steger & Frazier, 2005). Still, "religions in general, and Christianity in particular, are often perceived as anathema" to LGBTQ identity (O'Brien, 2004, p. 180). Countless studies have documented the persistence of heterosexist attitudes and policies within numerous religious groups including the Catholic church (Buchanan, Dzelme, Harris, & Hecker, 2001; Carballo-Dieguez, 1989), fundamentalist Christian sects (Barton, 2010), conservative Jewish sects (Kahn, 1989), the Mormon church (Cooper & Pease, 2009), and Islamic sects (Boellstorff, 2005). For example, in a recent qualitative study, one woman reflected upon growing up as a lesbian youth in the Pentecostal church and stated "[t]he preacher would preach on homosexuality. He would always group us in with the so-called perverts, you know, like child molesters and just awful people" (Barton, 2010, p. 472). Such a traumatizing early experience is depicted frequently in research with religious LGBTQ people (Califia, 2002; Gold, 2008; Truluck, 2000).

It is important to clarify, however, that stigma is not a unidirectional prejudice from religious groups to LGBTQ persons. Individuals who openly identify as both LGBTQ *and* religious may be met with stigma and mistrust from the LGBTQ community because "a flight from religious intolerance is a central aspect of personal 'coming out' stories" for many LGBTQ people (O'Brien, 2004, p. 184). As such, LGBTQ youth who may try to maintain their ties to religious institutions may feel as though they will not be fully welcomed into some LGBTQ communities. Potentially confronting "double stigma," religious LGBTQ youth often must undergo a solo journey to forge a path of spiritual understanding and self-acceptance. A growing body of research suggests that many LGBTQ people are able to (re)integrate their religious beliefs, overcome guilt and feelings of betrayal, and (if they choose to) find affirming spiritual groups and religious communities with whom they can (re)connect (Buchanan et al., 2001; Halderman, 2004; O'Brien, 2004). Other LGBTQ people may choose instead to explore expressions of spirituality that have not been affiliated historically with oppression such as Buddhism, Paganism, Wiccan, and some Native American traditions (Buchanan et al., 2001). Within East Asian and South Asian cultures, Buddhist ideology is tolerant of sexual orientation variance, and the Hindu belief system often does not take a clear stance on homosexuality (Nagarkar, 2008; Williams, 1994). Finally, some LGBTQ people may decide that they can be fulfilled without formal ties to an organized belief system (Barret & Barzan, 1996).

Socioeconomic Status

Social class and economic status are critical aspects of identity that shape the daily experiences of all individuals, and some evidence points to links between poverty and psychological distress for youth (Lott, 2002). Unfortunately, little scholarship has focused explicitly on the impact of social class, and the research that is available is limited in scope and clarity (Baker, 1996; Liu et al., 2004). Consistent with intersectionality approaches, scholars state that socioeconomic status (SES) must be considered within the context of its complex interactions with other salient identities (Smith, 2005).

Stigmatization of the poor is represented by the concept and practice of *classism*. Classism enables those of more privileged SES to exclude, discount, discriminate, stigmatize and disempower the poor (Lott, 2002). Much of the distancing between social classes is a derivative of stereotypes about the poor including being characterized as dishonest, lazy, incompetent, promiscuous, dirty, immoral, abusive, alcoholic, and violent (for a review, see Lott, 2002). The poor also are perceived as less intelligent and lacking merit when compared with higher-income groups (Chafel, 1997), a perception that is likely very damaging to the futures of school-aged economically disadvantaged LGBTQ youth. The persistence of these negative attitudes toward the poor place economically disadvantaged LGBTQ youth in a position to be the targets of multiple forms of discrimination. Specifically, wealth and SES inequalities have deepened substantially in the past decade, with such disparities magnified for racial/ethnic minority individuals and members of other marginalized groups (Bullock & Lott, 2001). Among the most "severely poor" families, homelessness rates are rising, with LGBTQ youth being among some of the most vulnerable to homelessness (Hammer, Finkelhor, & Sedlack, 2002; Reck, 2009). For instance, although LGBTQ persons comprise approximately 3–5% of the general U.S. population, LGBTQ youth have been estimated to represent as much as 35% of the homeless youth population (Cochran, Stewart, Ginzler, & Cauce, 2002; Yu, 2010). While not necessarily a product of familial poverty, some LGBTQ youth may be pushed out of their homes and lose the economic support of their family members because of their sexual orientation or gender identity. In these circumstances, LGBTQ youth may be forced to employ more extreme strategies (e.g., dealing drugs or prostitution) to obtain money for basic necessities (e.g., food and shelter; Kruks, 1991; Reck, 2009). The futures of homeless youth are bleak and characterized by access to few resources, low educational outcomes, minimal job opportunities, and unreliable social networks (Tyler, 2006). Some larger metropolitan areas may have greater resources and supports for LGBTQ homeless and poor youth, but many rural areas do not.

Urban Density

When reviewing research about LGBTQ people, it is important to recognize the urban bias that persists in reports and studies across the country (D'Augelli & Hart, 1987; Waldo, Hesson-McInnis, & D'Augelli, 1998). Specifically, most research has focused on the experiences of LGBTQ people who live in large cities and metropolitan regions across the U.S. as they tend to be easier to sample (Huang et al., 2010). A recent content analysis of literature from the past decade with racial/ethnic sexual minority individuals found that studies typically only included participants from the metropolitan regions of four states: California, Illinois, Florida, and New York; moreover, no studies included participants from 23 of the most rural states in the U.S. (Huang et al., 2010). Thus, knowledge about rural LGBTQ youth remains sparse and limited in scope, with even the terms "rural" and "urban" being poorly defined.[2]

Because of the emphasis on urban LGBTQ people, much less is known about the development of LGBTQ youth and families in suburban or rural areas (D'Augelli & Hart, 1987). The limited data available suggests that LGBTQ identities often remain invisible due to overarching fear and discomfort about community heterosexism in rural areas (D'Augelli & Hart, 1987). Oswald and Culton (2003) discuss the prevailing attitude that "rural" and "gay" are incompatible terms. This social distance can be further compounded by influential community leaders (e.g., church leaders, city officials) who may not acknowledge LGBTQ individuals or promote gay affirming perspectives (D'Augelli & Hart, 1987). Similarly, Waldo and colleagues (1998) underscore the tendency for rural communities to overlook rampant prejudice toward LGBTQ youth in schools. A national survey of LGBTQ secondary school students found that LGBTQ students from rural communities report experiencing more homophobic remarks and victimization related to sexual orientation and gender expression than students from urban areas (Kosciw, Greytak, & Diaz, 2009). Such experiences can lead to anxiety, depression, and even suicidal ideation for some sexual minority youth (Waldo et al., 1998).

Despite the potential prejudice and violence faced by their children, parents of LGBTQ youth in rural communities may have nowhere to go for support, no models for how to cope with their children's coming out, nor any local community support organizations, such as Parents, Families, and Friends of Lesbians and Gays (PFLAG; Oswald & Culton, 2003). Such resources are readily available in metropolitan areas and even midsized suburban regions across the country, but may be viewed as too controversial for more rural and religiously conservative communities. Parents in rural and religious communities may feel that they are unable to reach out for support for their LGBTQ child due to pervasive stigma and fear of further marginalization. Beyond community-level heterosexism, there are also barriers to establishing personal supports or networks of LGBTQ friends in some rural regions due to the limited number of people who openly identify as sexual/gender minority persons (D'Augelli & Hart, 1987). Further, making lasting friendships and relationships within the sexual/gender minority community may be challenging because LGBTQ people in sparsely populated regions may have little in common besides their sexual/gender minority statuses (Moses & Buckner, 1980). For rural LGBTQ adults, particularly men, some of the most accessible gay social opportunities may be centered in adult bookstores and gay bars. However, most of these venues are not accessible to (or appropriate for) LGBTQ youth under 18 (D'Augelli & Hart, 1987).

Rural LGBTQ youth may instead rely heavily on the Internet for their community support and connection or visit larger cities and suburbs (Oswald & Culton, 2003).

Conversely, many metropolitan areas are well known for their "gayborhoods" (e.g., Chelsea in New York City, Boystown in Chicago, West Hollywood in Los Angeles) in which identifying as a sexual/gender minority person is not just affirmed, but expected. Youth in these urban areas often have numerous opportunities to connect with other LGBTQ people if they choose. For example, in New York City, in addition to the numerous shelters for homeless and runaway LGBTQ youth, centers such as the Lesbian, Gay, Bisexual, and Transgender Community Center are accessible resources for LGBTQ youth (Rosario et al., 1996). Such agencies often provide a wide range of activities for LGBTQ youth (e.g., artistic activities, discussion groups), including support and psychoeducational groups that address topics pertinent to this population (e.g., coming out; Rosario et al., 1996). Larger cities also often have LGBTQ centered bookstores, coffee shops, art exhibitions, and gay pride celebrations—all venues that can facilitate social connections among LGBTQ youth. However, Wright's (2008) study with racial/ethnic minority queer youth in New York City highlighted that racial/ethnic minority LGBTQ youth may remain isolated within cultural and ethnic enclaves and not access such resources that are readily available to White LGBTQ youth.

Conclusion

This chapter's relatively brief overview of important diversity factors to consider with LGBTQ youth highlights the importance of attending to the within-group variability present with this population. The discussion of race/ethnicity, religion, SES, and level of urbanity illustrates the unique considerations that manifest when LGBTQ identity intersects with other important identity and/or social factors. In particular, this review highlighted the conflicts that may exist for LGBTQ youth when aspects such as religion are considered. In several instances, factors discussed represented buffers or anticipated protective aspects of experience while simultaneously representing challenges to well-being (e.g., family values and/or acceptance). It is important for school professionals to be aware of both the potential benefits and challenges inherent in various intersections of identity and to assist LGBTQ youth to understand these complexities when appropriate.

Finally, in considering the diversity across LGBTQ youth, it is essential to recognize the role of individual difference variables (e.g., acculturation level, personality factors, availability of internal and external resources). Although the information provided in this chapter can inform the understanding of diverse LGBTQ youth, overgeneralizations across groups must be avoided. As intersectionality models suggest, the multiple identities of LGBTQ youth, privileged and oppressed, as well as the social and environmental factors that help to shape those identities, are important considerations for school professionals.

Notes

1 In order to present information that would be most representative of the current U.S. population, we chose to discuss the four primary racial/ethnic minority groups identified in the 2010 U.S. Census, but recognize that this list is not inclusive of all races/ethnicities nor individuals who may identify with more than one racial/ethnic group.

2 For the purpose of this chapter, rural communities are conceptualized in line with McCarthy's (2000) definition that they are cohesive, autonomous, agrarian communities with residents reporting lower SES and education levels.

References

Adams, H., & Phillips, L. (2006). Experiences of two-spirit lesbian and gay Native Americans: An argument for standpoint theory in identity research. *Identity*, 6(3), 273–291. doi:10.1207/s1532706xid0603_4

Akerlund, M., & Cheung, M. (2000). Teaching beyond the deficit model: Gay and lesbian issues among African Americans, Latinos, and Asian Americans. *Journal of Social Work Education*, 36(2), 279–292.

Allen, P. G. (1986). *The sacred hoop: Recovering the feminine in American Indian traditions*. Boston, MA: Beacon Press.

Baker, N. L. (1996). Class as a construct in a "classless" society. In M. Hill & E. D. Rothblum (Eds.), *Classism and feminist therapy: Counting costs* (pp. 13–24). New York, NY: Harrington Park.

Barney, D. D. (2003). Health risk-factors for gay American Indian and Alaska Native adolescent males. *Journal of Homosexuality*, 46(1/2), 137–157. doi:10.1300/J082v46n01_04

Barret, R., & Barzan, R. (1996). Spiritual experiences of gay men and lesbians. *Counseling and Values*, 41(1–2), 4–15. doi:10.1002/j.2161-007X.1996.tb00858.x

Barton, B. (2010). "Abomination"—Life as a Bible belt gay. *Journal of Homosexuality*, 57(4), 465–484. doi:10.1080/00918361003608558

Beckstead, L., & Israel, T. (2007). Affirmative counseling and psychotherapy focused on issues related to sexual orientation conflicts. In K. J. Bieschke, R. M. Perez, & K. A. DeBord (Eds.), *Handbook of counseling and psychotherapy with lesbian, gay, bisexual and transgender clients* (2nd ed., pp. 81–105). Washington, DC: American Psychological Association.

Bernal, G., Cumba-Avilés, E., & Sáez Santiago, E. (2006). Cultural and relational processes in depressed Latino adolescents. In S. Beach & N. Kaslow (Eds.), *Relational processes and mental health* (pp. 221–224). Washington, DC: American Psychiatric Press.

Black, L. L., & Stone, D. (2005). Expanding the definition of privilege: The concept of social privilege. *Journal of Multicultural Counseling and Development*, 33(4), 243–255. doi:10.1002/j.2161-1912.2005.tb00020.x

Boellstorff, T. (2005). Between religion and desire: Being Muslim and gay in Indonesia. *American Anthropologist*, 107(4), 575–585. doi:10.1525/aa.2005.107.4.575

Bowleg, L., Huang, J., Brooks, K., Black, A., & Burkholder, G. (2003). Triple jeopardy and beyond: Multiple minority stress and resilience among Black lesbians. *Journal of Lesbian Studies*, 7(4), 87–108. doi:10.1300/J155v07n04_06

Bridges, S. K., Selvidge, M. M. D., & Matthews, C. R. (2003). Lesbian women of color: Therapeutic issues and challenges. *Journal of Multicultural Counseling and Development*, 31(2), 113–130. doi:10.1002/j.2161-1912.2003.tb00537.x

Buchanan, M., Dzelme, K., Harris, D., & Hecker, L. (2001). Challenges of being simultaneously gay or lesbian and spiritual and/or religious: A narrative perspective. *The American Journal of Family Therapy*, 29(5), 435–449. doi:10.1080/01926180127629

Bullock, H. E., & Lott, B. (2001). Building a research and advocacy agenda on issues of social justice. *Analyses of Social Issues and Public Policy*, 1(1), 147–162. doi:10.1111/1530-2415.00008

Califia, P. (2002). *Speaking sex to power: The politics of queer sex*. San Francisco, CA: Cleis Press.

Carballo-Dieguez, A. (1989). Hispanic culture, gay male culture, and AIDS: Counseling implications. *Journal of Counseling and Development*, 68(1), 26–30. doi:10.1002/j.1556-6676.1989.tb02487.x

Chafel, J. A. (1997). Societal images of poverty: Child and adult beliefs. *Youth & Society*, 28(4), 432–463. doi:10.1177/0044118X97028004003

Chan, C. (1989). Issues of identity development among Asian-American lesbians and gay men. *Journal of Counseling and Development, 68*(1), 16–20. doi:10.1002/j.1556-6676.1989.tb02485.x

Choi, K. H., Yep, G. A., & Kumekawa, E. (1998). HIV prevention among Asian and Pacific Islander American men who have sex with men: A critical review of theoretical models and directions for future research. *AIDS Education and Prevention, 10(Supplement 3)*, 19–30.

Cochran, B. N., Stewart, A. J., Ginzler, J. A., & Cauce, A. M. (2002). Challenges faced by homeless sexual/gender minorities: Comparison of gay, lesbian, bisexual, and transgender homeless adolescents with their heterosexual counterparts. *American Journal of Public Health, 92*(5), 773–777.

Cole, E. R. (2009). Intersectionality and research in psychology. *American Psychologist, 64* (3), 170–180. doi:10.1037/a0014564

Constantine, M. G., & Sue, D. W. (2006). Factors contributing to optimal human functioning in people of color in the United States. *The Counseling Psychologist, 34* (2), 228–244. doi:10.1177/0011000005281318

Cooper, B., & Pease, E. C. (2009). The Mormons versus the "armies of Satan": Competing frames of morality in the *Brokeback Mountain* controversy in Utah newspapers. *Western Journal of Communication, 73*(2), 134–156. doi:10.1080/10570310902856097

Crocker, J. (1999). Social stigma and self-esteem: Situational construction of self-worth. *Journal of Experimental Social Psychology, 35*(1), 89–107. doi:10.1006/jesp. 1998.1369

Croteau, J. M., Talbot, D. M., Lance, T. S., & Evans, N. J. (2002). A qualitative study of the interplay between privilege and oppression. *Journal of Multicultural Counseling and Development, 30*(4), 239–258. doi:10.1002/j.2161-1912.2002.tb00522.x

Daley, A., Solomon, S., Newman, P. A., & Mishna, F. (2007). Traversing the margins: Intersectionalities in the bullying of lesbian, gay, bisexual, and transgender youth. *Journal of Gay and Lesbian Social Services: Issues in Practice, Policy & Research, 19*(3–4), 9–29. doi:10.1080/10538720802161474

D'Augelli, A. R., & Hart, M. M. (1987). Gay women, men, and families in rural settings: Toward the development of helping communities. *American Journal of Community Psychology, 15*(1), 79–93. doi:10.1007/BF00919759

DeBlaere, C., Brewster, M. E., Sarkees, A., & Moradi, B. (2010). Conducting research with LGB people of color: Methodological challenges and strategies. *The Counseling Psychologist, 38*(3), 331–362. doi:10.1177/0011000009335257

Diamond, L. M., & Butterworth, M. (2008). Questioning gender and sexual identity: Dynamic links over time. *Sex Roles, 59*(5–6), 365–376. doi:10.1007/s11199-008-9425-3

Dovidio, J. F., Bringham, J. C., Johnson, B. T., & Gaertner, S. L. (1996). Stereotyping, prejudice, and discrimination: Another look. In C. N. Macrae, C. Stangor, & M. Hewstone (Eds.), *Stereotypes and stereotyping* (pp. 276–319). New York, NY: Guilford Press.

Duarte-Velez, Y., Bernal, G., & Bonilla, K. (2010). Culturally adapted cognitive-behavioral therapy: Integrating sexual, spiritual, and family identities in an evidence-based treatment of a depressed Latino adolescent. *Journal of Clinical Psychology: In Session, 66*(8), 895–906. doi:10.1002/jclp.20710

Forquera, R. (2001). *Issue brief: Urban Indian health.* Retrieved from http://www.kff.org/minorityhealth/loader.cfm?url=/commonspot/security/getfile.cfm&pageid=13909

Fukuyama, M. A., & Ferguson, A. D. (2000). Lesbian, gay, and bisexual people of color: Understanding cultural complexity and managing multiple oppressions. In R. M. Perez, K. A. DeBord, & K. J. Bieschke (Eds.), *Handbook of counseling and psychotherapy with lesbian, gay, and bisexual clients* (pp. 81–105). Washington, DC: American Psychological Association.

Garbarino, J. (1995). *Raising children in a socially toxic environment.* San Francisco, CA: Jossey-Bass.

Garnets, L. D. (2002). Sexual orientations in perspective. *Cultural Diversity and Ethnic Minority Psychology, 8*(2), 115–129. doi:10.1037/1099-9809.8.2.115

Gold, M. (2008). *Crisis: 40 stories revealing the personal, social, and religious pain and trauma of growing up gay in America.* Austin, TX: Greenleaf Book Group Press.

Greene, B. (1994). Ethnic-minority lesbians and gay men: Mental health and treatment issues. *Journal of Consulting and Clinical Psychology, 62*(2), 243–251. doi:10.1037/0022-006X.62.2.243

Greene, B., & Boyd-Franklin, N. (1996). African American lesbian couples: Ethnocultural considerations in psychotherapy. *Women and Therapy, 19*(3), 49–60. doi:10.1300/J015v19n03_06

Halderman, D. W. (2004). When sexual and religious orientations collide: Considerations in working with conflicted same-sex attracted male clients. *The Counseling Psychologist, 32*(5), 691–715. doi:10.1177/0011000004267560

Hammer, H., Finkelhor, D., & Sedlack, A. (2002, October). *Runaway/Thrownaway children: National estimates and characteristics.* Washington, DC: U.S. Department of Justice, Office of Juvenile Justice and Delinquency Prevention. Retrieved from https://www.ncjrs.gov/pdffiles1/ojjdp/196469.pdf

Ho, P. (1995). Male homosexual identity in Hong Kong: A social construction. *Journal of Homosexuality, 29*(1), 71–88. doi:10.1300/J082v29n01_04

Huang, Y., Brewster, M. E., Moradi, B., Goodman, M., Wiseman, M., & Martin, A. (2010). Content analysis of literature about LGB people of color: 1998–2007. *The Counseling Psychologist, 38*(3), 363–396. doi:10.1177/0011000009335255

Kahn, Y. (1989). The liturgy of gay and lesbian Jews. In C. Balka & A. Rose (Eds.), *Twice blessed: On being lesbian, gay, and Jewish* (182–197). Boston, MA: Beacon Press.

Kim, B. S. K., & Abreu, J. M. (2001). Acculturation measurement: Theory, current instruments, and future directions. In J. G. Ponterotto, J. M. Casas, L. A. Suzuki, & C. M. Alexander (Eds.), *Handbook of multicultural counseling* (2nd ed., pp. 394–424). Thousand Oaks, CA: Sage.

Kosciw, J. G., Greytak, E. A., & Diaz, E. M. (2009). Who, what, where, when, and why: Demographic and ecological factors contributing to hostile school climates for lesbian, gay, bisexual, and transgender youth. *Journal of Youth and Adolescence, 38*(7), 976–988. doi:10.1007/s10964-009-9412-1

Kruks, G. (1991). Gay and lesbian homeless/street youth: Special issues and concerns. *Journal of Adolescent Health, 12*(7), 515–518. doi:10.1016/0197-0070(91)90080-6

Kwok, J., Atencio, J., Ullah, J., Crupi, R., Chen, D., Roth, A. R., . . . Brondolo, E. (2011). The Perceived Ethnic Discrimination Questionnaire—Community Version: Validation in a multiethnic Asian sample. *Cultural Diversity and Ethnic Minority Psychology, 17*(3), 271–282. doi:10.1037/a0024034

Lang, S. (1998). *Men as women, women as men: Changing gender in Native American cultures.* Austin, TX: University of Texas Press.

Liu, W. M., Ali, S. R., Soleck, G., Hopps, J., Dunston, K., & Pickett, T. (2004). Using social class in counseling psychology research. *Journal of Counseling Psychology, 51*(1), 3–18. doi:10.1037/0022-0167.51.1.3

Lott, B. (2002). Cognitive and behavioral distancing from the poor. *American Psychologist, 57*(2), 100–110. doi:10.1037/0003-066X.57.2.100

McCarthy, L. (2000). Poppies in a wheat field: Exploring the lives of rural lesbians. *Journal of Homosexuality, 39*(1), 75–92. doi:10.1300/J082v39n01_05

Moradi, B., & DeBlaere, C. (2010). Replacing either/or with both/and: Illustrations of perspective alternation. *The Counseling Psychologist, 38*(3), 455–468. doi:10.1177/0011000009356460

Moradi, B., DeBlaere, C., & Huang, Y. (2010). Centralizing the experiences of LGB people of color in counseling psychology. *The Counseling Psychologist, 38*(3), 322–330. doi:10.1177/0011000008330832

Moradi, B., Wiseman, M., DeBlaere, C., Sarkees, A., Goodman, M., Brewster, M., & Huang, Y. (2010). LGB people of color and White individuals' perceptions of heterosexist stigma, internalized homophobia and outness: Comparisons of levels and links. *The Counseling Psychologist, 38*(3), 397–424. doi:10.1177/0011000009335263

Moses, A. E., & Buckner, J. A. (1980). The special problems of rural gay clients. *Human Services in the Rural Environment, 5*(5), 22–27.

Nagarkar, M. (2008). *Changing attitudes towards homosexuality in the Indian immigrant community.* Retrieved from https://digitalarchive.wm.edu/handle/10288/656

Newman, B., & Muzzonigro, P. (1993). The effects of traditional family values on the coming out process of gay male adolescents. *Adolescence, 28*(109), 212–226.

O'Brien, J. (2004). Wrestling the angel of contradiction: Queer Christian identities. *Culture and Religion, 5*(2), 179–202. doi:10.1080/143830042000225420

Oswald, R. F., & Culton, L. S. (2003). Under the rainbow: Rural gay life and its relevance for family providers. *Family Relations, 52*(1), 72–81. doi:10.1111/j.1741-3729.2003.00072.x

Parks, C. W. (2001). African-American same-gender-loving youths and families in urban schools. *Journal of Gay and Lesbian Social Services, 13*(3), 41–56. doi:10.1300/J041v13n03_03

Poon, M., & Ho, P. (2002). A qualitative analysis of cultural and social vulnerabilities to HIV infection among gay, lesbian, and bisexual Asian youth. *Journal of Gay and Lesbian Social Services, 14*(3), 43–78. doi:10.1177/0011000002239398

Purdie-Vaughns, V., & Eibach, R. P. (2008). Intersectional invisibility: The distinctive advantages and disadvantages of multiple subordinate-group identities. *Sex Roles, 59*(5–6), 377–391. doi:10.1007/s11199-008-9424-4

Reck, J. (2009). Homeless gay and transgender youth of color in San Francisco: "No One Likes Street Kids"—even in the Castro. *Journal of LGBT Youth, 6*(2–3), 223–242. doi:10.1080/19361650903013519

Reid, P. T. (1984). Feminism versus minority group identity: Not for Black women only. *Sex Roles, 10*(3–4), 247–255. doi:10.1007/BF00287778

Rosario, M., Meyer-Bahlburg, H., Hunter, J., Exner, T., Gwadz, M., & Keller, A. (1996). The psychosexual development of urban lesbian, gay, and bisexual youths. *The Journal of Sex Research, 33*(2), 113–126. doi:10.1080/00224499609551823

Rotheram-Borus, M. J., Rosario, M., Van-Rossem, R., Reid, H., & Gillis, R. (1995). Prevalence, course, and predictors of multiple problem behaviors among gay and bisexual adolescents. *Developmental Psychology, 31*(1), 75–85. doi:10.1037/0012-1649.31.1.75

Savin-Williams, R. C. (1994). Verbal and physical abuse as stressors in the lives of lesbian, gay male, and bisexual youths: Associations with school problems, running away, substance abuse, prostitution, and suicide. *Journal of Consulting and Clinical Psychology, 62*(2), 261–269. doi:10.1037/0022-006X.62.2.261

Smith, L. (2005). Psychotherapy, classism, and the poor: Conspicuous by their absence. *American Psychologist, 60*(7), 687–696. doi:10.1037/0003-066X.60.7.687

Steger, M. F., & Frazier, P. (2005). Meaning in life: One link in the chain from religiousness to well-being. *Journal of Counseling Psychology, 52*(4), 574–582. doi:10.1037/0022-0167.52.4.574

Travers, R., Guta, A., Flicker, S., Larkin, J., Lo, C., McCardell, S., & van der Meulen, E. (2010). Service provider views on issues and needs for lesbian, gay, bisexual, and transgender youth. *Canadian Journal of Human Sexuality, 19*(4), 191–198. Retrieved from http://www.mendeley.com/research/service-provider-views-issues-needs-lesbian-gay-bisexual-transgender-youth/

Truluck, R. (2000). *Steps to recovery from bible abuse.* Gaithersburg, MO: Chi Rho Press.

Tyler, K. (2006). A qualitative study of early family histories and transitions of homeless youth. *Journal of Interpersonal Violence, 21*(10), 1385–1393. doi:10.1177/0886260506291650

Venzant Chambers, T. T., & McCready, L. T. (2011). "Making Space" for ourselves: African American student responses to their marginalization. *Urban Education, 46*(6), 1352–1378. doi:10.1177/0042085911400322

Waldo, C. R., Hesson-McInnis, M. S., & D'Augelli, A. R. (1998). Antecedents and consequences of victimization of lesbian, gay, and bisexual young people: A structural model comparing rural university and urban samples. *American Journal of Community Psychology, 26*(2), 307–334. doi:10.1023/A:1022184704174

Walters, K. L. (1997). Urban lesbian and gay American Indian identity. *Journal of Gay & Lesbian Social Services, 6*(2), 43–65. doi:10.1300/J041v06n02_05

Williams, W. (1994). Sexual variance in Asian cultures. *Amerasia Journal, 20*(3), 87–94.

Wolitski, R. J., Jones, K. T., Wasserman, J. L., & Smith, J. C. (2006). Self-identification as "down low" among men who have sex with men (MSM) from 12 U.S. cities. *AIDS and Behavior, 10*(5), 519–529. doi:10.1007/s10461-006-9095-5

Wright, K. (2008). *Drifting toward love: Black, brown, gay, and coming of age on the streets of New York.* Boston, MA: Beacon Press.

Yoder, J. D., & McDonald, T. W. (1998). Measuring sexist discrimination in the workplace: Support for the validity of the Schedule of Sexist Events. *Psychology of Women Quarterly, 22*(3), 487–491. doi:10.1111/j.1471-6402.1998.tb00170.x

Yu, V. (2010). Shelter and transitional housing for transgender youth. *Journal of Gay and Lesbian Mental Health, 14*(4), 340–345. doi:10.1080/19359705.2010.504476

Zamora-Hernandez, C. E., & Patterson, D. G. (1996). Homosexually active Latino men: Issues for social work practice. *Journal of Gay and Lesbian Social Services, 5*(2/3), 69–91. doi:10.1300/J041v05n02_04

Part II

Applications in the Schools and Community

7   Law, Policy, and Ethics
What School Professionals Need to Know

Asaf Orr and Karen Komosa-Hawkins

The old adages of "boys will be boys" and "kids are cruel" are no longer acceptable responses to complaints of harassment, bullying, or discrimination of lesbian, gay, bisexual, transgender, and questioning (LGBTQ) youth in schools. Nor can school districts or administrators use the prejudices of school employees or the surrounding community to block an LGBTQ student group from forming or to prevent an LGBTQ student from being "out" at school. Yet, those phrases and actions, and others like them, occur daily in schools across the country. They appear in court case after court case and conclude with the school district paying hundreds of thousands of dollars or more in damages and attorneys' fees. However, the ripple effect caused by a hostile school environment extends far beyond legal liability. Condoning or failing to respond to the effects of a hostile school environment also may violate the ethical standards governing school professionals.

According to the National Education Association (NEA, 2002–2010, p. 1), educators believe in the "worth and dignity of each human being" and in "mak[ing] reasonable effort[s] to protect students from conditions harmful to learning, health," or "safety," which includes protecting the privacy of students and guaranteeing "equal educational opportunity for all." Moreover, school professionals are obligated to provide a certain standard of care (American School Counselor Association [ASCA], 2006, 2007, 2009, 2011; Graybill, Varjas, Meyers, & Watson, 2009; National Association of School Psychologists [NASP], 2006; Whitman, Horn, & Boyd, 2007). In fact, in *Bruff v. North Mississippi Health Services* (2001; as cited in Hermann & Herlihy, 2006), a court upheld an employer's decision to terminate a counselor for refusing to comply with those standards due to religious beliefs regarding lesbian, gay, bisexual, and transgender (LGBT) people. Beyond losing her job, if the client had filed a complaint with the licensing board or a lawsuit, that counselor could have lost her license or faced liability for the damage she caused by not meeting the required standard of care. Likewise, educators are expected to adhere to certain standards of professional conduct (e.g., nondiscriminatory and inclusive teaching practices). Thus, if professionals adhere to their professional organizations' standards of professional conduct, it is likely that they will have also met their legal obligations.

Compliance with the myriad laws and regulations relating to schools and education has always been an integral part of education. Not surprisingly, legal liability and professional ethics are often the driving force behind the creation of anti-discrimination and bullying policies, among many other policies adopted by school boards across the country in an attempt to foster a safe educational environment. However, judges and juries figured out long ago that creating those policies is not enough to ensure that the school environment will be safe, welcoming, and affirming for LGBTQ youth. Although this chapter cannot offer specific legal advice, it will create a roadmap that will assist school administrators and personnel in developing the types of policies and practices that foster safe school environments, which in turn, will limit exposure to legal liability and other negative consequences. More specifically, this chapter will cover anti-discrimination laws in the context of harassment and bullying, discipline, and transgender youth; the First Amendment rights of students, teachers, and schools; the Equal Access Act and formation of Gay-Straight Alliances (GSAs); the right to privacy and "outing" of LGBTQ students; laws affecting private schools; and the rights of LGBT parents and their children.

Even with a roadmap of legal and ethical obligations, that process can be difficult. The changes required will force everyone in the district, from the superintendent to the maintenance staff, to confront their own prejudices as well as those of the students and surrounding community. Throughout the process, it is important to keep in mind that the end result will be a better school environment for all students and an education that will better prepare them for functioning in a diverse world. Having this roadmap also will assist in addressing any uncooperative personnel or resistant parents who do not follow the school district's lead.

An Overview of Federal and State Anti-Discrimination Protections for LGBTQ Youth

Though state laws differ on whether they specify sexual orientation and gender identity as protected categories,[1] school districts also must comply with federal laws that ensure all students have safe and equitable access to education. Those federal laws fill voids left by state and local regulations. The specific nature of the discriminatory conduct will determine which federal and state laws may have been violated by a school district's actions or a school personnel's conduct. In addition to discrimination claims on the basis of sexual orientation and gender identity, claims by LGBTQ youth can include violations of the United States (U.S.) Constitution, Title IX, state anti-discrimination protections on the basis of disability, and state constitutions. Typically, those claims revolve around one or more of the following themes: (a) harassment and bullying; (b) discipline; and (c) accommodations for transgender youth. The ways federal and state laws protect LGBTQ youth in those circumstances are discussed below.

Harassment and Bullying

Harassment and bullying by students, teachers, and administrators pervade the daily lives of many LGBTQ youth. Failing to effectively address those incidents of harassment and bullying can have detrimental effects on the targeted student's ability to learn, interfere with the learning of other students, and expose the school and district to significant legal liability. Chapter 9 of this volume explicitly addresses the effects of bullying and harassment on LGBTQ students and families as well as recommended prevention and intervention strategies. The specific claims often used in these cases include violations of the Equal Protection and Due Process Clauses of the United States Constitution, Title IX, state constitutional provisions, and state anti-discrimination laws.

As indicated by its name, the Equal Protection Clause (1868) prohibits a school district or individual employees of a school or district from treating students differently based on personal characteristics, such as race, sex, and disability. School districts and school personnel can violate the Equal Protection Clause in a variety of ways when dealing with harassment and bullying of LGBTQ youth in their schools. For example, a school could violate a student's right to equal protection by failing to respond, investigate, or adequately address incidents of harassment reported by an LGBTQ student while consistently doing so for non-LGBTQ students. Those failures can be seen as discrimination on the basis of sexual orientation, but also on the basis of gender, particularly if there is evidence that the student was treated differently because he or she did not conform to gender stereotypes.

One example of this is the case of Jaime Nabozny, a gay student in Wisconsin, who was mercilessly harassed by students and administrators for several years. In 1996, a federal appeals court ruled that school officials were at least deliberately indifferent to Jaime's pleas for assistance, and in some instances, intentionally discriminated against him. Those actions equated to a denial of equal protection on the basis of gender and sexual orientation. The court based that decision on the following: evidence that reports of assaults on female students were handled differently than Jaime's reports of similar incidents; the repeated and persistent harassment experienced by Jaime despite the school district claiming strong enforcement of its anti-harassment policies; and statements made by school personnel that "Nabozny should expect to be harassed because he is gay" (*Nabozny v. Podlesny*, 1996, p. 457). At trial, the jury found that the school district violated federal law by discriminating against Jaime (Lambda Legal, 1995). Before the jury could determine the amount of damages to award Jaime, the school district settled the case for nearly a million dollars.

Unlike the Equal Protection Clause, the Due Process Clause of the Fourteenth Amendment of the United States Constitution (1868) prevents a school district or school employee from interfering with a person's life, liberty, or property. That protection is triggered by the fact that state laws across the country grant children of certain ages the right to an education and require school attendance (*Goss v. Lopez*, 1975). Moreover, the courts have recognized that people have an interest in being protected from harm in school (*Ingraham v. Wright*, 1977). Nonetheless, public schools do not exercise a sufficient level of control over their students to create a constitutional duty to protect. However, a school district or school employee may violate the Due Process Clause by taking actions to encourage or foster an environment where a student's due process rights are violated, even though the Constitution does not impose a general duty to protect (*Vernonia v. Acton*, 1995; *DeShaney v. Winnebago County*, 1989). For example, in *O.H. v. Oakland Unified School District* (2000), school personnel responded to O.H.'s complaints of harassment, discrimination, intimidation, and physical abuse, including three incidents of rape, by telling him to "be a man" and "to get over it" (p. 3). O.H. alleged that school personnel discriminated against him on the basis of gender and perceived sexual orientation. The court found that those responses constituted sufficient evidence that the defendants "affirmatively encouraged" the violence and discrimination against O.H. (p. 35). This case ultimately settled out of court for an undisclosed amount of money.

As noted earlier, the United States Constitution is not the only source of federal protections for LGBTQ youth. Title IX (1972) mandates that "no person in the United States shall, on the basis of sex, be excluded from participating in, be denied the benefits of, or be subjected to discrimination under any education program or activity receiving Federal financial assistance" (20 U.S.C. § 1681(a)). A student who brings a claim under Title IX on the basis of peer-to-peer harassment must show the following: (a) a school employee with the authority to address the harassment actually knew of the harassment; (b) that school employee's response was clearly unreasonable under the circumstances; and (c) harassment that is "so severe, pervasive, and objectively offensive, and that so undermines and detracts from the victims' educational experience, that the victim-students are effectively denied equal access to an institution's resources and opportunities" (*Davis v. Monroe County*, 1999, p. 651). However, the standard is slightly different if the harasser is a school employee. In those cases, the student must show the first two elements listed above, but not the third (*Gebser v. Lago Vista*, 1998). Additionally, unlike violations of a student's constitutional rights, the majority of courts do not permit students to sue individuals for violations of Title IX (*Norris v. Norwalk*, 2000).

The case of Dylan Theno from Tonganoxie, Kansas provides insight into what schools are required to do in order to avoid liability under Title IX. Dylan was perceived to be different than his male peers; he did not play "manly" sports like football and basketball, but wore earrings and styled his hair in atypical ways compared to his male peers (*Theno v. Tonganoxie Unified*, 2005). Though Dylan identified as straight, his peers responded to his gender expression by attacking him with a daily barrage of insults such as "fag," "flamer," and "queer" (*Theno v. Tonganoxie Unified*, 2005, p. 1305) and sexually explicit remarks. At trial, the school district demonstrated that it responded to some of the complaints made by Dylan and his father, but that evidence was outweighed by the many incidents in which school officials chose to do nothing or very little to ensure that the harassment would not continue. The jury awarded Dylan damages in the amount of $250,000, an award that was upheld by the trial court.

Not adequately addressing harassment and bullying of an LGBTQ student also may open the school district to legal liability under state laws. States differ in what an LGTBQ student would have to prove in order to demonstrate that the school district or its personnel violated state law. For example, California courts use the same standard used in the Title IX cases previously discussed (*Donovan v. Poway Unified*, 2008), while New Jersey courts attach liability where the school district "knew or should have known of the harassment but failed to take actions reasonably calculated to end the mistreatment and offensive conduct" (*L.W. v. Toms River*, 2007, p. 540). Unlike the California standard, the New Jersey standard requires action even if the school did not actually know of the harassment but should have known of its occurrence. Besides differing on what a student must prove at trial, state laws can differ in many other respects. For example, some states may choose to limit a school district's liability by prohibiting lawsuits against individuals (*Donovan v. Poway Unified*, 2008) or capping punitive damage awards, while other states may require a student to file a complaint with a state agency before filing a lawsuit in court (*Washington v. Pierce*, 2005). Similarly, other areas of state law may affect the obligations of school personnel in the context of bullying and harassment. Beginning in July 2012, California law compels school personnel who witness bias-related dis-crimination, harassment, or bullying in schools to take immediate action to intervene

(Cal. Ed. Code § 234.1(b) (1)). Irrespective of state-to-state differences, LGBTQ youth have successfully sued school districts under state anti-discrimination statutes.

In addition to being sued by a student, school district personnel also must be aware of enforcement actions being brought by the federal and state agencies, such as the United States Department of Justice (DOJ), the United States Department of Education (DOE), and the State Education Agency (i.e., state board of education). Enforcement actions can take a variety of forms, such as a formal investigation into an administrative complaint, and can lead to an equally wide range of outcomes, from fines and on-going compliance monitoring to withdrawal of funding and litigation (N.J. Stat. Ann. § 10:5-14.1a; 20 U.S.C. § 1682).

The DOJ's and DOE's investigation of the Tehachapi Unified School District in central California is a recent example of an enforcement action. Those agencies began investigating the Tehachapi Unified School District shortly after the highly publicized death of Seth Walsh, a thirteen year old student who was viciously harassed for years because of his sexual orientation and gender nonconforming behaviors (DOJ & DOE to R. L. Swanson, June 30, 2011). The investigation resulted in a finding that school officials violated Title IX because they were well aware of the harassment Seth experienced, but instead of intervening, left Seth to fend for himself. To avoid long, costly, and embarrassing litigation, Tehachapi entered into a resolution agreement with the DOJ and DOE that requires the school district to implement significant policy changes, undertake extensive training, and administer regular school climate surveys, among many other requirements (Resolution Agreement, June 30, 2011). Furthermore, those agencies will be monitoring Tehachapi's compliance with the agreement until July 2016, and will reopen the investigation in the event that Tehachapi does not comply.

Although the aforementioned examples are of school districts and personnel minimally responding to or participating in the bullying and harassment of LGBTQ youth, school districts and personnel also may violate the law by responding to bullying and harassment in a manner that treats LGBTQ students as the problem. Moving an LGBTQ student who reports harassment and bullying to an alternative education program, independent study curriculum, adult school, or similar program also can violate a school district's duty to not discriminate against LGBTQ students. That includes moving an LGBTQ student in the name of "protecting" that student from harassment and bullying. For example, Derek Henkle was moved from school to school on the condition that he would not be "out" at school (*Henkle v. Gregory*, 2001). Eventually, Derek was placed in an adult education program at the local community college, making him ineligible for a high school diploma. Derek sued his school district on the basis that the school district's conduct constituted discrimination and violated his constitutional rights. After a failed attempt to dismiss Derek's lawsuit, the school district and personnel settled the case for $451,000 (Lambda Legal, 2002).

Moreover, that rule may still apply where an LGBTQ student requested or agreed to such a placement. Despite being academically successful and heavily involved in extra-curricular activities, George Loomis' parents agreed to move him into an independent study program because of the intolerable harassment he experienced at school (*Gay-Straight Alliance Network v. Visalia Unified*, 2001). Once in that program, Loomis could not participate in extracurricular activities and was no longer eligible for admission into the University of California. Loomis presented evidence that the school district routinely ignored the eligibility criteria for the alternative education programs, pushing LGBTQ youth into those programs instead of addressing the harassment and bullying. The school district settled the matter, agreeing to implement sweeping policy changes, train staff and students, track harassment complaints, and pay damages in the amount of $130,000 (National Center for Lesbian Rights [NCLR] & Gay, Lesbian, and Straight Education Network [GLSEN], n. d.).

In a similar vein, providing or requiring an LGBTQ student to participate in services such as counseling designed to discourage LGBTQ students from being themselves and shaming them for identifying as LGBTQ would likely violate anti-discrimination protections afforded LGBTQ students (American Civil Liberties Union [ACLU], 2009). That conduct also would violate the ethical obligations of school personnel. Current best practices or standards of care dictate that ethical, culturally competent, and effective practitioners may associate LGBTQ status with risk, but never regard such an identity as deviant or disordered (American Psychological Association [APA], 2008; World Professional Association for Transgender Health [WPATH], 2011). Nor is there any support for reparative or conversion therapies (APA, 2008; Whitman, Glosoff, Kocet, & Tarvydas, 2006; WPATH, 2011). Rather, culturally competent professionals recognize that any signs of maladjustment for LGBTQ individuals are more often due to environmental factors (e.g., experiences of injustice and maltreatment) than intrapersonal factors. Ethical professionals promote awareness and acceptance wherein the dignity and rights of LGBTQ individuals are affirmed and protected and the needs of all individuals are met through appropriate preventative and responsive services.

Discipline

Responding to reports of harassment and bullying very often involves discipline. Even outside of the context of bullying, sexual minority students are more likely to be punished and receive harsher punishments for engaging in conduct similar to that of their heterosexual peers (Himmelstein & Brückner, 2010).[2] Consequently, discipline is another area where school districts and personnel often discriminate against LGBTQ youth. Like harassment and bullying, discrimination can take many different forms, such as inconsistently applying zero-tolerance disciplinary policies, doling out harsher punishments to LGBTQ youth for conduct that does not typically warrant that level of punishment, not accounting for mitigating factors such as a student acting in self-defense, and responding to conduct involving LGBTQ students differently than non-LGBTQ students.

Fed up with the constant harassment for refusing to conform to gender stereotypes of boys his age and with the school's failure to take his complaints seriously, Dylan Theno began fighting back against his harassers (*Theno v. Tonganoxie Unified*, 2005). Consistent with the school's indifference to Dylan's complaints, school officials either punished Dylan more severely than his harasser, or would not account for the harasser's role in instigating the fight when meting out punishment, instead preferring to "let that sleeping dog lie" (*Theno v. Tonganoxie Unified*, 2005, p. 1311). Jaime Nabozny experienced similar circumstances more than 10 years before Dylan. As previously noted in Jaime's case, school administrators did not bother to discipline his harassers at all (*Nabozny v. Podlesny*, 1996). Each of the claims that an LGBTQ student can raise in the context of harassment and bullying also could be raised in the context of discipline. Moreover, those claims would be in addition to any claims an LGBTQ student may have based on the school's response to the harassment and bullying faced by that student.

Transgender Youth

Transgender youth have specific and unique needs that schools and districts must address when developing policies in order to create a safe and supportive school environment. Those needs are: (a) use of chosen name and pronouns by *all* school and district personnel in all contexts, including substitute teachers; (b) protocols to ensure that the student's transgender identity remains private and confidential, the disclosure of which is controlled by the student and/or the student's family; (c) being allowed to dress in a manner consistent with the student's affirmed gender; and (d) restroom and locker room access that conforms with the student's gender identity. Besides addressing those basic needs, it is important for schools to ensure that their personnel treat transgender students according to the student's gender identity in all aspects, including participation in competitive sports. Failing to accommodate those needs places the transgender student in an unwelcoming and potentially unsafe educational environment and exposes the school district and personnel to legal liability.

Current state and federal laws and ethical standards support a transgender student's right to have a school district respect and use the student's chosen name and pronoun. In the states that have statutes specifically prohibiting discrimination on the basis of gender identity, a court would be hard pressed to interpret that statute in a manner that did not require schools to meet this basic need. That aside, by intentionally not referring to a transgender student by the student's chosen name and pronouns, the school district and its personnel will be creating a hostile school environment for that student, possibly exposing the school to legal liability under state anti-discrimination statutes prohibiting sex and/or disability discrimination, Title IX, and the Due Process and Equal Protection Clauses of the United States Constitution. Moreover, the conduct of the school personnel would reveal the student's transgender status to the student's peers, making that student a likely target for harassment, creating yet another possible avenue of legal liability if the school district or personnel do not address that harassment appropriately.

Similarly, regardless of whether a school must change the school's records to conform to the student's chosen name and gender identity, the school should take precautionary measures to ensure that the student's transgender status remains private and confidential. By not changing the student's records, a school is running the risk that a transgender student will be "outed" in a number of ways, such as by a substitute teacher who does not know the student or by a peer who happens to see the attendance sheet. The consequences of not changing a transgender student's school records or implementing protocols to safeguard that student's identity will lead to many, if not all, of the same outcomes previously detailed. As a result, the school district may be exposing itself to legal liability.

In addition to using a transgender student's affirmed name and pronouns, that student must be permitted to dress in a manner consistent with the student's gender identity. Thus, to the extent that a school has a dress code policy, that policy should be applied equally to transgender and nontransgender students, and transgender students should be asked to comply with the rules applicable to their affirmed gender. For example, in *Doe v. Yunits* (2000), the school district required Pat Doe, a transgender student, to report to the assistant principal's office to have her attire approved before she was permitted to attend school each day. If the assistant principal did not approve what she was wearing, Pat Doe was sent home to change. Notably, her attire was being judged against the rules applied to boys; thus, she was sent home for wearing any clothing and accessories typically worn by girls. As a result of that demeaning treatment, Pat Doe often would not return to school after being sent home. The following school year, the school district would not even allow her to enroll unless she agreed not to wear girls' clothing.

Pat Doe sued her school claiming that the school's conduct discriminated against her on the basis of a disability and constructively expelled her from the school, among other claims (*Doe v. Yunits*, 2000). On the disability claim, the court found that Gender Identity Disorder (GID),[3] a diagnosis commonly given to transgender people upon seeking medical or mental health services, is covered under the state anti-discrimination law's protection for people with disabilities, and therefore, denied the school district's attempt to dismiss that claim (*Doe v. Yunits*, 2001). Similarly, the court denied the school district's motion to dismiss the constructive expulsion claim. In that claim, Doe alleged that the school district's discriminatory application of its dress code made the school so unwelcoming and psychologically harmful that, for all intents and purposes, she had been expelled. The court agreed and ruled that meeting the school's requirements would cause her significant psychological harm, such that a reasonable person would have felt compelled to not attend school (*Doe v. Yunits*, 2001).

Access to restrooms and locker rooms in a manner consistent with a transgender student's gender identity is another critical component to ensuring that a school is creating a safe and affirming environment. A transgender student should be permitted to use the restroom and locker room that correspond with that student's gender identity, without limitation. That said, in the locker room context, a school may need to make some adjustments or accommodations if the student needs additional privacy (e.g., permission to change in the teacher's or nurse's office or creation of a different changing schedule). If there are circumstances that make using a restroom or locker room dangerous for a transgender student, the school should provide alternatives that are still gender affirming (e.g., access to a unisex restroom); however, a transgender student cannot be required to use those alternatives.

Both the law and school district policies are moving in the direction of supporting the needs of transgender students to have access to restrooms and locker rooms that affirm their gender identities. In June 2009, the Maine Human Rights Commission (MHRC) issued a groundbreaking investigation report finding that a school district discriminated against a transgender student by denying her access to the girls' restroom after a nontransgender male student followed her into the girls' restroom in an attempt to make a statement about her use of the girls' restroom (*Minor Student 1 v. School Union 87*, 2009). As of this printing, the case is still in litigation. Notably, the male student that caused the initial uproar also filed a discrimination complaint with the MHRC alleging that the school discriminated against him by punishing him in response to his entering the girls' restroom (*Minor Student 2 v. Asa Adams School*, 2009). The MHRC found that the school district did not discriminate against him because his gender identity is male and, as such, the school appropriately permitted him access to the boys' restrooms at the school, not the girls' restroom. In reaching that conclusion, the MHRC explicitly rejected the student's attempts to claim that he and the transgender student were similarly situated (i.e., that both of them are males entering a girls' restroom).

More recently, school districts are addressing the needs of transgender youth and school policies are incorporating language regarding appropriate restroom and locker room access. For example, the Los Angeles Unified School District (LAUSD), one of the largest school districts in the country, revised its policy on transgender youth to permit transgender students access to restrooms and locker rooms based on their gender identity. LAUSD's prior policy on transgender students had given principals discretion regarding access to sex-separated facilities. At the same time, the Gay, Lesbian, and Straight Education Network (GLSEN) and the National Center for Transgender Equality (NCTE) released a new model policy for addressing the needs of transgender and gender nonconforming youth with similar language regarding restroom and locker room access (GLSEN & NCTE, 2011).

Schools that are interested in creating a safe and welcoming environment for transgender youth also must ensure that transgender students are permitted to play on a sports team in a manner that is consistent with the student's gender identity. Both the Washington Interscholastic Activities Association (WIAA) and the National Collegiate Athletic Association (NCAA) have been leaders in this area. Since 2008, WIAA has successfully permitted transgender student-athletes to compete in sex-separated sports in a manner consistent with their gender identity (Griffin & Carroll, 2010). The policy requires that a transgender student's eligibility must remain confidential and sealed, unless the student's family requests otherwise, and includes an appeal procedure with review by a panel comprised of school professionals and professionals who work with transgender youth (WIAA, 2011).

The policy adopted by NCAA in August 2011 provides additional guidance regarding best practices for including transgender student-athletes. In particular, that policy requires coaches, teammates, and the school community to refer to transgender students by their chosen name and pronouns in all settings (Griffin & Carroll, 2011). Similarly, the policy stipulates that transgender student-athletes should be permitted to dress in a manner that is consistent with their gender identity, including uniforms. As for access to the locker room, restrooms, and shower facilities, the policy states that transgender student-athletes should use the facility consistent with their gender identity, and that each facility should have a private area for any student who would like to use that private area, but a transgender student-athlete cannot be required to use that area (Griffin & Carroll, 2011). When a team travels to another school to compete, it is the obligation of the coach and school personnel to obtain any accommodation a transgender student-athlete may require, but must do so in consultation with the student and in a manner that protects the student-athlete's right to privacy (Griffin & Carroll, 2011).

Finally, as hinted throughout this subsection, confidentiality is of the utmost importance. Beyond the effect on the school environment, "outing" a transgender student also may violate that student's right to privacy under federal and state law, a claim that will be discussed more in-depth in a subsequent section of this chapter.

Putting Anti-Discrimination Protections into Action

Although preventing or avoiding discrimination is not simple, the previously cited cases highlight clear steps schools can take to proactively address discrimination against

LGBTQ students. First and foremost, the school's policy and culture must specifically enumerate what constitutes prohibited conduct and encourage everyone to report incidents of harassment, bullying, and other forms of discrimination. Likewise, those reports must be taken seriously and account for the particular circumstances surrounding the complaint (e.g., the seriousness of the allegations, prior complaints, prior disciplinary actions). On the other end, there needs to be a quality control measure to ensure that school personnel are not exercising discretion to the disadvantage of LGBTQ youth, whether it is in areas such as discipline or enrollment in independent study programs.

In respect of the particular needs of transgender youth, schools should follow two basic rules: (1) treat transgender students as members of their affirmed gender in all aspects of school life; and (2) provide transgender students with the modifications they may need to feel safe and affirmed. Taking the student's lead will help build a trusting relationship between the student and the school as well as ensure that the school is not, consciously or unconsciously, relying on unfounded fears and prejudices in making decisions. Moreover, it is important to keep in mind that the logistics of meeting the needs of transgender youth are not difficult. Large and small school districts throughout the country are making the minor changes needed to make a big difference in the school experiences of transgender students; it just requires effort, thought, and a desire to help.

The First Amendment Inside the Schoolhouse Gates

At its core, the First Amendment seeks to create an "uninhibited marketplace of ideas" (*Virginia v. Hicks*, 2003, p. 119). Recognizing that that ideal may conflict with other legitimate governmental interests, courts permit the government to impose certain types of regulations on speech. In the context of schools, courts have tweaked the legal standards to account for the unique circumstances of the school environment and the purposes of public education. Nonetheless, "the vigilant protection of constitutional freedoms is nowhere more vital than in the community of American schools. The classroom is particularly the 'marketplace of ideas'" (*Keyishian v. Board of Regents*, 1967, p. 603). Thus, respecting the bounds of the First Amendment and maintaining a safe and affirming school environment for LGBTQ youth requires a delicate, but achievable, balance.

The Student Soapbox

One of the most difficult aspects of creating a safe, welcoming, and affirming environment for LGBTQ youth is balancing the right of LGBTQ youth to attend school in an environment in which they will be able to learn with the First Amendment rights of their peers. The complexity of this balancing act depends on the content and context of student expression, but the courts have developed a relatively clear and consistent approach to striking that balance. As a general rule, courts see the school environment as a training ground for students to express themselves and learn the boundaries of civility before entering the adult world where their First Amendment rights will appear limitless in comparison. Consequently, courts tend to be suspicious of attempts to limit student expression when it does not fall squarely within a specified exception, and courts interpret those few exceptions very narrowly.

There are four major cases that establish the legal framework for a school's authority to limit student speech. The first, and most cited, is *Tinker v. Des Moines Independent Community School District* (1969). This case involved a group of students who were wrongfully suspended for peacefully expressing their objection to the Vietnam War while at school. The United States Supreme Court established that a school is permitted to restrict student speech where

> conduct by the student, in class or out of it, which for any reason—whether it stems from time, place, or type of behavior—materially disrupts class work or involves substantial disorder or invasion of the rights of others is, of course, not immunized by the constitutional guarantee of freedom of speech.
> (*Tinker v. Des Moines Independent Community School District*, 1969, p. 513)

Moreover, to justify limiting student speech a school "must be able to show that its action was caused by something more than a mere desire to avoid the discomfort and unpleasantness that always accompany an unpopular viewpoint" (*Tinker v. Des Moines Independent Community School District*, 1969, p. 509). Otherwise known as the "substantial disruption" test, courts have been uniformly hesitant to permit schools to restrict the First Amendment rights of students absent significant evidence of actual or anticipated disruption. The following are some of the reasons courts have found insufficient to warrant restricting student speech: a large percentage of the student body boycotting school for a day (*Boyd County Gay Straight Alliance v. Board of Education of Boyd County*, 2003) and a higher incidence of physical fights precipitated by issues unrelated to the student's speech (*Chambers v. Babbitt*, 2001).

Nearly twenty years after *Tinker*, the Court gave school administrators permission to regulate vulgar and offensive speech. In *Bethel School District No. 403 v. Fraser* (1986), a student gave a speech at a school assembly that was replete with sexual innuendoes. In response, the school suspended the student for three days and removed his name from the list of potential student speakers for graduation. Finding in favor of the school, the Court grounded its ruling on the notion that "the process of educating our youth for citizenship in public schools is not confined to books, the curriculum, and the civics class; schools must teach by example the shared values of a civilized social order" (*Bethel School District No. 403 v. Fraser*, 1986, p. 683). Similarly, in *Hazelwood v. Kuhlmeier* (1988), the Court found that a school was permitted to censor the contents of a school newspaper as the newspaper bore the "imprimatur of the school" (p. 271) and could be considered "school-sponsored" speech (p. 271). In those instances, schools are permitted to restrict speech where the restrictions "are reasonably related to legitimate pedagogical concerns" (p. 273). Most recently, the Court upheld a school's authority to discipline student speech that promotes illegal drugs and illegal drug use (*Morse v. Frederick*, 2007).

In applying those standards to a student's right to be "out" at school, courts have uniformly found that schools have no legitimate justification for prohibiting students from identifying themselves as LGBTQ. For example, in *Henkle* (2001), the harassment case cited in the previous section, the court found that the rule created in *Tinker* was broad enough to encompass a student's right to express his or her sexual orientation, which Henkle had done through the buttons on his backpack and participating in a televised discussion about being gay in high school that aired on a local television station. Likewise, in *Nguon v. Wolf* (2007), a court reaffirmed the right of LGBTQ students to engage in expressive conduct with one another (e.g., hugging and kissing) provided such conduct stayed within the bounds of school rules regarding public displays of affection.

Courts also have had several opportunities to consider how the "substantial disruption" test applies where the student speech involves religious attitudes towards homosexuality. The first case involved a student who was prohibited from wearing a t-shirt with the slogan "Straight Pride" on the front and a picture of a man and woman holding hands on the back (*Chambers v. Babbitt*, 2001). Despite evidence of complaints about the t-shirt and evidence of fourteen prior fights that school year, which were not related to tensions surrounding LGBTQ issues, the court found in favor of the student. In so doing, the court empathized with LGBTQ youth with regard to their experiences in schools and commended the school's effort to create a positive learning environment for all of its students. Nevertheless, according to the court, the balance struck by the school infringed too much on the right of students with religious objections to homosexuality to express their views in a civil and respectful manner.

Standing in stark contrast to *Chambers*, is *Harper v. Poway Unified School District* (2006), which began when a student was asked to remove a t-shirt stating "Be Ashamed, Our School Embraced What God Has Condemned" and "Homosexuality is a Sin, Romans 1:27" (p. 1171). Relying on a school's authority to restrict student speech where it invades the rights of others, a federal appellate court held that "those who administer our public educational institutions need not tolerate verbal assaults that may destroy the self-esteem of our most vulnerable teenagers and interfere with their educational development" (*Harper v. Poway Unified School District*, 2006, p. 1179). In reaching that conclusion, the court cited not only the school's obligation to maintain a safe and affirming environment for LGBTQ youth and students of other protected groups, but also the overwhelming evidence documenting the detrimental educational effects that a hostile school environment has on LGBTQ youth.[4]

With *Chambers* and *Harper* marking the ends of the spectrum, *Nuxoll v. Indian Prairie School District* (2008) presents an example that is somewhere in between.[5] In this case, two students wore t-shirts with the phrase "Be Happy, Not Gay." The school sought to compromise on the language of the t-shirt stating that the school would not permit slogans that "negatively refer to being gay" (*Zamecnik v. Indian Prairie School District*, 2007, p. 18). Instead of agreeing to a compromise, the students filed a lawsuit in federal court. Although the trial court rejected the students' arguments, the appellate court reversed and found in favor of the students. The court characterized the students' t-shirts as "tepidly negative" (*Nuxoll v. Indian Prairie School District*, 2008, p. 676) and not rising to the level of a substantial disruption. Nevertheless, the court did note that if the school could demonstrate that the psychological effects of those t-shirts on students rose to the level of a substantial disruption, it may be entitled to a judgment in its favor at a later point in the litigation.

As one scholar points out, each of those cases appear to turn on whether the student's expression was a relatively bland statement of the student's belief that the Bible does not approve of homosexuality versus student expression that denigrates or shames LGBTQ youth using harsh language (Biegel, 2010). Consequently, Biegel (2010) suggests that "a simple 'Do unto others as you would have them do unto you' mindset can go a long way'" (pp. 104–105). That approach will not only help the school better express its position in a manner that may engender empathy among students, but also to a court, if needed.

Cyberbullying is another area in which schools must strike this delicate balance. Courts consistently apply *Tinker* to analyze whether the school had the authority to limit the student's speech, but differ on how to define the geographical reach of a school's authority to limit off-campus speech. For example, in *J.C. v. Beverly Hills Unified School District* (2010), a student created a disparaging video of another student while off-campus, posted the video on YouTube, and encouraged friends to view the video later that evening. The following day, the student targeted by the video complained to the school administration who then viewed the at-issue video on school computers and ultimately suspended J.C. According to the court, the school administrators were the only people known to have viewed the video at school. Despite that seemingly negligible connection to the school, the court applied the *Tinker* standard to analyze whether the school's decision to discipline J.C. for creating the video violated J.C.'s First Amendment rights. The court ultimately concluded that the incident did not result in a substantial disruption of school activities and therefore, the school improperly disciplined J.C. for speech that was protected by the First Amendment.

By contrast, several other courts considering similar cases imposed an additional requirement on the traditional *Tinker* standard. In those cases, the courts were reticent to permit a school to discipline a student for off-campus speech absent evidence that it was reasonably foreseeable that the speech would reach campus or that the student intended his or her speech to do so. However, the threshold for meeting that requirement appears to be relatively low. Courts have found that standard was met in the following cases: (a) a student's blog entry erroneously criticized the school for canceling an event and encouraged students and parents to call and complain (*Doninger v. Neihoff*, 2008); (b) a student who distributed an underground newspaper that encouraged students to hack the school's computers and provided instructions for readers to follow (*Boucher v. School Board*, 1998); and (c) a student who created a website with violent and derogatory comments about school officials, which he accessed on campus, and told friends about the website (*J.S. v. Bethlehem Area School District*, 2002). Thus, only the inadvertently disclosed speech or speech that meticulously disavowed a connection to the school will find safe harbor from the court's reach (*Thomas v. Board of Education*, 1979). Given the fluid nature of the Internet and the near ubiquitous access students have to the Internet, it is unclear how long those boundaries will last, especially with the proliferation of cyberbullying in recent years.

Dress to Express

With all of the tradition and "pomp and circumstance" surrounding the school prom, it is not surprising that high school students see the prom as a very important event. Yet, in the name of "tradition" several schools have sought to ban same-sex dates and/or regulate gender expression by requiring girls to wear dresses and boys to wear tuxedos. Those same "traditions" are carried over into sex-specific dress codes for senior yearbook pictures. Courts have consistently found those restrictions to violate a student's First Amendment right to freedom of expression.

After watching a fellow gay student unsuccessfully lobby to bring a same-sex date to prom the previous year, Aaron Fricke decided to follow in his friend's footsteps and asked permission to bring a same-sex date to the senior prom (*Fricke v. Lynch*, 1980). When the school refused, Fricke filed a lawsuit and sought a court order requiring the school district to allow him to bring a same-sex date to prom. In response, the principal asserted that the school's prom policy was based on concern about possible disruption and violence at prom in reaction to participation of a same-sex couple. Although the court did not doubt the sincerity of the principal's concern, the court found in Fricke's favor, stating that:

> some people might say that Aaron Fricke's conduct would infringe the rights of the other students, and is thus unprotected by *Tinker*. This view is misguided, however. Aaron's conduct is quiet and peaceful; it demands no response from others and in a crowd of some five hundred people can be easily ignored. Any disturbance that might interfere with the rights of others would be caused by those students who resort to violence, not by Aaron and his companion, who do not want a fight.
>
> (*Fricke v. Lynch*, 1980, p. 388)

The court went on to note that because "meaningful security measures are possible" (*Fricke v. Lynch*, 1980, p. 388) to prevent violence erupting at prom, "the First Amendment requires that such steps be taken to protect rather than to stifle free expression" of LGBT students (p. 388).

Despite the court's unequivocal decision in *Fricke*, that case did not settle the issue of same-sex dates and prom. In 2010, Itawamba Agricultural High School denied Constance McMillen's request to bring her girlfriend to the prom as her date and to wear a tuxedo (*McMillen v. Itawamba County School District*, 2010). Although the couple could have chosen to attend as individuals, the school refused to let them "slow dance" together as that would "push people's buttons" (*McMillen v. Itawamba County School District*, 2010, p. 701). Moreover, school officials informed McMillen that she and her girlfriend would be kicked out if their presence at prom made anyone uncomfortable. When McMillen filed a lawsuit against her school, the school decided to cancel prom.

Wanting to attend her prom, McMillen sought a preliminary injunction to require the school to hold the prom as planned. The court found that the school violated Constance's First Amendment rights by denying her requests, but ultimately decided not to issue the injunction because the parents had organized a prom, and the school assured the court that all of the school's students were welcome to attend. The prom planned by the parents turned out to be a cruel joke. McMillen and her girlfriend showed up to what they thought was their prom to find seven people there. Meanwhile, their classmates attended the "real" prom at another location approximately thirty miles away. McMillen hauled the school into court a second time after which the school agreed to settle the case, which included monetary damages, attorneys' fees, and policy changes.

Likewise, schools have been unable to protect sex-specific dress codes for senior yearbook photos (e.g., drape for girls and tuxedo for boys) from claims that those policies violate a student's constitutional rights. For example, Ceara Sturgis consistently dressed in clothing traditionally associated with boys. Thus, when it came time to take her senior yearbook photo, Ceara opted to wear the tuxedo as opposed to the drape, which went against school policy. In response, the school refused to print her photo in the senior portrait section of the yearbook. After a federal judge refused to dismiss Ceara's claims, the school district settled the matter and agreed to implement a gender-neutral policy that required all students to wear a cap and gown (ACLU, 2011).

Teacher Talk

From placing a "Safe Haven" sticker on their classroom door and being "out" in the school community to incorporating LGBTQ-inclusive materials into their teaching, teachers can have a profound effect on students and the school environment. Unfortunately, the ever-diminishing First Amendment rights of teachers discourage them from taking proactive steps to make the school environment a safe and welcoming place for LGBTQ students. In *Garcetti v. Ceballos* (2006), the United States Supreme Court held that when a public employee's speech is related to his or her "official duties" (p. 421) it is not protected by the First Amendment, meaning a public entity is permitted to discipline, retaliate, and terminate an employee for that speech.

Although the Court specifically noted that it was not addressing the extent to which that rule would apply in the education context, the lower courts have not hesitated to uphold a school's authority to discipline or terminate teachers based on their in-class speech. For example, in *Mayer v. County Community School Corporation* (2007), a court upheld a school's decision not to rehire a teacher for responding to a student's question regarding whether she ever participated in a political demonstration by recounting an experience where she drove by a demonstration and honked her horn upon seeing a sign stating "Honk for Peace." That exchange took place during a discussion of current events including anti-war demonstrations. The court observed that "the school system does not 'regulate' teachers' speech as much as it *hires* that speech. Expression is a teacher's stock in trade, the commodity she sells her employer in exchange for a salary" (*Mayer v. County Community School Corporation*, 2007, p. 479). According to the court, the purpose for such a restrictive rule is that the classroom presents teachers with a "captive audience," an opportunity that a teacher may use to indoctrinate students, which is a level of authority that is better vested in an elected or accountable body like a board of education. This rule is a double-edged sword because it limits the ability of a teacher to take initiative and include LGBTQ-positive materials into the classroom, but also prevents teachers from proselytizing in class (*Webster v. New Lenox School District No. 122*, 1990), which could negatively affect the school environment. That rule includes displays of information within the classroom environment. As will be discussed in detail in the following subsection, the First Amendment analysis is very different when the school or district chooses the curriculum and the parents object.

For speech that is unrelated to a teacher's "official duties," teachers have a little bit more leeway, but far from unfettered discretion. Teachers are permitted to speak as "citizens on matters of public concern" provided that, on balance, the teacher's speech does not unduly interfere with the "efficiency of the public services [the school district] performs through its employees" (*Pickering v. Board of Education*, 1968, p. 568). The protoypical example is a teacher who writes a letter to the editor in the local paper about a controversy surrounding the board of education (*Hall v. Marion School District*, 1994; *Seemuller v. Fairfax County School Board*, 1989; *McGee v. South Pemiscot School District*,

1984). However, the United States Supreme Court has extended protections to include private speech. In *Givhan v. Western Line Consolidated School District* (1979), the Court ruled that the First Amendment prohibited a school district from refusing to rehire a teacher who complained to the school principal about discriminatory employment practices in private meetings with the principal. Notably, in each of the examples, the place where the teacher's speech took place was not during instructional time.

Thus, despite having the appearance of more discretion, the line between the teacher as an employee and the teacher as a citizen is easily blurred, leaving teachers in an uncertain position that discourages them from speaking freely. For example, a court could deem a teacher's decision to put up a poster of Harvey Milk in his/her classroom as a citizen speaking on an issue of public concern (i.e., the invisibility of influential LGBTQ people), a decision that would have a negligible effect on the school's ability to function, if any at all. However, that same court could just as easily interpret the teacher's decision as overstepping bounds into an area that is at the discretion of district-level employees and elected board of education members. Not surprisingly, teachers hesitate to put up a "safe haven" sticker or take other proactive steps intended to make the school a safe and affirming environment for LGBTQ students unless the school administration indicates to them, directly or indirectly, that doing so will not cost them their job.

The connection between the First Amendment rights of school personnel and its effect on the school environment was at the heart of a federal lawsuit as well as investigations by the U.S. DOE and DOJ into the Anoka-Hennepin School District in Minnesota (NCLR, 2011). Prior to the lawsuit, school district policy prevented teachers from discussing issues of sexual orientation. That policy fostered a dangerous school environment where teachers did not intervene to stop or address the underlying causes of the pervasive anti-gay bullying and harassment in their schools. As a result, LGBTQ students were subjected to harassment on a daily basis, which included everything from being pushed into lockers to being urinated on in the bathroom. In response to the lawsuit, investigations by the federal government, and constant attention from national media, the school board revised its policy to adopt the Respectful Learning Environment Policy, which would permit teachers to take the actions needed to help create a safe and welcoming environment for LGBTQ youth (Baca, 2012). Moreover, the settlement included an extensive review of current district policies and oversight by the federal government for the next five years (NCLR, 2012). Not surprisingly, shortly after the settlement was announced, the students who brought the lawsuit noted that there had been a dramatic decrease in the bullying they experienced.

The analysis appears to be slightly different for teachers who decide to be "out" in the school environment. In *Weaver v. Nebo School District* (1998), a teacher alleged that the school violated her First Amendment rights by refusing to rehire her as the girls' volleyball coach because she responded truthfully when asked whether she was gay. The court ultimately did not consider the question of whether a teacher could come out in class, as both parties agreed that she could not. In light of *Garcetti*, it is unclear whether courts would consider identifying oneself as LGBT as a statement made as part of an employee's official duties or as a private citizen, and if so, whether that rule would be applicable in all contexts throughout the school. Although a teacher's First Amendment rights factor into a teacher's ability to be "out" at school, this phenomenon is largely a function of employment protections available to LGBT teachers, either under federal or state law (Biegel, 2010).

When Schools "Speak"

Schools have First Amendment rights too. Through their administrators, schools are constantly making decisions and taking particular actions that impart a specific message to their students. None of those decisions is more charged than the academic curriculum a school chooses to teach its children. Parents have sought the right to prohibit the use of curricula that conflict with the parents' religious beliefs or create all sorts of carve outs that essentially nullify the benefits of the curriculum.

The seminal case in this area is *Mozert v. Hawkins County Board of Education* (1987) in Tennessee, which involved born-again Christian parents who argued that the curriculum interfered with their freedom to practice their religion and impart religious beliefs on their children. In rejecting the parents' claims, the court reiterated that "governmental actions that merely offend or cast doubt on religious beliefs do not on that account violate free exercise [of religion]" (*Mozert v. Hawkins County Board of Education*, 1987, p. 1068). The critical component that was missing from the parents' claims was compulsion; the parents presented no evidence that their children were "*required* to participate beyond reading and discussing assigned materials, or were disciplined for disputing assigned materials" (*Mozert v. Hawkins County Board of Education*, 1987, p. 1068). Since the ruling was first issued, the court's opinion in this case has taken on a national character, with courts in other parts of the country reaching similar conclusions. For example, in a Massachusetts case, *Brown v. Hot, Sexy, and Safer Productions, Inc.* (1995, p. 534), the court stated that:

> If all parents had a fundamental constitutional right to dictate individually what the schools teach their children, the schools would be forced to cater the curriculum for each student whose parents had a genuine moral disagreement with the school's choice of subject matter. We cannot see that the Constitution imposes such a burden on state educational systems.

In 2006, two families sued their school district for exposing their children, a kindergartener and second grader, to books that contain positive portrayals of same-sex couples and families (*Parker v. Hurley*, 2008). Those families alleged that the books interfered with their freedom of religious expression and their right to raise their children in the manner that they see fit. In both instances, the school rejected the parents' requests to opt out of any instruction or materials that included positive portrayals of homosexuality. Relying on cases such as *Mozert*, both the trial court and appellate court dismissed the complaint. The court found that the parents had not presented evidence that the books burdened either their right to raise their children or their children's right to free exercise of religion.

In addition to expressing itself through curriculum, the books and materials in the school library make a statement about the breadth of information provided to its students. In a New York case, *Board of Education, Island Trees Union Free School District v. Pico* (1982), the Board of Education removed "objectionable" books from school libraries in the district. Students upset with the board's decision to restrict their access to information sued, contending that the board's action violated their First Amendment rights. The United States Supreme Court agreed and held that:

> our Constitution does not permit the official suppression of *ideas*. Thus whether [the Board's] removal of books from their school libraries denied [students] their First Amendment rights depends upon the motivation behind [the Board's] actions. If [the Board] *intended* by their removal decision to deny [students] access to ideas with which [the Board] disagreed, and if this intent was the decisive factor in [the Board's] decision, then [the Board members] have exercised their discretion in violation of the Constitution.
>
> (p. 871)

However, the court did note that the school could still remove books that were "pervasively vulgar" or educationally unsuitable. It is important to note, that the Court did not determine whether the students could compel a school to purchase certain books for the school library, a question the Court has not revisited.

With the proliferation of information available on the Internet that particular question may be moot, but the underlying issue remains. More specifically, schools use filters to restrict student access to obscene content or content that would not otherwise be protected by the First Amendment; however, using filtering software that is overly restrictive may run afoul of the principle articulated in *Pico*. As the ACLU has documented, many of the software filters will block students from accessing the websites of LGBTQ community centers and organizations, but will permit students to view websites for groups that promote harmful reparative therapies for LGBTQ people (Hampton, 2011). Schools and software companies have quickly realized that there is no justifiable reason for restricting access to those websites and have worked to fix the problem instead of facing litigation.

Finally, hosting events that explore and celebrate diversity is another form of school "speech." In those situations, a school's First Amendment obligations are determined by the structure of the program. If the school retains total control of the program such that students are not involved in any of the presentations, the school is engaging in "government speech." In *Downs v. Los Angeles Unified School District* (2000), the school district created and disseminated posters and other materials to be used in schools throughout the district during Gay and Lesbian Awareness Month. Displeased with the content of the display, Robert Downs commandeered the bulletin board outside his classroom to display information expressing his religious views decrying homosexuality. When Downs was ordered to remove the materials, he sued the school district for violating his First Amendment rights. The appellate court rejected Downs's claim because the district maintained control of the message being portrayed at all times, whether through the materials it created or the authority it vested in the school principal. In fact, the court characterized the bulletin boards as "an expressive vehicle for the school board's policy of 'Educating for Diversity'" (*Downs v. Los Angeles Unified School District*, 2000, p. 1012).

On the flip side, when a school district opens up a forum for private speech and debate, including that of students, courts apply the rule established in *Kuhlmeier* (1988), a rule that is typically deferential to the authority of schools. However, in *Hansen v. Ann*

Arbor Public Schools (2003), the court rejected the school's proffered "legitimate pedagogical concerns" (p. 780), finding that the school's conduct violated Hansen's First Amendment rights. In that case, the school decided to host a "Diversity Week," a series of events planned by the school's Student Council, including a panel put together by the school's GSA on reconciling homosexuality and religion. In part, the school refused Hansen's request to participate on the panel or designate an adult as a panelist to present the view that homosexuality and religion are irreconcilable. The court found the school's position to constitute viewpoint discrimination as opposed to advancing "legitimate pedagogical concerns." A similar analysis can be applied to a school permitting students to organize a *Day of Silence* or, its religious counterpart, the *Day of Dialogue*. Those events would likely be considered "school-sponsored" speech and thus the school could not prohibit student speech based on the viewpoint being expressed. That does not mean that students have free-reign to say whatever they would like. Instead, if a school wants to place limitations on student speech, the pedagogical basis for those limitations must be unrelated to the viewpoint being expressed.

To date, no court has decided the related, but equally pressing, question of whether permitting students to organize a *Day of Silence* requires a school to permit students to organize a counter event, such as the *Day of Dialogue*. However, at least one scholar has argued that "one does not follow the other" (Biegel, 2010, p. 95). More specifically, the purpose of the *Day of Silence* is to raise awareness of the harassment and bullying that LGBTQ youth face in schools and the silencing effect it has on the voices of LGBTQ students. Conversely, programs like the *Day of Dialogue* seek to inform members of the school community of a particular interpretation of the Bible that homosexuality is a sin and irreconcilably in conflict with their religious beliefs. That said, the court's opinion in *Hansen* indicates the issue may not be that straightforward.

The lessons learned from the cases discussed in this subsection can be distilled into succinct guidelines for schools to follow. Although certainly easier said than done, safeguarding the right of LGBTQ students to learn and that of their peers to express views that are critical of the LGBTQ community requires a measured approach. Absent statements that clearly go beyond a student's First Amendment rights or strong evidence of actual or likely disruption, schools must tread lightly when considering disciplining a student for speech or expressive conduct. That does not mean that the school cannot use the opportunity as a "teachable moment" to counteract the negative affects that anti-gay speech can have on the school environment. Similarly, schools should not permit students and community members to exercise a "Heckler's Veto" over speech or expressive conduct (e.g., same-sex dates at prom) that protects the rights of LGBTQ students and fosters a positive school environment.

As the aforementioned cases demonstrate, when it comes to teachers and the schools themselves, the law gives schools a lot of leeway. Thus, it is particularly important to make decisions based on what is going to be best for the students, a consideration that is at the heart of a school professional's ethical obligations. To that end, schools should encourage teachers to take steps to make their classrooms a safe environment for LGBTQ youth by putting up posters of influential LGBTQ people, including LGBTQ issues into the curriculum, and even "coming out" to their students in an age-appropriate manner. Chapter 9 of this volume focuses on creating safe school climates; Chapter 10 of this volume explores how to create supportive and responsive classrooms; while Chapter 11 of this volume addresses how to establish inclusive school environments for LGBT families and their children. On the school-wide level, schools should take opportunities to educate students about the diversity of people and ideas that exist in our society and give them access to information that will allow them to broaden their perspective on the world around them. Again, it is important that schools do not allow the objections of parents to steer them away from taking those strides to support and foster a safe, welcoming, and affirming school environment for LGBTQ youth.

The Equal Access Act and Gay-Straight Alliances on Campus

In 1984, Congress passed the Equal Access Act with the intent to clarify the right of students to organize student groups, specifically religious or prayer groups. More recently, due to the broad language of the statute, students interested in starting GSAs have been able to rely on the Equal Access Act to counter the actions of hostile school administrators. Courts have routinely held in favor of students seeking to start GSAs, rejecting the varied arguments made by school districts attempting to block the creation of GSAs.

Under the Equal Access Act (1984), any secondary school that receives federal funding is not permitted "to deny equal access or a fair opportunity to, or discriminate against, any students who wish to conduct a meeting . . . on the basis of the religious, political, philosophical, or other content of the speech at such meetings" (§ 4071a). This prohibition is triggered if the school allows "one or more noncurriculum related student groups to meet on school premises during noninstructional time" (§ 4071b). The United States Supreme Court has defined "noncurriculum related student group" as "any student group that does not directly relate to the body of courses offered by the school" (*Board of Education v. Mergens*, 1990, p. 239). Courts also have interpreted the phrase "noninstructional time" to include the lunch period (*Ceniceros v. San Diego Unified School District*, 1997) and a school created "activity period" (*Donovan v. Punxsutawney Area School Board*, 2003). Moreover, it is important to note that the statute defines "secondary school" by relying on state law (*Ceniceros v. San Diego Unified School District*, 1997); thus, the scope of students who are protected under the Equal Access Act may vary from state to state.

Even if a school permits noncurriculum related student groups to meet at school, students do not have an entirely automatic right to form a student group. The group must meet each of the following criteria: (a) the meeting is voluntary and student-initiated; (b) the school, the government, or its agents or employees are not sponsoring the meeting; (c) employees or agents of the school or government are present at religious meetings only in a nonparticipatory capacity; (d) the meeting does not materially and substantially interfere with the orderly conduct of educational activities within the school; and (e) nonschool persons do not direct, conduct, control, or regularly attend activities of student groups (Equal Access Act, 1984). Similarly, the requirements of the Equal Access Act do not limit a school district's authority "to maintain order and discipline on school premises, to protect the well-being of students and faculty, and to assure that attendance of students at meetings is voluntary" (§ 4071f). Combined, those are the only criteria under which a school can prevent the formation of a student group.

School districts have attempted to use several of those criteria to thwart student attempts to form GSAs. In one instance, a school claimed that the GSA constituted a curriculum-related group because it covered the topic of human sexuality, a topic taught in the school's health class (*Colín v. Orange Unified School District*, 2000). The court rejected the school's claim because the club's stated purpose was to discuss tolerance, treating one another with respect, and combating prejudice, and therefore there was not enough of an overlap to justify considering the GSA a curriculum-related group. Relying on the "substantial interference" element, another school district claimed that the community uproar following approval of the GSA permitted the school district to rescind that approval (*Boyd County Gay Straight Alliance v. Bd. of Educ. of Boyd County*, 2003). The backlash included droves of phone calls from parents, a protest of approximately 100 students the day before school began, and one day when approximately one half of the student body did not attend school in protest. However, the evidence demonstrated that the uproar did not affect the day-to-day operations of the school and that the supporters of the GSA were not involved in any of the incidents. Thus, the court rejected the school district's argument because the limitation contained in the Equal Access Act applies to situations where the members of the group seeking recognition are causing the interference.

Similarly, another school district argued that permitting a GSA would harm the well-being of the students and also interfere with the school district's obligation to maintain order (*Gonzalez v. Sch. Bd. of Okeechobee County*, 2008). In particular, the school district argued that the rejection of the GSA:

> 1) is necessary to maintain the integrity of the abstinence only program, 2) will avoid unhealthy premature sexualization of students, 3) will protect GSA members from the risk of contact with potentially dangerous outside adult influences, and 4) will ensure that GSA members do not have access to adult only materials.
>
> (p. 1263)

The court rejected each of the school district's arguments as unfounded and speculative as the mission of the GSA is to promote tolerance, which does not undermine the school district's "abstinence only" program or have any connection to any of the other concerns raised by the school district.

However, school districts have not been wholly unsuccessful in limiting "noncurriculum related student groups." In those cases, the proposed student group either violated the school's anti-discrimination policies by placing burdensome criteria on group membership or endorsed inappropriate and explicit materials. Given the inclusive mission of GSAs, a school district has yet to argue that a GSA violated the school's anti-discrimination policy.[6] In *Caudillo v. Lubbock Independent School District* (2004), the court ruled that the school district was permitted to reject an application to start a student group because the group's website contained links to websites that displayed what the court deemed to be "sexually explicit material."

Equality under the Equal Access Act provides more than just permission to hold meetings in the school. All student groups should have the same level of access to advertise the group's events and meetings. For example, Osseo Area Schools designated its Cheerleading and Synchronized Swimming groups as "curriculum related student groups" and, as such, allowed them to advertise events over the public announcement system and the school's "scrolling screen," have a page in the school yearbook, fundraise, and participate in field trips (*Straights & Gays for Equality v. Osseo Area Sch.*, 2006). "Noncurriculum related student groups" were not allowed those same privileges. Finding that the Cheerleading and Synchronized Swimming groups were in fact "noncurriculum related student groups," the court ruled it was impermissible for the school to permit those two groups to have access to avenues of communication that were unavailable to other "noncurriculum related student groups." Notably, had those groups legitimately been "curriculum related student groups," those distinctions would have been permissible under the Equal Access Act.

As noted by the United States Supreme Court, there are two ways to entirely sidestep the Equal Access Act: reject federal funding or limit student groups to "curriculum related student groups" (*Board of Education v. Mergens*, 1990). Even still, schools run the risk that one of the "curriculum related student groups" will be declared by a court to be noncurricular, thereby requiring the school's compliance with the Equal Access Act. That is exactly what happened to the Board of Education of Salt Lake City School District. In February 1996, the Board of Education issued a policy limiting student groups to curriculum-related groups (*East High Gay/Straight Alliance v. Board of Education*, 1999). Despite the board's attempt to restrict the formation of student groups, the court found that one of the student groups at the high school constituted a "noncurriculum related student group," thus requiring the board to comply with the Equal Access Act. Likewise, in *Boyd County Gay Straight Alliance v. Board of Education of Boyd County* (2003), the court held that the school district was required to comply with the Equal Access Act, in part, because there was evidence that the Bible Club continued meeting during noninstructional time after the school district eliminated "noncurriculum related student groups," and the meetings were held in a manner that the school district should have known those meetings were occurring.

As in the other areas previously discussed, a student's right to bring a claim under the Equal Access Act does not limit the student's ability to allege violations of other federal and state laws, such as the First Amendment. Thus, although not explicitly addressed in the Equal Access Act, students forming a "noncurriculum related student group" have a right to choose the group's name, provided the name stays within the bounds of protected speech. In fact, a court rebuffed a school district's attempt to condition approval of a GSA on the students' agreeing to change the group's name to "Tolerance Club" or "Tolerance for All" (*Colin v. Orange Unified School District*, 2000).

In sum, secondary schools have two choices when it comes to the formation of a GSA: (1) allow the group to form without interference provided it meets each of the basic requirements and treat the group as any other "noncurriculum related student group" or (2) go to the great lengths required to not have to comply with the Equal Access Act (i.e., reject federal funding or prohibit "noncurriculum related student groups") and risk the possibility of litigation. Given that GSAs have been shown to improve the school environment for LGBTQ students, which is discussed in detail in Chapter 15, the choice appears to be relatively straightforward.

Law, Policy, and Ethics 113

The Right to Privacy and "Outing" Students

In addition to the right to speak out and organize student groups, LGBTQ students have a right to privacy regarding their sexual orientation and gender identity. That right to privacy is recognized under the United States Constitution (*Whalen v. Roe*, 1977; *Roe v. Wade*, 1973; *Eisenstadt v. Baird*, 1972; *Griswold v. Connecticut*, 1965), as well as the law of many states (Alaska Const. art. I, § 22; Ariz. Const. art. II, § 8; Cal. Const. art. I § 1; Fla. Const. art. I, § 23; Haw. Const. art. I, § 6; Ill. Const. art. I, § 6; La. Const. art. I, § 5; Mont. Const. art. II, § 10; S.C. Const. art. I, § 10; Wash. Const. art. I, § 7). Whether someone's right to privacy has been violated hinges on that person's "reasonable expectation of privacy," which is balanced against the need for disclosing that information and the manner in which that disclosure was made (*Whalen v. Roe*, 1977; *T.L.S. v. Montana Advocacy Program*, 2006; *Winfield v. Division. of Pari-Mutuel Wagering*, 1985). Courts uniformly agree that a person's sexual orientation and gender identity are entitled to protection as private information (*Nguon v. Wolf*, 2007; *Sterling v. Borough of Minersville*, 2000; *Powell v. Schriver*, 1999). Revealing the assigned sex of a transgender student also may trigger a right to privacy over medical information (*Gunnerud v. State*, 1980; *Hill v. National Collegiate Athletic Association*, 1994; *King v. State*, 2000; *Naipo v. Border*, 2011). Those protections remain in place even if that information is known in certain contexts (*U.S. Dep't of Justice v. Reporters Comm. for Freedom of the Press*, 1989). For example, in *Nguon v. Wolf* (2007), the court held that even though a student did not have a reasonable expectation of privacy regarding her sexual orientation at school because she had been engaging in public displays of affection with her girlfriend on school grounds, that fact did not surrender her right to keep that information private from her parents who were unlikely to be on campus or otherwise know about those public displays of affection. That same analysis could be applied to a transgender student who lives as his or her affirmed gender at school, but lives consistent with his or her assigned sex while at home.

The scope of legitimate interests for disclosing a student's sexual orientation and gender identity are limited, especially when accounting for the implications of that disclosure (e.g., increased bullying in school or parental disapproval of student). Despite finding the student had a protected expectation of privacy, the court in *Nguon v. Wolf* (2007) held that a school district did not violate the student's right to privacy by telling her parents that she was a lesbian because the school district was required to provide her parents with enough information to allow them to properly defend her in a school disciplinary proceeding. Notably, however, the court did not explain why the student's sexual orientation was such vital information to warrant the intrusion on the student's right to privacy, as well as that of her girlfriend. Although courts may be willing to give school districts some leeway in the disclosure of a student's sexual orientation or gender identity, it is hard to imagine a factual scenario where those legitimate interests would become so compelling as to specifically require the disclosure of a student's sexual orientation or gender identity.

Moreover, even if a school district demonstrates a legitimate interest in disclosing a student's private information, revealing that information may still violate that student's right to privacy if the disclosure was not made in a manner that safeguarded against future or unintended disclosures. For example, the United States Supreme Court relied on the various privacy protections built into a school district's drug-testing system to uphold the constitutionality of that system (*Vernonia v. Acton*, 1995). Similarly, although the court in *Nguon* did not undertake that specific analysis, assuming the student's sexual orientation was vital information, the school district could have given the student an opportunity to discuss her sexual orientation with her parents on her own terms and provided the support she needed to do that before the school intervened.

In the context of privacy rights, school districts also must ensure that their employees are complying with the Family Educational Rights and Privacy Act (FERPA, 1974), a federal law that enumerates the specific conditions under which a school can disclose student information. More specifically, unless the disclosure fits into one of the exceptions, FERPA requires prior written consent from a parent or student, if the student is over eighteen years old, to disclose student information. However, a student cannot allege a violation of FERPA in a lawsuit (*Gonzaga Univ. v. Doe*, 2002), but the United States Department of Education can bring an enforcement action against a school district (FERPA, 1974).

Considering the significant levels of peer and familial rejection faced by LGBTQ youth, respecting LGBTQ students' right to privacy regarding their sexual orientation and gender identity is critical. Although the student in *Nguon* was lucky to have a supportive family, countless others do not or are too scared to find out. In fact, an eighteen year old gay high school student took his own life after a local police officer threatened to tell the student's grandfather that the student was gay (*Sterling v. Borough of Minersville*, 2000).

"Outing" an LGBTQ student can happen in ways too numerous to list. The best way to avoid violating a student's right to privacy is not to share any information that the student has not expressly permitted to be shared, unless a legal obligation requires the disclosure (e.g., mandated reporting laws). Even in situations where school personnel are permitted or required to share information regarding a student, it is critical to go through the following analysis: can the necessary information be conveyed or reported without revealing the student's sexual orientation or gender identity? If not, what can be done to ease the effect of that disclosure on the student (e.g., giving the student advance notice)? Moreover, what measures or safeguards are needed to ensure that the information shared is not redisclosed (e.g., confidentiality agreements, written protocols regarding disclosure of private information)? By protecting the privacy of students, professionals are upholding their ethical obligation of promoting the moral principles of beneficence (doing good) and nonmaleficence (avoiding harm; Whitman et al., 2006). Furthermore, any behavior that intentionally or unintentionally harms a student could be grounds for a complaint to the professional's licensing board or a malpractice suit.

Private Schools Do Not Get a Free Pass on Everything

The legal protections available to LGBTQ youth attending private and parochial schools vary widely from state to state. Like public schools, if private schools accept any federal funding those schools would be required to comply with federal laws such as Title IX. Depending on the scope of the applicable state anti-discrimination statute, private schools may or may not fall within the reach of that statute as a public accommodation. For example, a court upheld a parochial school's authority to expel two students for having "a bond of intimacy . . . characteristic of a lesbian relationship" (*Doe v. California Lutheran High School Association*, 2009) because the school could not be considered a business under the state's anti-discrimination law. Moreover, religious institutions have been successful in obtaining exemptions from state anti-discrimination statutes where those mandates conflict with the institution's religious beliefs either through explicit statutory exceptions (e.g., N.Y. EXEC. LAW § 296(11)) or judicially created ones (e.g., *Wazeerud-Din v. Goodwill Home & Missions, Inc.*, 1999).

That said, LGBTQ youth who attend private schools do have some protections outside of anti-discrimination laws. Depending on the circumstances, an LGBTQ student may be able to sue a private school for torts (i.e., personal injury) such as infliction of emotional distress, negligent supervision, or invasion of privacy. However, in the context of religious institutions, those institutions may be able to use their religious beliefs as a defense to those claims (e.g., *Paul v. Watchtower Bible & Tract Society*, 1987). It is imperative, then, for professionals working in parochial schools to lean heavily on their ethical standards and accepted standard of care when faced with the need to balance the various competing interests involved.

LGBT Parents Have Rights Too

Although this chapter has focused mostly on the rights of students and a school district's legal and ethical obligation to create a safe and affirming school environment, a school's attitude and conduct towards LGBT parents is equally important because of its effect on LGBT parents, the school community, and the children of LGBT parents. Many of the same laws that protect LGBTQ students also safeguard the rights of LGBT parents. In some instances, the protections afforded LGBT parents may be even clearer and easier to enforce than their younger counterparts by virtue of their status as parents.

It is well established that children benefit socially, emotionally, and academically from collaborative school–family partnerships (Bryan & Holcomb-McCoy, 2007; Esler, Godber, & Christenson, 2008), and LGBT parents participate in the education of their children at rates that are significantly higher than the national average (Kosciw & Diaz, 2008). Yet, Kosciw and Diaz found that LGBT parents still felt excluded and invisible at their child's school. In particular, some LGBT parents reported that school employees refused to recognize one of the parents as a parent or questioned his/her parenting ability because of that parent's LGBT status.

Currently, there are no published cases of LGBT parents that have sued a school district for discriminating against them because of their LGBT status. However, that does not mean that there are no circumstances where an LGBT parent could bring a successful claim against a school district. For example, a school employee who refuses to respect the parental rights of an adoptive LGBT parent, despite the fact that the state permits second-parent adoptions by same-sex couples, may be violating that parent's rights under federal and state law. Similarly, an LGBT parent may be able to successfully sue a school district that permits other parents to volunteer in the classroom but rejects the LGBT parent's requests to volunteer.

Conclusion

Aside from telling a cautionary tale of the significant financial costs of failing to adequately address the needs of LGBTQ youth in school, the cases cited throughout this chapter provide clear guidance to school districts on the steps needed to create the type of school environment that will allow students to access and benefit from their education. That guidance can be encapsulated in two words: respect and leadership. By respecting LGBTQ students and parents, school districts will make significant strides in creating a safe, welcoming, and affirming environment for LGBTQ people. From that respect flows support of a student's right to be "out" and affirmed at school, to receive an education free from harassment and bullying, and to organize student groups, among others. In order for that respect to permeate the school environment, district- and school-level administrators and personnel must demonstrate leadership. For administrators, that means encouraging and supporting teachers, counselors, and other school personnel to take proactive measures that foster positive educational environments; responding appropriately to complaints of harassment; permitting all students to express themselves in a respectful manner; and modeling the level of respect that is expected of members of the school community. For teachers, counselors, and other school personnel it requires intervening to stop harassment and bullying, incorporating positive portrayals of LGBT people into the classroom, creating a safe haven for LGBTQ students, and advocating for LGBTQ students when members of the school community are not treating them with the respect they deserve.

Both the law and society expect a lot from schools, an expectation that reflects the importance of education. Unfortunately, schools have been asked to meet those high standards on ever-shrinking budgets and resources. In that context, compliance with the laws discussed in this chapter may seem overwhelming. Anecdotally, however, school districts across the country are meeting the needs of their LGBTQ students without difficulty and financial strain. Moreover, the prophylactic efforts undertaken by those school districts are cheaper than paying attorneys' fees for the school district and student's attorneys as well as monetary damages to the student. Thus, in this regard, the needs of LGBTQ students to attend school in a safe and affirming environment and the interest of district and school administrators to reduce expenses complement one another.

Moreover, school personnel who aspire to the ethical standards of their profession, understand students' legal rights, and take a leadership role in ensuring those rights are protected by: not discriminating against LGBTQ students (NEA, 2002–2010); developing and implementing comprehensive school-wide violence and/or bullying prevention programs; advocating on behalf of and protecting all students, particularly those who are marginalized, both in and outside the school district (American Association of School Administrators [AASA], 2007; ASCA, 2007); actively pursuing and implementing/ enforcing nondiscrimination policies that explicitly reference LGBTQ students; recogniz- ing and ameliorating societal and school-based obstacles or risks that may negatively impact the development of LGBTQ students (i.e., address any inequities and remove any barriers); and increasing awareness and sensitivity in all stakeholders, including oneself (ASCA, 2006, 2007, 2009, 2011; Graybill et al., 2009; NASP, 2006; Whitman et al., 2007). Additionally, the American School Counselor Association (ASCA) suggests that pro- fessionals not only model inclusive language, but also address any inappropriate language and behavior from students and adults (ASCA, 2007).

By simply upholding their legal and ethical obligations to reduce bullying and discri- mination, school personnel are actively preventing risks or vulnerabilities associated with sexual minority status, thereby addressing the developmental needs of students proactively (Masten, Herbers, Cutuli, & Lafavor, 2008). Educators are encouraged to seek out the existing ethical codes/standards that stipulate professional roles and responsibilities related to working with LGBTQ youth in order to guide their professional behavior (see Appendix).

Notes

1 To date, fourteen states and the District of Columbia protect students from discrimination on the basis of sexual orientation and gender identity. Those states are: California, CAL. EDUC. CODE § 220; Colorado, COLO. REV. STAT. ANN. § 24-34-601; Connecticut, CONN. GEN. STAT. ANN. § 10-15c; Illinois, 775 ILL. COMP. STAT. ANN. § 5/5-102; Iowa, IOWA CODE § 216.9; Maine, ME. REV. STAT. ANN. tit. 5, § 4592; Massachusetts, 2011 Massachusetts House Bill No. 3810 (Effective Jul. 1, 2012); Minnesota, MINN. STAT. ANN. § 363A.13; Nevada, Nev. Rev. Stat. § 651.070; New Jersey, N.J. STAT. ANN. 10:5-4; New Mexico, N.M. STAT. ANN. § 28-1-7; Oregon, ORE. REV. STAT. ANN. § 659.850; Vermont, VT. STAT. ANN. tit. 9, § 4502; Washington, WASH. REV. CODE ANN. § 28A.642.010; and the District of Columbia, D.C. CODE ANN. § 2-1402.41. Additionally, Arkansas, Maryland, New York, and North Carolina have statutes that protect students from harassment, bullying and intimidation on the basis of sexual orientation and gender identity (i.e., ARK. CODE ANN. § 6-18-514; MD. CODE ANN. EDUC. § 7-424(a); N.Y. EDUC. LAW § 12 (Effective Jul. 1, 2012); N.C. GEN. STAT. § 115C-407.15). Some states prohibit discrimination on the basis of sexual orientation, but not gender identity.
2 There is no specific study on transgender and/or gender nonconforming youth.
3 In the absence of any other state anti-discrimination laws specifically protecting the rights of transgender individuals, attorneys have relied on disability anti-discrimination claims to protect the rights of gender nonconforming individuals. GID is currently an accepted diagnosis under the DSM-IV-TR (American Psychiatric Association, 2000); however, the World Professional Association for Transgender Health (WPATH, 2011) argues that rather than pathologizing gender nonconformity, it is more appropriate to recognize that any psychological distress is socially constructed as opposed to inherent to the individual. See Chapter 5 of this volume for a more in-depth discussion of optimizing the health and mental health of transgender students and WPATH's standards of care.
4 It is important to note that the United States Supreme Court initially agreed to hear this case, but ultimately dismissed it based on procedural grounds and vacated the appellate court's opinion. Thus, the appellate court opinion does not have precedential value, but can be persuasive and instructive to courts who are faced with similar issues.
5 *Nuxoll* is a continuation of another case, *Zamecnik v. Indian Prairie School District* (2007).
6 Cases that fall within this category often involve religious student groups that seek to limit group membership based on some objective measure of religious conviction. For example, *Truth v. Kent Sch. Dist.*, 542 F.3d 634, 639, 648 (9th Cir. 2008) held that the school district had proper motive to reject a student group's application for recognition where a group sought to limit membership to those who expressed a "true desire to grow in a relationship with Jesus Christ."

References

ALA. CODE § 16-40A-2(c)(8) (West 2008).
ALASKA CONST. art. I, § 22.
American Association of School Administrators. (2007). *Code of ethics: AASA's statement of ethics for educational leaders*. Arlington, VA: Author. Retrieved from http://www.aasa.org/ SchoolAdministratorArticle.aspx?id=10544&terms=Code+of+Ethics
American Civil Liberties Union. (2009, May 18). High school student takes on anti-gay harassment—and wins [Press release]. Retrieved from http://www.aclu.org/lgbt-rights_hiv-aids/high-school-student-takes-anti-gay-harassment%E2%80%94and-wins

American Civil Liberties Union. (2010, July 20). Mississippi school agrees to revise policy and pay damages to lesbian teenager denied chance to attend prom [Press release]. Retrieved from http://www.aclu.org/lgbt-rights/mississippi-school-agrees-revise-policy-and-pay-damages-lesbian-teenager-denied-chance-a

American Civil Liberties Union. (2011, December 7). Mississippi school district and ACLU reach agreement over student whose tuxedo photo was excluded from senior portrait section of yearbook [Press release]. Retrieved from https://www.aclu.org/lgbt-rights/mississippi-school-district-and-aclu-reach-agreement-over-student-whose-tuxedo-photo-was

American Psychiatric Association. (2000). *Diagnostic and statistical manual of mental disorders, fourth edition, text revision* (pp. 576–582). Washington, DC: Author.

American Psychological Association. (2008). *Just the facts about sexual orientation and youth: A primer for principals, educators, and school personnel.* Washington, DC: Author. Retrieved from http://www.apa.org/pi/lgbc/publications/justthefacts.html

American Psychological Association. (2010). *Ethical principles of psychologists and code of conduct.* Washington, DC: Author. Retrieved from http://www.apa.org/ethics/code/index.aspx

American School Counselor Association. (2006). *The professional school counselor and equity for all students* [Position Statement]. Alexandria, VA: Author. Retrieved from http://asca2.timberlakepublishing.com//files/PS_Equity.pdf

American School Counselor Association. (2007). *The professional school counselor and LGBTQ youth* [Position Statement]. Alexandria, VA: Author. Retrieved from http://asca2.timberlakepublishing.com//files/PS_LGBTQ.pdf

American School Counselor Association. (2009). *The professional school counselor and cultural diversity* [Position Statement]. Alexandria, VA: Author. Retrieved from http://asca2.timberlakepublishing.com//files/CulturalDiversity.pdf

American School Counselor Association. (2011). *The professional school counselor and the promotion of safe schools through conflict resolution and bullying/harassment prevention* [Position Statement]. Alexandria, VA: Author. Retrieved from http://asca.membershipsoftware.org//files/SafeSchl.pdf

Ariz. Const. art. II, § 8.

Ariz. Rev. Stat. Ann. § 15-716(c)(1) to (3) (West 2008).

Baca, M. E. (2012, February 14). Anoka-Hennepin School Board votes to replace neutrality policy. *The Star Tribune.* Retrieved from http://www.startribune.com/local/north/139244228.html

Bethel School District No. 403 v. Fraser, 478 U.S. 675, 683 (1986).

Biegel, S. (2010). *The right to be out: Sexual orientation and gender identity in America's public schools.* Minneapolis, MN: University of Minnesota Press.

Board of Education, Island Trees Union Free School District v. Pico, 457 U.S. 853, 871 (1982).

Board of Education of the Westside Community School v. Mergens, 496 U.S. 226, 239, 240–41 (1990).

Boucher v. School Board of the School District of Greenfield, 134 F.3d 821 (7th Cir. 1998).

Boyd County Gay Straight Alliance v. Board of Education of Boyd County, 258 F. Supp. 2d 667, 688, 673–75, 691 (E.D. Ky. 2003).

Brown v. Hot, Sexy, and Safer Productions, Inc., 68 F.3d 525, 534 (1st Cir. 1995).

Bryan, J. & Holcomb-McCoy, C. (2007). An examination of school counselor involvement in school-family-community partnerships. *Professional School Counseling, 10*(5), 441–454.

Cal. Const. art. I § 1.

Cal. Ed. Code § 234.1(b) (1).

Caudillo v. Lubbock Independent School District, 311 F. Supp. 2d 550, 561 (N.D. Tex. 2004).

Ceniceros v. Board of Trustees of the San Diego Unified School District, 105 F.3d 878, 880–81 (9th Cir. 1997).

Chambers v. Babbitt, 145 F. Supp. 2d 1068 (D. Minn. 2001).

Colin v. Orange Unified School District, 83 F. Supp. 2d 1135, 1143–46 (C.D. Cal. 2000).

Davis v. Monroe County Bd. of Educ., 526 U.S. 629, 650–51 (1999).

Department of Education, Office of Civil Rights. (2011, October 26). Dear Colleague Letter. Retrieved from http://www2.ed.gov/about/offices/list/ocr/letters/colleague-201010.pdf

Department of Justice and Department of Education. (2011, June 30). Letter to Richard L. Swanson, Ph.D., Superintendent Tehachapi Unified School District. Retrieved from http://www.justice.gov/crt/about/edu/documents/tehachapiletter.pdf

DeShaney v. Winnebago County Department of Social Services, 489 U.S. 189 (1989).

Doe v. California Lutheran High School Association, 170 Cal. App. 4th 828, 833 (2009).

Doe v. Clark County Sch. Dist., 2008 U.S. Dist. LEXIS 71204 (D. Nev. Sep. 17, 2008).

Doe v. Yunits, 2000 Mass. Super. LEXIS 491, at *2–3 (Mass. Super. Ct. Oct. 11, 2000).

Doe v. Yunits, 2001 Mass. Super. LEXIS 327, at *15–16, 18–22 (Mass. Super. Ct. Feb. 26, 2001).

Doninger v. Neihoff, 527 F.3d 41 (2d Cir. 2008).

Donovan v. Poway Unified School District, 167 Cal. App. 4th 567, 581, 584 (4th Dist. 2008).

Donovan v. Punxsutawney Area Sch. Bd., 336 F.3d 211, 214 (3rd Cir. 2003).

Downs v. Los Angeles Unified School District, 228 F.3d 1003, 1012 (9th Cir. 2000).

East High Gay/Straight Alliance v. Board of Education of the Salt Lake City School District, 81 F. Supp. 2d 1166, 1168, 1180 (D. Utah 1999).

Eisenstadt v. Baird, 405 U.S. 438 (1972).

Equal Access Act, 20 U.S.C. § 4071(a, b, c, f), 4072(1, b) (1984).

Esler, A. N., Godber, Y., & Christenson, S. L. (2008). Best practices in supporting school-family partnerships. In A. Thomas & J. Grimes (Eds.), *Best practices in school psychology V* (pp. 917–936). Bethesda, MD: The National Association of School Psychologists.

Family Educational Rights and Privacy Act, 34 C.F.R. § 99.30–31, 99.66–67 (1974).

Fla. Const. art. I, § 23.

Flores v. Morgan Hill Unified School District, 324 F.3d 1130, 1132–34 (9th Cir. 2003).

Fricke v. Lynch, 491 F. Supp. 381 (D.R.I. 1980).

Garcetti v. Ceballos, 547 U.S. 410, 421 (2006).

Gay-Straight Alliance Network v. Visalia Unified School District, 262 F. Supp. 2d 1088, 1094–97 (E.D. Cal. 2001).

Gay, Lesbian, and Straight Education Network & National Center for Transgender Equality (n.d.). *Model district policy on transgender and gender nonconforming students*. Washington, DC: GLSEN & NCTE. Retrieved from http://www.glsen.org/binary-data/GLSEN_ATTACHMENTS/file/000/001/1978-1.pdf

Gebser v. Lago Vista Independent School District, 524 U.S. 274, 290 (1998).

Givhan v. Western Line Consolidated School District, 439 U.S. 410 (1979).

Gonzaga University v. Doe, 536 U.S. 273, 276 (2002).

Gonzalez v. School Board of Okeechobee County, 571 F. Supp. 2d 1257, 1263–68 (S.D. Fla. 2008).

Goss v. Lopez, 419 U.S. 565, 573 (1975).

Graybill, E. C., Varjas, K., Meyers, J., & Watson, L. B. (2009). Content-specific strategies to advocate for lesbian, gay, bisexual, and transgender youth: An exploratory study. *School Psychology Review, 38*(4), 570–584. Retrieved from http://www.nasponline.org/publications/spr/pdf/spr384graybill.pdf

Griffin, P., & Carroll, H. J. (2010). *On the team: Equal opportunity for transgender student athletes*. San Francisco, CA: NCLR. Retrieved from http://www.nclrights.org/site/DocServer/TransgenderStudentAthleteReport.pdf?docID=7901

Griffin, P., & Carroll, H. (2011). *NCAA inclusion of transgender student-athletes* (NCAA Office of Inclusion Resource). Retrieved from http://www.class.uh.edu/lgbt/docs/Transgender_Handbook_2011_Final.pdf

Griswold v. Connecticut, 318 U.S. 479 (1965).

Gunnerud v. State, 611 P.2d 69, 72 (Alaska 1980).

Hall v. Marion School District, 31 F.3d 183 (4th Cir. 1994).

Hampton, C. (2011). *Don't filter me interim report*. New York, NY: ACLU. Retrieved from http://www.aclu.org/files/assets/dontfilterme_report.pdf

Hansen v. Ann Arbor Public Schools, 293 F. Supp. 2d 780 (D. Mich. 2003).

Harper v. Poway Unified School District, 445 F.3d 1166, 1171, 1179 (9th Cir. 2006), *vacated*, 549 U.S. 1262 (2007).

HAW. CONST. art. I, § 6.

Hazelwood v. Kuhlmeier, 484 U.S. 260, 271 (1988).

Henkle v. Gregory, 150 F. Supp. 2d 1067, 1070 (D. Nev. 2001).

Hermann, M. A., & Herlihy, B. R. (2006). Legal and ethical implications of refusing to counsel homosexual clients. *Journal of Counseling and Development, 84*(4), 414–418. doi:10.1002/j.1556-6678.2006.tb00425.x

Hill v. National Collegiate Athletic Association, 865 P.2d 633 (Cal. 1994).

Himmelstein, K. E. W., & Brückner, H. (2010). Criminal-justice and school sanctions against nonheterosexual youth: A national longitudinal study. *Pediatrics, 127*, 49–57. doi:10.1542/peds.2009-2306

ILL. CONST. art. I, § 6.

Ingraham v. Wright, 430 U.S. 651, 674 (1977).

J.C. v. Beverly Hills Unified School District, 711 F. Supp. 2d 1094 (C.D. Cal. 2010).

J.S. v. Bethlehem Area School District, 569 Pa. 638, 807 A.2d 847 (2002).

Keyishian v. Board of Regents of the University of the State of New York, 385 U.S. 589, 603 (1967).

King v. State, 535 S.E.2d 492 (Ga. 2000).

Kosciw, J. G., & Diaz, E. (2008). *Involved, invisible, ignored: The experiences of lesbian, gay, bisexual and transgender parents and their children in our nation's K-12 schools* (pp. 25–43, 77–89). New York, NY: GLSEN. Retrieved from http://www.glsen.org/binary-data/GLSEN_ATTACHMENTS/file/000/001/1104-1.pdf

Kosciw, J. G., Greytak, E. A., Diaz, E. M., & Bartkiewicz, M. J. (2010). *The 2009 National School Climate Survey: The experiences of lesbian, gay, bisexual and transgender youth in our nation's schools*. New York, NY: GLSEN. Retrieved from http://www.glsen.org/binary-data/GLSEN_ATTACHMENTS/file/000/001/1675-2.pdf

LA. CONST. art. I, § 5.

Lambda Legal (1995, January 1). *Nabozny v. Podlesny* [Online forum content]. Retrieved from http://www.lambdalegal.org/in-court/cases/nabozny-v-podlesny.html

Lambda Legal (2002, August 28). Groundbreaking legal settlement is first to recognize constitutional right of gay and lesbian students to be out at school and protected from harassment [Press release]. Retrieved from http://www.lambdalegal.org/news/pr/ca_20020828_groundbreaking-legal-settlement-first-to-recognize.html

L.W. v. Toms River Regional School Board of Education, 915 A.2d 535, 540 (N.J. 2007).

Masten, A. S., Herbers, J. E., Cutuli, J. J., & Lafavor, T. L. (2008). Promoting competence and resilience in the school context. *Professional School Counseling, 12*(2), 76–84. Retrieved from http://schoolcounselor.metapress.com/content/rp3rv814qjh1m878/fulltext.pdf

Mayer v. County Community School Corporation, 474 F.3d 477, 479 (7th Cir. 2007).

McGee v. South Pemiscot School District, 712 F.2d 339 (8th Cir. 1984).

McMillen v. Itawamba County School District, 702 F. Supp. 2d 699, 701 (N.D. Miss. 2010).

Minor Student 1 v. School Union 87, Compl. No. 08-0239 (Me. Human Rts. Comm'n Jun. 5, 2009).

Minor Student 2 v. Asa Adams School, Compl. No. 08-0415 (Me. Human Rts. Comm'n Jun. 5, 2009).

MONT. CONST. art. II, § 10.

Morse v. Frederick, 551 U.S. 393, 397 (2007).

Mozert v. Hawkins County Board of Education, 827 F.2d 1058, 1064, 1068 (1987).

Nabozny v. Podlesny, 92 F.3d 446, 453–58, 460–61 (7th Cir. 1996).

Naipo v. Border, 251 P.3d 594 (Haw. 2011).

National Association of School Psychologists. (2006). *Gay, lesbian, bisexual, transgender, and questioning (GLBTQ) youth* [Position Statement]. Bethesda, MD: Author. Retrieved from http://www.nasponline.org/about_nasp/positionpapers/GLBQYouth.pdf

National Center for Lesbian Rights. (2011, July 21). NCLR and SPLC File Lawsuit Challenging Hostile Anti-LGBT Environment for Students in Minnesota's Anoka-Hennepin School District [Press release]. Retrieved from http://www.nclrights.org/site/PageServer? pagename=press_2011_Minn_Lawsuit_Filing_072111

National Center for Lesbian Rights. (2012, March 5). Civil Rights Organizations Announce Agreement to Resolve Anoka-Hennepin School District Bullying Lawsuits [Press release]. Retrieved from http://www.nclrights.org/site/PageServer?pagename= press_2012_Agreement_to_Resolve_AnokaHennepin_030512

National Center for Lesbian Rights & Gay, Lesbian Straight Education Network. (n.d.). *Fifteen expensive reasons why safe schools legislation is in your state's best interest*, 1–6. Retrieved from http://www.nclrights.org/site/DocServer/15reasons.pdf?docID=1621

National Education Association. (2002–2010). *Code of ethics*. Washington, DC: Author. Retrieved from http://www.nea.org/home/30442.htm

N.J. STAT. ANN. 10:5-14.1a.

Nguon v. Wolf, 517 F. Supp. 2d 1177, 1191, 1195–96 (C.D. Cal. 2007).

Norris v. Norwalk Public School, 124 F. Supp. 2d 791, 794–98 (D. Conn. 2000).

Nuxoll v. Indian Prairie School District, 523 F.3d 668, 674, 676 (7th Cir. 2008).

N.Y. EXEC. LAW § 296(11).

O.H. v. Oakland Unified School District, No. C-99-5123 JCS, 35 (N.D. Cal. Apr. 17, 2000).

Parker v. Hurley, 514 F.3d 87 (1st Cir. 2008).

Paul v. Watchtower Bible & Tract Society, 819 F.2d 875 (9th Cir. 1987).

Pickering v. Board of Education of Township High School, 205, 391 U.S. 563, 568 (1968).

Powell v. Schriver, 175 F.3d 107 (2d Cir. 1999).

Resolution Agreement, U.S. Department of Justice–U.S. Department of Education–Tehachapi Unified School District, Jun. 30, 2011. Retrieved from http://www.justice.gov/crt/about/edu/documents/tehachapiagreement.pdf

Roe v. Wade, 410 U.S. 113 (1973).

S.C. CONST. art. I, § 10.

Seemuller v. Fairfax County School Board, 878 F.2d 1578 (4th Cir. 1989).

Sterling v. Borough of Minersville, 232 F.3d 190, 192-93, 196 (3d Cir. 2000).

Straights & Gays for Equality v. Osseo Area School, 471 F.3d 908, 910, 912–13 (8th Cir. 2006).

TEX. STAT. HEALTH & SAFETY CODE ANN. § 85.007 (2008).

Theno v. Tonganoxie Unified School District, No. 464, 394 F. Supp. 2d 1299–1312 (D. Kan. 2005).

Thomas v. Board of Education, Granville Central School District, 607 F.2d 1043 (2d Cir. 1979).

Tinker v. Des Moines Independent Community School District, 393 U.S., 513 (1969).

Title IX Education Amendments, 20 U.S.C. § 1681(a), 1682 (1972).

T.L.S. v. Mont. Advocacy Program, 144 P.3d 818, 824 (Mont. 2006).

U.S. Const. amend. XIV § 1 (1868).

U.S. Department of Justice v. Reporters Committee for Freedom of the Press, 489 U.S. 749, 770 (1989).

Vernonia School District 47J v. Acton, 515 U.S. 646, 655 (1995).

Virginia v. Hicks, 539 U.S. 113, 119 (2003).

WASH. CONST. art. I, § 7.

Washington Interscholastic Activities Association (WIAA) (2011). *WIAA 2011–2012 Official Handbook* (pp. 49–50). Retrieved from http://www.wiaa.com/ConDocs/Con951/Handbook%20%28Web%29.pdf

Washington v. Pierce, 895 A.2d 173, 186 (Vt. 2005).

Wazeerud-Din v. Goodwill Home & Missions, Inc., 737 A.2d 683 (N.J. App. Div. 1999).

Weaver v. Nebo School District, (D. Utah 1998).

Webster v. New Lenox School District, No. 122, 917 F.2d 1004 (7th Cir. 1990).

Whalen v. Roe, 429 U.S. 589 (1977).

Whitman, J. S., Glosoff, H. L., Kocet, M. M., & Tarvydas, V. (2006, May 22). *Ethical issues related to conversion or reparative therapy* [Press release]. Retrieved from http://www.counseling.org/PressRoom/NewsReleases.aspx?AGuid=b68aba97-2f08-40c2-a400-0630765f72f4

Whitman, J. S., Horn, S. S., & Boyd, C. J. (2007). Activism in the schools: Providing LGBTQ affirmative training to school counselors. *Journal of Gay & Lesbian Psychotherapy, 3*(4), 143–154. doi:10.1300/J236v11n03_08

Winfield v. Div. of Pari-Mutuel Wagering, 477 So. 2d 544, 548 (Fla. 1985).

World Professional Association for Transgender Health (WPATH) (2011). Standards of care for the health of transsexual, transgender, and gender nonconforming people (7th ed.). Retrieved from http://www.wpath.org/publications_standards.cfm

Zamecnik v. Indian Prairie School District, Dkt. No. 07 C 1586, at *18 (N.D. Ill. Apr. 17, 2007).

APPENDIX

American Association of School Administrators. (2007). *Code of ethics: AASA's statement of ethics for educational leaders.* Arlington, VA: Author. Retrieved from http://www.aasa.org/SchoolAdministratorArticle.aspx?id=10544&terms=Code+of+Ethic

American Counseling Association. (ACA) (2005). *ACA code of ethics.* Alexandria, VA: Author. Retrieved from http://www.counseling.org/Counselors/ [ACA download: ACA_2005_Ethical_Code-2.pdf].

American School Counselor Association. (ASCA) (2010). *Ethical standards for school counselors.* Alexandria, VA: Author. Retrieved from http://asca2.timberlakepublishing.com//files/EthicalStandards2010.pdf

American Psychological Association. (APA) (2010). *Ethical principles of psychologists and code of conduct.* Washington, DC: Author. Retrieved from http://www.apa.org/ethics/code/index.aspx

National Association of School Psychologists. (NASP) (2010). *NASP principles for professional ethics.* Bethesda, MD: Author. Retrieved from http://www.nasponline.org/standards/2010standards/1_%20Ethical%20Principles.pdf

National Association of Social Workers. (NASW) (2008). *Code of ethics of the national association of social workers.* Washington, DC: Author. Retrieved from https://www.socialworkers.org/pubs/code/code.asp

National Education Association. (2002–2010). *Code of ethics.* Washington, DC: Author. Retrieved from http://www.nea.org/home/30442.htm

National School Boards Association. (2009). *Beliefs and policies of the national school boards association.* Alexandria, VA: Author. Retrieved from http://www.nsba.org/About/NSBAGovernance/BeliefsandPolicies.pdf

8 Training School Professionals to Work with Lesbian, Gay, Bisexual, Transgender, and Questioning Students and Parents

Joy S. Whitman

Creating schools that are safe and provide a learning environment relatively free of violence and harassment for lesbian, gay, bisexual, transgender, and questioning (LGBTQ) students and students with lesbian, gay, bisexual, and transgender (LGBT) parents takes a community of professional adults actively advocating for and implementing safe school policies and interventions. Administrators, teachers, school counselors, social workers, school psychologists, and other school personnel[1] have a responsibility to these students; yet how prepared these school professionals are to meet that responsibility is debatable. Without proper pre-service and in-service training, school professionals likely will not know how to create a safe school or offer support to LGBTQ students and families. The issues of preparation of school professionals in their pre-service programs and in their various positions in schools are addressed in this chapter. Additionally, recommendations are offered for preparation programs across disciplines and for in-service trainings. Existing national and state workshops and trainings will be reviewed.

LGBTQ Pre-Service Training of School Professionals

Given the relatively recent social and psychological shift in perspective related to LGBTQ individuals, it is understandable that school professional preparation programs are still catching up to these changes, to the needs of LGBTQ individuals, and to the adaptations required in school district and state policies. It is no longer ethical or professional to ignore LGBTQ students in the preparation of school professionals. However, there is variation among professional training programs in regard to how they educate their pre-service students, which speaks to the wide range of mandates from their professional organizations representing the variety of school personnel. Additionally, most of the focus on training to date has been directed toward infusion of lesbian and gay issues rather than gender identity, though a growing body of research is indicating a trend toward addressing the needs of bisexual and transgender individuals (Goodrich & Luke, 2009; Graff & Stufft, 2011; McCabe & Rubinson, 2008; Walker & Prince, 2010).

School-Based Mental Health Professionals

Major professional organizations for school-based mental health professionals, such as the American Counseling Association (ACA), the American Psychological Association (APA), and the National Association of Social Workers (NASW) have position statements about ethical mental health treatment of LGBTQ individuals. More specifically, each organization addresses LGBTQ issues in the schools and the ethical responsibilities of practitioners within the school (see Chapter 7 of this volume for more information). To this end, mental health practitioner preparation programs must address these issues in their curriculum and practice-based courses (e.g., practicum, fieldwork, and internship).

The reality, however, is that preparation programs are uneven in their attention to LGBTQ issues in their curriculum. Often the inclusion of LGBTQ issues is found in courses focused on multicultural counseling as a single lecture topic or included as a one-time lecture in other classes (Israel & Selvidge, 2003; Savage, Prout, & Chard, 2004; Sherry, Whilde, & Patton, 2005). Graduate students and practicing mental health professionals frequently report absence of LGBTQ issues in their training programs (Bahr, Brish, & Croteau, 2000; McCabe & Rubinson, 2008; Walker & Prince, 2010). Attention to LGBTQ issues in practice-based courses is limited, with few studies indicating an intentional approach to ensuring school-based mental health professionals are prepared to deliver affirmative counseling services to or to advocate for LGBTQ students (Buhrke & Douce, 1991; Goodrich & Luke, 2009; Messinger, 2004).

Studies on the inclusion of LGBTQ issues in school-based mental health preparation programs indicate there is much work to be done in this area. In a study of 288 school psychologists, Savage et al. (2004) found that though relatively positive attitudes were held by participants, knowledge of specific LGBTQ student issues was low to moderate, and "85% reported no preparation or education in training programs related to lesbian and gay male issues" (p. 204). Though 75% of the respondents stated they felt prepared to serve LGBTQ students, they also reported lack of knowledge about academic success as it relates to sexual orientation. In a study of counseling students introduced to a training module on LGBTQ issues and counseling, Rutter, Estrada, Ferguson, and Diggs (2008) found an increase in students' knowledge and skills but not in their awareness. Research in social work offers mixed results in terms of knowledge, attitude, and skill change after educational interventions (Cramer, 1997; Dongvillo & Ligon, 2001; Lim & Johnson, 2001).

Preparation programs in counseling, social work, and psychology have begun to respond to this need, and overall, there has been an increase in separate courses on LGBTQ issues, either as full- or partial-credit courses or workshops (Israel & Hackett, 2004; Pearson, 2003; Whitman, 1995). Common among most of these courses are the following topics: ethical and professional responsibilities of serving LGBTQ clients; basic information about LGBTQ individuals; exploration of pre-service mental health professionals' biases and stereotypes; appropriate and affirmative counseling interventions; and information about advocacy and social justice practices to make communities safer for LGBTQ clients. Courses in counseling and psychology often follow the model of multicultural competence, which includes a focus on knowledge, awareness, and skills (Sue, Arredondo, & McDavis, 1992). These components have been well studied in regard to the development of competence in serving ethnically and racially diverse populations of clients and are just beginning to be understood as critical components for inclusion in LGBTQ affirmative counseling (Bidell, 2005; Grove, 2009; Israel & Selvidge, 2003).

It is clear from this brief review of the literature that school-based mental health professional preparation is still nascent in addressing an intentional and comprehensive integration of LGBTQ issues in its curriculum. Though mandated by their respective professional organizations to be affirmative in the treatment of LGBTQ individuals, the preparation of these professionals to do so remains an area of needed curriculum, program evaluation, and advocacy for inclusive training.

Educators

In 1991, Sears studied the attitudes of pre-service teachers toward lesbian and gay individuals and found that 8 out of 10 felt negatively toward these populations and that knowledge about lesbian and gay issues was minimal. He called for the profession to better serve sexual minority youth and for teacher preparation programs to adequately prepare educators to do so. Now 20 years later, where does the profession stand in regard to pre-service teacher preparation of LGBTQ issues in the schools?

Research indicates movement forward but still much work to be done. Studies across the Unites States (U.S.) of pre-service teachers still show educators need to be educated about specific issues and to explore and develop their attitudes toward LGBTQ individuals. Koch's (2000) study in Illinois of 813 pre-service teachers found that only 35% answered the knowledge section of the survey correctly with over 50% acknowledging a need for more training on LGBTQ issues to effectively work with students. Sherwin and Jennings (2006) reviewed public secondary teacher preparation programs for inclusion of sexual orientation material in curriculum and found that 40% of the programs studied (77 programs) did not include any information. Wyatt, Oswalt, White, and Peterson's (2008) survey of 334 teacher candidates in Texas revealed that 69.2% were only moderately informed about sexuality issues. In a study of 200 pre-service teachers from the Midwest regarding their attitudes, level of homophobia, and knowledge of LGBTQ issues, Mudrey and Medina-Adams (2008) found results consistent with earlier studies that more knowledge did not translate into more positive attitudes and perceptions.

Szalacha (2004) offered a review of the research in teacher preparation and programs around LGBTQ issues and noted that most programs took one of three approaches to inclusion in curriculum: safety, equity, or critical theory. She observed that the majority of preparation programs focused on safety and equity in schools and incorporated LGBTQ issues in courses on cultural diversity and education. Sherwin and Jennings' (2006) national study of teacher preparation programs was consistent with Szalacha's review, noting that 90.3% of the programs included the topic of sexual orientation in their foundation courses. However, they pointed out that inclusion in teaching and practica courses was only present in 17.9% of the programs, a stark contrast to the number of programs including other forms of diversity in these practice courses (92.3%). They concluded that "even among inclusive programs, it appears that sexual orientation as a diversity topic tended to be isolated in foundation courses" (p. 213) and that "the closer preservice teachers moved to actual interactions with sexual-minority students and parents/guardians (as well as homophobic/heterosexist school cultures), the less instruction regarding sexual orientation diversity they received" (pp. 213–214).

Given that the inclusion of sexual orientation is typically isolated to foundation courses, Athanases and Larrabee (2003) explored the effectiveness of this approach by analyzing the responses of 97 students after having been introduced to lesbian and gay (LG) issues in three education classes with an equity perspective. Toward the later part of the course, classes were devoted to engaging students via the use of discussions, readings, guest speaker, video, and weekly reflections around LG issues in the schools. Athanases and Larrabee found that students valued gaining knowledge about LG youth and issues in schools and that as a result of the class, "60 students (or 61.9%) reported ways that they were beginning to wear the mantle of advocate for LG youth" (p. 249).

A recently developed training offered through a teacher education program at Syracuse University's School of Education (SOE) and primarily created as a vehicle for professional development for in-service teachers, is called Reduction of Stigma in Schools (RSIS) (Payne & Smith, 2011). The program is creative in its vision of utilizing graduate education students and professors in the SOE to deliver workshops and trainings to teachers in the schools (a more complete discussion of the program is offered later in the chapter). Notably, in regard to training of teachers, the program utilizes graduate education students as facilitators of the workshops. These students are in a unique position to not only learn about LGBTQ issues in schools, but also through active engagement and partnership with professors, to deliver that information to teachers. This model has the potential for greater impact, and potentially could be infused throughout teacher education programs.

Administrators

Research on the training of school administrators around LGBTQ issues reveals a similar picture to the preparation of the other school professionals discussed in this chapter. The advent of a social justice and equity focus for educational administration preparation programs is relatively new, and as a result, there exists no stand-alone course with a specific focus on LGBTQ issues. In general, preparation programs focus on equity issues for all students and prepare administrators to be leaders for social justice (McKenzie et al., 2008). The aim is to abide by the Association for Supervision and Curriculum Development's (ASCD) position to address the needs of the whole child and to do so by providing an environment that is "safe, supportive, and caring" (2005, third paragraph) and that attends to students' health and well-being.

Capper et al., (2006) reviewed the literature on the inclusion of sexual orientation in educational leadership preparation and found only five articles that address this topic. Courses focused on equity embedded LGBTQ issues in the schools in a manner similar to how these issues were included in courses on multicultural education and counseling (Brown, 2006; Capper et al. 2006; McKenzie, et al., 2008). In response to the dearth of attention specific to LGBTQ issues in educational leadership, Capper et al. (2006) offered a comprehensive discussion regarding their recommendations about how to include these issues in preparation programs from the social justice perspective consistent in the literature. Many of these recommendations were similar to ones found in other school professional programs, and will be included in the following section of this chapter.

Critical Components of LGBTQ Preparation and In-service Programs

There are a variety of key components necessary to include in the training of pre-service and practicing school professionals around LGBTQ issues. Research of existing pre-service and professional development programs repeatedly indicates that education, across professional disciplines, needs to include the following: specific information about appropriate language and terminology; issues of identity development; information on the school experiences of LGBTQ youth; opportunities to explore one's biases and misconceptions; information on federal, state, and district laws and policies; methods of advocating for change; and mechanisms for providing support (Capper et al., 2006; Israel & Selvidge, 2003; McCabe & Rubinson, 2008; Szalacha, 2004). Often what is recommended, particularly derived from the school-based mental health field, is that professionals gain knowledge, awareness, and skill to deliver culturally competent services to LGBTQ individuals. It also is recommended that adult learning styles be taken into consideration during professional development activities (Fisher & Kennedy, 2012).

Adult Learning

How information is delivered to adult learners is equally as important as the content of the training. For practicing school professionals, trainings offered by school professionals in their respective discipline are recommended whenever possible (Biegel, 2010; Payne & Smith, 2011). This is especially significant for teachers who respond better to in-services delivered by other educators who can "establish trust and convince educators that heteronormativity is an educational issue that is relevant for their daily classroom practice" (Payne & Smith, 2011, p. 185). Supplementing this approach is the suggestion to offer repeated in-service and follow up workshops (Szalacha, 2004). Biegel (2010) suggests fostering "collaborative dialogue between educators" (p. 134) which facilitates "brainstorming among them regarding new strategies and follow up meetings to share results" (p. 134). For preparation programs, this can be similar to the concept of infusing LGBTQ issues throughout the program, including practicum and internship classes, rather than isolating the topic in one course or to one or two class sessions within a course (Bahr et al., 2000; Logie, Bridge, & Bridge, 2007; Matthews, 2005; Savage et al., 2004). Additional mechanisms for information delivery will be discussed in conjunction with the content that follows.

Knowledge

There are a variety of topics about LGBTQ issues in general and specific to schools that can be included in any training of school professionals. The following discussion is not exhaustive of these topics, and other chapters of this volume provide additional ideas for content.

Language and Terminology. A basic step in working with LGBTQ individuals is the use of appropriate language and terminology to communicate effectively and respectfully. As the social and political LGBTQ movements have progressed, language has changed, and as a vehicle to connect with LGBTQ students and families, it is important that school professionals use terms that are current, communicate acceptance and inclusivity, and create safety.

Graff and Stufft (2011) recommend that open discussions addressing language be incorporated in pre-service teacher education. These kinds of discussions can be initiated by offering all pre-service and in-service professionals basic handouts of current terminology (Whitman, Horn, & Boyd, 2007). Lists of appropriate terms can be found in safe space trainings (see section of this chapter on existing professional development programs), and terminology match-up exercises are often incorporated into trainings, offering adult learners an opportunity to interactively and in a consultative manner learn appropriate language for LGBTQ individuals.

Identity Development and Resources. Development of sexual and gender identity for LGBTQ youth is crucial to the understanding of working with LGBTQ individuals. There are a variety of models of sexual and transgender identity development (see Chapters 3 and 5 of this volume), and inclusive in many models of identity development are ways in which professionals and allies can intervene to facilitate healthy development of these identities (Chun & Singh, 2010; Lev, 2004; Troiden, 1989). Important to attend to are the multiple identities youth embody, and Athanases and Larrabee (2003) recommend connecting these identities during trainings. By doing so, school professionals begin to understand how cultural, racial, and ethnic identities can complicate the development of healthy sexual and gender identities and be a source of resilience.

Knowledge of resources LGBTQ students will need at the various stages of identity development is equally important to include in training. These resources can be both internal to the school, such as a Gay-Straight Alliance (GSA), and external to the school, such as a chapter of Parents, Families, and Friends of Lesbians and Gays (PFLAG). Given the limited resources schools often have for LGBTQ students, age appropriate community resources can facilitate the healthy incorporation of an LGBTQ identity and can offer support for school professionals and families. Local resources that serve LGBTQ individuals of color can be referenced and, if possible, members invited to speak. If local resources or guest speakers are difficult to obtain, high quality online resources or videos can be utilized.

Information about identity development can be introduced through guided readings and didactic instruction using the literature cited above. Additionally, research has shown the effectiveness of the use of panels and guest speakers in LGBTQ trainings in the service of creating empathy for the experience of LGBTQ individuals and their families and in making the information personal and accessible to school professionals (Athanases & Larrabee, 2003; Nelson & Krieger, 1997; Swank & Raiz, 2007). Through dialogue, LGTBQ youth and individuals can discuss real life examples of their own development and ways in which they have been positively affected by ally intervention, and PFLAG members can present ways in which they have offered support to families and school professionals. Doing so provides trainees an opportunity to make personal connections with LGBTQ individuals, and the research cited above continues to indicate that knowing someone who is LGBTQ can create change in attitude for heterosexual individuals.

It is suggested that videos of LGBTQ youth and families be offered in educational programs and professional workshops to augment the inclusion of guest speakers in trainings (Capper et al., 2006; Whitman et al., 2007). Often recommended videos are *It's Elementary* (Chasnoff, 1996), *Let's Get Real* (Cohen, 2004), *That's a Family* (Cohen, 2000), and *Gay Youth* (Walton, 1992).

LGBTQ Issues. There are a variety of social and psychological consequences with which LGBTQ students may grapple as a result of coming out in a heterosexist and homoprejudice environment, and other chapters of this volume offer detailed accounts of these issues. Including information about these topics in the training of school professionals is crucial to ensure appropriate intervention and advocacy is instituted in schools.

Specifically, all trainings must present the statistics and signs of depression, suicidality, homelessness, and substance abuse for LGBTQ youth, and given the epidemic of bullying leading to depression, suicide, and academic failure (e.g., Kosciw, Greytak, Diaz, & Bartkiewicz, 2010), school professionals need to be aware of the connection between these behaviors and consequences. Information about recent legal cases as a result of anti-gay violence and the resulting impact on school policy is equally important to include (Biegel, 2010; Capper et al., 2006; National School Boards Association [NSBA], 2004). This knowledge will build empathy and provide data school professionals can use to advocate for change in their schools. School climate reports are useful to integrate into pre- and in-service trainings as they offer national data on the lived experiences of LGBTQ students (GLSEN and Harris Interactive, 2008; Kosciw et al., 2010). State and local information, when available, ought to be included to make personal these crucial issues.

Though the data is critical to present, how it is presented to adult learners is important to consider. Certainly guided readings of reports and articles are needed and act as resources for future use. Incorporation of videos as previously discussed will provide a more personal approach. Whitman et al. (2007) also offer an interactive mechanism of data delivery included in an intensive training for school professionals. Through the use of a modified Jeopardy game, statistics and basic information are presented, and teams of school professionals compete against one another as they learn about the experiences of LGBTQ students.

Finally, it is only recently that research has begun to offer information about LGBTQ youth resilience in the face of these daunting statistics (see Chapter 4 of this volume). How youth use their experiences of oppression and discrimination to gain strength and succeed needs to be presented to school professionals in order to offer a balanced picture of LGBTQ individuals' lives. In doing so, school professionals can integrate a strengths-based approach into their interventions and offer a more optimistic perspective with their students and in their schools and classrooms. Inviting professionals from the various disciplines to discuss how they integrated a strengths-based perspective into their work can offer trainees concrete ways in which they can incorporate this approach into theirs.

Awareness

An outcome of engaging pre-service and school professionals in conversations about LGBTQ issues is the uncovering of their attitudes about LGBTQ individuals. These conversations are provocative in activating feelings about sexuality and gender, specifically as they relate to marginalized identities. Therefore, it is difficult to discuss these topics without attention to the thoughts and feelings school professionals have about LGBTQ individuals, and avoiding these issues is not beneficial. Additionally, given the research on the negative beliefs and attitudes school professionals often report about LGBTQ individuals (Logie, et al., 2007; McCabe & Rubinson, 2008; Riggs, Rosenthal, & Smith-Bonahue, 2011; Swank & Raiz, 2007), it is crucial to any training that attitudes be addressed. Included in these discussions can be attention to the sexual and gender identity development of pre-service and school professionals.

Biases and Misconceptions. Exploring biases, assumptions, stereotypes, and attitudes about LGBTQ individuals requires a delicate balance between creating a learning environment safe enough to allow open discussions of reactions and beliefs and one that facilitates evaluation of these perspectives. Inviting school professionals to be curious about their attitudes and to question the origin of their perspectives is integral to training. Instruction can include questions for professionals to consider and can consist of the following:

• How are you aware of your heterosexism, sexism, biphobia, transphobia, and homoprejudice?
• How do your cultural and religious values impact your views?
• Given what you have learned about LGBTQ people, what misinformation did you previously acquire and how did that impact your beliefs and attitudes?
• How do you see your own sexual and gender identity development impacting your understanding of LGBTQ individuals?
• What experiences have you had with LGBTQ individuals that have informed your values and attitudes?

Implicit in these questions is the belief that none of us are exempt from integrating these stereotypes, biases, and attitudes into our understanding of LGBTQ individuals and that we are capable of changing them. Use of values clarification exercises have been effective in facilitating this type of exploration and conversation (Graff & Stufft, 2011).

It is during these points in training when engaging in empathy building activities can be effective. An often-used tool to create empathy is a guided imagery exercise of the world as predominately LGBTQ and the experience of someone who identifies as heterosexual facing the obstacles often presented to LGBTQ individuals. This includes being attracted to someone of the opposite gender, deciding to come out as heterosexual, managing the fear and relational consequences of that decision, managing prejudice and harassment, and so on. This exercise can help school professionals understand the psychological and social implications of coming out and managing a marginalized identity, and the often reported impact on mental health and academic failure.

Other means to help school professionals appreciate the struggles faced by LGBTQ individuals and assist in debunking their stereotypes and challenging their values are through the use of videos and guest speakers (Athanases & Larrabee, 2003; Dessel, 2010). Included in the list of guest speakers can be religious leaders to address those professionals for whom religious values conflict sharply with accepting LGBTQ individuals. These guests can speak to this issue and more personally explore how school professionals can be both religious and supportive of LGBTQ issues.

Finally, role-playing various school scenarios can facilitate the creation of empathy and allow for pre-service and school professionals to experience the perspectives of LGBTQ individuals while also practicing appropriate responses (Kocarek & Pelling, 2003). An example of a role-play could be a coming out scenario in which a queer teen comes out to a school counselor when discussing his fear of coming out to his parents and consequently being homeless. Role-plays can be tailored to the various pre-service professional disciplines and target real issues presented within the context of school professionals' work places.

Awareness of One's Own Sexual and Gender Identity Development. Frequently individuals who do not experience marginalization because of sexual orientation or gender identity do not explore their own sexual and gender identity development (Buhrke & Douce, 1991). As a result, they are not aware of the intentional process involved in identity discovery or of their own beliefs about their sexual orientation and gender identity. Consequently, they may not be attentive to how these beliefs can impact the experiences of LGBTQ individuals with whom they interact.

Exposure to the literature on sexual identity and gender identity development is an important training component for school professionals, and discussing their developmental processes in light of this information can be a helpful training process. Guided exercises that map professionals' journeys of sexual and gender identity development can be included, as well as activities that address how they manifest their gender identity (Butler, 1990). Highlighting how sexuality and gender are enacted in one's life can bring to awareness how significant these identities are to one's self-concept.

Skill

Preparation and training programs for school professionals must include components targeted toward transforming knowledge and awareness into action. Doing so offers these professionals tools to effect change, to facilitate growth for LGBTQ students, and to promote safety in their schools. There are similar and unique skills required across disciplines, and this section will discuss what is needed for all school professionals and what is specific to each.

Mechanisms of Support. It is essential that LGBTQ students receive support from school professionals, as it is often the case that the presence of a supportive adult in school results in higher academic achievement (Kosciw et al., 2010). Being visible as an ally is critical, and trainings can offer simple advice on how to do so. For example, regardless of the school professional's discipline, displaying LGBTQ symbols, books, posters, and other visibly identifiable ally indicators communicates to all students that she or he is a safe person with whom students can connect. Chapter 14 of this volume provides in-depth information about school professionals as allies and advocates.

It is not unusual for LGBTQ students to come out to teachers and school-based mental health professionals whom they perceive as safe (Kosciw et al., 2010; McCabe & Rubinson, 2008). Learning how to listen to these youth, provide resources appropriate for their needs, and support them as they navigate potential challenges with their families, peers, faculty, and staff are critical skills for all school professionals. School professionals who have successfully implemented these skills can be invited to speak, especially if these individuals are from the schools in which the trainings occur. For administrators, learning to listen and problem solve with students and parents so as to fully grasp the full picture of what is occurring rather than reacting prematurely to parents' or personnel's complaints or students' difficulties is particularly important (Goodman, 2005).

For school-based mental health professionals, information about affirmative counseling practices must be integrated into preparation programs and in-service trainings (see Chapter 12 of this volume). Using case studies and role-plays typical of issues encountered by LGBTQ students provides pre-service and school professionals the opportunity to apply their newly acquired knowledge, awareness, and techniques. Appropriate and ethical use of assessment and diagnosis is imperative to guard against misdiagnosis of LGBTQ students whose anxiety or depression may be natural psychological reactions to the challenges of coming out and managing multiple identities (Bahr, et al., 2000; Logie et al., 2007).

Policy and Advocacy. Taking a social justice stance and enacting change in schools requires an intentional action plan. Chapters 9 and 14 of this volume provide school professionals with specific ways in which they can make schools safe and advocate for change. Preparation programs and in-service trainings can include the suggestions included in these chapters. This would comprise of a review of the current policies around sexual orientation and gender expression. Pre-service and in-service trainings can facilitate what Capper et al. (2006) describe as an "LGBT equity audit" (p. 5) of their school. Such an audit includes exploring district and school anti-harassment policies as they pertain to sexual and gender identity, reviewing holdings in the library related to LGBTQ issues, evaluating forms to see if they are inclusive of LGBTQ families, and assessing the treatment of staff who identify as LGBTQ.

Building on a school inclusion and safety assessment, training can guide school professionals toward taking action. There are various ways in which this can be conducted, and many of the workshops for school professionals include action plans (see professional development section). One organization to use as a resource is the Midwest Academy (n.d.), an institute that teaches strategic planning and ways to take action. Their chart for strategic planning can be introduced as a mechanism for school professionals to collaborate across disciplines and to map a layered plan for the school. This concrete and hands-on activity clarifies what resources schools possess, what changes are needed, what is needed to make these changes, who is responsible, and what partners are needed for action.

Educators can begin these changes by making their classrooms safer. Both in teacher preparation programs and professional development workshops, it is important to address how LGBTQ issues are included in the curriculum, how teachers intervene when anti-LGBTQ language is used, and how LGBT families are integrated into the school. Teachers who have successfully navigated these issues can be invited to discuss obstacles and concerns and how they worked with administrators and parents to make these changes. Transforming curriculum during a professional development workshop will offer teachers tangible results which they can bring back to their classrooms and use to advocate for change with their colleagues. Teacher preparation programs can easily incorporate inclusion of LGBTQ issues in all courses addressing curriculum planning and instruction as well as practice courses. Chapter 10 of this volume addresses LGBTQ-responsive classroom curriculum.

School-based mental health professionals can evaluate the forms and psychological assessments they use to ensure they are inclusive and respectful of LGBTQ individuals, and trainings can provide opportunities for discussion and examples of inclusive material. School-based mental health professionals can ensure they offer large group guidance and classroom lessons that address bullying, that include language that does not assume heteronormative behavior, and that speak to the unique needs and challenges facing LGBTQ students (Goodrich & Luke, 2009). Examples of these lessons can be included in preparation and professional development programs, and school-based mental health professionals who have successfully delivered these lessons in schools can be invited to present their work.

Finally, administrators are in unique positions to make the widest systemic change ensuring safety and inclusion for LGBTQ students, families, and staff. Capper et al. (2006) offer a comprehensive approach to integrating LGBTQ issues in educational leadership preparation programs, and many of their suggestions can be incorporated into professional development workshops as well. With respect to advocacy, preparation programs and professional trainings can focus on assisting leaders to better understand and keep current with legal responsibilities toward LGBTQ individuals, to implement necessary changes, and to speak to parents who might object to these changes. Incorporating readings that address these issues (e.g., National School Boards Association, 2004; GLSEN and Harris Interactive, 2008) and engaging in dialogue with principals who have actively made changes in their schools can be considered.

Existing Professional Development Programs

Both nationally and locally, programs have been developed to provide training to school professionals. Through state and national organizations, school professionals can gain post-graduate trainings that will include many of the components discussed in this chapter. School professionals can contact either national or local organizations for consultation and training.

National Organizations. One of the most recognized organizations addressing LGBTQ issues in schools is the Gay, Lesbian, and Straight Education Network (GLSEN), established in 1990. It "strives to assure that each member of every school community is valued and respected regardless of sexual orientation or gender identity/expression" (2011, para 1). In doing so, GLSEN has conducted national research on the experiences of LGBTQ students and students with LGBT parents and created trainings and resources for school professionals in order to institute greater safety and learning opportunities. They have created both a Safe Space Kit (GLSEN, n.d.), which offers ways in which educators can create safety in their schools and be allies to their students, and a packaged training, called the GLSEN Lunchbox (2005), focused chiefly on the preparation of school professionals and community members. Inclusive in the Lunchbox are more than 40 exercises that can be tailored to the needs of the professional and of the school. Components include but are not exclusive to (a) exploration of one's own biases and stereotypes about sexual orientation and gender; (b) instruction focused on appropriate terminology and facts about LGBTQ individuals; (c) education about bullying, anti-harassment, and mental health and social needs; and (d) engagement in advocacy and policy assessment. Use of the major components of adult education is infused throughout the various modules, such as inclusion of speaker panels, interactive exercises, and didactic instruction. The Lunchbox also addresses the needs at various levels of education so that school professionals in elementary, middle, and high school can tailor their professional development activities to the age-level of the students with whom they work.

GLSEN is the only national organization expressly focused on the experiences of LGBTQ students and students with LGBT parents in schools. However, a national organization that addresses the needs of LGBTQ individuals of all ages and their families is Parents, Families, and Friends of Lesbians and Gays (PFLAG). Within its structure, PFLAG offers a certification program to its members called *Cultivating Respect* (PFLAG, n.d.), a training program that equips them to enter into schools to provide professional development. The program prepares members to present personal stories, factual information, and mechanisms for policy and school change. Because PFLAG has state and community chapters, it can tailor the information to the policies and laws current for the school in which it offers the training.

The National Education Association (NEA), an association for educators and school staff, offers professional development to build safe learning communities for LGBTQ students. The training is one that addresses safety, bias, and LGBT issues and consists of four workshops, either offered as a series or as stand-alone programs (NEA, 2010). All but one module are directed toward all school professionals and focus on (a) how bias is created, is maintained, and can be combated in schools; (b) how LGBT issues intersect with race and gender; (c) how communication around LGBT issues is crucial and ways to effectively engage in these conversations; and (d) how to infuse LGBT issues into curriculum. The mechanisms for delivery of the information include use of videos, hands-on activities, and modeling of effective strategies.

Regional/Local Programs. In 1993, the state of Massachusetts, at the direction of the Department of Elementary and Secondary Education and the Governor's Commission on Gay and Lesbian Youth, created the Safe Schools Program (SSP) for gay and lesbian students. According to the Commission, "teachers, guidance counselors, and all school staff should be equipped with the training necessary to respond to the needs of gay and lesbian students, including protecting them from harassment and violence, and intervening to prevent suicide and dropping out" (1993, p. 29). The SSP is at the forefront of programs that address the safety of lesbian and gay students and has a four-prong approach to its mission. One of these components includes professional development for school professionals, ranging from one-hour sessions to half-day retreats. Workshops are designed to help school professionals to explore their attitudes toward LGBTQ individuals, to avoid discriminatory attitudes, to provide information about mental health and other needs of lesbian and gay youth, and to offer resources for responding to LGBTQ student needs.

Just four years after the initiation of the SSP in Massachusetts, the Out for Equity Program in the Saint Paul Public School District in Minnesota was adopted (Horowitz & Loehnig, 2005). It offers a variety of programs in the service of creating safety in schools for LGBTQ students, one of which is directed toward staff development. This service includes topics similar to other trainings, such as inclusion of LGBTQ issues in curriculum, management of homophobic harassment, discussion of LGBTQ issues at all school levels, and institution of school policy to create safety. The organization created a Safe Schools Manual (Horowitz & Loehnig, 2005), which incorporates a variety of training activities. These activities help professionals explore their own attitudes and behaviors and help them create GSAs/support groups and address family issues.

In Illinois, the Illinois Safe Schools Alliance (ISSA) is an organization whose mission is similar to other organizations focused on creating safety in schools for LGBTQ students. The ISSA offers trainings for school professionals in their schools and provides a three-day workshop for educators called the Summer Institute (Whitman et al., 2007).

Although school-based trainings vary in regard to length (from two hours to day-long trainings depending on need and request), all trainings, including the Summer Institute, include basic and necessary information, such as LGBTQ terminology, legal responsibilities of school professionals, data on bullying and anti-gay behavior in schools, and activism toward policy and climate change. Interactive and didactic activities are utilized to address adult learning, and the Summer Institute offers a hands-on exercise to facilitate school-specific action planning for attendees.

Using the existing literature and programs focused on educating school professionals on LGBTQ issues, Payne and Smith (2011) created the Reduction of Stigma in Schools Program (RSIS) in 2006. This program connects schools with university educators and pre-service teachers at Syracuse University in New York in order to provide professional development in the schools. Innovative in its use of connecting the School of Education at Syracuse University with schools in its surrounding communities, Payne and Smith's use of an "educator-to-educator model" (p. 176) brings tailored trainings to schools and makes contact with teachers who might not typically or voluntarily attend a workshop addressing safety for LGBTQ students. These professional development workshops leverage the needs of the schools against potentially resistant school professionals and do so by "creating opportunities for colleagues to engage in dialogue about how the material applies to their specific context" (p. 176). Initially focused on reaching high school teachers, the program has extended its outreach to include administrators, counselors, psychologists, and social workers in the schools, has expanded its topics to address transgender youth, and has begun to include middle and elementary schools. It also bases its trainings less on legal obligations of schools to create safety for LGBTQ students and more on sociological research and the experiences within the school. In doing so, real-life examples of bullying and anti-gay attitudes and the resulting effect on the school community serve as motivators for change. Finally, presentations are research based and include topics focusing on stigma, school climate and academic success, heteronormativity, and mechanisms for change. Film clips of LGBTQ students' experiences are embedded within these presentations.

Online Training. Several organizations offer online training modules that can be used for professional development efforts in schools or in preparation programs. Through their website, the National Association of School Psychologists (NASP; www.nasponline.org/advocacy/glb.aspx) offers a series of four training modules on LGBTQ issues, including: social challenges; self-acceptance and coming out; mental health issues and counseling; and creating a positive school climate. The National LGBT Health Education Center, which is part of The Fenway Institute, also offers a series of online training modules (www.lgbthealtheducation.org/training/learning-modules). Though these modules are designed for healthcare professionals, they contain information that can be easily adapted for use in schools. The modules include information on: ending invisibility; taking a history and providing risk reduction counseling; health promotion and disease prevention; caring for LGBTQ youth; and promoting the health of LGBT families.

Conclusion

Pre-service and in-service training of school professionals are critical steps in changing the school climate for LGBTQ students and students with LGBT parents School professionals can only truly work effectively with LGBTQ individuals once they understand their biases and misconceptions, have knowledge about LGBTQ individuals' experiences, and develop strategies to make all school environments safe and inclusive. Through intentional training in these issues, school professionals will have the tools to transform their practices.

Note

1 School professionals refers to administrators, teachers, school counselors, social workers, and psychologists. School-based mental health professionals refers to school counselors, social workers, and psychologists.

References

Association for Supervision and Curriculum Development. (2005). The whole child: A framework for education in the 21st century. Retrieved from http://www.ascd.org/publications/newsletters/policy-priorities/feb05/num40/toc.aspx

Athanases, S. Z., & Larrabee, T. G. (2003). Toward a consistent stance in teaching for equity: Learning to advocate for lesbian and gay-identified youth. *Teaching and Teacher Education, 19*, 237–261. doi:10.1016/S0742-051X(02)00098-7

Bahr, M. W., Brish, B., & Croteau, J. M. (2000). Addressing sexual orientation and professional ethics in the training of school psychologists in school and university settings. *School Psychology Review, 29*(2), 217–230. Retrieved from http://www.nasponline.org/publications/spr/abstract.aspx?ID=1541

Bidell, M. P. (2005). The sexual orientation counselor competency scale: Assessing attitudes, skills, and knowledge of counselors working with lesbian, gay, and bisexual clients. *Counselor Education and Supervision, 44*, 267–279.

Biegel, S. (2010). *The right to be out: Sexual orientation and gender identity in America's public schools*. Minneapolis, MN: University of Minnesota Press.

Brown, K. M. (2006). Leadership for social justice and equity: Evaluating a transformative framework and andragogy. *Educational Administration Quarterly, 42*(5), 700–745. doi:10.1177/0013161X06290650

Buhrke, R. A., & Douce, L. A. (1991). Training issues for counseling psychologists in working with lesbian women and gay men. *The Counseling Psychologist, 19*, 216–234. doi:10.1177/0011000091192006

Butler, J. (1990). *Gender trouble*. New York, NY: Routledge.

Capper, C. A., Alston, J., Gause, C. P., Koschoreck, J., Lopez, G., Lugg, C. A., & McKenzie, K. B. (2006). Integrating gay/lesbian/bisexual/transgender topics and their intersections with other areas of difference into the leadership preparation curriculum: Practical ideas and strategies. *Journal of School Leadership, 16*(2), 142–157. Retrieved from https://rowman.com/page/JSL

Chasnoff, D. (Producer). (1996). *It's elementary : Talking about gay issues in school*. [DVD]. United States: GroundSpark.

Chun, K., & Singh. A. A. (2010). The bisexual youth of color intersecting identities development model: A contextual approach to understanding multiple marginalization experiences. *Journal of Bisexuality, 10*(4), 429–451. doi:10.1080/15299716.2010.521059

Cohen, H. S. (Producer). (2000). *That's a family*. [DVD]. United States: GroundSpark.

Cohen, H. S. (Producer). (2004). *Let's get real*. [DVD]. United States: GroundSpark.

Cramer, E. (1997). Effects of an educational unit about lesbian identity development and disclosure in a social work methods course. *Journal of Social Work Education, 33*, 461–472.

Dessel, A. G. (2010). Effects of intergroup dialogue: Public school teachers and sexual orientation prejudice. *Small Group Research, 41*(5), 556–592. doi:10.1177/1046496410369560

Dongvillo, J., & Ligon, J. (2001). Exploring the effectiveness of teaching techniques with lesbian and gay content in the social work curriculum. *The Journal of Baccalaureate Social Work, 6*, 115–124.

Fisher, E. S., & Kennedy, K. S. (2012). *Responsive school practices to support lesbian, gay, bisexual, transgender, and questioning students and families.* New York, NY: Routledge Publishing.

Gay, Lesbian, and Straight Education Network. (n.d.). *Safe Space Kit.* Retrieved from http://www.glsen.org/cgi-bin/iowa/all/library/record/1641.html?state=tools&type=tools

Gay, Lesbian, and Straight Education Network. (2005). *GLSEN Lunchbox: A Comprehensive Training Program for Ending Anti-LGBT Bias in Schools.* Retrieved from http://www.glsen.org/cgi-bin/iowa/all/library/record/1748.html?state=tools&type=tools

Gay, Lesbian, and Straight Education Network. (2011). *Our mission.* Retrieved from http://www.glsen.org/cgi-bin/iowa/all/about/history/index.html

Gay, Lesbian, and Straight Education Network and Harris Interactive. (2008). *The principal's perspective: School safety, bullying and harassment, a survey of public school principals.* New York, NY: GLSEN.

Goodman, J. M. (2005). Homophobia prevention and intervention in elementary schools: A principal's responsibility. *Journal of Gay & Lesbian Issues in Education, 3*(1), 111–116. doi:10.1300/J367v03n01_12

Goodrich, K. M., & Luke, M. (2009). LGBTQ responsive school counseling. *Journal of LGBT Issues in Counseling, 3*(2), 113–127. doi:10.1080/15538600903005284

Governor's Commission on Gay and Lesbian Youth. (1993). Making schools safe for gay and lesbian youth: Breaking the silence in schools and in families. Boston, MA: Author.

Graff, C., & Stufft, D. (2011). Increasing visibility for LGBTQ students: What schools can do to create inclusive classroom communities. *Current Issues in Education, 14*(1). Retrieved from http://cie.asu.edu/ojs/index.php/cieatasu/article/view/636

Grove, J. (2009). How competent are trainee and newly qualified counsellors to work with lesbian, gay, and bisexual clients and what do they perceive as their most effective learning experiences? *Counselling & Psychotherapy Research, 9*, 78–85. doi:10.1080/14733140802490622

Horowitz, A., & Loehnig, G. (2005). *Safe schools manual.* Saint Paul, MN: Out for Equity of the Saint Paul Public Schools.

Israel, T., & Hackett, G. (2004). Counselor education on lesbian, gay and bisexual issues: Comparing information and attitude exploration. *Counselor Education and Supervision, 43*, 179–191. Retrieved from Academic Search Premier database

Israel. T., & Selvidge, M. D. (2003). Contributions of multicultural counseling to counselor competence with lesbian, gay, and bisexual clients. *Journal of Multicultural Counseling and Development, 31*, 84–98.

Kocarek, C. E., & Pelling, N. J. (2003). Beyond knowledge and awareness: Enhancing counselor skills for work with gay, lesbian, and bisexual clients. *Journal of Multicultural Counseling and Development, 31*, 99–112. Retrieved from Academic Search Premier database

Koch, C. (2000). *Attitudes, knowledge, and anticipated behaviors of pre-service teachers toward individuals with different sexual orientations.* Unpublished doctoral dissertation. The George Washington University, Washington, DC.

Kosciw, J. G., Greytak, E. A., Diaz, E. M., & Bartkiewicz, M. J. (2010). *The 2009 National School Climate Survey: The experiences of lesbian, gay, bisexual and transgender youth in our nation's schools.* New York, NY: GLSEN.

Lev, A. I. (2004). *Transgender emergence: Therapeutic guidelines for working with gender-variant people and their families.* New York, NY: Hayworth Press.

Lim, H. S., & Johnson, M. M. (2001). Korean social work students' attitudes toward homosexuals. *Journal of Social Work Education, 37,* 545–554. Retrieved from Academic Search Premier database

Logie, C., Bridge, T. J., & Bridge, P. D. (2007). Evaluating the phobias, attitudes, and cultural competence of master of social work students toward the LGBT populations. *Journal of Homosexuality, 53*(4), 201–221. doi:10.1080/00918360802103472

Matthews, C. (2005). Infusing lesbian, gay, and bisexual issues into counselor education. *Journal of Humanistic Counseling, Education & Development, 44,* 168–184. Retrieved from Academic Search Premier database

McCabe, P. C., & Rubinson, F. (2008). Committing to social justice: The behavioral intention of school psychology and education trainees to advocate for lesbian, gay, bisexual, and transgendered youth. *School Psychology Review, 37*(4), 469–486. Retrieved from http://www.nasponline.org/publications/spr/abstract.aspx?ID=1873

McKenzie, K. B., Christman, D. E., Hernandez, F., Fierro, E., Capper, C. A., Dantley, M., . . . Scheurich, J. J. (2008). From the field: A proposal for educating leaders for social justice. *Educational Administration Quarterly, 44,* 111–138. doi:10.1177/0013161X07309470

Messinger, L. (2004). Field education in social work out in the field: Gay and lesbian social work students' experiences in field placement. *Journal of Social Work Education, 40*(2), 187–204.

Midwest Academy. (n.d.). Midwest academy strategy chart. Retrieved from http://www.tcsg.org/sfelp/toolkit/MidwestAcademy_01.pdf

Mudrey, R., & Medina-Adams, A. (2008). Attitudes, perceptions, and knowledge of pre-services teachers regarding the educational isolation of sexual minority youth. *Journal of Homosexuality, 51*(4), 63–90. doi:10.1300/J082v51n04_04

National Education Association. (2010). *National training program on safety, bias, and GLBT issues* [Pamphlet]. Washington, DC: Author.

National School Boards Association. (2004). *Dealing with legal matters surrounding students' sexual orientation and gender identity.* Alexandria, VA: Author.

Nelson, E. S., & Krieger, S. L. (1997). Changes in attitudes toward homosexuality in college students: Implementation of a gay men and lesbian peer panel. *Journal of Homosexuality, 33*(2), 63. doi:10.1300/J082v33n02_04

Parents, Families, and Friends of Lesbians and Gays. (n.d.). Cultivating Respect. Retrieved from http://community.pflag.org/page.aspx?pid=1030

Payne, E. C., & Smith, M. (2011). The reduction of stigma in schools: A new professional development model for empowering educators to support LGBTQ students. *Journal of LGBT Youth, 8*(2), 174–200. doi:10.1080/19361653.2011.563183

Pearson, Q. M. (2003). Breaking the silence in the counselor education classroom: A training seminar on counseling sexual minority clients. *Journal of Counseling and Development, 81,* 292–300.

Riggs, A. D., Rosenthal, A. R., & Smith-Bonahue, T. (2011). The impact of a combined cognitive-affective intervention on pre-service teachers' attitudes, knowledge, and anticipated professional behaviors regarding homosexuality and gay and lesbian issues. *Teaching and Teacher Education, 27,* 201–209. doi:10.1016/j.tate.2010.08.002

Rutter, P. A., Estrada, D., Ferguson, L. K., & Diggs, G. A. (2008). Sexual orientation and counselor competency: The impact of training on enhancing awareness, knowledge and skills. *Journal of LGBT Issues in Counseling, 2,* 109–125. doi:10.1080/1553860080212547

Savage, T. A., Prout, H. T., & Chard, K. M. (2004). School psychology and issues of sexual orientation: Attitudes, beliefs, and knowledge. *Psychology in the Schools, 41,* 201–210. doi:10.1002/pits.10122

Sears, J. T. (1991). Educators, homosexuality, and homosexual students: Are personal feelings related to professional beliefs? *Journal of Homosexuality, 22,* 29–79.

Sherry, A., Whilde, M. R., & Patton, J. (2005). Gay, lesbian, and bisexual training competencies in American Psychological Association accredited graduate programs. *Psychotherapy: Theory, Research, Practice, Training, 42,* 116–120. doi:10.1037/0033-3204.42.1.116

Sherwin, G., & Jennings, T. (2006). Feared, forgotten, or forbidden: Sexual orientation topics in secondary teacher preparation programs in the USA. *Teaching Education, 17*(3), 207–223. doi:10.1080/10476210600849664

Sue, D. W., Arredondo, P., & McDavis, R. J. (1992). Multicultural counseling competencies and standards: A call to the profession. *Journal of Multicultural Counseling and Development, 20,* 64–88.

Swank, E., & Raiz, L. (2007). Explaining comfort with homosexuality among social work students: The impact of demographic, contextual, and attitudinal factors. *Journal of Social Work Education, 43*(2), 257–279. doi:10.5175/JSWE.2007.200500560

Szalacha, L. A. (2004). Educating teachers on LGBTQ issues. *Journal of Gay & Lesbian Issues in Education, 1*(4), 67–79. doi:10/1300/J367v01n0407

Troiden, R. R. (1989). The formation of homosexual identities. *Journal of Homosexuality, 17*(1/2), 43–73. doi:10.1300/J082v17n01_02

Walker, J. A., & Prince, T. (2010). Training considerations and suggested counseling intervention for LGBT individuals. *Journal of LGBT Issues in Counseling, 4,* 2–17. doi:10.1080/15538600903552756

Walton, P. (Producer). (1992). *Gay youth* [DVD]. United States: New Day Films.

Whitman, J. S. (1995). Providing training about sexual orientation in counselor education. *Counselor Education & Supervision, 35,* 168–176.

Whitman, J. S., Horn, S. S., & Boyd, C. J. (2007). Activism in the school: Providing LGBTQ affirmative training to school counselors. *Journal of Gay & Lesbian Psychotherapy, 11*(3–4), 143–154. doi:10.1300/J236v11n03_08

Wyatt, T., Oswalt, S., White, C., & Peterson, F. (2008). Are tomorrow's teachers ready to deal with diverse students? Teacher candidates' attitudes toward gay men and lesbians. *Teacher Education Quarterly, 35*(2), 171–185. Retrieved from http://www.teqjournal.org/TEQ%20Website/Back%20Issues/Volume%2035/Volume%035%20Number%202.html

9 Safe Schools

Prevention and Intervention for Bullying and Harassment

Dorothy L. Espelage and Mrinalini A. Rao

This chapter reviews school-based bullying and harassment prevention and intervention efforts with a particular focus on lesbian, gay, bisexual, transgender, and questioning (LGBTQ) youth. We first discuss the prevalence of bullying and harassment experienced by LGBTQ students and then we explore the psychological and educational outcomes associated with these negative experiences. Next we discuss school-based bullying prevention frameworks and approaches and conduct a brief review of the literature on bullying prevention and intervention efforts. We also discuss some promising programs and initiatives addressing anti-LGBTQ bullying and harassment, as well as anti-bullying and anti-discrimination policies. We end the chapter with some recommendations for practice and future research.

Prevalence of Victimization Among LGBTQ Youth

Research has consistently shown that sexual minority youth report high rates of peer victimization (Robinson & Espelage, 2011). The Gay, Lesbian, and Straight Education Network's (GLSEN) 2009 National School Climate Survey of 7,261 middle and high school students found that, at school, nearly 90% of lesbian, gay, bisexual, and transgender (LGBT) students experienced harassment in the past year; nearly 61% felt unsafe because of their sexual orientation; and 30% skipped at least one day of school in the past month because of safety concerns (Kosciw, Greytak, Diaz, & Bartkiewicz, 2010). In a different study, D'Augelli, Pilkington, and Hershberger (2002) found that 59% of lesbian, gay, and bisexual (LGB) youth reported verbal abuse in high school because of sexual orientation, 24% were threatened with violence, 11% had objects thrown at them, 11% were physically assaulted, 2% were threatened with weapons, and 20% had been threatened with being outed. Individuals whose sexual orientation was more publicly known during high school or who exhibited less gender-typical behavior reported more verbal abuse (D'Augelli, Pilkington, & Hershberger, 2002). This is not a new development, with studies over the past two decades documenting as many as 70% of sexual minority youth reporting some sort of harassment including rude comments, discrimination, profanities written on lockers, and threats from students' parents (Telljohann & Price, 1993).

Indeed, sexual minority youth have been found to be at greater risk for bullying and peer victimization than their heterosexual counterparts, even after adjusting for age, race/ethnicity, and weight (Berlan, Corliss, Field, Goodman, & Austin, 2010; Bontempo & D'Augelli, 2002; Hanlon, 2004; Poteat, Mereish, DiGiovanni, & Koenig, 2011). As compared to their peers, sexual minority adolescents were more likely to report being physically threatened, injured with a weapon, fearful of attending school, as well as having property stolen or damaged by peers; 33% were threatened with a weapon at school compared to 7% of other youth; and 50% reported property damage as compared to 29% of other youth (Berlan et al., 2010; Garofalo, Wolf, Kessel, Palfrey, & DuRunat, 1998; Robinson & Espelage, 2011). Thus, LGBTQ youth are a particularly vulnerable group for peer victimization ranging from name-calling to serious physical threats and assaults.

Research on sexual minority youth often groups lesbian, gay, bisexual, and transgender youth together in their analyses. However, each of these groups undoubtedly has their own unique concerns and challenges. Some studies have attempted to disaggregate victimization experiences by sexual identity. For example, Espelage, Aragon, Birkett, and Koenig (2008) found that lesbian, gay, bisexual, and questioning (LGBQ) students reported greater general peer victimization and homophobic teasing than heterosexual peers, with questioning students reporting more victimization experiences than LGB youth. A British study found that levels of bully victimization did not vary with sexual orientation when comparing 53 7th–9th graders who were attracted to the same sex in comparison to 53 7th–9th graders who were attracted to the opposite sex (Rivers & Noret, 2008). However, they did find that same-sex attracted students were significantly more likely to drink alone, report higher levels of hostility, and report higher levels of loneliness than opposite-attracted students (Rivers & Noret, 2008).

Less research has focused on the victimization experiences of transgender youth. However, recently, McGuire, Anderson, Toomey, and Russell (2010) conducted a survey with 68 transgender youth and also conducted focus groups with 35 of these youth. The results of this study suggest that harassment due to transgender identity is pervasive and associated with negative perceptions of school. Similarly, the 2009 GLSEN survey found that transgender students were more likely than all other groups to report feeling unsafe at school because of their sexual orientation and gender expression (Kosciw et al., 2010). They also were more likely than all other groups to avoid school bathrooms and locker rooms because they felt unsafe or uncomfortable in those spaces (Kosciw et al., 2010). Transgender students generally were more likely than all other students to have negative experiences at school; they were more likely to be physically harassed or assaulted at school based on their sexual orientation and gender expression/identity (Kosciw et al., 2010).

Rivers' (2001) findings from a retrospective study suggest that victimization among LGBTQ youth remains quite salient into adulthood. In this study, 82% of 190 LGBT adolescents and adults who were bullied during their schooling retrospectively reported experiences of homophobic verbal abuse, 60% reported physical assault, 58% reported teasing, 59% reported being the victim of rumors, and 27% experienced social isolation. They also reported that the bullying occurred over an extended period of time with an average duration of five years and, when they were bullied, the perpetrators were groups of kids not just one individual.

Gender and race differences have been found in the rates of peer victimization and homophobic harassment across LGBTQ youth. Poteat, Aragon, Espelage, and Koenig (2009) found that boys reported higher general peer victimization (not necessarily homophobic slurs) than girls among heterosexual and questioning students. In addition, levels of victimization were significantly higher for questioning boys than for gay, bisexual, and heterosexual boys. Likewise, questioning girls were victimized more than lesbian and bisexual girls, who, in turn, were victimized more than heterosexual girls. In a national survey of LGBT secondary school students, female youth were less likely to report victimization than male youth, and both were less likely to experience victimization than transgender youth (Kosciw, Greytak, & Diaz, 2009).

In a national survey of LGBT secondary school students, Kosciw, Greytak, and Diaz (2009) found that African-American and Asian-American youth were less likely to hear homophobic remarks than White youth. African-American youth were also less likely to report victimization based on sexual orientation than White youth. LGBT youth in rural communities and communities with lower adult educational attainment faced more hostile school climates. Finally, older youth were less likely to report at-school victimization based on sexual orientation or gender expression. Thus, younger, White, questioning and transgender males in rural and less educated communities seem to be the most frequent targets of victimization.

These trends have been found across international samples as well (Finlinson, Colón, Robles, & Soto, 2008; Warner et al., 2004). LGBTQ adolescents in a Canadian school-based sample reported more bullying, peer sexual harassment, and peer physical abuse over a two-month period than heterosexual students (Williams, Connolly, Pepler, & Craig, 2003). Additionally, within a British study, researchers found significant increases in rates of LGBT bullying over two decades (Ellis & High, 2004). Compared to 1981, youth in 2001 were four times more likely to feel isolated at school, seven times more likely to be teased, and five times more likely to experience verbal abuse (Ellis & High, 2004).

Thus, it is clear that sexual and gender minority youth are at greater risk for bullying and peer victimization than heterosexual youth. This difference has been theorized to be a result of prevailing homophobic beliefs and attitudes (Poteat & DiGiovanni, 2010). Thus, it is simply not the case that sexual orientation or gender identity contributes to the greater risk, but the fact that these students are growing up in environments that are homophobic (and transphobic) and promote heteronegativity (Horn, Kosciw, & Russell, 2009). Evidence of the pervasiveness of homophobic attitudes can be seen in a 2008 report from GLSEN where 42% of students with LGBT parents had been verbally harassed at school because of their parents' sexual orientation and 28% had heard teachers or staff make negative comments about LGBT families (Kosciw & Diaz, 2008). Indeed, as youth enter adolescence and puberty, the content of bullying begins to include commentary about gender expression and sexual orientation (Poteat & Espelage, 2005). Homophobic attitudes in schools and communities place LGBTQ youth at risk for victimization, isolation, and marginalization. Homophobic teasing and use of biased language also are associated with endorsing sexual prejudices among adolescent populations (Poteat & DiGiovanni, 2010). Furthermore, general bullying perpetration has been found to be predictive of future homophobic teasing and bullying in a middle school sample (Espelage, Rao, Little, & Rose, 2011).

Psychological and Academic Outcomes

Peer victimization and homophobic teasing have been found to impact educational and psychological outcomes for LGBTQ youth (D'Augelli et al., 2002; Poteat et al., 2011;

Robinson & Espelage, 2011; Warner et al., 2004). A study by the California Safe Schools Coalition (CSSC) and 4-H Center for Youth Development (2004) examined bullying based on actual or perceived sexual orientation. As compared to students who were not bullied, bullied students in this study reported more grades at or below C (24% versus 17%) and more frequent absenteeism (27% versus 7%). Other studies have documented as many as 72% of bullied LGBT students being truant and/or playing sick to avoid at-school victimization (Birkett, Espelage, & Koenig, 2009; Rivers, 2000).

In addition to the educational costs endured by victimized LGBTQ adolescents, studies have documented more substance abuse, depression, and suicidality among LGBTQ students than heterosexual students (Birkett et al., 2009; Bontempo & D'Augelli, 2002; Espelage et al., 2008; Poteat et al., 2009). Within a sample of youth bullied for their perceived or actual sexual orientation, 45% seriously considered suicide and 35% developed a plan for suicide in the year prior to the survey (CSSC & 4-H Center for Youth Development, 2004). D'Augelli et al. (2002) found that 9% of the variance in mental health of LGB high school students was accounted for by victimization. Bullying victimization has been found to mediate the relation between gender-role nonconformity and suicidality in gay male adolescents, with this relation being present across grade levels but strongest in the middle school years (Friedman, Koeske, Silvestre, Korr, & Sites, 2006). Additionally, bullied LGBT students were twice as likely to engage in risky behaviors (CSSC & 4-H Center for Youth Development, 2004). Although some demographic differences have been found, such as homophobic victimization being more strongly associated with suicidality for LGBTQ White youth than for LGBTQ youth of color (Poteat et al., 2011), in general, victimization of LGBTQ youth increases the risk for negative psychological outcomes.

An examination of the protective factors that may buffer LGBTQ youth from negative outcomes is warranted (a thorough examination of these factors can be found in Chapter 4 of this volume). Psychological outcomes for LGBTQ and heterosexual high school students exposed to bullying and homophobic attitudes were found to depend on the social support system present in their environment (Espelage et al., 2008; Safren & Heimberg, 1999). Some research has begun to document variables in the individual, peer, family, and school context that may protect LGBTQ youth from the negative consequences of peer victimization. For example, family support and self-acceptance has been found to mediate the relation between victimization and mental health in LGBT youth (Hershberger & D'Augelli, 1995).

School-level variables also have been found to play an important role in the differential psychosocial adjustment of victimized LGBTQ youth. Poteat et al. (2011) found that suicidality and school belongingness mediated the relations between homophobic victimization and grades, truancy, and importance of graduating in a high school sample. Although homophobic bullying had negative effects on school belongingness for all groups (Poteat et al., 2011), a positive school climate was found to moderate the association between bullying and psychological consequences including depression, suicidality, and drug use (Birkett et al., 2009; Espelage et al., 2008; Poteat et al., 2011).

General school safety and greater school belongingness are important, but schools that have specific programs related to sexual identity and gender expression also appear to be important for preventing adverse outcomes for LGBTQ youth. Gay-Straight Alliances (GSAs) are extracurricular student-led clubs that often advocate for improved school climate, educate the larger school community about issues pertinent to LGBTQ people, and support LGBTQ students and their allies (Goodenow, Szalacha, & Westheimer, 2006; Russell, 2002). The presence of GSAs or similar student clubs has been found to be related to less hostile experiences for LGBTQ youth, including less victimization, greater safety, and greater school connectedness (Bochenek & Brown, 2001; Kosciw et al., 2009). Furthermore, adolescents attending schools with LGBTQ support groups have been found to report lower rates of at-school victimization and suicide attempts (Goodenow et al., 2006; Heck, Flentje, & Cochran, 2011). They also were less likely to miss school because of concerns for physical safety than those attending a school without a GSA (Walls, Kane, & Wisneski, 2010). The behaviors of the individuals at the schools also impacted LGBTQ youths' psychosocial adjustment. More specifically, among a sample of 202 Massachusetts students across 50 high schools, LGB youth reported less victimization and suicidality in schools with support groups compared to LGB youth in schools with no support groups (Goodnow et al., 2006). However, although a majority of teachers are aware of homophobic bullying, they report being either unable or unwilling to address the phenomenon (Warwick, Aggleton, & Douglas, 2001).

School-Based Bullying Prevention Frameworks and Approaches

A multitude of school-based bullying prevention/intervention efforts, programs, and frameworks are available, but relatively few have been systematically evaluated. These prevention efforts range from simple one-time efforts (e.g., theater, guest speakers, musical groups) to comprehensive school-wide approaches (e.g., Positive Behavior Intervention Supports (PBIS); Ross & Horner, 2009; Ross, Horner, & Stiller, 2008) and comprehensive primary prevention programs that address bullying through explicit social and emotional learning instruction (e.g., *Steps to Respect* and *Second Step*; Committee for Children, 2008, 2001).

Universal Prevention Programs

Social-emotional Learning. One approach that is gaining more attention in bullying prevention is the social-emotional learning (SEL) approach (Frey et al., 2005). SEL is a framework that emerged from influences across different movements which focused on resilience and teaching social and emotional competencies to children and adolescents (Elias et al., 1997). In response, advocates for SEL use social skill instruction to address behavior, discipline, safety, and academics in order to help youth become self-aware, manage their emotions, and build social skills such as empathy, perspective-taking, respect for diversity, friendship skills, and decision-making (Zins, Weissberg, Wang, & Walberg, 2004). An SEL framework includes five interrelated skill areas: self-awareness, social awareness, self-management and organization, responsible problem-solving, and relationship management (Zins et al., 2004). Recently, a meta-analytic study of more than 213 programs found that if a school implements a quality SEL curriculum, it can expect better student behavior and an 11 percentile point increase in academic test scores (Durlak, Weissberg, Dymnicki, Taylor, & Schellinger, 2011). The gains that schools see in achievement come from a variety of factors: students feel safer and more connected to school and academics, SEL programs build work habits in addition to social skills, and students and teachers develop stronger relationships (Zins et al., 2004).

Specific Bullying Prevention Programs. Whole-school or primary preventive interventions for bullying have been slowly introduced over the past few decades, following the introduction of the Norway-based *Olweus Bullying Prevention Program* (OBPP; Olweus, Limber, & Mihalic, 2000) and *Steps to Respect: A Bullying Prevention Program* (STR; Committee for Children, 2001) which was designed to help students build supportive relationships with one another (Brown, Low, Smith, & Haggerty, 2011; Committee for Children, 2001). Although widely implemented in America, the OBPP has extremely limited empirical support in United States (U.S.) schools despite established efficacy in other countries (Ttofi, Farrington, & Baldry, 2008). In contrast, STR is demonstrating positive changes in U.S. schools (Brown et at., 2011).

STR promotes a whole-school primary- and secondary-level approach to bullying prevention by addressing factors at four levels: (a) school staff, (b) peer group membership or friendships, (c) individual child, and (d) family (Committee for Children, 2008). Program developers believe that intervening at multiple levels is the most effective way to reduce school bullying (Committee for Children, 2008). Frey et al. (2005) demonstrated empirical support for STR in terms of its effectiveness as a bullying prevention program among 3rd to 6th graders. Furthermore, they found reductions in acceptance of bullying behavior, playground bullying, and argumentative behavior for those students who participated in the STR program as compared to students who did not receive the STR program. At the same time, these researchers found increases in agreeable interactions and perceptions that adults will be responsive to bullying incidents in comparison with control schools (Frey et al., 2005). More recently, researchers have found that STR participation was associated with higher teacher ratings of peer social skills and reductions in observed aggression, as well as reductions in bystanders assisting the bully in directing aggression toward the victim among elementary school children (3rd to 6th graders) (Brown et al., 2011; Hirschtein & Frey, 2006; Hirschtein, Edstrom, Frey, Snell, & MacKenzie, 2007). However, it is not clear whether STR and similar programs make an impact specifically on the homophobic bantering or victimization directed toward LGBTQ youth.

Contraindications

Some things are contraindicated in bullying prevention. For example, researchers have found zero tolerance policies (policies that provide for punishment regardless of the basis of the problem behavior) are ineffective in curbing aggressive behaviors (Casella, 2003), and expulsion appears to be equally ineffective (Morrison, Redding, Fisher, & Peterson, 2006). Despite this, Furlong, Morrison, and Grief (2003) noted that most formalized legislation addressing bullying and peer aggression in schools continues to emphasize taking action with bullies to the exclusion of addressing the needs of victims or addressing the larger school climate. For example, many bullying interventions have tended to allocate more resources to identifying individual bullies and addressing their behavior than to developing universal programs that address the entire student body. Interventions that may be effective with other types of violence, such as conflict resolution, peer mediation, and group therapy, do not translate into effectiveness with bullying (Espelage & Horne, 2008). These approaches fail to shift the negative school climate that might be contributing to the elevated rates of victimization or homophobia in a school.

Research Support for Bullying Prevention

Meta-Analytic Studies

Despite a long history of published studies on what predicts bullying involvement in school-age children and adolescents (e.g., Espelage, Bosworth, & Simon, 2000; Espelage & Holt, 2001), systematic evaluations of large-scale prevention programs are only now appearing in the literature. In 2008, Merrell, Gueldner, Ross, and Isava conducted a meta-analytic investigation of 16 studies published from 1980 to 2004 that yielded disappointing results regarding the impact of anti-bullying programs. This meta-analysis included data from over 15,000 students (grades Kindergarten to 12) in Europe, Canada, and the U.S. Positive effect sizes were found for only one-third of the study variables, which primarily reflected favorable changes in knowledge, attitudes, and perceptions of bullying. No changes were found for actual bullying behaviors. These authors tentatively indicated that school bullying interventions showed modest evidence of enhancing student social competence, self-esteem, and peer acceptance. In addition, it appears that programs shifted teachers' knowledge of effective practices and efficacy of intervening and responding to incidences at school in a positive direction. Given that teachers spend a substantial amount of time with students and are often the adults that children look to for socialization of attitudes and behaviors, it makes sense that effective bullying prevention must improve teachers' knowledge, competence, and behavioral repertoire to identify and intervene when they witness bullying.

Ttofi et al. (2008) simultaneously conducted a meta-analysis that included more studies. In a report for the Swedish National Council for Crime Prevention, they evaluated 44 bullying intervention studies being implemented across the globe. Results indicated that bullying and victimization were reduced by 17–23% in schools with interventions compared to control schools. Ttofi et al. (2008) found that reductions in bullying were associated with classroom rules, classroom management, parent training, increased playground supervision, home–school communication, and the use of training videos. Further, the strongest effects were found for programs that included several of these components, rather than just one or two.

Research on Bystanders

Increasingly, school-based bullying prevention programs are focusing their attention on encouraging bystanders (i.e., students and teachers who are witnessing bullying situations or know about the bullying) to intervene in preventing or stopping bullying. Such interventions are demonstrating efficacy in reducing bullying rates in schools (Newman, Horne, & Bartolomucci, 2000; Polanin, Espelage, & Pigott, 2012; Rigby & Johnson, 2006; Salmivalli, Kärnä, & Poskiparta, 2010). These studies found an association between increases in the amount of bystander intervening behavior and concomitant decreases in bullying. Indeed, a recent small-scale meta-analysis conducted by Polanin et al. (2012) found support for the effectiveness of bullying prevention programs in altering bystander behavior to intervene in bullying situations. Evidence from 12 school-based interventions in this study, involving 12,874 students, revealed that overall the programs were successful, with larger effects for high school samples compared to K-8 samples. Thus, this meta-analysis indicated that programs were effective at changing bystander intervening behavior, both on a practical and statistically significant level.

Despite this promising small-scale meta-analysis, much research needs to be conducted to understand the complex nuances of bystander intervention in order to give bystanders practical strategies for intervening effectively. In most of the prevention programs, bystanders or onlookers (sometimes called allies, upstanders, and reinforcers) are encouraged to either report an incident of bullying or to confront students who are bullying other students. A recent empirical study found that greater bullying perpetration within one's peer group was highly predictive of less individual willingness to intervene, suggesting that any prevention efforts to address bystander or defender intervention must first reduce the level of bullying within peer groups (Espelage, Green, & Polanin, 2011). Thus, it is imperative that both basic and applied research is conducted on bystander intervention.

In a more public health approach, the National School Climate Center (NSCC; n.d.) also has developed a program to address bullying and harassment in schools named *Bully Bust*, which was launched in 2009 to facilitate bystander intervention and help students and adults become "upstanders," or individuals who support victims or targets of bullying, teasing, and harassment. Overall, the NSCC's goal is to create positive academic and social environments in schools by offering a variety of professional development programs and services to support K-12 schools, afterschool settings, educators, parent advocate groups, and states to sustain school climate improvement efforts. To date, there are no efficacy or effectiveness data available on the impact of Bully Bust or other public health initiatives on reducing bullying in our schools and society.

Future Directions in Bullying Research

Indeed, there is a huge gulf between research and practice in bullying prevention and intervention. We believe that the next generation of bullying scholarship needs to move beyond a focus that is solely on individual children within schools, and instead attempt to change the contextual variables that are promoting bullying within schools and in our society. For example, the fields of sports psychology, medicine, law, social justice, gender studies, history, political science, ethnic studies, and even teacher education should contribute to the discourse about the historical and sociological nature of bullying. Many of these groups are starting to understand their role in bullying prevention at the national level.

None of the studies included in the aforementioned meta-analyses assessed victimization directed toward LGBTQ youth, and none of the studies assessed homophobic teasing and bullying. Thus, it is not clear whether these programs can reduce homophobic teasing and bullying in particular. Given the vulnerability of sexual minority youth, very little research has focused on the effectiveness of "generic" bullying prevention efforts with subgroups, such as LGBTQ youth or ethnically diverse populations. "Generic" refers to programs that do not address specifically (beyond a mention that certain subgroups of individuals can be bullied) bias-based bullying related to race/ethnicity, sexual orientation, cultural/religious practices, students with disabilities, gender expression, or gender. However, we believe that these programs are failing in large part because they are neglecting to address a very prevalent form of bullying—that directed toward LGBTQ youth. Adapting bullying prevention programs to address diversity in sexual orientation and gender expression and the use of homophobic epithets that create hostile school environments is a necessary next step. Thus, if educators choose to implement an existing evidence-based universal prevention program, they will need to complement these programs with materials that are relevant to LGBTQ youth in particular or supplement an existing program. Some of the materials that could be used to complement the generic bully prevention programs are discussed next.

Programs and Initiatives Specifically Addressing Anti-LGBTQ Bullying and Harassment

Because extant bullying prevention programs do not specifically address LGBTQ youth, educators will need to utilize the following resources to modify prevention program practices. Several independent organizations have been concerned with the climate of schools for LGBTQ and gender nonconforming youth for decades. However, much of their efforts have been slow to reach the hallways of K-12 schools because of resistance to discuss sexuality and gender identity within schools and due to the obvious political landscape in which these issues are often couched. In spite of these roadblocks, active steps have been taken to address the issue of bullying and harassment of LGBTQ youth in schools, and increasingly more attention has been given to preventing widespread discriminatory and prejudiced beliefs. Some of these organizations and programs are described below.

The Gay, Lesbian, and Straight Education Network

The Gay, Lesbian, and Straight Education Network (GLSEN) is a national organization that seeks to end discrimination, harassment, and bullying based on sexual orientation, gender identity and gender expression in K-12 schools (http://www.glsen.org/cgi-bin/iowa/all/home/index.html). GLSEN's work targets policy makers, educators, community leaders, and students, and provides these stakeholders with the information, skills trainings, and outreach programming to advance their mission of creating safer schools for LGBTQ youth. Some of GLSEN's programming includes nationwide awareness campaigns such as the *National Day of Silence* and the *No Name Calling Week*. In addition, there are GLSEN chapters and GSAs to organize and educate at the local community level. Participants in these chapters are trained to be effective advocates of GLSEN's mission. In combination with their outreach and activism, GLSEN conducts national-level research examining the experiences of LGBT youth, identifying positive and negative practices and policies that impact school environments for LGBT youth and examining the effectiveness of their own programs. GLSEN also has a strong online presence through which it creates awareness and opportunities for involvement in the organization.

GLSEN has received funding from the Center for Disease Control (CDC) to implement its *Safe Space* initiative, a school-based program that provides educators with strategies for creating a positive learning environment for LGBT students, supporting LGBT students beyond academics, and reducing anti-LGBT bias in the larger school population. It also has a similar program, the *GLSEN Lunchbox*, that provides strategies to address the negative outcomes of anti-LGBT biases in schools.

GroundSpark

Movies, videos, and other forms of multimedia also are used in bullying prevention efforts. GroundSpark creates films and educational campaigns that address gender identity and gender expression to improve relations across diverse groups of youth (GroundSpark, n.d.). It offers a comprehensive set of resources for educators and service providers, including award-winning documentary films, high-quality curriculum guides, and a comprehensive workshop series for professionals and community members (GroundSpark, n.d.). GroundSpark targets a broad audience including children, youth, and adults. Its stated goals include: (a) to challenge stereotypes and help individuals make connections between various prejudice and bias issues; (b) to promote respect and equity as early as possible and on a regular basis to prevent prejudices from becoming entrenched and harmful; (c) to reduce bullying and violence among youth; and (d) to create inclusive, welcoming school and community environments where everyone, regardless of identity and background, can thrive (GroundSpark, n.d.). Some of these films include *Straightlaced—How Gender's Got Us All Tied Up*, about the gender and sexuality pressures that teens and young adults face today, *It's Elementary—Talking About Gay Issues in School*, about addressing LGBT issues in elementary and middle school, and *Let's Get Real*, a film about bias and bullying.

Anti-Defamation League

An initiative that was originally formed to stop the defamation of Jewish people is the Anti-Defamation League (ADL), which has expanded its focus to address all forms of prejudice and bigotry. The ADL's "ultimate purpose is to secure justice and fair treatment to all citizens alike and to put an end forever to unjust and unfair discrimination against and ridicule of any sect or body of citizens" (ADL, n.d.). The ADL has developed a school assembly program, *Step Up!*, to address bullying and harassment in middle and high schools. This program aims to give voice to the experiences of the victims of bullying and harassment, to build empathy in the bullies, and to empower bystanders to take a stand against bullying.

The Illinois Safe Schools Alliance

The Illinois Safe Schools Alliance (the Alliance) states that its mission is to promote safety, support, and healthy development for LGBTQ youth in Illinois schools and communities through advocacy, education, youth organizing, and research (Illinois Safe Schools Alliance, n.d.). The goals of the Alliance include: (a) educating and involving schools, community organizations, parents, public officials, youth, and the general public in Illinois regarding sexual orientation and gender identity issues and the needs of LGBTQ youth in schools; (b) engaging youth across the state of Illinois to become leaders in the LGBTQ safe schools movement and to be agents of change in their own schools and communities; and (c) conducting advocacy activities that will result in the inclusion of sexual orientation and gender identity issues in the programs and policies that support the safety and well-being of youth (Illinois Safe Schools Alliance, n.d.). In order to achieve these goals the Alliance has developed several programs targeting different audiences such as school personnel, social service providers, and government officials. In addition, they organize and empower youth through programs such as youth leadership summits, the *Day of Silence/Night of Noise* awareness programming, and GSA networks in schools and communities. The Alliance also is involved in policy development, advocacy, research, and evaluation related to the discrimination that LGBTQ youth face in schools.

Anti-Bullying and Anti-Discrimination Policies

Regardless of what curriculum or materials are employed for bullying prevention, it is critical that anti-bullying legislation and policies are comprehensive and enumerate specific characteristics of targets to be protected, including actual or perceived sexual orientation and gender identity/expression (Kosciw et al., 2010). Research suggests that specific and comprehensive laws and policies are more effective than "generic" laws and policies (Kosciw, Diaz, & Greytak, 2008). When students report that their schools have inclusive policies that explicitly address protection based on sexual orientation and gender identity, they feel safer at school, experience less anti-LGBTQ harassment, and report higher levels of resilience (Russell, 2010). Stakeholders and community members are encouraged to support legislation that provides funding to implement anti-bullying and anti-discrimination policies that specifically include protections based on students' actual or perceived sexual orientation and gender identity.

Putting the Pieces Together

Educators are urged to make comprehensive school-wide anti-bullying and anti-discrimination a priority. As discussed in this chapter, this includes not only increasing awareness amongst all stakeholder groups, but also updating existing policies and equipping school personnel and students with concrete and realistic strategies to both prevent and respond to anti-LGBTQ bullying and harassment. An ideal program or framework would include training for all students, staff, administrators, and parents on the school and district policies on harassment, intimidation, and bullying. It is imperative that all stakeholders understand the rights to a safe school environment. Students and teachers need to understand how bias-based bullying in schools creates a negative climate. Schools should support GSAs, infuse LGBTQ content in curriculum (addressed in Chapter 10 of this volume), and work with students on gender, gender nonconformity, and traditional masculinity and femininity. Students also need to have ample opportunities to develop strong interpersonal skills through social emotional learning activities. Only then will youth come to respect one another and work together to promote a safe school for all individuals.

However, additional research is needed to help direct and shape intervention programs for bullying prevention and intervention with LGBTQ youth. LGBTQ students face unique risks associated with being targets of bias-based bullying, however, most anti-bullying programs do not address the specific needs of these populations. In fact, in a study of 23 comprehensive anti-bullying programs aimed at middle and high school students, none of them covered issues of sexual orientation, homophobia, sexual harassment, and sexual violence sufficiently enough to warrant any efficacy related to LGBTQ youth outcomes (Birkett, Espelage, & Stein, 2008). Although the research is inconclusive as to the impact of anti-bullying prevention programs on students in general, and completely lacking for LGBTQ students, there are steps that educators can take to make positive systemic changes in order to create safer schools. Thus, it is imperative that bullying prevention programs or approaches include discussions around diversity, sexual identity, and gender expression.

References

Anti-Defamation League. (n.d.). Retrieved from http://www.adl.org/main_Education/default.htm

Berlan, E. D., Corliss, H. L., Field, A. E., Goodman, E., & Austin, S. B. (2010). Sexual orientation and bullying among adolescents in the growing up today study. *Journal of Adolescent Health, 46,* 366–371. doi:10.1016/j.jadohealth.2009.10.015

Birkett, M., Espelage, D. L., & Koenig, B. (2009). LGB and questioning students in schools: The moderating effects of homophobic bullying and school climate on negative outcomes. *Journal of Youth and Adolescence, 38,* 989–1000. doi:10/1007/S10964-008-9389-1

Birkett, M. A., Espelage, D. L., & Stein, N. (2008, August). Have School Anti-Bullying Programs Overlooked Homophobic Bullying? Poster presented at the American Psychological Association Annual Convention, Boston, MA.

Bochenek, M., & Brown, A. W. (2001). *Hatred in the hallways: Violence and discrimination against lesbian, gay, bisexual, and transgender students in US schools.* New York, NY: Human Rights Watch.

Bontempo, D. E., & D'Augelli, A. R. (2002). Effects of at-school victimization and sexual orientation on lesbian, gay, or bisexual youths' health risk behavior. *Journal of Adolescent Health, 30,* 364–374. doi:10.1016/S1054-139X(01)00415-3

Brown, E. C., Low, S., Smith, B. H., & Haggerty, K. P. (2011). Outcomes from a school-randomized controlled trial of Steps to Respect: A school bullying prevention program. *School Psychology Review, 40,* 423–443. doi:10.1177/0143034311406813

California Safe Schools Coalition & 4-H Center for Youth Development, University of California, Davis. (2004). Safeplace to learn: Consequences of harassment based on actual or perceived sexual orientation and gender non-conformity and steps to making schools safer. San Francisco and Davis, CA: Authors.

Casella, R. (2003). Zero tolerance policy in schools: Rationale, consequences, and alternatives. *Teachers College Record, 105,* 872–892. doi:10.1111/1467-9620.00271

Committee for Children. (2001). *Steps to Respect: A Bullying Prevention Program.* Seattle, WA: Author.

Committee for Children. (2008). *Second Step: Student Success through Prevention Program.* Seattle, WA: Author.

D'Augelli, A. R., Pilkington, N. W., & Hershberger, S. L. (2002). Incidence and mental health impact of sexual orientation victimization of lesbian, gay, and bisexual youths in high school. *School Psychology Quarterly, 17,* 148–167. doi:10.1521/scpq.17.2.148.20854

Durlak, J. A., Weissberg, R. P., Dymnicki, A. B., Taylor, R. D., & Schellinger, K. B. (2011). The impact of enhancing students' social and emotional learning: A meta-analysis of school-based universal interventions. *Child Development, 82,* 405–432. doi:10.1111/j.1467-8624.2010.01564.x

Elias, M. J., Zins, J. E., Weissberg, K. S., Greenberg, M. T., Haynes, M., Kessler, R., et al. (1997). *Promoting social and emotional learning: Guidelines for educators.* Alexandria, VA: Association for Supervision and Curriculum Development.

Ellis, V., & High, S. (2004). Something more to tell you: Gay, lesbian or bisexual young people's experiences of secondary schooling. *British Educational Research Journal, 30,* 213–225. doi:10.1080/0141192042000195281

Espelage, D. L., Aragon, S. R., Birkett, M., & Koenig, B. W. (2008). Homophobic teasing, psychological outcomes, and sexual orientation among high school students: What influence do parents and schools have? *School Psychology Review, 37,* 202–216.

Espelage, D. L., Bosworth, K., & Simon, T. R. (2000). Examining the social context of bullying behaviors in early adolescence. *Journal of Counseling and Development, 78,* 326–333. doi: 10.1002/j.1556-6676.2000.tb01914.x

Espelage, D. L., Green, H. D., & Polanin, J. (2011). Willingness to intervene in bullying episodes among middle school students: Individual and peer-group influences. *Journal of Early Adolescence.* Online first doi:10.1177/0272431611423017

Espelage, D. L., & Holt, M. L. (2001). Bullying and victimization during early adolescence: Peer influences and psychosocial correlates. *Journal of Emotional Abuse, 2*(3), 123–142. doi:10.1300/J135v02n02_08

Espelage, D., & Horne, A. (2008). School violence and bullying prevention: From research based explanations to empirically based solutions. In S. Brown & R. Lent (Eds.), *Handbook of counseling psychology,* 4th edition (pp. 588–598). Hoboken, NJ: John Wiley and Sons.

Espelage, D. L., Rao, M., Little, T., & Rose, C. A. (2011, August). *Linking bullying perpetration to homophobic name-calling during early adolescence.* Poster presented at the annual meeting of the American Psychological Association, Washington, DC.

Finlinson, H. A., Colón, H. M., Robles, R. R., & Soto, M. (2008). An exploratory study of Puerto Rican MSM drug users: The childhood and early teen years of gay males and transsexual females. *Youth & Society, 39,* 362–384. doi:10.1177/0044118x07305998

Frey, K. S., Hirschstein, M. K., Snell, J. L., Edstrom, L. V., MacKenzie, E. P., & Broderick, C. J. (2005). Reducing playground bullying and supporting beliefs: An experimental trial of the Steps to Respect program. *Developmental Psychology, 41,* 479–491. doi:10.1037/0012-1649.41.3.479

Friedman, M. S., Koeske, G. F., Silvestre, A. J., Korr, W. S., & Sites, E. W. (2006). The impact of gender-role nonconforming behavior, bullying, and social support on suicidality among gay male youth. *Journal of Adolescent Health, 38,* 621–623. doi:10.1016/j.jadohealth.2005.04.014

Furlong, M. J., Morrison, G. M., & Greif, J. L. (2003). Reaching an American consensus: Reactions to the special issue on school bullying. *School Psychology Review, 3,* 456–470.

Garofalo, R., Wolf, R., Kessel, S., Palfrey, J., & DuRant, R. (1998). The association between health risk behaviours and sexual orientation among a school-based sample of adolescents. *Pediatrics, 101,* 895–902. doi:10.1542/peds101.5.895

Gay, Lesbian, Straight Education Network. (n.d.). Retrieved from http://www.glsen.org/cgi-bin/iowa/all/antibullying/index.html

Goodenow, C., Szalacha, L., & Westheimer, K. (2006). School support groups, other school factors, and the safety of sexual minority adolescents. *Psychology in the Schools, 43,* 573–589. doi:10.1002/pits.20173

GroundSpark. (n.d.). Retrieved from http://www.groundspark.org

Hanlon, B. M. (2004). 2003 Massachusetts youth risk behavior survey results, Massachusetts Department of Education, Malden, MA. Retrieved from http://www.gaydata.org/02_Data_Sources/ds007_YRBS/Massachusetts/ds007_YRBS_MA_Report_2003.pdf

Heck, N. C., Flentje, A., & Cochran, B. N. (2011). Offsetting risks: High school gay-straight alliances and lesbian, gay, bisexual, and transgender (LGBT) youth. *School Psychology Quarterly, 26,* 161–174. doi:101.1037/a0023226

Hershberger, S. L., & D'Augelli, A. R. (1995). The impact of victimization on the mental health and suicidality of lesbian, gay, and bisexual youths. *Developmental Psychology, 31,* 65–74. doi:10.1037/0012-1649.31.1.65

Hirschstein, M. K., Edstrom, L. V. S., Frey, K. S., Snell, J. L., & MacKenzie, E. P. (2007). Walking the talk in bullying prevention: Teacher implementation variables related to initial impact of the Steps to Respect program. *School Psychology Review, 36,* 3–21.

Hirschstein, M. K., & Frey, K. S. (2006). Promoting behavior and beliefs that reduce bullying: The Steps to Respect program. In S. Jimerson & M. Furlong (Eds.), *The handbook of school violence and school safety: From research to practice* (pp. 309–323). Mahwah, NJ: Erlbaum.

Horn, S. S., Kosciw, J. G., & Russell, S. T. (2009). Special issue introduction: New research on lesbian, gay, bisexual, and transgender youth: Studying lives in context. *Journal of Youth and Adolescence, 38,* 863–866.

Illinois Safe Schools Alliance. (n.d.). Retrieved from http://www.illinoissafeschools.org/

Kosciw, J. G., & Diaz, E. M. (2008). *Involved, Invisible, Ignored: The Experiences of Lesbian, Gay, Bisexual and Transgender Parents and Their Children in Our Nation's K–12 Schools.* New York, NY: GLSEN.

Kosciw, J. G., Diaz, E. M., & Greytak, E. A. (2008). *The 2007 National School Climate Survey: The experiences of lesbian, gay, bisexual, and transgender youth in our nation's schools.* New York, NY: GSLEN.

Kosciw, J. G., Greytak, E. A., & Diaz, E. M. (2009). Who, what, where, when, and why: Demographic and ecological factors contributing to hostile school climates for lesbian, gay, bisexual, and transgender youth. *Journal of Youth and Adolescence, 38,* 976–988. doi:10.1007/s10964-009-9412-1

Kosciw, J. G., Greytak, E. A., Diaz, E. M., & Bartkiewicz, M. J. (2010). The 2009 National School Climate Survey: The experiences of lesbian, gay, bisexual and transgender youth in our nation's schools. New York, NY: GLSEN Retrieved from http://www.glsen .org/cgi-bin/iowa /all/ research/index .htm

McGuire, J. K., Anderson, C. R., Toomey, R. B., & Russell, S. T. (2010). School climate for transgender youth: A mixed method investigation of student experiences and school responses. *Journal of Youth and Adolescence, 39,* 1175–1188. doi:10.1007/s10964-010-9540-7

Merrell, K. W., Gueldner, B. A., Ross, S.W., & Isava, D. M. (2008). How effective are school bullying intervention programs? A meta-analysis of intervention research. *School Psychology Quarterly, 23,* 26–42. doi:10.1037/1045-3830.23.1.26

Morrison, G. M., Redding, M., Fisher, E., & Peterson, R. (2006). Assessing school discipline. In S. R. Jimerson & M. Furlong (Eds.), *Handbook of school violence and school safety: From research to practice* (pp. 211–220). Mahwah, NJ: Erlbaum.

National School Climate Center. (n.d.). Retrieved from http://www.schoolclimate.org/bullybust/

Newman, D. A., Horne, A. M., & Bartolomucci, C. L. (2000). *Bully Busters: A teacher's manual for helping bullies, victims, and bystanders.* Champaign, IL: Research Press.

Olweus, D., Limber, S. P., & Mihalic, S. (2000). *The Bullying Prevention Program: Blueprints for violence prevention* (Vol. 10). Boulder, CO: Center for the Study and Prevention of Violence.

Polanin, J., Espelage, D. L., & Pigott, T. D. (2012). A meta-analysis of school-based bullying prevention programs' effects on bystander intervention behavior and empathy attitude. *School Psychology Review, 41*(1), 47–65.

Poteat, V. P., Aragon, S. R., Espelage, D. L., & Koenig, B. W. (2009). Psychosocial concerns of sexual minority youth: Complexity and caution in group differences. *Journal of Consulting and Clinical Psychology, 77,* 196–201. doi:10.1037/a0014158

Poteat, V. P., & DiGiovanni, C. D. (2010). When biased language use is associated with bullying and dominance behavior: The moderating effect of prejudice. *Journal of Youth and Adolescence, 39,* 1123–1133. doi:10.1007/s10964-010-9565-y

Poteat, V. P., & Espelage, D. L. (2005). Exploring the relation between bullying and homophobic verbal content: The Homophobic Content Agent Target (HCAT) Scale. *Violence and Victims, 20*, 513–528. doi:10.1891/vivi.2005.20.5.513

Poteat, V. P., Mereish, E. H., DiGiovanni, C. D., & Koenig, B.W. (2011). The effects of general and homophobic victimization on adolescents' psychosocial and educational concerns: The importance of intersecting identities and parent support. *Journal of Counseling Psychology,* Online First Publication, August 22, 2011. doi:10.1037/a0025095

Rigby, K., & Johnson, B. (2006). Expressed readiness of Australian schoolchildren to act as bystanders in support of children who are being bullied. *Educational Psychology, 26*, 425–440. doi:10.1080/01443410500342047

Rivers, I. (2000). Social exclusion, absenteeism and sexual minority youth. *Support for Learning, 15*, 13–18. doi:10.1111/1467-9604.00136

Rivers, I. (2001). The bullying of sexual minorities at school: Its nature and long-term correlates. *Educational and Child Psychology, 18*, 32–46.

Rivers, I., & Noret, N. (2008). Well-being among same-sex and opposite-sex-attracted youth at school. *School Psychology Review, 37*, 174–187.

Robinson, J. P., & Espelage, D. L. (2011). Inequities in educational and psychological outcomes between LGBTQ and straight students in middle and high school. *Educational Researcher, 40*, 315–330. doi:10.3102/0013189x11422112

Ross, S., & Horner, R., (2009). Bully prevention in positive behavior support. *Journal of Applied Behavior Analysis, 42*(4), 747–760. doi:10.1901/jaba.2009.42-747

Ross, S., Horner, R., & Stiller, B. (2008). *Bully prevention in positive behavior support.* Eugene, OR: Educational and Community Supports. Retrieved from http://www.pbis.org/common/pbisresources/publications/bullyprevention_ES.pdf

Russell, S. (2010, September). Memorandum for discussion at the Research workshop on issues in education research, Washington, DC.

Russell, S. T. (2002). Queer in America: Citizenship for sexual minority youth. *Applied Developmental Science, 6*(4), 258–263.

Safren, S. A., & Heimberg, R. G. (1999). Depression, hopelessness, suicidality and related factors in sexual minority and heterosexual adolescents. *Journal of Consulting and Clinical Psychology, 67*, 859–866. doi:10.137/0022-006x.67.6.859

Salmivalli, C., Kärnä, A., & Poskiparta, E. (2010). Development, evaluation, and diffusion of a national anti-bullying program, KiVa. In B. Doll, W. Pfohl, & J. Yoon (Eds.), *Handbook of Youth Prevention Science* (pp. 240–254). New York, NY: Routledge.

Telljohann, S. K., & Price, J. H. (1993). A qualitative examination of adolescent homosexuals' life experiences: Ramifications for secondary school personnel. *Journal of Homosexuality 26*, 41–56. doi:10.1300/J082v26n01_04

Ttofi, M. M., Farrington, D. P., & Baldry, A. C. (2008). *Effectiveness of programmes to reduce school bullying.* Stockholm: Swedish Council for Crime Prevention, Information, and Publications.

Walls, N. E., Kane, S. B., & Wisneski, H. (2010). Gay-straight alliances and school experiences of sexual minority youth. *Youth and Society, 41*, 307–332. doi:10.1177/0044118x09334957

Warner, J., McKeown, É., Griffin, M., Johnson, K., Ramsay, A., Cort, C., & King, M. (2004). Rates and predictors of mental illness in gay men, lesbians and bisexual men and women: Results from a survey based in England and Wales. *British Journal of Psychiatry, 185*, 479–485. doi:10.1192/bjp.185.6.479

Warwick, I., Aggleton, P., & Douglas, N. (2001). Playing it safe: Addressing the emotional and physical health of lesbian and gay pupils in the U.K. *Journal of Adolescence. Special Issue: Gay, Lesbian, and Bisexual Youth, 24*, 129–140. doi:10.1006/jado.2000.0367

Williams, T., Connolly, J., Pepler. D., & Craig, W. (2003). Questioning and sexual minority adolescents: High school experiences of bullying, sexual harassment and physical abuse. *Canadian Journal of Community Mental Health, 22*, 47–58.

Zins, J. E., Weissberg, R. P., Wang, M. C., & Walberg, H. J. (Eds.). (2004). *Building school success through social and emotional learning.* New York, NY: Teachers College Press.

10 Responsive Classroom Curriculum for Lesbian, Gay, Bisexual, Transgender, and Questioning Students

Emily A. Greytak and Joseph G. Kosciw

Ideally school provides opportunities for youth to learn new skills, engage in intellectual exploration, and develop valuable social connections. However, for lesbian, gay, bisexual, transgender, and questioning (LGBTQ) youth, schools are often sites of exclusion and victimization. Anti-LGBTQ language, such as referring to something undesirable or boring as "gay," is omnipresent in school hallways and classrooms (Kosciw, Greytak, Diaz, & Bartkiewicz, 2010). Many LGBTQ youth are regularly bullied and harassed by their peers merely because of their sexual orientation or gender identity (D'Augelli, Pilkington, & Hershberger, 2002; Kosciw et al., 2010). Even the very adults tasked with protecting them may do nothing in the face of blatant homophobia and transphobia,[1] and at times, may participate in anti-LGBTQ language themselves (Bochenek & Brown, 2001; Kosciw et al., 2010; Smith & Smith, 1998). Beyond individual educators' actions (or inaction), school policies often may prove exclusionary, such as forbidding couples of the same sex from attending the prom or insisting students wear gender-specific graduation attire. Less blatant, but perhaps more pervasive and insidious, are the everyday practices that reinforce heterosexuality and gender norms, such as assuming a student will want to marry someone of a different gender, that render LGBTQ students invisible and send the message that they are not "normal." Whether through overt violence, official policies, or educator practices, heterosexism, homophobia, and transphobia manifest themselves in the school environment, giving LGBTQ youth the impression that they are not welcome in their schools.

The combination of the egregious harassment, pervasive biased language, and discriminatory policies and practices makes school, the place where most youth spend the majority of their waking hours, a very unwelcoming, and even hostile, environment for LGBTQ youth. Not only does a hostile school climate limit these students' ability to participate fully in their educational experience (Diaz, Kosciw, & Greytak, 2010; Centers for Disease Control and Prevention [CDC], 2011), but it also can significantly impact their academic achievement (Kosciw et al., 2010), physical health (Gruber & Fineran, 2008; Russell, Ryan, Toomey, Diaz, & Sanchez, 2011), and emotional well-being (Kosciw, et al., 2010; Russell & Joyner, 2001). These negative impacts have led to significant disparities in educational success and well-being between LGBTQ youth and non-LGBTQ youth (CDC, 2011; Kosciw et al., 2010). For example, the CDC (2011) found that heterosexual students were less likely to have skipped school because they felt unsafe than were gay, lesbian, or bisexual students. Therefore, LGBTQ youth in hostile school environments are being deprived of their right to an education, as well as their opportunity to develop into healthy, supported young adults.

Fortunately, there are a number of steps schools can implement to ensure that LGBTQ youth are safe, respected, and prepared to learn, such as supporting student clubs that address LGBTQ issues (e.g., Gay-Straight Alliances [GSAs]), instituting bullying and harassment policies that explicitly protect LGBTQ students, and incorporating LGBTQ issues into the curriculum. In the last decade, increased attention has been paid to the role of student clubs and bullying/harassment policies (see Chapter 9 of this volume, as well as Kosciw et al., 2010; Russell, Kosciw, Horn, & Saewyc, 2010), but there is less information available about specific strategies to ensure that curriculum is inclusive of LGBTQ people and issues (hereafter referred to as *inclusive curriculum*). In addition to supporting LGBTQ youth, these strategies can also help to create a safe and welcoming environment for students with LGBTQ family members who also may experience discrimination and marginalization at school (Kosciw & Diaz, 2008).

LGBTQ-Inclusive Curriculum

Emily Style (1996) from the National Seeking Educational Equity and Diversity Project uses the imagery of windows and mirrors to describe the two important functions of curriculum that includes diverse people and perspectives—curriculum serves as a mirror by reflecting individuals and their experiences back to themselves, while at the same time it functions as a window into the experiences and perspectives of others. Although Style (1996) used the metaphor in advocating specifically for the inclusion of women and people of color in the curriculum, this metaphor of windows and mirrors aptly captures the importance of LGBTQ inclusion as well. By serving as a mirror for LGBTQ youth, inclusive curriculum validates the existence of an often invisible population, reinforcing the value of LGBTQ individuals themselves and sending a strong message to LGBTQ students about their worth. Teaching about LGBTQ-related issues and incorporating LGBTQ people in the curriculum provides other students a window into a world they might not otherwise have access to, raising the awareness of all students and promoting a general tone of acceptance. Research on LGBTQ-inclusive curriculum lends evidence to the notion that these mirrors and windows help to create a more positive environment for LGBTQ students (Kosciw et al., 2010). In fact, the *National School Climate Survey*, a biennial survey of LGBTQ youth in school in the United States (U.S.), demonstrates that inclusive curriculum was related to a more positive school environment for LGBTQ youth (Kosciw et al., 2010). Specifically, compared to those without inclusive curriculum, LGBTQ students in schools that taught about LGBTQ people, history, and events:

- heard less anti-LGBTQ language (e.g., homophobic remarks like "fag" or "dyke");
- felt safer at school because of their sexual orientation or gender expression;
- were less likely to be harassed or assaulted because of their sexual orientation or gender expression; and
- missed less school because of safety concerns.

In addition to being less likely to experience a hostile school climate, LGBTQ students in schools with inclusive curriculum also had more positive experiences, as they:

- felt more connected to their school community;
- believed their peers to be more accepting of lesbian, gay, bisexual, and transgender (LGBT) people;
- were more likely to report that their peers intervened when others made homophobic remarks; and
- were more comfortable talking with teachers about LGBT issues and more likely to have talked with teachers about these issues.

Despite the positive benefits of inclusive curriculum, it appears that very few schools actually do incorporate these issues into the curriculum—less than one in five (17.9%) of LGBTQ students in the 2009 *National School Climate Survey* reported LGBT-related topics being included in their textbooks or assigned readings and only one in ten (11.7%) had been specifically taught positive representations of LGBT people, history, or events in their classes (Kosciw et al., 2010).

LGBTQ people and issues can be incorporated into a multitude of subjects, including social studies (Crocco, 2001; Jennings, 2006), English (Blackburn & Buckley, 2005; Rockefeller, 2009), and art (Lampela, 2001, 2007), but two specific fields are ideally suited for inclusion: multicultural education and sexuality education. Although both of these fields provide natural opportunities for LGBTQ inclusion, far too often they fail to include LGBTQ people or address LGBTQ issues (Blumenfeld, 2010).

LGBTQ Inclusion in Multicultural Education

Multicultural education can be broadly described as the teaching of diverse people and perspectives. Although there are numerous ways it has been defined and implemented (Gay, 1994), multicultural education is a field ripe for the inclusion of LGBTQ people and issues. Multicultural education is not situated in one specific discipline and can be addressed in any subject (for example, see Zaslavsky, 1996 for LGBTQ-inclusion in math classes). Returning to Style's (1996) metaphor of mirrors and windows, multicultural education has the opportunity to reflect back diverse groups of students' identities, histories, and lives while simultaneously providing students with insight into others' backgrounds and experiences. Of course, multicultural education can, and should, go further than merely representing various groups of people. It should educate about the context of these people in our society, highlighting the power held by some groups and the oppression of others and providing a social justice framework for students to learn about the world. Multicultural teaching should include perspectives that are both historical and current and construct knowledge that is both abstract and deeply personal. In the context of LGBTQ inclusion, this means that multicultural education should not only discuss LGBTQ individuals, but also address related personal and institutional prejudices such as homophobia and transphobia.

Historically, multicultural education efforts have focused on race, ethnicity, nationality, and, to a lesser extent, religion, while LGBTQ issues, along with gender, socioeconomic class, and disability issues, have been largely absent (Asher, 2007; Letts, 2002). More recently some multicultural education materials have begun to incorporate LGBTQ topics (e.g., Griffin, Hahn d'Errico, Haro, & Schiff, 2007; Mayo, 2010), although this content is mostly focused on lesbian and gay people and issues. Bisexual topics are somewhat less likely to be addressed and transgender content remains largely absent (see Catalano, McCarthy, & Shlasko, 2007 for an exception). Even in instances where transgender people or issues are acknowledged, it is too often in name only, with content actually only reflecting lesbian, gay, and bisexual people or issues related to sexual orientation (McCarthy, 2003). Despite the more recent inclusion of sexual orientation issues, and to a lesser extent transgender issues in some cases, LGBTQ issues still remain invisible or relegated to the margins of most multicultural education efforts (Blumenfeld, 2010; Mayo, 2010). Higher education, including teacher preparation courses, generally fails to address these issues—multicultural education textbooks rarely include LGBTQ content (Jennings & Macgillivray, 2008; Mathison, 1998) and teacher education on multicultural issues is unlikely to address LGBTQ topics (Jennings, 2007; Letts, 2002). In K-12 schools themselves where multicultural education would have the most direct impact on youth's school experiences, LGBTQ issues continue to be largely ignored. A national survey of public school principals found that while approximately 40% of principals reported that their staff and students were educated on multicultural issues, only 4% indicated the same of LGBT issues (GLSEN & Harris Interactive, 2008). The inclusion of diverse people and perspectives in professional development and classroom curriculum is laudable, yet it makes the omission of LGBTQ people and issues all the more glaring. In addition to leaving school professionals without the skills and knowledge to adequately respond to anti-LGBTQ bias, this omission deprives LGBTQ youth of the ability to see themselves reflected in their school environment and denies all students the opportunity to learn about LGBTQ people as an integral part of society. The exclusion of LGBTQ issues in multicultural education perpetuates a heterosexist and gender normative system that continually disenfranchises LGBTQ youth. However, by ensuring the inclusion of LGBTQ issues in multicultural efforts, educators instead could play an important role in dismantling homophobia and transphobia in schools, and in turn, our society.

There are multiple ways that LGBTQ issues could be incorporated into multicultural education curriculum. Banks (1995) proposed five dimensions of multicultural education: content integration, knowledge construction, equity pedagogy, prejudice reduction, and empowering school culture. The majority of Banks' work predominantly has focused on diversity as related to race, ethnicity, nationality, religion, social class, disability and gender, and by and large has not included LGBTQ content. Recently, however, Banks has begun addressing LGBTQ issues, as evidenced by the inclusion of a chapter about sexual and gender minorities (Mayo, 2010) in the seventh edition of his popular text, *Multicultural Education: Issues and Perspective* (Banks & Banks, 2010). Banks' commonly referenced dimensions of multicultural education provide a useful framework for exploring how educators can incorporate LGBTQ issues into the curriculum.

Content Integration

Content integration refers to the use of a diverse array of people and groups in the curriculum specifically when providing examples to demonstrate a concept or theme in the regular course of teaching a given subject (Banks, 1995). LGBTQ people, history, and events can be inserted into already established topics. Examples include: in a math word problem that uses an example of a family, use a same-sex couple; include the persecution of gays and lesbians when teaching the Holocaust; acknowledge Keith Haring's gay identity or Frieda Kahlo's bisexuality when viewing their work in art class; use works with LGBTQ themes and/or by LGBTQ authors (and mention the sexual orientation or gender identity of the author) in literature classes (see Blackburn & Buckley, 2005 for examples of literature addressing same-sex attractions and Rockefeller, 2009 for an extensive list of transgender-inclusive young adult fiction titles).

Knowledge Construction

While content integration is an important step, merely incorporating LGBTQ people and events into existing subjects is not enough. Educators also must address the values and norms that perpetuate LGBTQ exclusion. The knowledge construction dimension describes instruction that helps students identify and understand the cultural biases and assumptions that shape the way knowledge is constructed (Banks, 1995). Educators can question common assumptions of heterosexuality that arise throughout the curriculum by presenting examples of lesbian, gay, and bisexual people and relationships and gender-neutral examples of dating and relationships (e.g., asking "Who is the lucky person you are going to prom with?" as opposed to "Who is the lucky boy you are going to prom with?"). They also can challenge the concept that everyone is one of two genders, male or female, and that these genders align with the biological sex assigned at birth and remain static across the lifespan for everyone (i.e., the gender binary system). This example could be addressed in a biology course.

Equity Pedagogy

Integrating specific materials and knowledge construction is important, but how one teaches is just as important as what one teaches. The equity pedagogy dimension refers to specific ways of teaching that foster the inclusion and success of diverse groups of students (Banks, 1995). LGBTQ-responsive pedagogy ensures that teaching methods are inclusive and relevant to all students, regardless of sexual orientation or gender identity. For example, teachers should take care to avoid gender-specific groupings whenever possible. Although it is often seen as a relatively easy and simple way to divide students, it may reinforce the heterosexist notion that girls and boys are polar opposites, and that there are only two acceptable genders. It may inadvertently punish boys who may be more comfortable working with girls, and vice-versa. It may perpetuate stereotypes and essentialist thinking by sending a message that there is a "girls' viewpoint" or "girls' way of learning" and a "boys' viewpoint" or "boys' way of learning." In addition, forcing students to choose between joining a boys' group or a girls' group may be particularly challenging for transgender students who may feel forced to select a gender with which they do not identify.

Prejudice Reduction

Prejudice reduction attempts to educate students specifically about bias with the intention of increasing tolerance and respect of diverse people (Banks, 1995). It goes beyond the basic level of acceptance and includes analysis of the development, function, and impact of prejudice in our society. Education about homophobia and transphobia can happen both proactively and reactively. School professionals need to speak up when witnessing anti-LGBTQ language (e.g., students using the phrases "that's so gay" or "no homo") and intervene in anti-LGBTQ bullying and harassment. It is not enough to stop the victimization or punish the perpetrators, but educators must take the teachable moment to specifically name the behavior as homophobic or transphobic and explain why it is unacceptable. Doing so will not only serve to educate the student committing the offense, but also it will send a powerful message to both the victim and bystanders that anti-LGBTQ behavior is not tolerated. For specific suggestions of how to intervene in these types of incidents see Gay, Lesbian, and Straight Education Network's (GLSEN's) *Safe Space Kit* (GLSEN, 2009).

In addition to responding when witnessing LGBTQ bias, prejudice reduction requires educators to work proactively to diminish stereotypes and prejudice of LGBTQ people. There are multiple ways to do this, including:

- bringing in LGBTQ-identified speakers' panels;
- showing relevant films (see www.groundspark.org for examples); and
- using specific lessons about LGBTQ bias (e.g., *Think B4 You Speak Educator's Guide* [GLSEN, 2008]).

Although educating about anti-LGBTQ bias and its effects on LGBTQ people is an important component of LGBTQ-inclusive curriculum, it should not be the sole, or even the predominant, representation of LGBTQ people and issues (Britzman & Gilbert, 2004). Care must be taken to avoid portraying LGBTQ people (and especially LGBTQ youth) as mere victims. Instead, educators should present LGBTQ people and communities in their full humanity—as complex, vibrant, and even mundane. A truly inclusive curriculum acknowledges their persecution, their resilience, their triumph, and their common every-day existence.

Empowering School Culture

Empowering school culture requires going beyond the classroom and addressing the school community as a whole (Banks, 1995). School professionals can work to ensure that school practices and policies are LGBTQ-inclusive. In addition to enacting LGBTQ-inclusive curriculum in their own classrooms, there are a variety of school-wide efforts that educators can advocate for in order to help make schools safer and responsive to LGBTQ students:

- Ongoing Assessment: regular surveying of school climate (e.g. student behavior surveys) that includes information about anti-LGBTQ behaviors in school (e.g., bullying and harassment) and provides ways to assess school climate for LGBTQ students (i.e., including questions that, in addition to gender and race, assess sexual orientation and transgender status);

- Inclusive Policies: discrimination, bullying, and harassment policies that specifically name sexual orientation, gender expression, and gender identity among protected characteristics;
- Professional Development: staff training on how to address anti-LGBTQ behaviors and how to be responsive to LGBTQ students;
- Inclusive Bullying Prevention Strategies: bullying prevention efforts, including student education programs and staff training, that specifically discuss anti-LGBTQ bullying, along with other types of bias-based bullying (e.g., bullying based on race, religion, socioeconomic class, disability, etc.);
- Gender-Neutral Policies: eliminating gender-specific assignments for dress codes (including graduation gowns and yearbook photos) and allowing students to bring dates of any gender for school dances;
- Specific Policies and Practices to Support Transgender Youth: written guidelines for how staff should treat transgender youth; for example, using students' preferred name and pronouns in the classroom and ensuring safe, respectful, and convenient bathroom and locker room options. For more specific recommendations, see Chapters 5 and 7 of this volume; and
- Student Leadership: support of GSAs and similar student-led clubs working to combat LGBTQ bias in schools, and of student actions designed to raise awareness of LGBTQ people and issues, such as the *Day of Silence*.

Chapter 14 of this volume provides more specific guidance on how to be an ally and advocate for LGBTQ students. In addition to addressing these issues directly themselves, educators can inspire their students to do the same, which would have the dual benefit of educating individual students as well as improving the school environment.

LGBTQ Inclusion in Sexuality Education

Whereas multicultural education is an approach that can, and should, be infused throughout all disciplines, one specific subject, sexuality education, is also ripe for LGBTQ inclusion. Sexuality education, one component of the larger discipline of health education, addresses sexual health and development, generally contains information about reproduction, and often also includes content about sexual and romantic relationships. Thus, sexuality education curriculum is an important source, and in some cases, the only source, of information for our nation's youth about a variety of critical topics—including puberty, anatomy, pregnancy and contraception, HIV/AIDS and other sexually transmitted infections, dating and marriage, gender roles, rape/sexual assault, and intimate partner violence. Classroom curricula vary in the breadth with which they cover these topics. Some may cover only pregnancy prevention, while others may include an intensive curriculum that includes more relationship-oriented topics and social issues. Regardless of the breadth or depth of the curriculum, any discussion of sexuality education should, by its nature, incorporate LGBTQ issues. The subject matter affords an opportunity for specific discussion of sexual identity or orientation, and even if sexual identities/orientations are not specifically addressed as a topic, sexuality should certainly be inclusive of nonheterosexual people and behaviors by merely acknowledging gay, lesbian, bisexual, and/or questioning people and same-sex sexual or romantic behaviors in their discussions and materials. In addition, discussions regarding issues of sex and gender should include, or at the very least, allow for the possibility of transgender people. However, despite the myriad opportunities for LGBTQ-inclusion, much of the sexuality education in U.S. schools excludes LGBTQ people and issues (Fisher, 2009; Kosciw et al., 2010). And even when sexual identities or behaviors other than heterosexual are acknowledged, they may be presented in ways that stigmatize or marginalize LGBTQ people (Advocates for Youth, 2002; Lipkin, 1993/1994). Specifically, in regards to LGBTQ people and issues, sexuality education has tended to reflect four types of approaches: ignoring, demonizing, stigmatizing, and/or transgender excluding.

The "Ignoring" Approach to LGBTQ Content in Sexuality Education

The curriculum ignores the existence of LGBTQ people and nonheterosexual behaviors completely. Not only is there an omission of LGBTQ people and related topics, but heterosexuality is put forth as the norm and only conceivable option. This may occur in the content of the curriculum with only heterosexual sexual activity or romantic relationships acknowledged. Even the very definition of sex used in some curricula applies only to heterosexuals (Bay-Cheng, 2003). For example, "sex" is defined by one curriculum, *Sex Respect*, as "the physical and personal act of male and female genital union, sexual intercourse" (Mast, n.d., as cited in Yakush, 2007, p. 17).

The "Demonizing" Approach to LGBTQ Content in Sexuality Education

The curriculum includes, yet demonizes, LGBTQ people and nonheterosexual behaviors. For example, two national studies indicated that a small portion of sexuality education explicitly teaches that homosexuality is wrong—8% of health teachers (Telljohann, Price, Poureslami, & Easton, 1995) and, more recently, 1% of public secondary school principals (National Public Radio, Kaiser Family Foundation, & Kennedy School of Government, 2004) reported that their curriculum included this message. In addition to such direct negative statements about homosexuality, curriculum also can implicitly communicate that being LGBTQ is undesirable and unacceptable. For example, certain curricula have equated homosexuality with child sexual abuse (Cahill & Jones, 2001) and others have insinuated that gay men are responsible for the AIDS epidemic (Advocates for Youth, 2002).

The "Stigmatizing" Approach to LGBTQ Content in Sexuality Education

While perhaps not outright condemning LGBTQ people or any nonheterosexual feelings or behaviors, curriculum may still be stigmatizing to LGBTQ youth. For instance, LGBTQ people may be mentioned only when discussing sexually transmitted infections. This portrays LGBTQ people as dangerous and their sexual behaviors as risky and abnormal (Fisher, 2009; Lipkin, 1993/1994).

The "Transgender Excluding" Approach to LGBTQ Content in Sexuality Education

Regardless of how (or if) sexuality education curricula portray lesbian, gay, and bisexual (LGB) people or nonheterosexual feelings or behaviors, transgender topics are rarely addressed at all (Green, 2010). Even curriculum that includes LGB people and nonheterosexuality in an affirming, respectful manner, generally excludes transgender people and issues completely, negating their existence and value.

These aforementioned approaches are not necessarily mutually exclusive in any given sexuality curriculum. A curriculum could encompass all four of the approaches in various aspects of the curriculum. For example, a curriculum could ignore the existence of LGB people by discussing dating in a heterosexist manner, while, at the same time, could acknowledge, yet demonize, gay and bisexual males by asserting that they were responsible for the spread of HIV/AIDS.

Abstinence-Only Sexuality Education

One of the most common and well-funded, albeit controversial, brands of sexuality education in United States secondary schools is abstinence-only education. By its very definition abstinence-only cannot be LGBTQ inclusive, as it instructs that people should abstain from sex until legally married, an option not available for same-sex couples in all but a few U.S. states. Although leading organizations such as the American Public Health Association (2006), Sexuality Information and Education Council of the U.S. (Yakush, 2007), and the Society for Adolescent Medicine (Santelli et al., 2006) have condemned abstinence-only education for its lack of LGBT inclusivity, among other things, it continues to persist throughout U.S. schools. More than a third (39.7%) of LGBT students reported being taught abstinence-only (and an additional 22.8% did not know if their school's sex education curriculum was abstinence-only or not) (Kosciw, Diaz, & Greytak, 2008). Although the Obama administration's recent guidelines for the federal funding stream for abstinence-based programs encourages states receiving funds to "consider the needs of lesbian, gay, bisexual, transgender, and questioning youth and how their programs will be inclusive of and nonstigmatizing toward such participants" (Title V State Abstinence Education Grant Program, 2010, p. 9), funding recipients are not mandated to do so. In fact, one might wonder exactly how any abstinence-only program could, given the illegality of same-sex marriage in most U.S. states, be inclusive and nonstigmatizing of LGBTQ youth. One such program, WAIT (*Why Am I Tempted?*), that has asserted its appropriateness for gay and lesbian youth, has come under fire for this claim, given its lack of specific mention of gays or lesbians and its heterosexist messages (Kopsa, 2011; Yakush, 2007).

Given the exclusionary and biased messaging inherent in abstinence-only curriculum, it is not surprising that use of this type of curriculum has been related to negative educational outcomes for LGBTQ youth. LGBTQ youth who reported receiving an abstinence-only based sex education were (Kosciw et al., 2008):

- less likely to feel safe at school due to their sexual orientation or their gender expression;
- more likely to miss school because they felt unsafe;
- less likely to feel comfortable talking about LGBT issues with school personnel; and
- less likely to be able to identify school personnel who were supportive of LGBT students.

Abstinence-only curriculum does not have the monopoly on excluding LGBTQ students, and even sex education that is more comprehensive can utilize any of the four approaches previously discussed (ignoring, demonizing, stigmatizing, and/or transgender exclud-ing). Although a majority of LGBTQ students were not taught an abstinence-only curriculum or did not know if the curriculum was abstinence-only (37.5% and 22.8%, respectively), when asked whether they were taught about LGBT people, history, or events in any of their subjects, only 4.3% reported that their health classes included this information (Kosciw et al., 2008). Thus, it appears that the vast majority of middle and high schools, regardless of whether they follow an abstinence-only approach, are teaching sexuality education that is not LGBTQ inclusive.

LGBTQ-Inclusive Sexuality Education Curriculum

Although, unfortunately, most sexuality education is not LGBTQ-inclusive, there are some health educators who are addressing these issues, and many more who are interested in doing so (Telljohann et al., 1995). Educators and curriculum developers alike should keep in mind a number of key guidelines to help ensure that sexuality education curriculum appropriately incorporates LGBTQ people and issues.

Do not assume heterosexuality. Curriculum should use gender-neutral language, such as "partner," when appropriate and should include examples of same-gender romantic and sexual activity.

Avoid relegating LGBTQ issues to "special topics." Educators striving to ensure that their sexuality education curriculum is truly LGBTQ-inclusive will make certain that LGBTQ people and concerns are reflected throughout all aspects of the curriculum, not relegated to one specific session or unit. Although having topic-specific units on "sexual orientation" or "gender identity" may be appropriate, this should not be the only time LGBTQ issues are incorporated into the curriculum. Furthermore, in discussions of sexual orientation, heterosexuality should be discussed alongside of homosexuality, bisexuality, and asexuality, and in discussions about gender identity, cisgender individuals (people whose sex assigned at birth aligns with their gender identity and gender expression, i.e., non-transgender people) should be discussed along with transgender individuals. The Sexuality Information and Education Council of the United States' (SIECUS) *Comprehensive Sexuality Education Framework* (2004), for example, incorporates LGB people in units on families, romantic relationships, and gender roles, and LGBT people in the sexuality and religion unit in addition to specific units on sexual orientation/identity and gender identity.

Pay more than token attention to transgender people and concerns. Curriculum should avoid the four approaches previously enumerated (ignoring, demonizing, stigmatizing, transgender excluding) and utilize an approach that is fully LGBTQ-inclusive by incorporating nonheterosexual behaviors and LGBTQ people in an affirming, respectful manner. Whereas there has been some discussion of the components of a sex education curriculum that is genuinely inclusive of nonheterosexual people and behaviors (see Elia & Eliason, 2010), there has been little attention paid to what a transgender-inclusive sex education curriculum would specifically contain. Instead, much of the literature about LGBTQ-inclusive sexuality education pays mere lip service to the "T," only discussing topics related to sexual orientation, such as the dangers of promotion of heterosexual marriage as the only acceptable realm for sexual activity and the potential damage done by stigmatizing or vilifying same-sex sexual behaviors.

Although these issues may prove relevant for some transgender youth, they may not for others (e.g., transgender youth who are heterosexual). Yet, there are other topics that should be included in order for a curriculum to truly be trans-inclusive, such as the differentiation between sex and gender.

Use inclusive definitions of sexual activity. Definitions of sex should not be based upon the gender of those involved (i.e., "the physical and personal act of male and female genital union, sexual intercourse" (Mast, n.d., as cited in Yakush, 2007, p. 17)). Even more specific definitions of sex such as penetration of the vagina by a penis excludes gays and lesbians, and some bisexual and transgender people, from sex altogether, not to mention exempting a variety of activities engaged in by heterosexual cisgender people. Instead of using a restrictive definition of sex, various types of penetrative sex (oral, anal, with fingers, with other objects such as sex toys) and nonpenetrative sex (mutual masturbation) could be included.

Avoid discussing LGBTQ people and same-gender sexual activity only in the context of risk. While accurate information should be provided about certain sexual behaviors that may put youth at higher risk, the focus should be on the behavior (e.g., unprotected anal sex) not the sexual orientation or gender identity of the individuals engaging in the behavior.

Avoid using gender-specific activities when possible. As previously mentioned, separating male and female students by dividing them into separate groups (e.g., boys' discussions and girls' discussions) or giving them different activities or assignments may reinforce heterosexuality, promote essentialist gender stereotypes, foster divisiveness (i.e., "battle of the sexes"), and endorse the idea that there are only two acceptable genders. It may also create a hostile environment for transgender youth or youth who are unsure about their gender identity as they may be forced to come out to their peers or to choose a group with which they do not identify. If educators choose to divide students into groups, they can choose other methods, such as by birthday month or having students count off by numbers.

Do not reinforce gender stereotypes. Much of sexuality education continues to frame males as seekers of sexual pleasure and females as seekers of romantic relationships (Fine & McClelland, 2006; Yakush, 2007). This perpetuates damaging and limiting notions of both male and female desire, stigmatizing anyone who falls outside these narrow conceptions of femininity and masculinity.

Sexuality education should strive to benefit all students, providing LGBTQ students with accurate and useful information that is relevant to their sexual health and development. Curriculum that fails to do so leaves these students at disproportionate risk. This inadequate sex education may account for some of the sexual health disparities so widely reported, including increased risk of sexually transmitted infections (CDC, 2011), sexual abuse (Saewyc, Bearinger, Blum, & Resnick, 1999), and pregnancy involvement (CDC, 2011; Saewyc et al., 1999) among non-heterosexual youth and HIV infection among transgender individuals[2] (Grant et al., 2011). Along with depriving LGBTQ youth of important factual and practical information, noninclusive sexuality education curriculum denies LGBTQ youth that critical mirror in which they can see themselves reflected as valuable human beings. In addition, it fails to provide that window to non-LGBTQ youth, squandering the opportunity to increase awareness, dispel myths, and broaden the worldview of the majority of students.

Barriers to LGBTQ Inclusion in Curriculum

Given the demonstrated value of inclusive curriculum for LGBTQ students, and the variety of ways of including LGBTQ people and issues into the curriculum, it is disappointing that these issues are so rarely incorporated into the school curriculum. There are a number of barriers to LGBTQ-inclusive education, both formal and informal. One of the most obvious barriers is specific legislation or policies that actually prohibit LGBTQ inclusion. As previously discussed, abstinence-only sex education policies ignore the needs, and often even the existence, of LGBTQ youth. To date, eight states[3] have enacted laws that prohibit positive portrayals of homosexuality in schools (i.e., "no promo homo" laws), virtually outlawing any LGBTQ inclusive curriculum (or at least any that did not explicitly stigmatize LGBTQ people).[4] In addition, local school districts have employed policies that forbid discussion of LGBTQ people or issues. For example, the "Sexual Orientation Curriculum Policy" (2009) of the Minnesota School District Anoka-Hennepin states, "teaching about sexual orientation is not a part of the district adopted curriculum; rather, such matters are best addressed within individual family homes, churches, or community organizations" (p. 1). Even in the absence of formal laws or policies restricting LGBTQ inclusion, educators may face resistance from school or district administration, parents, or the community (Lai, 2011; Maher & Sever, 2007).

A more personal barrier to including LGBTQ content in the curriculum may be concerns of the educators themselves. For LGBTQ teachers, incorporating these issues may pose specific risks, and some may choose to refrain from discussing LGBTQ issues in their classroom for fear of being outed and potentially losing their jobs (Bliss & Harris, 1998; Lampela, 2001). This is one of the reasons job protections for LGBTQ school employees and anti-discrimination laws that include sexual orientation, gender expression, and gender identity are so important.

Another concern of educators that may inhibit LGBTQ inclusion is the false belief that talking about LGBTQ people and issues requires discussion of sexual behaviors (Lampela, 2001). Educators also may lack the knowledge, skills, or resources necessary to incorporate LGBTQ issues (Kim, 2009), either not being aware of the importance of doing so or feeling ill equipped to do so. They are unlikely to be prepared by their pre-service or in-service education to address LGBTQ issues (GLSEN & Harris Interactive, 2008; Rands, 2009; Sherwin & Jennings, 2006).

Promoting LGBTQ Inclusion in Curriculum

In spite of the aforementioned barriers, many educators persevere and integrate LGBTQ issues and people into their teaching (see Athanases, 1996 for examples). There are a number of measures that can be taken to support and facilitate LGBTQ inclusion.

Preparation and Professional Development

Pre-service and ongoing in-service education should be provided to all school personnel on LGBTQ issues. In addition to the basic information that all personnel should receive—knowledge about the school environment for LGBTQ students and ways to respond to anti-LGBTQ bias—educators will benefit from having concrete opportunities to practice discussing these issues in the classroom and planning how to integrate LGBTQ issues into their instruction. Similarly, professional development for curriculum development staff can focus on ways to address LGBTQ issues in curriculum materials and standards. Schools, districts, and pre-service institutions (be they traditional university teacher education programs or alternative certification routes, e.g., Teach for America) must proactively provide education on LGBTQ issues, seeking out research-based and tested resources and training programs whenever possible (for examples see Greytak & Kosciw, 2010 and Payne & Smith, 2010). These institutions also must ensure that any professional development on bullying, sexuality education, and multicultural education substantively address LGBTQ issues.

Curricular Resources

In addition to receiving professional development on LGBTQ issues, educators can proactively seek out resources to help ensure their curriculum is LGBTQ-inclusive. There are a variety of existing resources that address LGBTQ issues available for use in classrooms, such as:

- GLSEN's website for educators (http://www.glsen.org/educator), which provides a wealth of curricular resources including lessons for elementary and secondary grade levels;
- *Unheard Voices*, a recently released curriculum by the Anti-Defamation League, GLSEN, and StoryCorps (2011), which uses oral histories to teach about LGBTQ history (available at http://www.glsen.org/educator);
- Meyer's *Gender and Sexual Diversity in Schools* (2010), which provides user-friendly concrete suggestions for including LGBTQ issues in a variety of different subjects (including math, biology, fine and performing arts);
- GroundSpark (http://www.groundspark.org), which provides videos with educator discussion guides, such as *Straightlaced: How Gender's Got Us All Tied Up* (Chasnoff & Chen, 2009); and
- The Milk Foundation, which offers curriculum for educating about Harvey Milk (http://www.milkfoundation.org).

Professional Associations

Many of the leading education associations have worked to advocate on behalf of LGBTQ students to create resources, develop position statements, and support legislation and policies to ensure safe and respectful school environments for these youth. For example:

- The National Education Association (NEA) published a report on LGBT people in education (Kim, 2009) and offers a training program, "Safety, Bias, and GLBT Issues" for educators;
- The American Federation of Teachers provides a special section on their website for information related to LGBT people (http://www.aft.org/yourwork/tools4teachers/bullying/specialpops.cfm); and

- A number of professional education associations, including the School Social Work Association of America, the National Association of Secondary School Principals, and the American School Counselor Association, endorsed a publication about sexual orientation and youth for school personnel (Just the Facts Coalition, 2008) and have endorsed proposed federal legislation that protects LGBT students from bullying and discrimination (The National Safe Schools Partnership, 2007).

Information and position statements from these associations may provide individual educators with support and legitimacy when faced with opposition from their local administration or community.

Educator Groups

Educators have formed both formal and informal groups to support each other in creating LGBTQ-inclusive schools. Examples include:

- NYQueer (http://www.nycore.org/nyqueer), a working group of the New York Collective of Radical Educators;
- GLSEN's Educator Forum on Facebook;
- The National Association of School Psychologist's Gay, Lesbian, and Bisexual Issues Workgroup; and
- The National Education Association's Gay, Lesbian, Bisexual, and Transgender Caucus.

In addition to a sense of community, these groups can provide much needed tools and support to individual educators.

Curricular Standards

Just as laws and policies can be used to prohibit or restrict inclusion of LGBTQ people and issues in the curriculum, they also can serve to promote LGBTQ inclusion. For example, California's recent FAIR (Fair, Accurate, Inclusive and Respectful) Education Act mandates that LGBT people and history are included in social science education, and it prohibits the adoption of instructional materials that discriminate against LGBT people (California Department of Education, 2011). On a local level, public school districts, such as Montgomery County, MD and New York City, NY, have implemented sexuality education curriculum that explicitly includes discussion of LGBTQ people and issues (de Vise, 2007; Santos & Phillips, 2011).

This chapter touches on the multitude of ways educators can ensure that their teaching is LGBTQ-inclusive. In addition to those teaching in the classroom, all those working in schools, especially in the realms of sexuality education and multicultural education, must take affirmative steps to ensure that LGBTQ people and issues are included. Curriculum developers, administrators, textbook publishers, scholars, education reformers, and policymakers must be sure to integrate LGBTQ people and issues into their work, ensuring that multicultural education, sexuality education, and schools in general are LGBTQ inclusive. If they do not, LGBTQ students will continue to receive a subpar education, one that results in educational disparities and a lack of safety, ultimately depriving these students of access to an equal education and potentially stunting their development into healthy, productive adults.

Notes

1 For the purposes of this chapter, homophobia is defined as the irrational fear of or aversion to homosexuality or lesbian, gay, or bisexual people, and transphobia is defined as an irrational fear of or aversion to transgender people or those who are perceived to break or blur societal norms regarding gender identity or gender expression.
2 We refer to "transgender individuals" as opposed to "transgender youth" because the data on sexual health disparities between transgender and cisgender youth are confined to adults; to date there is little information on sexual health disparities between transgender and cisgender youth.
3 States that prohibit the positive portrayal of homosexuality in schools include: Alabama, Arizona, Louisiana, Mississippi, Oklahoma, South Carolina, Texas, and Utah (Kosciw et al., 2010).
4 While "no promo homo" laws do not necessarily preclude educators from portraying transgender people and issues in a positive light in school, it is our assumption that educators who are prohibited from presenting homosexuality in a positive light would not be including positive representations of transgender people/issues in the classroom. Thus, we believe that "no promo homo" laws also may stigmatize transgender individuals and restrict transgender youth from learning about themselves and their communities in school.

References

Advocates for Youth. (2002). Abstinence-only-until-marriage education: Abandoning responsibility to GLBTQ youth. *Transitions, 14*(4), 8–9.

American Public Health Association. (2006). *Abstinence and U.S. abstinence-only education policies: Ethical and human rights concerns* (Policy Statement Number: 200610). Retrieved from http://www.apha.org/advocacy/policy/policysearch/default.htm?id=1334

Anti-Defamation League, GLSEN, & StoryCorps. (2011). *Unheard voices: Stories of LGBT history*. Retrieved from GLSEN website: http://www.glsen.org/educator

Asher, N. (2007). Made in the (multicultural) U.S.A.: Unpacking tensions of race, culture, gender, and sexuality in education. *Educational Researcher, 36*(2), 65–73. doi:10.3102/0013189X07299188

Athanases, S. Z. (1996). A gay-themed lesson in an ethnic literature curriculum: Tenth graders' responses to "Dear Anita." *Harvard Educational Review, 66*(2), 231–257.

Banks, J. A. (1995). Multicultural education: Historical development, dimensions, and practice. In J. A. Banks & C. A. M. Banks (Eds.), *Handbook of research on multicultural education* (pp. 3–24). New York, NY: Macmillan.

Banks, J., & Banks, C. (Eds.). (2010). *Multicultural education: Issues and perspectives* (7th ed.). New York, NY: Wiley.

Bay-Cheng, L. Y. (2003). The trouble of teen sex: The construction of adolescent sexuality through school-based sexuality education. *Sex Education, 3*(1), 61–74. doi:10.1080/1468181032000052162

Blackburn, M. V., & Buckley, J. (2005). Teaching queer-inclusive English language arts. *Journal of Adolescent & Adult Literacy, 49*(3), 202–212. doi:10.1598/JAAL.49.3.4

Bliss, G. K., & Harris, M. B. (1998). Experiences of gay and lesbian teachers and parents with coming out in a school setting. *Journal of Gay & Lesbian Social Services, 8*(2), 13–28. doi:10.1300/J041v08n02_02

Blumenfeld, W. J. (2010). How comprehensive is multicultural education?: A case for LGBT inclusion. *Journal of Multiculturalism in Education, 5*(2), 1–20.

Bochenek, M., & Brown, A. W. (2001). *Hatred in the hallways: Violence and discrimination against lesbian, gay, bisexual, and transgender students in U.S. schools.* New York, NY: Human Rights Watch.

Britzman, D. P., & Gilbert, J. (2004). What will have been said about gayness in teacher education? *Teaching Education, 15*(1), 81–96. doi:10.1080/1047621042000180004

Cahill, S., & Jones, K. T. (2001). *Leaving our children behind: Welfare reform and the gay, lesbian, bisexual, and transgender community.* Washington, DC: National Gay and Lesbian Task Force.

California Department of Education. (2011, July 14). State schools chief Tom Torlakson releases statement on Senate Bill 48. *California Department of Education News Release #11-49.* Retrieved from http://www.cde.ca.gov/nr/ne/yr11/yr11rel49.asp

Catalano, C., McCarthy, L., & Shlasko, D. (2007). Transgender oppression curriculum design. In M. Adams, L. A. Bell, & P. Griffin (Eds.), *Teaching for diversity and social justice: A sourcebook* (pp. 219–246). New York, NY: Routledge.

Centers for Disease Control and Prevention [CDC]. (2011). Sexual identity, sex of sexual contacts, and health-risk behaviors among students in grades 9–12: Youth risk behavior surveillance, selected sites, United States, 2001–2009. *MMWR* (Vol. 60). Atlanta, GA: Author.

Chasnoff, D., & Chen, S. (Director, Producer). (2009). *Straightlaced: How gender's got us all tied up.* USA: GroundSpark.

Crocco, M. S. (2001). The missing discourse about gender and sexuality in the social studies. *Theory into Practice, 40*(1), 65–71. doi:10.1207/s15430421tip4001_10

D'Augelli, A. R., Pilkington, N. W., & Hershberger, S. L. (2002). Incidence and mental health impact of sexual orientation victimization of lesbian, gay, and bisexual youths in high school. *School Psychology Quarterly, 17*(2), 148–167.

de Vise, D., (2007, January 10). Board of Education approves new sex-ed curriculum. *The Washington Post.* Retrieved from http://www.washingtonpost.com/wp-dyn/content/article/2007/01/09/AR2007010901707.html

Diaz, E. M., Kosciw, J. G., & Greytak, E. A. (2010). School connectedness for lesbian, gay, bisexual, and transgender youth: In-school victimization and institutional supports. *The Prevention Researcher, 17*(3), 15–17.

Elia, J. P., & Eliason, M. (2010). Discourses of exclusion: Sexuality education's silencing of sexual others. *Journal of LGBT Youth, 7*(1), 29–48. doi:10.1080/19361650903507791

Fine, M., & McClelland, S. I. (2006). Sexuality education and desire: Still missing after all these years. *Harvard Educational Review, 76*(3), 297–338.

Fisher, C. M. (2009). Queer youth experiences with abstinence-only-until-marriage sexuality education: "I can't get married so where does that leave me?" *Journal of LGBT Youth, 6*(1), 61–79. doi:10.1080/19361650802396775

Gay, G. (1994). A synthesis of scholarship in multicultural education. *Urban Education Monograph Series:* Retrieved from http://www.ncrel.org/sdrs/areas/issues/educatrs/leadrshp/le0gay.htm

GLSEN. (2008). *ThinkB4YouSpeak educator's guide: For discussing and addressing anti-gay language among teens.* Retrieved from http://www.thinkb4youspeak.com/ForEducators/GLSEN-EducatorsGuide.pdf

GLSEN. (2009). *Safe Space Kit.* New York, NY: Author.

GLSEN & Harris Interactive. (2008). *The principal's perspective: School safety, bullying and harassment, a survey of public school principals.* New York, NY: GLSEN.

Grant, J. M., Mottet, L. A., Tanis, J., Harrison, J., Herman, J. L., & Keisling, M. (2011). *Injustice at every turn: A report of the National Transgender Discrimination Survey.* Retrieved from National Center for Transgender Equality and National Gay and Lesbian Task Force website: http://www.thetaskforce.org/downloads/reports/reports/ntds_full.pdf

Green, E. R. (2010). Shifting paradigms: Moving beyond "Trans 101" in sexuality education. *American Journal of Sexuality Education, 5*(1), 1–16. doi:10.1080/15546121003748798

Greytak, E. A., & Kosciw, J. G. (2010). *Year one evaluation of the New York City Department of Education Respect for All training program.* New York, NY: GLSEN.

Griffin, P., Hahn d'Errico, K., Haro, B., & Schiff, T. (2007). Heterosexism curriculum design. In M. Adams, L. A. Bell, & P. Griffin (Eds.), *Teaching for diversity and social justice: A sourcebook* (pp. 195–218). New York, NY: Routledge.

Gruber, J., & Fineran, S. (2008). Comparing the impact of bullying and sexual harassment victimization on the mental and physical health of adolescents. *Sex Roles, 59*(1), 1–13. doi:10.1007/s11199-008-9431-5

Jennings, K. (2006). "Out" in the classroom: Addressing lesbian, gay, bisexual and transgender (LGBT) issues in social studies curriculum. In W. E. Ross (Ed.), *The social studies curriculum: Purposes, problems, and possibilities* (3rd ed., pp. 255–282). Albany, NY: State University of New York Press.

Jennings, T. (2007). Addressing diversity in US teacher preparation programs: A survey of elementary and secondary programs' priorities and challenges from across the United States of America. *Teaching and Teacher Education, 23,* 1258–1271.

Jennings, T., & Macgillivray, I. K. (2008, March). *A content analysis of LGBT topics in multicultural education textbooks.* Paper presented at the Annual Conference of the American Educational Association, New York, NY.

Just the Facts Coalition. (2008). *Just the facts about sexual orientation and youth: A primer for principals, educators, and school personnel.* Retrieved from American Psychological Association website: http://www.apa.org/pi/lgbc/publications/justthefacts.html

Kim, R. (with Sheridan, D., & Holcomb, S.) (2009). *A report on the status of gay, lesbian, bisexual and transgender people in education: Stepping out of the closet, into the light.* Washington, DC: National Education Association.

Kopsa, A. (2011, August 9). Abstinence-only funding was refused, but that didn't stop a state school-board member. *Westword News.* Retrieved from http://www.westword.com/2011-08-11/news/abstinence-only-education-colorado/

Kosciw, J. G., & Diaz, E. M. (2008). *Involved, invisible, ignored: The experiences of lesbian, gay, bisexual and transgender parents and their children in our nation's K–12 schools.* New York: GLSEN.

Kosciw, J., Diaz, E., & Greytak, E. (2008). *The 2007 national school climate survey: The experiences of lesbian, gay, bisexual, and transgender youth in our nation's schools.* New York, NY: GLSEN.

Kosciw, J., Greytak, E., Diaz, E., & Bartkiewicz, M. J. (2010). *The 2009 national school climate survey: The experiences of lesbian, gay, bisexual, and transgender youth in our nation's schools.* New York, NY: GLSEN.

Lai, A. (2011). Tango or more? From California's Lesson 9 to the constitutionality of a gay-friendly curriculum in public elementary schools. *Michigan Journal of Gender & Law, 17*(2), 315–348.

Lampela, L. (2001). Lesbian and gay artists in the curriculum: A survey of art teachers' knowledge and attitudes. *Studies in Art Education, 42*(2), 146–162. doi:10.2307/1321030

Lampela, L. (2007). Including lesbians and gays in art curricula: The art of Jeanne Mammen. *Visual Arts Research, 1*(64), 34–43.

Letts, W. (2002). Revisioning multiculturalism in teacher education: Isn't it queer? In R. M. Kissin (Ed.), *Getting ready for Benjamin: Preparing teachers for sexual diversity in the classroom* (pp. 199–132). New York, NY: Rowman & Littlefield.

Lipkin, A. (1993/1994). The case for a gay and lesbian curriculum. *The High School Journal, 77*(1/2), 95–107.

Maher, M. J., & Sever, L. M. (2007). What educators in Catholic schools might expect when addressing gay and lesbian issues: A study of needs and barriers. *Journal of Gay & Lesbian Issues in Education, 4*(3), 79–111. doi:10.1300/J367v04n03_06

Mathison, C. (1998). The invisible minority: Preparing teachers to meet the needs of gay and lesbian youth. *Journal of Teacher Education, 49*(2), 151–155. doi:10.1177/0022487198049002008

Mayo, C. (2010). Queer lessons: Sexual and gender minorities and multiculturalism. In J. Banks & C. Banks (Eds.), *Multicultural education: Issues and perspectives* (7th ed., pp. 209–227). New York, NY: Wiley.

McCarthy, L. (2003). What about the "T"? Is multicultural education ready to address transgender issues? *Multicultural Perspectives, 5*(4), 46–48. doi:10.1207/S15327892MCP0504_11

Meyer, E. J. (2010). *Gender and sexual diversity in schools.* New York, NY: Springer. doi:10.1007/978-90-481-8559-7

National Public Radio, Kaiser Family Foundation, & Kennedy School of Government. (2004). *Sex education in America: Principals survey.* Retrieved from http://www.kff.org/newsmedia/upload/Sex-Education-in-America-Principals-Survey-Toplines.pdf

Payne, E., & Smith, S. (2010). Reduction of stigma in schools: An evaluation of the first three years. *Issues in Teacher Education, 19*(2), 11–36.

Rands, K. E. (2009). Considering transgender people in education. *Journal of Teacher Education, 60*(4), 419–431. doi:10.1177/0022487109341475

Rockefeller, E. I. (2009). Selection, inclusion, evaluation and defense of transgender inclusive fiction for young adults: A resource guide. *Journal of LGBT Youth, 6*(2–3), 288–309. doi:10.1080/19361650902962641

Russell, S. T., & Joyner, K. (2001). Adolescent sexual orientation and suicide risk: Evidence from a national study. *American Journal of Public Health, 91*(8), 1276–1281. doi:10.2105/AJPH.91.8.1276

Russell, S. T., Kosciw, J. G., Horn, S., & Saewyc, E. (2010). Safe schools policy for LGBTQ students. *Society for Research in Child Development 24*(4), 1–25.

Russell, S. T., Ryan, C., Toomey, R. B., Diaz, R. M., & Sanchez, J. (2011). Lesbian, gay, bisexual, and transgender adolescent school victimization: Implications for young adult health and adjustment. *Journal of School Health, 81*(5), 223–230. doi:10.1111/j.1746-1561.2011.00583.x

Saewyc, E. M., Bearinger, L. H., Blum, R. W., & Resnick, M. D. (1999). Sexual intercourse, abuse and pregnancy among adolescent women: Does sexual orientation make a difference? *Family Planning Perspectives, 31*(3), 127–131. doi: 10.2307/2991695

Santelli, J., Ott, M. A., Lyon, M., Rogers, J., Summers, D., & Schleifer, R. (2006). Abstinence and abstinence-only education: A review of U.S. policies and programs. *Journal of Adolescent Health, 38*(1), 72–81.

Santos, F., & Phillips, A. M. (2011, August 9). New York City will mandate sex education. *The New York Times.* Retrieved from http://www.nytimes.com/2011/08/10/nyregion/in-new-york-city-a-new-mandate-on-sex-education.html?_r=2

Sexuality Information and Education Council of the United States [SIECUS]. (2004). *Guidelines for comprehensive sexuality education: Kindergarten–12th grade* (3rd ed.). Retrieved from http://www.siecus.org/_data/global/images/guidelines.pdf

Sexual Orientation Curriculum Policy 604.11. Anoka-Hennepin School District (2009). Retrieved from Anoka-Hennepin School District website: http://www.anoka.k12.mn.us/education/components/docmgr/default.php?sectiondetailid=223568&fileitem=48585&catfilter=15049

Sherwin, G., & Jennings, T. (2006). Feared, forgotten, or forbidden: Sexual orientation topics in secondary teacher preparation programs in the USA. *Teaching Education, 17*(3), 207–223. doi: 10.1080/10476210600849664

Smith, G. W., & Smith, D. E. (1998). The ideology of "fag": The school experience of gay students. *The Sociological Quarterly, 39*, 309–335. doi:10.1111/j.1533-8525.1998.tb00506.x

Style, E. (1996). Curriculum as window & mirror. *Social Science Record, 33*(2), 21–28.

Telljohann, S. K., Price, J. H., Poureslami, M., & Easton, A. (1995). Teaching about sexual orientation by secondary health teachers. *Journal of School Health, 65*(1), 18–22. doi:10.1111/j.1746-1561.1995.tb03333.x

The National Safe Schools Partnership. (2007). *Bridging the gap in federal law: Promoting safe schools and improved student achievement by preventing bullying and harassment in our schools.* Retrieved from GLSEN website: http://www.glsen.org/binary-data/GLSEN_ATTACHMENTS/file/000/000/912-1.pdf

Title V State Abstinence Education Grant Program HHS-2010-ACF-ACYF-AEGP-0123 (2010). Retrieved from U.S. Department of Health and Human Services Administration for Children & Families website: http://www.acf.hhs.gov/grants/open/foa/view/HHS-2010-ACF-ACYF-AEGP-0123

Yakush, J. H. (2007). *Legalized discrimination: The rise of the marriage-promotion industry and how federally funded programs discriminate against lesbian, gay, bisexual, and transgender youth and families.* Retrieved from SIECUS website: http://www.siecus.org/policy/SpecialReports/Legalized-Discrimination.pdf

Zaslavsky, C. (1996). *Multicultural math classroom: Bringing in the world.* Portsmouth, NH: Heinemann.

11 Creating Inclusive School Environments for Lesbian, Gay, Bisexual, and Transgender Headed Families and their Children

Alicia L. Fedewa and Ashley Candelaria

Every day millions of children attend school and overhear homophobic epithets, experience bullying and harassment, and feel ostracized from classroom discussions regarding their families (Stacey & Biblarz, 2001; Sutter, Daas, & Bergen, 2008). For children whose families do not fit the mother–father–child prototype, schools can be a place where they feel marginalized and ignored. Children with same-sex parents are one such population whose families are, in the majority of school contexts, not accepted (Baker, 2002). Despite the increasing numbers and visibility of same-sex parents (Landau, 2009), the school continues to be an institution that often is unwelcoming and hostile to lesbian, gay, bisexual, and transgender (LGBT) headed families (Kosciw & Diaz, 2008).

The research is clear that even in a hostile societal context, same-sex parents raise children who are just as psychologically and physically healthy as children with heterosexual parents (Crowl, Ahn, & Baker, 2008). Yet given that schooling is mandatory for children in the United States (U.S.) and that schools often reflect the beliefs and cultural values of the larger societal system in which they are embedded, same-sex parents and their children have unique challenges and often meet hostile environments within the school setting (Baker, 2002). In fact, the vast majority of same-sex parents report specific and very intentional strategies for navigating the school context in order to protect their children from harassment, discrimination, and bullying (Bower, 2008; Lindsay et al., 2006; Ryan & Martin, 2000). This chapter will explore the harassment, discrimination, and unwelcoming environments often faced by LGBT-headed families. Additionally, recommendations for training school personnel in the use of appropriate language and terminology for LGBT-headed families will be discussed. This chapter will conclude by building on the information provided in Chapter 10 of this volume, addressing strategies for creating supportive and inclusive classroom environments for LGBT-headed families (including parents as well as children whose parents identify as LGBT).

School Experiences of LGBT-Headed Families

Bullying experiences of children with same-sex parents have been a dominant theme among researchers when investigating children's perceptions of the school environment. Although there have been different findings depending on the age and school context of the child, research generally has found that children with same-sex parents are bullied about their parents' sexual orientation but experience no more bullying or harassment than other children their age (Golombok, Tasker, & Murray, 1997; Vanfraussen, Ponjaert-Kristoffersen, & Breweys, 2002). However, more in-depth studies using interviews and open-ended questionnaires find that lesbian mothers take proactive measures to prevent their children's experiences of bullying and discrimination in the first place (Lindsay et al., 2006; Mercier & Harold, 2003). Thus, while researchers have uncovered similar levels of bullying for children across sexual minority and heterosexual parents, findings may be misinterpreted given the preventative lengths same-sex parents often take when selecting schools and preparing their children for combating bullying in school.

There are two general strategies used by same-sex parents when navigating the school systems: choosing schools with a reputation for diversity and openness to their family structure or using "self-imposed invisibility" such that school personnel are unaware of their sexual orientation (Lindsay et al., 2006; Mercier & Harold, 2003). Same-sex parents often use this self-imposed invisibility as an adaptive strategy for navigating schools in which parents perceive little tolerance or acceptance toward their family structure. In the first large scale study to be conducted on the school experiences of children with a sexual minority parent, the Gay, Lesbian, and Straight Education Network (GLSEN) found that nearly half of parents surveyed worried that their children would have problems in school solely because of their own sexual orientation (Kosciw & Diaz, 2008). Kosciw and Diaz (2008) also found that approximately 32% of sexual minority parents worry that their child will be ostracized or have a difficult time making friends due to their parents identifying as gay or lesbian.

Sexual minority parents have a right to express concern and take significant efforts to prevent an unwelcoming and unsupportive school climate for their children, as many authors have shown that sexual minority parents and their children have experiences with schools that are similar to the experiences of sexual minority adolescents: hostile and homophobic (Jeltova & Fish, 2005; Ryan & Martin, 2000). In the 2008 GLSEN study, 72% of students with same-sex parents reported hearing homophobic remarks, while 51% of students reported feeling unsafe at school (Kosciw & Diaz, 2008). Although students should feel as though they can turn to teachers for help and support, many students with same-sex parents felt quite the opposite. Kosciw and Diaz (2008) found that almost 40% of students with same-sex parents reported hearing homophobic remarks from their teachers and that when teachers would hear homophobic comments about the students' parents, 62% of teachers would ignore it or choose not to intervene.

Given these pervasive concerns and the conscious efforts same-sex parents make to thwart unwelcoming and harsh school environments for their children, it is little wonder why the vast majority of research in this area calls for multicultural training programs within schools. It is clear from the research with same-sex parents and their children that a welcoming and respectful school climate leads to positive experiences for both parents and children (Jeltova & Fish, 2005; Kosciw & Diaz, 2008; Ryan & Martin, 2000). Further, educators have a tremendous impact on their students' lives and experiences in school.

The Role of Diversity Training in Schools

While teachers are expected to be accepting of diversity and able to instruct with a certain degree of cultural competency, many report feeling unprepared by traditional education in recognizing and promoting diversity in the classroom (Hagan & McGlynn, 2004; Laduke, 2009). Additionally, while training in regards to racial and ethnic diversity is becoming more prevalent, two main areas that are frequently left out of the pre-educator diversity preparedness are sexual identity and sexual orientation (Capper et al., 2006). Providing diversity training to school personnel to fill this gap is a requisite in creating a positive and welcoming environment for all families.

Nationwide, many states have already passed legislature specifically requiring diversity training that addresses diverse sexual orientations. In California, the Safe Place to Learn Act (AB 394) and the California Student Safety and Violence Prevention Act of 2000 (AB 537) mandate protection of LGBT students from harassment and other forms of discrimination (Knotts, 2009). The statutes require that schools make available to staff and other personnel various trainings and resources to combat discrimination based on sexual orientation. Specifically, the state of California requires that trainings "effectively address bias-motivated discrimination and harassment in schools" (Knotts, 2009, p. 602).

Additionally, the Safe Schools Program, first launched in Massachusetts in 2001, mandates the same educator training related to anti-discrimination as well as school-wide training in prevention of violence and suicide (Cahill & Cianciotto, 2004). These acts were founded on the premise that educators should operate from a *social justice* perspective, one that upholds equality for all (Capper et al., 2006). While these acts were created with LGBT students in mind, children of LGBT-headed families certainly can benefit from the protections and increased awareness as well.

Prior to implementing any type of diversity training, school administrators may wish to conduct a formal needs assessment to gauge the current knowledge base and comfort levels of the staff as a whole in regards to LGBT cultural competency (Capper et al., 2006). Questions might reflect the extent of prior trainings and familiarity with various LGBT issues, as well as information regarding personnel's past and present experiences in working with children from LGBT-headed households and families. Information from these assessments may then guide the focus of subsequent trainings.

The selected diversity training should involve a component that addresses such issues as increasing teacher comfort in using the words *lesbian*, *gay*, and *homosexual*, as well as teaching of other less familiar language related to sexual orientation, gender identity, the LGBT community, and other aspects of diversity (Rimalower & Caty, 2009). Beginning diversity trainings with this type of basic foundation in terminology creates a safer environment for further discussion among personnel, students, and families. Additionally, opening up a dialogue to explore the common myths and facts of the LGBT community as well as common stereotypes and misunderstandings is beneficial before commencing further training (Rimalower & Caty, 2009).

Models of Diversity Training

Several examples of effective diversity training programs exist in the literature. Capper et al. (2006) describe several pedagogical approaches to introducing the conversation about sexual orientation diversity to school personnel. They refer to their program as a "leadership preparation course." The first strategy involves having staff brainstorm current obstacles that exist on the part of the school that may be preventing a fully inclusive and welcoming school environment. Once several ideas are generated, staff members then shape and modify the list to create a single representative document of the targeted issues surrounding discrimination in their school. Every staff member has an active role in this process, allowing for a non-hierarchical system of change.

An additional exercise utilized in the leadership preparation training involves the use of vignettes and role-play. School personnel first are instructed in various principles of equality and appropriate interactions with individuals from diverse backgrounds. This involves bringing in professional representatives who are capable of providing effective training in diversity issues and may include inviting LGBT community members (Capper et al., 2006). School personnel are given the opportunity to watch a role-played situation modeled incorrectly and then modeled correctly by trainers. Staff, themselves, then may be asked to participate in role-play activities to practice previously learned skills, followed by a feedback session. While the authors hold that this interactive approach to diversity training is effective in working with teachers, assessment of actual teaching practices post-training is lacking (Capper et al., 2006). Thus, in order to ensure that diversity principles are maintained in school contexts, follow-up and review sessions may be necessary to determine the extent to which personnel are actually applying the principles conveyed in the diversity training.

Further training in interpersonal communication and empathy also may add to school personnel's repertoire of cultural competency. Lu, Dane, and Gellman (2005) discuss a model of training that builds empathy and cultural competence into existing interpersonal skills, particularly in reference to the student–teacher relationship. This training involves role play, experiential learning, and coaching to promote awareness of others. The material is presented through a two-day workshop in which teachers participate in hands-on activities and discussion to facilitate cultural sensitivity. The overall outcome of this program and others like it includes a reported increase in the ability to "let go" of the power of which various cultures are awarded and an improvement in the ability to openly communicate with others in a more effective manner (Lu et al., 2005). This empathy training in conjunction with training in the principles of diversity may provide a solid foundation of cultural competency among staff members, thus improving the social climate for LGBT families.

Teachers and administrators are not the only staff involved with LGBT families. School psychologists and other personnel who typically provide mental health and other interpersonal services in the schools especially should be encouraged to attend diversity and empathy trainings. Choi, Thul, Berenhaut, Suerken, and Norris (2005) found that as few as 30% of school psychologists have reported receiving training that specifically addressed LGBT issues, while 47.5% reported only receiving a total of four hours of training or less on the subject. However, nearly 60% of school psychologists indicated that they knew of and/or worked directly with children in their schools who were from LGBT-headed families (Choi et al., 2005). The discrepancy between these numbers could be remedied through the implementation of more frequent and more in depth trainings on working with both LGBT families and children.

School-Wide Harassment Training and Policies

Training staff to recognize and respond appropriately to harassment based on sexual orientation has been shown to increase the likelihood of reporting such harassment, as well as higher levels of intolerance of harassment (Estrada & Laurence, 2009).

An additional step classroom teachers and school personnel may take in facilitating a harassment-free school environment for all children and families is to immediately address situations in which homophobic epithets are heard or harassment is seen (Souto-Manning & Hermann-Wilmarth, 2008). Rather than ignoring these situations or simply responding with verbal reprimands, teachers are encouraged to use the situation as an opportunity for discussion. Asking questions, such as why the student used a particular term and educating that student on the history of the derogatory term, allows for further understanding of the ways in which words affect others. Additionally, taking appropriate disciplinary action when necessary conveys the message that harassment will not be tolerated.

School-based harassment training should prepare teachers to identify harassment based on sexual orientation both from students and adults in the school. A disconnect is often inherent between personnel's ability to recognize homophobic bullying, taunting, and other forms of harassment and the decision to report such instances based on personal comfort levels and confusion about the proper protocol for reporting (Souto-Manning & Hermann-Wilmarth, 2008). Including additional information regarding when, where, how, and to whom to report these instances is necessary to facilitate a systems-wide procedure, as is reassurance from administration that such reports will be taken seriously.

Harassment Training Models

Several agencies nationwide provide sexual orientation harassment training specifically targeting teachers and school personnel, often at low costs or free of charge. The Safe Schools Coalition, in addition to GLSEN and the American Civil Liberties Union (ACLU), provides trainings which focus on identifying harassment, familiarizing staff with legal repercussions of harassment, as well as promoting various resources to support the concepts learned during training (Phoenix et al., 2006). Specifically, the ACLU provides sexual orientation harassment training to schools and other public organizations who wish to decrease instances of homophobic harassment (Otto, Middleton, & Freker, 2002). The training is designed for school faculty and staff and strives to promote a school environment in which students are able to reach their potential. The ACLU program is unique in that it has three main components: a panel of LGBT individuals, a panel of attorneys and other legal professionals, and a series of role-play opportunities. While no research to date has evaluated the outcomes of this type of harassment training, the workshops certainly expose faculty and staff to a variety of facts and strategies to use in dealing with sexual orientation harassment at school and could be effective in improving the school climate for LGBT families.

Finally, staff may be encouraged to seek professional development opportunities available to them outside of the school whenever possible. For instance, disseminating amongst faculty information about various books, films, or other community resources available for increasing LGBT awareness creates the opportunity for professional development, as well as shows support for those interested in pursuing cultural competence. Two examples of the various media resources available for professional development opportunities are the documentaries *It's Elementary: Talking about Gay*

Issues in School (1996) and *In My Shoes: Stories of Youth with LGBT Parents* (2005), which provide footage of public schools that already have begun the dialogue about LGBT issues and the successes and struggles that have subsequently occurred. These documentaries and others like them also may be appropriate for older children and adolescents.

Parent-Centered Diversity and Harassment Training

School personnel are not the only adults involved with the school who may feel ill-prepared in diversity issues, especially those of the LGBT community. The parents of other students at school may benefit from the same diversity training teachers receive, as nearly 23% of students from same-sex parented households have reported hearing harassing statements from classmates' parents regarding parental sexual orientation (GLSEN, 2008).

Recent studies have shown that LGBT parents are more likely to volunteer at and be involved in school activities as compared to the general parent population (67% versus 42%; GLSEN, 2008). The high rate at which LGBT parents are involved with their children's school experiences provides additional opportunities for training of staff as well as parents, through school committees such as the parent–teacher organization or parent–teacher association (PTO/PTA). Providing a school–community seminar addressing these issues is an effective way of spreading awareness throughout the school and community and building a partnership against discrimination of LGBT-headed families.

Student-Centered Diversity and Empathy Training

Educating teachers and other school professionals in the importance of non-discrimination policies and cultural competence is critical in creating a welcoming and accepting school climate. Yet students also need to be exposed to similar trainings or learning modules which focus on teaching acceptance and eliminating harassment. Periodically reminding students of the school's code of conduct regarding these issues by dedicating instructional time to review policies (assuming districts have adopted such policies) ensures all children are knowledgeable of the school-wide regulations on discrimination (Knotts, 2009). Many districts already incorporate a guidance component into the curriculum with the purpose of promoting student social, academic, and emotional growth. Receiving this guidance portion of the curriculum has been shown to improve academic and social-emotional outcomes, and, in particular, increases in student self-concept have been found (Ma, Guo, & Shen, 2009). This natural time of exploring feelings and emotions in the classroom may prove to be an opportunity to incorporate a variety of activities for cultural competence and acceptance of all peers and families.

Empathy training for students is another strategy to implement during the discussion of diversity awareness and anti-harassment behaviors. Working with students in understanding the feelings of others and what it might feel like to be teased or harassed opens up the lines of communication regarding diversity even further. The REACH Beyond Tolerance Program (Respect, Empathy, Attitude, Cultural Knowledge, Hold your Ground) was developed with these goals in mind (Hollingsworth, Didelot, & Smith, 2003). The program was designed to increase children's tolerance of individuals from diverse backgrounds while promoting the concepts of fairness, empathy, and respect for all individuals. Exposure to the REACH Program and others like it increases positive interactions between students and their capacity to relate to individuals from a wide variety of backgrounds (Hollingsworth et al., 2003). While the potential effects of diversity and empathy training on students' acceptance of peers from diverse backgrounds is clear, it also is evident that these programs must be ongoing and repeated to ensure long-term results (Robertson, 2007).

Updating School Forms and Policies

In addition to providing opportunities for staff and students to become more familiar and comfortable with discussing the language of diversity, a focus also may be placed on harassment policies. A national survey by GLSEN (2008) found that over 45% of LGBT-parented households sought out information about a prospective school's policies specifically regarding LGBT issues and response to harassment before enrolling a child, and of those families, 78% reported that the policy had a large effect on the decision to enroll. Providing diversity and harassment training is only one step to ensuring a positive and welcoming school environment for same-sex parents and their children. In addition, school personnel should advocate for the rights of these students and families by implementing non-discriminatory or "safe schools" policies in order to create a safer and more supportive environment (Daniel & Bondy, 2008). A solid school-wide anti-discrimination policy with specific mention of discrimination based on sexual orient-ation and gender identity is necessary to support any additional training provided to school personnel. While training of this nature has clear benefits, not only for children of LGBT-headed households, but also for all families and household compositions, only 10% of parents surveyed reported being aware of teacher and school personnel training in these areas (GLSEN, 2008).

In order for school-wide training to be effective in promoting diversity, staff must be trained upon hiring and introduced early to school policies on diversity. Further, it is recommended that new and existing staff be frequently updated on the policies (Landers, Mimiaga, & Krinsky, 2010). Developing a school environment that is welcoming to parents of all sexual orientations and gender identities also may involve updating previously used professional forms and paperwork to reflect acceptance of diverse family compositions, including LGBT-headed families. For instance, rather than having school forms include the traditional *Mother's name/Father's name* option, a more inclusive *Parent's/Guardian's name* is recommended. These standard school forms also can provide the opportunity for reporting other adults who may be involved in the care-giving of that particular student but who are not legal or biological parents (Ryan & Martin, 2000). In a similar vein, interview forms typically utilized in collecting information on the social and developmental history of a child can be inclusive of a variety of pregnancy, adoption, and surrogate experiences typical of children from LGBT-headed families and families in general (Telingator & Patterson, 2008). Including questions about various possible experiences in becoming parents also can be considered as opposed to simply providing a space for checking off whether or not pregnancy and delivery were "normal."

Additionally, accepting signatures from all parents of an LGBT-headed family and providing forms that can be filled out to allow parents without guardianship rights to participate in routine school activities is another way to reflect cultural acceptance at school. Similar adjustments can be made during interactions with a student that may involve asking questions about his or her parent versus asking about his or her mother and father or even better, asking about important adults in his or her life. Using parent-neutral terms when directly addressing a student avoids possible feelings of exclusion.

In addition to modifying the school's forms and policies to support acceptance and inclusion, educators also may wish to adapt school-wide pledges to reflect the same principles. Many schools begin the day by reciting a personal pledge, often in unison, over the public announcement (PA) system (e.g., a pledge against bullying or a pledge to strive for personal best). Modifying that pledge to also reflect acceptance of diversity and an inclusive atmosphere is an additional measure to promote a safe and welcoming school environment. Acceptance of LGBT-headed families also can be expressed through the recognition and inclusion of parents in school traditions: adding a Parent's Day celebration, for example, displays school-wide acceptance of LGBT-headed families.

From a systemic perspective, administrators may consider revising the school mission statement and code of conduct to reflect the school's goal of diversity and acceptance of all families (Landers et al., 2010). The updated statement may be made readily available to all staff and parents and can be posted on the school website and in the code of conduct. Included in the updated code of conduct also should be a policy on familial privacy. Many LGBT-headed families choose to keep the family's identity private (Lindsay et al., 2006). During situations in which a parent's sexual identity is revealed or discovered, school personnel are encouraged to keep that information confidential and respect the family's decision to do so. Similarly, it is important to avoid using the terms *gay families* or *lesbian families* so as to refrain from placing labels upon or making assumptions about children from those families (Ryan & Martin, 2000). A more appropriate alternative may be to say *same sex-parented families* as this term captures the range of existing family compositions.

Creating a Welcoming Environment

In addition to modifying school forms, it may be beneficial to arrange the front office, conference room, and other publicly viewed areas in the school to promote a positive message of belonging and welcoming. Displaying posters with encouraging statements of diversity and images of various types of families also conveys the beliefs of a school in terms of acceptance and inclusion. Similarly, school counselors, psychologists, and other school personnel may display LGBT-friendly images or symbols to express acceptance (e.g., the rainbow image/triangle).

Educators also may consider developing a repertoire of resources for LGBT parents. Establishing a collection of literature, magazines, brochures, and other helpful materials for parents conveys a feeling of inclusiveness and a willingness to communicate. Resources may include pamphlets, brochures, and contact information for key organizations, such as GLSEN (http://www.glsen.org), COLAGE (http://www.colage.org), the Gay-Straight Alliance Network (http://www.gsanetwork.org), and the Human Rights Campaign (http://www.hrc.ogr; Phoenix et al., 2006). The Human Rights Campaign's

Welcoming Schools Guide and materials are available for access at http://www. welcomingschools.org.

A final strategy that educators may utilize in an effort to create an inclusive and welcoming school environment is to conduct an annual assessment of the degree to which harassment and other instances of intolerance are occurring (Phoenix et al., 2006). Information should come from both students and faculty. These assessments may include information such as the number of occurrences of bullying based on sexual orientation, specific epithets used, feelings about the degree of support offered at school for students from LGBT-headed families and LGBT students themselves, and further descriptive information. Administrators are then able to analyze this data and make decisions about necessary revision of policies, trainings, and overall school climate.

Reframing the Curriculum

Globally, public school curriculum and literature tends to have heterosexist undertones and a preference for separating that which is "normal" from that which is "abnormal" (Temple, 2005). While the issue of infusing diverse sexual orientations and gender identities into the school curriculum has been contested, the potential benefits of developing an overall more diverse and inclusive curriculum cannot be denied (Davis, 2007). There is a need for schools to teach students about families that may not fit the "typical" family model (although one might argue that the "typical" family is a misnomer given the vast configurations of families in contemporary society). This "anti-oppressive" teaching style challenges teachers to recognize diversity and actively work to infuse it in the classroom curriculum (Rothing, 2008). In this case, students of same-sex parents would be made to feel validated by the material covered in class because it is neither excluding of their family composition nor expressing a negative message about it. By remaining aware of such instances of diversity amongst students, the teacher is increasing both self as well as student awareness of acceptance of others by delivering a positive message (Rothing, 2008).

Opportunities for infusing diversity into the curriculum exist across subjects. Including historical events in the LGBT community as a part of the natural history of America provides students with a background of the culture that may not have been available otherwise. In middle and high school history courses, students may study landmark cases in the history of LGBT rights, such as *Baker v. Vermont* of 1999 which was one of the first rulings in the ongoing struggle for equal marriage rights (Romano, 2010). Moreover, studying various sexual minority historical figures and the inherent controversy in other areas, such as Walt Whitman in English or language arts courses, provides a continuity of diverse curriculum (Champagne, 2008). Current events provide another opportunity to include the legislature on same-sex marriages and the continued struggle for equality with respect to legal and healthcare access rights, such as the recent repeal of California's Proposition 8 which previously banned same-sex marriage.

Important events in the history of the gay and lesbian community also may be shared through popular media. For instance, students in middle and high school may benefit from watching various documentaries on the history of sexual orientation rights, such as *Before Stonewall* (1984) and *Brother Outsider: The Story of Bayard Rustin* (2003). These documentaries illustrate the political relevance and personal struggle of individuals fighting for LGBT rights in America (Capper et al., 2006). Further, depending on the developmental level of the student, a number of activities can be incorporated into the classroom curriculum. For example, encouraging students to include one or both LGBT parents in classroom activities, such as constructing a family tree or genealogy, sends a message to students that school is a safe place to share such information. Students may also participate in a "my town" project, in which pictures or drawings of various family members as well as narrative stories and poems are combined to create portfolios of their lives (Hunter, 2008). This portfolio can then be shared with the class and later displayed in the classroom, hallway, or media center. Further, all families can be invited to attend a show-and-tell or a diversity day celebration in which the classroom-created projects are presented, and families participate in various activities related to diversity awareness and acceptance.

Choosing a general book that will spark class-wide conversation about familial diversity, such as *Is Your Family Like Mine?* (Abramchik, 1996) for pre-school and elementary students, or *Between Mom and Jo* (Peters, 2006) for adolescents, often provides built-in questions and opportunities for students to examine their own families and decide if they are similar to or different than those of their peers (Souto-Manning & Hermann-Wilmarth, 2008). Following up with activities such as those described previously sends a positive message about diverse families and allows for a closer connection and more open dialogue about diversity amongst classmates.

Modifying Classrooms to Promote Diversity

Additional classroom modifications also may be made to promote acceptance and inclusion of all students and families. For example, designating an area of the classroom as the diversity or "peace" area by decorating with images of various types of families among other images of diversity and providing a safe place to ask questions and discuss a variety of issues allows students to explore while promoting acceptance (Hunter, 2008). On display in this area may be a bulletin board depicting student artwork as well as positive messages that embody acceptance and diversity. The *Safe Space Kit* (GLSEN, 2010) is available online and provides tools for educators in creating welcoming environments for all, as well as stickers and posters for display.

Classrooms also may benefit by adding resources for both the student and his or her family. GLSEN endorses several books that promote positive messages specifically about gay or lesbian parented households for students of all ages including *Jenny Lives with Eric and Martin* (Bosche, Hansen, & MacKay, 1983), *Families: A Celebration of Diversity, Commitment and Love* (Jenness, 1993), and *One Dad, Two Dads, Brown Dad, Blue Dads* (Valentine & Sarecky, 2004). Adding these books to existing school and classroom libraries increases the amount of positive exposure students receive regarding diverse families. Additionally, compiling a list of resources for interested students and parents ensures accessibility for school personnel, students, and parents.

Incorporating a Gay-Straight Alliance (GSA)

Involving the general school clubs and programs in diversity awareness is an additional strategy for ensuring that the school's positive message is being conveyed through extracurricular activities. This may occur, for example, through encouraging school clubs or teams to volunteer with and seek out sponsorships from organizations that have affiliation with the LGBT community. While a number of schools also currently offer a Gay-Straight Alliance (GSA) at school, some offer no such group that children may join for support. Studies conducted through the Safe Schools initiatives have found that students who are actively involved in GSAs at school benefit through a positive academic outcome, an increased feeling of belonging to the school, a heightened sense of safety within the school, and the development of coping strategies for dealing with others' assumptions regarding their sexual orientation (Cahill & Cianciotta, 2004). While the GSA is a group typically associated with LGBTQ youth, and the outcomes for children of same-sex parents have not been studied per se, joining such a club as a child of an LGBT parent can provide a sense of belonging and shared experience as well (Walls, Kane, & Wisneski, 2010).

In addition to incorporating a GSA, schools also may wish to participate in various diversity celebrations throughout the school year (Otto et al., 2002). For instance, the month of October is deemed *LGBT History Month*, and the first Friday in October is established as *National Diversity Day*. Recently, GLSEN sponsored *No Name Calling Week*, which takes place every January and encourages activities to end name calling amongst elementary, middle, and high school students. Incorporating these events into existing holiday and awareness celebrations helps to increase acceptance and the promotion of diversity.

Conclusion

Providing a safe and welcoming environment for all students and families is a critical role of all school personnel. However, with as many as 72% of students hearing homophobic remarks at school and 51% of students with same-sex parents feeling unsafe at school, it is clear that a gap exists between the ideal and actual school environment for children of LGBT-headed households. With as many as 32% of sexual minority parents worrying that their children will be ostracized due to their parents' sexual orientation, it is no wonder that schools are being called to action. As discussed, the first step in creating a welcoming school environment for all students and families requires providing teacher, staff, student, and parent training in the principles of anti-harassment, cultural competence, diversity, and empathy. Implementing a school-wide policy against harassment based on sexual orientation and gender identity, as well as adjusting current school forms, websites, and manuals to reflect such policies, is essential. Additionally, providing opportunities for students to learn and discuss with each other the dynamics of their families as well as the history of the LGBTQ community provides children of LGBT-headed households a safe place for sharing. Finally, as previously emphasized, educators can improve upon existing organizations or create student associations such as GSAs to promote acceptance of diverse students and families. The call to action has been made; it is the responsibility of administrators, teachers, and other school personnel to adopt these strategies in an effort to improve the school experience for all students.

References

Abramchik, L. (1996). *Is your family like mine?* Brooklyn, NY: Open Heart, Open Mind.

Baker, J. (2002). *How homophobia hurts children: Nurturing diversity at home, at school, and in the community.* New York, NY: Harrington Park Press.

Bosche, S., Hansen, A., & MacKay, L. (1983). *Jenny lives with Eric and Martin.* London, England: Gay Men's Press.

Bower, L. A. (2008). Standing up for diversity: Lesbian mothers' suggestions for teachers. *Kappa Delta Pi Record, 44*(4), 181–183.

Cahill, S., & Cianciotto, J. (2004). U.S. policy interventions that can make schools safer. *Journal of Gay and Lesbian Issues in Education, 2*(1), 3–17. doi:10.1300/J367v02n01_02

Capper, C., Alston, J., Koschoreck, J., Lopez, G., Lugg, C., & McKenzie, K. (2006). Integrating lesbian/gay/bisexual/transgender topics and their intersections with other areas of difference into the leadership preparation curriculum: Practical ideas and strategies. *Journal of School Leadership, 16*(2), 142–157.

Champagne, J. (2008). Walt Whitman, our great gay poet? *Journal of Homosexuality, 55*(4), 648–664. doi:10.1080/00918360802421676

Chasnoff, D., & Cohen, H. (1996). *It's elementary: Talking about gay issues in school* [Documentary]. United States: New Day Films.

Choi, H., Thul, C., Berenhaut, K., Suerken, C., & Norris, J. (2005). Survey of school psychologists' attitudes, feelings, and exposure to gay and lesbian parents and their children. *Journal of Applied School Psychology, 22*(1), 87–107. doi:10.1300/J008v22n01_05

Crowl, A. L., Ahn, S., & Baker, S. A. (2008). A meta-analysis of developmental outcomes for children of same-sex and heterosexual parents. *Journal of GLBT Family Studies, 4*(3), 385–407. doi:10.1080/15504280802177615

Daniel, Y., & Bondy, K. (2008). Safe schools and zero tolerance: Policy, program and practice in Ontario. *Canadian Journal of Educational Administration and Policy, 70*, 1–20. Retrieved from http://www.eric.ed.gov/PDFS/EJ806990.pdf

Davis, J. (2007). Making a difference: How teachers can positively affect racial identity acceptance. *Social Studies, 98*(5), 209–214. doi:10.3200/TSSS.98.5.209-216

Estrada, A., & Laurence, J. (2009). Examining the impact of training on the homosexual conduct policy for military personnel. *Military Psychology, 21*(1), 62–80. doi:10.1080/08995600802565751

Gilomen, J. (2005). *In my shoes: Stories of youth with LGBT parents* [Documentary]. United States: COLAGE Youth Leadership and Action Program.

GLSEN (2008). *Involved, invisible, ignored: The experiences of lesbian, gay, bisexual, and transgender parents and their children in our nation's K–12 schools.* Retrieved from http://www.glsen.org/binary-data/GLSEN_ATTACHMENTS/file/000/001/1104-1.pdf

GLSEN (2010). *The jump start guide: Building and activating your GSA or similar student club.* Retrieved from http://www.glsen.org/cgi-bin/iowa/all/library/record/2226.html

GLSEN (2010). *The safe space kit.* Retrieved from http://safespace.glsen.org/

Golombok, S., Tasker, F., & Murray, C. (1997). Children raised in fatherless families from infancy: Family relationships and the socioemotional development of children of lesbian and single heterosexual mothers. *Journal of Child Psychology and Psychiatry, 38*(4), 783–791. doi:10.1111/j.1469-7610.2004.00847.x

Hagan, M., & McGlynn, C. (2004). Moving barriers: Promoting learning for diversity in initial teacher education. *Intercultural Education, 15*(3), 244–253. doi:10.1080/1467598042000262545

Hollingsworth, L., Didelot, M., & Smith, J. (2003). REACH beyond tolerance: A framework for teaching children empathy and responsibility. *Journal of Humanistic Counseling, Education, and Development, 42*(2), 139–151.

Hunter, T. (2008). Creating a culture of peace in the elementary classroom. *Education Digest, 74*(1), 54–58.

Jeltova, I., & Fish, M.C. (2005). Creating school environments responsive to gay, lesbian, bisexual, and transgender families: Traditional and systemic approaches for consultation. *Journal of Educational and Psychological Consultation, 16*(1/2), 17–33. doi:10.1207/s1532768xjepc161&2_2

Jenness, A. (1993). *Families: A Celebration of Diversity.* Boston, MA: Houghton-Mifflin.

Knotts, G. (2009). Undoing gender through legislation and schooling: The case of AB 537 and AB 394 in California. *International Review of Education, 55*(5/6), 597–614. doi: 10.1007/s11159-009-9138-z

Kosciw, J. G., & Diaz, E. M. (2008). *Involved, invisible, ignored: The experiences of lesbian, gay, bisexual and transgender parents and their children in our nation's K–12 schools.* New York, NY: GLSEN.

Laduke, A. (2009). Resistance and renegotiation: Preservice teacher interactions with and reactions to multicultural education course content. *Multicultural Education, 16*(3), 37–44. Retrieved from http://www.eric.ed.gov/PDFS/EJ847143.pdf

Landau, J. (2009). Straightening out (the politics of) same-sex parenting: Representing gay families is US print news stories and photographs. *Critical Studies in Media Communication, 26*(1), 80–100. doi:10.1080/15295030802684018

Landers, S., Mimiaga, M., & Krinsky, L. (2010). The open door project task force: A qualitative study on LGBT aging. *Journal of Gay & Lesbian Social Services, 22*(3), 316–336. doi:10.1080/10538720903426438

Lindsay, J., Perlesz, A., Brown, R., McNair, R., De Vaus, D., & Pitts, M. (2006). Stigma or respect: Lesbian-parented families negotiating school settings. *Sociology, 40*(6), 1059–1077.

Lu, Y., Dane, B., & Gellman, A. (2005). An experiential model: Teaching empathy and cultural sensitivity. *Journal of Teaching in Social Work, 25*(3/4), 89–103. doi:10.1300/J067v25n03_06

Ma, K., Guo, H., & Shen, D. (2009). An experimental study on enhancing the academic emotions of 2nd graders of junior high school by systematic intervention. *Psychological Science, 32*(4), 778–782.

Mercier, L. R., & Harold, R. D. (2003). At the interface: lesbian-parent families and their children's schools. *Children & Schools, 25*(1), 35–47.

Otto, N., Middleton, J., & Freker, J. (2002). *Making schools safe: An anti-harassment training program from the lesbian and gay rights project of the American civil liberties union.* Retrieved from http://www.eric.ed.gov/PDFS/ED475204.pdf

Peters, J. A. (2006). *Between mom and Jo.* New York, NY: Hachette Book Group.

Phoenix, T., Hall, W., Weiss, M., Kemp, J., Wells, R., & Chan, A. (2006). A report from the safe schools NC organization. *Homophobic Language and Verbal Harassment in North Carolina High Schools.* Retrieved from http://www.eric.ed.gov/PDFS/ED491454.pdf

Rimalower, L., & Caty, C. (2009). The mamas and the papas: The invisible diversity of families with same sex parents in the United States. *Sex Education, 9*(1),17–32. doi:10.1080/14681810802639921

Robertson, E. (2007). Promoting the acceptance of sexual diversity in a class of fifth grade boys. *Journal of LGBT youth, 5*(1), 15–25. doi:10.1300/J524v05n01_03

Romano, M. (2010). Same-sex marriage Massachusetts and Iowa: Templates for legalization. *New England Journal of History, 67*(1), 19–33. Retrieved from http://web.ebscohost.com.ezproxy.uky.edu/ehost/

Rothing, A. (2008). Homotolerance and heteronormativity in norwegian classrooms. *Gender and Education, 20*(3), 253–266. doi:10.1080/09540250802000405

Ryan, D., & Martin, A. (2000). Lesbian, gay, bisexual, and transgender parents in the school systems. *The School Psychology Review, 29*(2), 207–216. Retrieved from http://web.ebscohost.com.ezproxy.uky.edu/ehost/

Schiller, G., & Rosenberg, R. (1984). *Before Stonewall* [Documentary]. United States: Before Stonewall, Inc.

Singer, B., & Kates, N. D. (2003). *Brother outsider: The life of Bayard Rustin* [Documentary]. United States: Bayard Rustin Film Project.

Souto-Manning, M., & Hermann-Wilmarth, J. (2008). Teacher inquiries into gay and lesbian families in early childhood classrooms. *Journal of Early Childhood Research, 6*(3), 263–280. doi:10.1177/1476718X08094450

Stacey, J., & Biblarz, T. J. (2001). (How) does the sexual orientation of parents matter? *American Sociological Review, 66*(2), 159–183.

Sutter, E. A., Daas, K. L., & Bergen, K. M. (2008). Negotiating lesbian family identity via symbols and rituals. *Journal of Family Issues, 29*(1), 26–47. doi:10.1177/0192513X07305752

Telingator, C., & Patterson, C. (2008). Children and adolescents of lesbian and gay parents. *American Academy of Child and Adolescent Psychiatry, 47*(12), 1364–1368. doi: 10.1097/CHI.0b013c31818960bc

Temple, J. (2005). "People who are different from you": Heterosexism in Quebec high school textbooks. *Canadian Journal of Education, 28*(3), 271–294. Retrieved from http://www.eric.ed.gov/PDFS/EJ728342.pdf

Valentine, J., & Sarecky, M. (2004). *One dad, two dads, brown dad, blue dads.* Boston, MA: Alyson Books.

Vanfraussen, K., Ponjaert-Kristoffersen, I., & Brewaeys, A. (2002). What does it mean for youngsters to grow up in a lesbian family created by means of donor insemination? *Journal of Reproduction and Infant Psychology, 20*(4), 237–252. doi:10.1080/0264683021000033165

Walls, E., Kane, S., & Wisneski, H. (2010). Gay-straight alliances and school experiences of sexual minority youth. *Youth & Society, 41*(3), 307–332. doi: 10.1177/0044118X09334957

12 Counseling Lesbian, Gay, Bisexual, Transgender, and Questioning Students

Grady L. Garner, Jr. and Dennis M. Emano

In recent years, there has been greater attention directed toward the needs of lesbian, gay, bisexual, transgender, and questioning (LGBTQ) students and the impact that discrimination, bullying, and harassment have on their well-being. School-based counseling can serve to promote positive development for LGBTQ students when mental health professionals provide affirmative and responsive services. At the core of all counseling services is the moral/ethical principle of non-maleficence or do no harm (Rowson, 2001). Yet, many mental health professionals risk violating this principle and potentially harming LGBTQ students due to inadequate training in LGBTQ issues (Walker & Prince, 2010), a lack of understanding of the systemic prejudice and ignorance that exists in the counseling profession related to LGBTQ issues (Pearson, 2003), and the failure to effectively address LGBTQ harassment in schools (Russell, Kosciw, Horn, & Saewyc, 2010).

Graduate programs historically have failed to adequately prepare school professionals, including school-based mental health professionals, in providing LGBTQ-affirmative services (Biaggo, Orchard, Larson, Petrino, & Mihara, 2003; Callahan, 2001; Fontaine, 1998; Israel & Hackett, 2004; Phillips & Fisher, 1998; Savage, Prout, & Chard, 2004; Sherry, Whiled & Patton, 2005). In a qualitative study conducted with graduate students in school counseling, school psychology, and teacher preparation programs, McCabe and Rubinson (2008) found that graduate students did not view lesbian, gay, bisexual, and transgender (LGBT) individuals as an oppressed group, did not view themselves as change agents in schools, and were unlikely to correct injustices against LGBT individuals. Additionally, participants reported receiving minimal to no exposure to LGBT topics in their graduate programs. Similarly, Savage, Prout, and Chard (2004) found that school psychologists reported lacking the preparation from graduate programs to address gay and lesbian issues. See Chapter 8 of this volume for an in depth review of pre-service training for school professionals.

School-based mental health professionals need to be adequately equipped to provide effective individual and group counseling services to LGBTQ students, as well as to serve as system change agents. This chapter focuses on important areas to consider when counseling LGBTQ students, including: the need for counseling, ethically and culturally competent counseling, LGBTQ-affirmative counseling approaches, supporting sexual and gender identity development, suicide prevention, and expanding counseling roles. Notably, not all counseling involving LGBTQ youth will focus on sexual or gender identity development or related concerns as LGBTQ youth may present with a variety of problems similar to their heterosexual peers (Fisher et al., 2008). Nonetheless, given the increased life-stressors LGBTQ students may face due to discrimination and harassment and the associated risks, it is critical to ensure that culturally competent and affirmative counseling practices are employed.

A Need for Counseling

Prevalence of Mental Disorders

Lesbian, gay, and bisexual (LGB) youth historically have shown higher rates of mental disorders compared to heterosexual youth (Fergusson, Horwood, & Beautrais, 1999; Fergusson, Horwood, Ridder, & Beautrais, 2005), which is consistent with research on LGB individuals as a whole (Bostwick, Boyd, Hughes, & McCabe, 2009; King et al., 2008). King et al. (2008) conducted a meta-analysis of 25 studies from around the world that involved samples of both LGB adolescents and adults and found that mental disorders occur at a higher rate in these populations as compared to heterosexual adolescents and adults. However, that is not to say that sexual minority status predicts mental health disorders; but rather, sexual minority status is associated with an increased propensity or vulnerability to experience maladjustment if risk factors far outweigh protective factors for any given individual at any particular time. Notably, the higher prevalence of mental health disorders is likely attributable to the heightened environmental stressors experienced by LGBTQ individuals along with a limited availability of adequate supports or resources.

Studies using population-based samples show that LGB individuals are at higher risk for depression and suicide (Fergusson et al., 1999; Hatzenbuehler, Keyes, & Hasin, 2009; Russell & Joyner, 2001; Udry & Chantala, 2005). These results were confirmed in a recent study by Lucassen et al. (2011) who evaluated data from a population-based survey of New Zealand youth health and well-being, finding that adolescents who reported same-sex attraction or attraction to both sexes were more likely to report having experienced suicidality, self-harming behavior, and depression compared with adolescents attracted to the opposite sex. Population-based studies improve external validity or the generalizability of the results to a defined population—in this case LGB youth—because they are based on large cohort samples.

Research suggests that bisexual adolescents may experience even higher rates of mental health problems than their lesbian and gay (LG) peers, and they may be less likely to get help with their concerns (Lucassen et al., 2011). One possible explanation for this is that bisexual youth have different experiences from LG and heterosexual youth and may feel marginalized by both heterosexual and LG groups (Lucassen et al., 2011). Bostwick et al. (2009) suggest that bisexual individuals often are misunderstood and stereotyped by heterosexual and LG individuals, resulting in a "double stigma" (p. 6). Similarly, many myths and misconceptions about bisexual individuals abound, which may contribute to further misunderstanding and marginalization (Kennedy & Fisher, 2010).

Research also suggests that questioning youth may experience unique risks associated with mental health problems (Birkett, Espelage, & Koenig, 2009). In two large studies of high school students, youth who were confused about their sexual orientation reported greater levels of truancy, homophobic teasing, peer victimization, alcohol/marijuana use, and depression/suicidality compared with LGB and heterosexual students (Birkett et al., 2009; Espelage, Aragon, Birkett, & Koenig, 2008). This could be explained by the availability of social support, such that heterosexual and LGB youth have identified supportive communities which may help reduce isolation and substance use, whereas questioning students do not fit with either group (Espelage et al., 2008). Yet, contrary to these results, the national study by Lucassen et al. (2011) showed that questioning youth were at a lower risk for depressive symptoms and suicidality. These inconsistent results point to the need for further research into this population and their differences from LGB individuals.

Transgender students, who are managing gender identity issues along with possible issues of sexual orientation, are another group that are potentially at risk for mental health problems due to victimization from harassment and assault. According to the Gay, Lesbian, and Straight Education Network (GLSEN)'s *2007 National School Climate Survey* of 13 to 20 year old transgender students, 90% reported hearing negative comments from other students in school about someone's gender expression, and 39% reported hearing them from school personnel (Greytak, Kosciw, & Diaz, 2009). In addition, transgender students reported verbal harassment (87%), physical harassment (53%), physical assault (26%), and feeling unsafe at school (65%) due to their gender expression. When levels of harassment were high, there was an increase in poor academic performance, a decrease in educational aspirations, and an increase in absenteeism. A full review of the needs of transgender students can be found in Chapter 5 of this volume.

Suicide Risk

A review of the literature shows that there is a relationship between sexual orientation and suicidal behavior (Haas et al., 2011; Lucassen et al., 2011). While the exact nature of this relationship has been questioned in the past due to research limitations (e.g., studies using non-representative samples and inadequate measures), more recent studies using population-based studies have helped to confirm and clarify this risk (Haas et al., 2011; King et al., 2008; Remafedi, 1999; Russell, 2003). A meta-analysis of studies examining the prevalence of suicide attempt, suicidal ideation, mental disorders, and substance misuse revealed that LGB adolescents and adults are approximately 2.5 times more likely to report a suicide attempt (in both lifetime and 12 month period) than heterosexual peers (King et al., 2008).

Savin-Williams and Ream (2003), however, argue that the literature should move away from the question of whether gay youth are suicidal to the question of "which youth are suicidal and how being a sexual minority informs that experience" (p. 522). Research has demonstrated that when LGBTQ students' needs either go unmet or far exceed the support provided, symptoms likely worsen and might render the adolescent less able to cope (Savin-Williams & Ream, 2003).

Certain LGBTQ subgroups may be at higher risk than others, although research is not always consistent in this finding (e.g., Mustanski, Garofalo, & Emerson, 2010; Saewyc et al., 2007). In their meta-analysis, King et al. (2008) found that the lifetime prevalence of suicide attempts for LGB individuals was higher than their heterosexual peers. However, when comparing men and women, the rate for gay and bisexual males was even higher than for lesbian and bisexual females. Similarly, Lucassen et al. (2011) found that bisexuals were at greater risk for suicide and self-harm than individuals reporting same-sex attraction. Students questioning their sexual orientation or gender identity may also be at greater risk for suicidal behavior (Birkett et al., 2009; Poteat, Aragon, Espelage, & Koenig, 2009). Continued research is needed in order to clarify these findings, but there is no doubt that assessing and addressing suicide risk is an important part of counseling with LGBTQ students.

Ethical and Culturally Competent Counseling

One step toward improving conditions for LGBTQ students is for school-based mental health professionals to invest in and adopt an affirmative approach to treating LGBTQ students. Professional organizations have provided mental health professionals with a clear ethical path to follow related to counseling LGBTQ students.

According to the National Association of Social Workers (NASW, 2008), the American Counseling Association (ACA, 2005), and the National Association of School Psychologists (NASP, 2006), LGBTQ youth have the right to equal access to clinical services that foster the development and expression of a personal identity free from discrimination, harassment, violence, and abuse. More directly, the American School Counselor Association (ASCA, 2007) reissued the following position statement:

> Professional school counselors promote affirmation, respect and equal opportunity for all individuals regardless of sexual orientation or gender identity. Professional school counselors also promote awareness of issues related to sexual orientation/ gender identity among students, teachers, administrators, parents and the community. Professional school counselors work to eliminate barriers that impede student development and achievement and are committed to the academic, career and personal/social development of all students.
>
> (p. 29)

Therefore, mental health professionals must engage in self-discovery and determine if they unwittingly espouse heteronormative attitudes and biases (McGeorge & Carlson, 2011). In addition to critical self-exploration, increased awareness and knowledge are essential. Therefore, mental health professionals are responsible for securing training, consultation, and supervision to ensure competent service delivery (Fassinger, 1991; Israel, Ketz, Detrie, Burke, & Shulman, 2003; Kocarek and Pelling, 2003).

One of the more contentious LGBTQ-related counseling issues is the use of conversion therapy, also known as reparative or coercive therapy. It is arguably unethical and remains a concern given traditional religious and political efforts to publically promote a heterocentrist paradigm. This unsanctioned therapeutic approach is dedicated to eliminating a homosexual identity and promoting a heterosexual identity along with its concomitant heteronormative worldview. Proponents of this approach have argued that gay men are simply having difficulty realizing their full masculine identity, and to that end, continue searching for it in the pursuit of male–male homosexual relationships— referred to as a *gender identity deficit* (Nicolosi, 1991). Robinson (2006) found the following regarding the effectiveness of conversion therapies: (a) most therapists do not accept any of them; (b) at no time in the past were they accepted by most therapists;

(c) only a minority of therapists or clergy are using or have used them; and (d) there is no meaningful evidence to support their utility. A bounty of evidence reveals conversion therapy to be harmful, damaging, and potentially resulting in serious psychological trauma (APA, 2009; Beckstead, 2003; Beckstead & Morrow, 2004; Blackwell, 2008; Cianciotto & Cahill, 2006; Shidlo & Schroeder, 2002).

As a result, a coalition of 13 education, health, mental health, and religious organizations including the APA, ACA, ASCA, NASP, and the American Association of School Administrators (AASA), among others, published a booklet, entitled *Just the Facts about Sexual Orientation and Youth: A Primer for Principals, Educators, and School Personnel*, that addresses the health and well-being of all students including LGBTQ students in the wake of a rapid increase in efforts to change individuals' LGBTQ sexual orientation through psychotherapy and religious ministries (Just the Facts Coalition, 2008). The coalition reported that the use of conversion therapy is potentially harmful to LGB students and "exacerbate[s] the risk of marginalization, harassment, harm, and fear experienced by lesbian, gay, and bisexual students" (p. 10) and thereby may lead to "potential legal liability for school districts and officials" (p. 11).

The ACA addressed the issue of reparative therapy directly. As reported in Just the Facts Coalition (2008), the ACA adopted the following resolution in 1998:

> [The ACA] opposes portrayals of lesbian, gay, and bisexual youth and adults as mentally ill due to their sexual orientation; and supports the dissemination of accurate information about sexual orientation, mental health, and appropriate interventions in order to counteract bias that is based on ignorance or unfounded beliefs about same-gender sexual orientation. Further, in April 1999, the ACA Governing Council adopted a position opposing the promotion of "reparative therapy" as a "cure" for individuals who are homosexual.
>
> (p. 6)

Therefore, mental health professionals must consider the policy positions of ACA, ASCA, NASP, and APA in support of LGBTQ students' right to develop a positive sense of self, including a positive sexual orientation in an equally supportive, protective, and harassment-, violence-, and stigma-free educational environment, similar to that of their heterosexual contemporaries. In addition, mental health professionals need to refer to the APA's (2009) Task Force report which concluded that "the appropriate application of affirmative therapeutic interventions for those who seek Sexual Orientation Change Efforts (SOCE) involves therapist acceptance, support, and understanding of clients and the facilitation of clients' active coping, social support, and identity exploration and development, without imposing a specific sexual orientation identity outcome" (p. v).

LGBTQ-Affirmative Counseling

In spite of the nation's growing tolerance of LGBTQ individuals, LGBTQ youth are more likely than their heterosexual contemporaries to experience additive psychosocial distress during key developmental periods in childhood and throughout adolescence because of sexual orientation, same or both sex attraction, and/or gender identity-based oppression, victimization, and feelings of differentness (Callahan, 2001; Cooley, 1998;

D'Augelli, 1998; Henning-Stout, James, & Mcintosh, 2000; Richardson, Myers, Bing, & Satz, 1997; Whitman, Horn, & Boyd, 2007). When LGBTQ students experience sexual orientation, same or both sex attraction, and/or gender identity-based distress, counseling can help shape and enhance healthy development of youths' sense-of-self.

Therefore when LGBTQ students seek counseling, mental health professionals will need to assess the extent to which these students experience sexual orientation, same or both sex attraction, and/or gender identity-based discrimination, harassment, and/or internalized heterosexism, and to what extent, if any, these experiences contribute to students' presenting clinical problems like anxiety, depression, suicidal ideation, and social isolation (Fisher et al., 2008). When sexual orientation, same or both sex attraction, and/or gender identity appear to be at the heart of the presenting concern, mental health professionals should focus on ensuring client safety and facilitating the development of a healthy sense of self, which will in turn foster positive sexual orientation, same or both sex attraction, and/or gender identity development. We consider the latter goal to be driven by affirming and guiding identity integration in the face of socially hostile heterosexist environments. Heterosexism is covered in the next section of this chapter. Sexual and gender identity development are covered in Chapters 3 and 5 of this volume.

Theoretical Approach

The twenty-first century has ushered in a growing debate contrasting ethically affirmative LGB-oriented therapy and LGB-affirmative therapy. According to Langdridge (2007), the debate rests on the following distinctions: ethically affirmative therapy is a form of therapy whereby LGB identities are valued as much as heterosexual ones with an equitable consideration of LGB cultures; whereas LGB-affirmative therapy goes beyond simply recognizing the LGB individual's value. The LGB-affirmative therapeutic approaches also involve: affirming lived experiences, eradicating the influence of internalized heterosexism, and encouraging the development of supportive networks. Furthermore, this approach emphasizes the development of an integrated and positive sense of self with respect to individual expression and experience of sexual orientation, same or both sex attraction, and/or gender identity (Langdridge, 2007; McGeorge & Carlson, 2011; Whitman et al., 2007). The focus of this section will be on LGBTQ-affirmative therapy.

Regardless of theoretical orientation, mental health professionals who integrate LGBTQ affirmation into their therapeutic work with youth likely will see favorable outcomes in the development of a positive LGBTQ sense of self (Cornett, 1993; McGeorge & Carlson, 2011; Whitman et al., 2007). In addition to heterosexual mental health professionals (and school professionals) being allies to LGBTQ youth (Ji, 2007), mental health professionals have a unique opportunity and ethical obligation to provide affirming, direct clinical service to LGBTQ youth and develop in-service educational opportunities for school staff and administrators. As it relates to LGBTQ student mental health, the utility of affirmative therapy is an effective way of addressing issues specific to this population (Clark, 1987; Langdridge, 2007; McGeorge & Carlson, 2011; Perez, DeBord, & Bieschke, 2000; Safren & Rogers, 2001).

Gay-Affirmative Therapy, in particular, has enjoyed positive growth and acceptance as a viable approach for use with sexual minority clients since its inception in the late 1990s (Leslie, 1995). At its core, gay-affirmative therapy engenders affirmation of the individual's LGBTQ sense of self germane to improving his or her lived experience. This approach requires the mental health professional to explore and possess a deeper understanding of the nexus of intrapsychic processes and maladaptive sociocultural homophobic, heterosexist, and heteronormative messages—at both the individual and institutional level (Glassgold & Drescher, 2007; Leslie, 1995; McGeorge & Carlson, 2011). The aforementioned terms *homophobia, heterosexism,* and *heteronormative* typically are used interchangeably yet their differences connote distinct meanings worth exploring.

The term *homophobia* has been subject to many interpretations, and, in fact, is the most difficult of terms to operationalize in empirical research (Smith, Oades, & McCarthy, 2012). Clinically, the term represents an irrational fear of homosexuals. From an exhaustive literature search of the term, Smith et al. (2012) found that the problem with the term *homophobia* is that it is so ambiguous that it leads to many interpretations: fear of, dislike, hatred, contempt, negative attitudes, prejudice, discrimination, harassment, violence, marginalization, disenfranchisement, oppression, and ignorance toward homosexual, bisexual, transgender, and questioning individuals. Due to this lack of precision, the term is replaced here with *heterosexism.*

Heterosexism is a more accurate and appropriate term to use in defining sexual orientation, same and both sex attraction, and gender identity-based discrimination with subsequent negative outcomes experienced by members of homosexual, bisexual, and transgender communities. According to Smith et al. (2012), *heterosexism* does a better job of capturing the social pathology behind the maladaptive personal attitudes toward non-heterosexuals. Herek (1990) defined *heterosexism* as an ideological mechanism used to deny, denigrate, and otherwise stigmatize non-heterosexuals' ways of being. Of key interest here is how the term *heterosexism* moves us away from individual pathologies to a larger cultural or societal illness that can unknowingly contribute to negative individual and institutional beliefs, attitudes, and acts against LGBTQ youth.

Heteronormative assumptions are the offspring, if you will, of heterosexism. They tend to be reinforced by a more liberal-humanistic perspective that focuses on similarities between lesbian, gay, and heterosexual individuals in an effort to be more tolerant of lesbians and gay men. At one end of the spectrum, the dominant group holds positive attitudes toward LGBTQ individuals (relatively speaking) but still within the context of a heterosexual norm. On the other end of the spectrum, LGBTQ individuals are dehumanized, discriminated against, denied, and disregarded based on a rigid adherence to a socially sanctioned heterosexual norm. Either way, LGBTQ individuals are not afforded a distinct expression of sexual orientation, same or both sex attraction, and/or gender identity that is valued in the absence of the heterosexual norm. Heteronormative assumptions relegate LGBTQ individuals to sexual orientation, attraction, and/or gender identity-based oppression and discrimination and promote heterosexual privilege (McGeorge & Carlson, 2011).

In conclusion, if mental health professionals lack an awareness of both heterosexual privilege and the negative impact of heteronormative assumptions (or heterosexism), the result can be devastating for LGBTQ students. These students may be subjected to comparing and valuing their sense of self and well-being in relation to their heterosexual peers. It is logical then to conclude that facilitating an LGBTQ student's self-exploration in a safe, supportive, affirming environment is essential to a healthy developmental experience. Creating that space for the student may be challenging indeed, especially one absent of social pressure to measure his or her value against that of the heterosexual and gender identity norms. Therefore, school professionals are encouraged to consider LGBTQ students as individuals with personal histories, ambitions, concerns, and developmental needs that should be validated, given their vulnerability to subtle forms of harassment, bullying, and physical violence as they relate to oppression of LGBTQ individuals.

Similarly, mental health professionals are ethically obligated to create and maintain an environment of respect, support, and affirmation, and one that is free of heterosexism and gender conformity. To maximize effective care of LGBTQ students, we recommend that school mental health professionals do the following: (a) become aware of the oppression that LGBTQ individuals experience; (b) engage in their own self-exploration examining their beliefs about varying expressions of sexuality; and (c) explore their own heteronormative and gender conforming assumptions. The next section of this chapter will explore how school professionals and mental health providers can engage in this process. A therapeutic model is detailed and recommended as a process from which both school and school-based mental health professionals can benefit.

Theory into Practice

The American Psychological Association has developed guidelines for clinical practice when working with LGB clients (APA, 2000, 2012), which we recommend for your review. More specifically, the therapeutic model proposed by McGeorge and Carlson (2011) is designed to address unconscious and, in some cases, conscious heterosexist/heteronormative assumptions in the treatment of LGBTQ individuals. One can quite easily interject gender identity assumptions in the ensuing line of questioning as well. Future scholars may consider adapting this model to specifically address gender identity. Also keep in mind that even though the model is developed for mental health providers, all school professionals can benefit from this process of self-exploration.

As mentioned earlier, it is the mental health professionals' ethical responsibility to at least explore their heteronormative assumptions, such as assuming that students are heterosexuals and/or in heterosexual relationships. In fact, for examples of heteronormative assumptions that are often times unintentional and unconscious, one only needs to turn to pop culture, literature, film, advertisements, video games, and school-sanctioned heterosexual events (e.g., dances, prom, and homecoming). Moreover, the media is replete with cycles of national monologues proposing a ban of gay marriage and civil unions of same-sex partners, which contributes considerably to the invalidation of non-heterosexual expressions of love thereby reinforcing the heteronormative status quo. Mental health providers are encouraged to consider the following model and how this barrage of non-affirming and anti-homosexual, -bisexual, or -transgender messaging might impact the self-esteem and the development of a healthy sense of self for LGBTQ students.

McGeorge and Carlson (2011) offer a universal Three-Step Model or approach to becoming an optimally affirming mental health professional for LGB (and we have added transgender and questioning, or LGBTQ) individuals. We propose that this three-step model is used not only by heterosexual therapists, but also homosexual, bisexual, and transgender mental health professionals who may engage in the mental health treatment of LGBTQ youth. At the heart of this model is a deepening and critical self-exploration of how heterosexism can influence all parties' personal and professional understanding and attitude towards LGBTQ clients. McGeorge and Carlson's (2011) three-step model addresses this through the mental health professionals' exploration of (1) heteronormative assumptions, (2) heterosexual privilege, and (3) a heterosexual sexual identity. This approach represents the essential first steps in therapeutic work with youth grappling with their sexual orientation, sexual attractions, and/or gender identities.

McGeorge and Carlson (2011) recommend that mental health professionals use this model not only to challenge their internal dialogue, but also as accountability dialogue with which they can support mental health colleagues and student trainees as they challenge their own unconscious beliefs, attitudes, and practices. Again, we recommend that this process is brought to bear on all mental health professionals and school professionals (perhaps in the form of an in-service activity) regardless of professionals' sexual orientation, attractions, or gender identity. In fact, it is recommended that anyone who has meaningful and influential contact with school-aged youth engage in this level of self-awareness and exploration. The following three sections are a description of McGeorge and Carlson's (2011) self-exploration guide. In each of the three steps, we have modified some of the sample questions in order to make them more applicable to transgender and questioning individuals (indicated by the term "modified" following the question). We also have added school-based questions for consideration (indicated by the term "add-on" following the question).

Step 1: Exploring Heteronormative Assumptions. As previously discussed, heterosexual assumptions are the unconscious and automatic activation of beliefs and expectations of an ideal psychosexual norm centered on heterosexuality and heterosexual relationships (Ingraham, 2006; Oswald et al., 2005).

Mental health professionals should consider and reflect on the following sample questions originally proposed by McGeorge and Carlson (2011, p.17):

1. Were sexual orientation and same-sex and bisexual relationships talked about in my family? If so, what values were communicated? If not, what did that silence communicate?
2. Are there any LGBTQ members in my family? If so, how were/are they talked about and treated in my family? (modified)
3. If appropriate, what did/does my religious or spiritual community teach me about sexual orientation and same-sex and bisexual relationships? What do the religious or spiritual texts of my particular faith teach me about sexual orientation and same-sex relationships?
4. What are my beliefs about how a youth "becomes" gay, lesbian, bisexual, transgender, queer, or questioning? (modified)
5. What are my beliefs about why I did not "become" gay, lesbian, bisexual, transgender, queer, or questioning? (modified)
6. When I first meet a student, how often do I assume that s/he is heterosexual? What values and beliefs inform this assumption? (modified)

7. Do I believe that healthy personal development includes exploring one's sexual orientation and gender identity in a safe social space that normalizes all forms of sexual orientation, attractions, and gender identity? If so, how did I come to this realization? If not, why not? (add on)

It is helpful to consider that LGBTQ youth are faced with developing a sense of self in social environments that are often not supportive or safe, which can significantly affect LGBTQ youths' personal and academic development.

Step 2: Exploring Heterosexual Privilege. McGeorge and Carlson (2011) succinctly conceptualize heterosexual privilege as an experience of "unearned benefits" (p. 18). For example, they note that heterosexuals can see positive representations of themselves in many places including television, movies, and publicly endorsed displays of affection. LGBTQ mental health professionals can modify some of the following questions, as appropriate, to help them think more deeply about heterosexual privilege (McGeorge & Carlson, 2011, p.19):

1. How has your involvement in heterosexual relationships been encouraged, rewarded, acknowledged, and supported by your family, friends, and the larger society?
2. As a child, how were you encouraged to play according to heterosexual norms?
3. Have you ever had to question your heterosexuality? Has a family member, friend, or colleague ever questioned your heterosexuality?
4. Have you ever had to defend your heterosexuality in order to gain acceptance among your peers or colleagues?
5. Have you ever worried that you might lose your job because of your heterosexuality?
6. When you were young, did you ever experience internal conflict about who to ask to the dance, prom, or homecoming? Was that person of the same sex? Can you imagine the degree of worry, dread, and risk of losing your social status among your peers by taking a same-sex date? (add on)
7. Have you ever wondered why you were born heterosexual? Whether you could change your heterosexuality?
8. As a youth, did you ever worry that if you sought therapy your therapist might try to change your heterosexuality? (modified)
9. Have you ever worried that you might be "outed" as a heterosexual?
10. Have you ever feared that you would be physically harmed based solely on your heterosexuality?

Step 3: Exploring Heterosexual Identity. The final step that can lead to a more affirmative therapeutic process for heterosexual mental health professionals involves a critical self-exploration of heterosexual identity. Worthington, Savoy, Dillon, and Vernaglia (2002) refer to a heterosexual identity as one in which the individual not only identifies as such but also engages in its expression. McGeorge and Carlson (2011) argue that once heterosexual therapists explore their own identity, they are less likely to allow heteronormative assumptions and heterosexism to influence the therapeutic process. The following are recommended sample questions for reflection and consideration (McGeorge & Carlson, 2011, p. 20):

1. How do you describe your sexual identity? How do you explain how you came to identify as a heterosexual? Why do you think you identify as a heterosexual?
2. What role does your sexual identity play in who you are as a person?
3. What factors were most important or influential to your development of a heterosexual identity?
4. What societal beliefs or norms influenced your development of a heterosexual identity?
5. What spiritual or religious beliefs influenced your development of a heterosexual identity?
6. What family beliefs or norms influenced your development of a heterosexual identity?
7. When you were in your youth, when did you have your first opposite sex sexual attraction? What meaning did you assign to that attraction? If you experienced that attraction as natural or normative, where did those beliefs come from? (modified)
8. Have you experienced attraction to members of the same sex? If so, how did you make sense of those attractions? If not, how do you make sense of not having attractions to members of the same sex?
9. How does your identification as a heterosexual influence how you make sense of how a person comes to identify as an LGBTQ individual? How does your identification as a heterosexual influence how you perceive LGBTQ-identified individuals? (modified)
10. How does your identification as a heterosexual influence the way you do therapy with all of your young clients (regardless of their sexual orientation)? (modified)

Application. McGeorge and Carlson (2011) recommend the following guidelines for a mental health professional to create a more LGBTQ-affirmative counseling environment: (a) within the first session, identify as someone who is committed to providing services to all clients including LGBTQ individuals; (b) adopt non-heteronormative language and gender-neutral language (e.g., significant other, partner, etc.) until sexual orientation, attraction, and/or gender identity has been established; and (c) have a variety of magazines, brochures, and books in the waiting area, including some that are LGBTQ-friendly. Equally important, McGeorge and Carlson (2011) suggest that next steps include "coming out" as an LGB(TQ) affirming therapist and ally. This can be accomplished by posting an LGBTQ affirming symbol outside one's office, indicating a "safe space" for LGBTQ students. This should also involve publicly advocating for LGBTQ students' rights and needs. During therapy, where appropriate, address the presence and unconscious influence of heterosexism and the development of a healthy and positive sense of self.

Supporting Sexual and Gender Identity Development

The previous sections outlined the underlying process by which heterosexual therapists— and we would argue all therapists regardless of sexual orientation—become aware of the presence and impact of heterosexism on the therapeutic process. The previous section also addressed the specific application of an LGBTQ-affirming approach regardless of therapeutic orientation. This universal perspective also applies to specific treatment goals in the development of healthy sexual and gender identities. For example, rapport building is essential, including identifying oneself as someone who treats clients of all expressions of sexuality. Respecting clients' right to privacy and confidentiality also is essential, in addition to assessing the extent to which sexual orientation, sexual attraction, and/or gender identity play a role in the presenting psychological distress. If they do play a role, it is important to focus on helping the person become aware of the presence and impact of heterosexism on his or her sexual and/or gender identity. In an effort to appreciate the distinction, sexual and gender identity will be described.

Sexual Identity Development

Scholars seem to agree that the ultimate end-state of sexual identity development is self-acceptance/integration (e.g., Cass, 1979; Coleman, 1985; D'Augelli & Patterson, 2001; Fassinger, 2000; Troiden, 1979), although for many individuals there are shorter-term goals that may be the focus of school-based counseling. As mental health professionals work to promote healthy identity development, they must take into consideration the tremendous hardships LGBTQ students may be encountering both at school and home, which may substantially increase and/or sustain the likelihood of internalizing hetero-sexist messages. Lacking strategies to effectively manage these negative messages, students may use alternative coping mechanisms including hyper-investment in academics, private and public denial of sexual orientation, attraction, and/or gender identity, hyper-heterosexual attitude and behavior, anti-homosexual attitude and behavior, discretion, controlled disclosure, substance abuse/use, and/or suicide (Pachankis & Goldfried, 2004). To help students develop the internal resources to counter homonegative messages and to support self-acceptance/integration of sexuality and gender identity, mental health professionals will need to keep the developmental stage of LGBTQ students in mind as they conceptualize the case and develop and implement theory-based interventions (Savin-Williams, 2001). See Chapter 3 of this volume for a comprehensive review of sexual identity development.

Gender Identity Development

Chapter 5 of this volume provides a comprehensive review of transgender, intersex, gender identity, and gender identity disorder (GID). In providing counseling services for students who are managing gender identity issues, school-based mental health professionals are encouraged to examine their beliefs about whether or not GID should be classified as a mental disorder. The definition of GID often fails to capture the lived internal experience of transgender individuals, and evidence suggests that adolescents and adults diagnosed with GID function just as well as non-clinical populations (Cohen-Kettenis & Pfäfflin, 2010; Meyer-Bahlburg, 2009). In fact, it is likely that the American Psychiatric Association (APA, 2011) will make significant changes to the language used and diagnostic criteria related to gender dysphoria and GID in the coming years.

For school-based mental health professionals, a helpful place to begin is to understand that children and adolescents with gender identity dysphoria are those who present with a "strong and persistent cross-gender identification" (APA, 2000, p. 581), also understood as an incongruence between expressed and experienced gender and assigned gender. Factor and Rothblum (2008) give a rather comprehensive account of the complexities of gender expression and identity including: male to female (MtF), female to male (FtM), gender queer, sex radical, gender blender and more. Understandably, assigning labels unilaterally can be both uninformative and arresting to client autonomy. Another source worth considering is Devor's (2004) 14-stage model of transsexual and transgender identity formation. He posits that there are stages of development through which one moves from an observation that one is different to a stage of confusion, and, ultimately to integrating identity into one's sense of self.

Suicide Prevention and Risk Assessment

Given the increased risk for suicide among LGBTQ youth, the issue of prevention becomes a necessary and critical focus. Suicide prevention strategies exist at the national level, but their efficacy has not been adequately studied (Mann et al., 2005). Therefore, through a narrative synthesis of 93 studies (i.e., meta-analyses, quantitative studies, and population-based studies) related to suicide prevention, Mann et al. (2005) found that the most effective strategies for reducing suicide rates were primary care provider education (e.g., informing providers about suicide risk factors), suicide means restriction (e.g., enacting laws to control firearms), and gatekeeper education (e.g., informing school personnel, clergy, or first responders of suicide risk factors). However, Haas et al. (2011) reported that the suicide prevention strategies used at the national or state level have not been sufficiently developed or evaluated for LGBT individuals.

In an effort to identify suicide prevention programs that focus on LGBT youth, the Suicide Prevention Resource Center (SPRC, 2008) found only one program of this kind, *The Trevor Project*, which offers a national 24-hour crisis and suicide lifeline, a safe space for LGBT youth to find community and support, advocacy for mental health and suicide prevention programs, and educational resources (see http://www.thetrevorproject.org/Programs). *The Trevor Project* has received recent media coverage as a benefactor of the *It Gets Better* campaign, (see http://www.itgetsbetter.org/pages/about-it-gets-better-project/; Savage & Miller, 2011).

Although *The Trevor Project* may begin to fill the void in suicide prevention programming for LGBTQ youth, national suicide prevention programs otherwise have yet to fulfill their obligation to incorporate LGBTQ concerns into suicide prevention (Haas et al., 2011). As a result, in order to improve suicide prevention programs, Haas et al. (2011) recommended that national and state prevention programs, LGBT organizations, and general suicide prevention programs specifically address LGBT suicide risk and that program staff who may come into contact with suicidal individuals receive training specific to LGBT suicide risk and prevention.

When youth begin to experience isolation, rejection, victimization, and other factors related to being LGBTQ in a world that is non-affirming of LGBTQ individuals, they become at increased risk for suicidal behavior (SPRC, 2008). At that moment, it becomes critical for mental health professionals to ask LGBTQ students if they have ever thought about hurting themselves or taking their own lives. Mental health professionals need to conduct a thorough suicide risk assessment to determine how to best help the struggling

202 Grady L. Garner, Jr. and Dennis M. Emano

students. The literature on suicide risk assessment is rich with protocols for conducting assessments that identify certain at-risk groups, but it often fails to include LGBTQ youth in this at-risk category (e.g., Berman, Jobes, & Silverman, 2006; Sanchez, 2001; Simon, 2004; White, 2011). Nonetheless, there are some universal procedures that apply regardless of the population being assessed. We will briefly summarize them in the following paragraph as we integrate some of the more idiosyncratic issues specific to LGBTQ youth.

In assessing for suicide risk, Bryan and Rudd (2006) identified several areas that are important to address based on empirical support: (a) precipitating factors; (b) predisposition to suicidality; (c) current symptomatology; (d) history of suicide attempts; (e) nature of suicidal thoughts; (f) impulse control; (g) hopelessness; and (h) protective factors. The precipitants vary from person to person. However, in the case of LGBTQ youth, it could be harassment from peers, bullying, or being "outed" by someone against their will. Sadly, these precipitants were true in the cases of Billy Lucas, Seth Walsh, Tyler Clementi, and Asher Brown, whose suicides reached national attention and propelled the *It Gets Better* campaign (Savage & Miller, 2011). When an LGBTQ student is getting bullied in school or exhibiting great emotional distress, it is incumbent upon school mental health professionals to inquire about suicidal ideation and conduct a suicide risk assessment when necessary.

Issues of safety supersede confidentiality when students report suicidal ideation with a specific plan, even when students request that their report be held in confidence. This might create an ethical dilemma for mental health professionals as they need to maintain confidentiality about students' sexual or gender identity (Janson, 2002). Therefore, so long as an adolescent is deemed competent and not a danger to self or others, confidentiality is maintained by the mental health professional (Swann & Herbert, 1999). However, if mental health professionals need to break confidentiality to ensure students stay safe, they should take care to avoid unnecessarily revealing information about students' sexual or gender identity.

Expanding the Counseling Role

In addition to providing LGBTQ-affirmative counseling, school-based mental health professionals are encouraged to engage in efforts that foster social change through advocacy and outreach (APA, 2009; Russell et al., 2010; Vera & Speight, 2003; Whitman et al., 2007). Indeed, advocacy work is essential in helping students who are at risk of harassment, poor academic performance, and problems with identity development (Whitman et al., 2007). Professional organizations expound on the necessity of advocacy work, and ASCA goes so far to state, "professional school counselors ... monitor and expand personal multicultural and social justice advocacy awareness, knowledge and skills ... [and] strive for exemplary cultural competence by ensuring personal beliefs or values are not imposed on students or other stakeholders" (ASCA, 2010, section E.2.a.). With this shift in emphasis, mental health professionals can lead the process of school climate change and pave the path for a safer and more affirmative environment for LGBTQ students. The other chapters in this volume provide excellent recommendations and make reference to resources that will aid professionals in undertaking systemic change.

In conclusion, mental health professionals in schools play a pivotal role in an era when issues of bullying, harassment, and heterosexism continue to exist but also face greater public scrutiny as more and more victimized LGBTQ individuals and their allies are speaking out. School-based counseling potentially can be an effective means of promoting healthy development for LGBTQ students when it is ethical, affirming, compassionate, empathic, and responsive. Through a greater awareness, understanding, and prevention of homophobic, heteronormative, and heterosexist school environments, and the psychological impact these have on LGBTQ youth, mental health professionals can assist in turning this potential for healthy LGBTQ development into a reality. Indeed, mental health professionals can assist in saving young lives.

References

American Counseling Association. (2005). *American Counseling Association Code of Ethics.* Retrieved from http://www.counseling.org/Resources/CodeOfEthics/TP/Home/CT2.aspx

American Psychiatric Association. (2000). *Diagnostic and Statistical Manual of Mental Disorders* (4th ed., text rev.). Washington, DC: Author.

American Psychiatric Association. (2011). *P 00 Gender Dysphoria in Children.* Arlington, VA: Author. Retrieved from http://www.dsm5.org/ProposedRevisions/Pages/proposedrevision.aspx?rid=192#

American Psychological Association. (2000). Guidelines for Psychotherapy with Lesbian, Gay, and Bisexual Clients. *American Psychologist, 55 (12),* 1440–1451. doi:10.1037//0003-066X.55.12.1440

American Psychological Association. (2012). Guidelines for Psychological Practice with Lesbian, Gay, and Bisexual Clients. *American Psychologist, 67(1),* 10–42. Retrieved from http://www.apa.org/pi/lgbt/resources/guidelines.aspx

American School Counselor Association. (2007). *The professional school counselor and LGBTQ youth* (Position Statement). Alexandria, VA: Author. Retrieved from http://asca2.timberlakepublishing.com//files/PS_LGBTQ.pdf

American School Counselor Association. (2010). *Ethical Standards for School Counselors.* Retrieved from http://www.schoolcounselor.org/files/EthicalStandards2010.pdf

APA Task Force on Appropriate Therapeutic Responses to Sexual Orientation. (2009). *Report of the Task Force on Appropriate Therapeutic Responses to Sexual Orientation.* Washington, DC: American Psychological Association. Retrieved from http://www.apa.org/pi/lgbt/resources/sexual-orientation.aspx

Beckstead, A. L. (2003). Understanding the self-reports of reparative therapy "success." *Archives of Sexual Behavior, 32,* 421–423. doi:10.1177/0011000004268877

Beckstead, A. L., & Morrow, S. L. (2004). Mormon clients' experiences of conversion therapy: The need for a new treatment approach. *The Counseling Psychologist, 32,* 651–690. doi:10.1177/0011000004267555

Berman, A. L., Jobes, D. A., & Silverman, M. M. (2006). *Adolescent suicides: Assessment and intervention.* Washington, DC: American Psychological Association.

Biaggo, M., Orchard, S., Larson, J., Petrino, K., & Mihara, R. (2003). Guidelines for gay/lesbian/bisexual-affirmative educational practices in graduate psychology. *Professional Psychology: Research & Practice, 34*(5), 548–554. doi:10.1037/0735-7028.34.5.548

Birkett, M., Espelage, D. L., & Koenig, B. (2009). Lesbian, gay, bisexual and questioning students in schools: The moderating effects of homophobic bullying and school climate on negative outcomes. *Journal of Youth and Adolescence, 38,* 989–1000. doi:10.1007/s10964-008-9389-1

Blackwell, C. W. (2008). Nursing implications in the application of conversion therapies on gay, lesbian, bisexual, and transgender clients. *Issues in Mental Health Nursing, 29,* 651–665. doi:10.1080/01612840802048915

Bostwick, W. B., Boyd, C. J., Hughes, T. L., & McCabe, S. E. (2009). Dimensions of sexual orientation and the prevalence of mood and anxiety disorders in the United States. *American Journal of Public Health, 100*(3), 468–475. doi:10.2105/AJPH.2008.152942

Bryan, C. J., & Rudd, M. D. (2006). Advances in the assessment of suicide risk. *Journal of Clinical Psychology: In Session, 62*(2), 185–200. doi:10.1002/jclp.20222

Callahan, C. (2001). Protecting and counseling gay and lesbian students. *Journal of Humanistic Counseling, Education & Development, 40*(1), 5–10. doi:10.1002/j.2164-490X.2001.tb00097.x

Cass, V. C. (1979). Homosexual identity formation: A theoretical model. *Journal of Homosexuality, 4,* 219–235. doi:10.1300/J082v04n03_01

Cianciotto, J., & Cahill, S. (2006). *Youth in the crosshairs: The third wave of ex-gay activism.* New York, NY: National Gay and Lesbian Task Force.

Clark, D. (1987). *The new loving someone gay.* Berkeley, CA: Celestial Arts.

Cohen-Kettenis, P. T., & Pfäfflin, F. (2010). The DSM diagnostic criteria for gender identity disorder in adolescents and adults. *Archives of Sexual Behavior, 39,* 499–513. doi:10.1007/s10508-009-9562-y

Coleman, E. (1985). Developmental stages of the coming out process. In J. C. Gonsiorek (Ed.), *A guide to psychotherapy with gay and lesbian clients* (pp. 31–44). New York, NY: Harrington Park Press.

Cooley, J. (1998). Gay and lesbian adolescents: Presenting problems and the counselor's role. *Professional School Counseling, 1*(3), 30–34. Retrieved from http://www.schoolcounselor.org/content.asp?pl=325&sl=132&contentid=235

Cornett, C. (1993). *Affirmative dynamic psychotherapy with gay men.* Northvale, NJ: Jason Aronson.

D'Augelli, A. (1998). Development implications of victimization of lesbian, gay, and bisexual youths. In G. M. Herek (Ed.), *Stigma and sexual orientation: Understanding prejudice against lesbians, gay men, and bisexuals* (pp. 187–210). Thousand Oaks, CA: Sage Publications.

D'Augelli, A. R., & Patterson, C. J. (2001). *Lesbian, gay, and bisexual identities and youth: Psychological perspectives.* New York, NY: Oxford University Press.

Devor, A. H. (2004). Witnessing and mirroring: A fourteen stage model of transsexual identity formation. *Journal of Gay and Lesbian Psychotherapy, 8*(1–2), 41–67. doi:10.1300/J236v08n01_05

Espelage, D. L., Aragon, S. R., Birkett, M., & Koenig, B. W. (2008). Homophobic teasing, psychological outcomes, and sexual orientation among high school students: What influence do parents and schools have? *School Psychology Review, 37*(2), 202–216. Retrieved from http://www.nasponline.org/

Factor, R., & Rothblum, E. (2008). Exploring gender identity and community among three groups of transgender individuals in the U.S.: MTFs, FTMs, and genderqueers. *Health Sociology Review, 17*(3), 235–253. doi:10.5172/hesr.451.17.3.235

Fassinger, R. E. (1991). The hidden minority: Issues and challenges in working with lesbian women and gay men. *The Counseling Psychologist, 19,* 157–176. doi:10.1177/0011000091192003

Fassinger, R. E. (2000). Applying counseling theories to lesbian, gay, bisexual clients: Pitfalls and possibilities. In R. M. Perez, K. A. DeBord, & K. J. Bieschke (Eds.), *Handbook of psychotherapy with lesbians, gay, and bisexual clients* (pp. 107–131). Washington, DC: American Psychological Association.

Fergusson, D. M., Horwood, L. J., & Beautrais, A. L. (1999). Is sexual orientation related to mental health problems and suicidality in young people? *Archives of General Psychiatry, 56,* 876–880. doi:10.1001/archpsyc.56.10.876

Fergusson, D. M., Horwood, L. J., Ridder, E. M., & Beautrais, A. L. (2005). Sexual orientation and mental health in a birth cohort of young adults. *Psychological Medicine, 35*, 971–981. doi:10.1017/S0033291704004222

Fisher, E. S., Komosa-Hawkins, K., Thomas, G. M., Saldaña, E., Rauld, M., Hsiao, C., & Miller, D. (2008). Promoting school success for lesbian, gay, bisexual, transgendered, and questioning students: Primary, secondary, and tertiary prevention and intervention strategies. *The California School Psychologist, 13*, 79–91. Retrieved from http://www.caspsurveys.org/NEW/pdfs/journal08.pdf#page=79

Fontaine, J. (1998). Evidencing a need: School counselors' experiences with gay and lesbian students. *Professional School Counseling, 1*(3), 8–14. Retrieved from http://www.schoolcounselor.org/

Glassgold, J. M., & Drescher, J. (2007). Activism and LGBT psychology: An introduction. *Journal of Gay & Lesbian Psychotherapy, 11*(3/4), 1–8. doi:10.1300/J236v11n03_01

Greytak, E. A., Kosciw, J. G., & Diaz, E. M. (2009). *Harsh Realities: The experiences of transgender youth in our nation's schools.* New York, NY: GLSEN.

Haas, A. P., Eliason, M., Mays, V. M., Mathy, R. M., Cochran, S. D., D'Augelli, A. R., . . . Clayton, P. J. (2011). Suicide and suicide risk in lesbian, gay, bisexual, and transgender populations: Review and recommendations. *Journal of Homosexuality, 58*, 10–51. doi:10.1080/00918369.2011.534038

Hatzenbuehler, M. L., Keyes, K. M., & Hasin, D. S. (2009). State-level policies and psychiatric morbidity in LGBT populations. *American Journal of Public Health, 99*(12), 2275–2281. doi:10.2105/AJPH.2008.153510

Henning-Stout, M., James, S., & Mcintosh, S. (2000). Reducing harassment of lesbian, gay, bisexual, transgender, and questioning youth in schools. *School Psychology Review, 29*(2), 180–191. Retrieved from http://www.nasponline.org/publications/spr/ index.aspx?vol=40&issue=4

Herek, G. M. (1990). The context of anti-gay violence: Notes on cultural and psychological heterosexism. *Journal of Interpersonal Violence, 5*, 316–333. doi:10.1177/088626090005003006

Ingraham, C. (2006). Thinking straight, acting bent: Heteronormativity and homosexuality. In K. Davis, M. Evans, & J. Lorber (Eds.), *Handbook of gender and women's studies* (pp. 307–321). Thousand Oaks, CA: Sage.

Israel, T., & Hackett, G. (2004). Counselor education on lesbian, gay, and bisexual issues: Comparing information and attitude exploration. *Counselor Education and Supervision, 43*(3), 179–191. doi:10.1002/j.1556-6978.2004.tb01841.x

Israel, T., Ketz, K., Detrie, P. M., Burke, M. C., & Shulman, J. L. (2003). Identifying counselor competencies for working with lesbian, gay, and bisexual clients. *Journal of Gay & Lesbian Psychotherapy, 7*(4), 3–21. doi:10.1300/J236v07n04_02

It Gets Better Project. (2012). About the it gets better project. Retrieved from http://www.itgetsbetter.org/pages/about-it-gets-better-project/

Janson, G. R. (2002). Family counseling and referral with gay, lesbian, bisexual, and transgendered clients: Ethical considerations. *The Family Journal: Counseling and Therapy for Couples and Families, 10*(3), 328–333. doi:10.1177/10680702010003010

Ji, P. (2007). Being a heterosexual ally to the lesbian, gay, bisexual, and transgendered community: Reflections and development. *Journal of Gay & Lesbian Psychotherapy, 11*(3/4), 173–185. doi:10.1300/J236v11n03_10

Just the Facts Coalition. (2008). *Just the facts about sexual orientation and youth: A primer for principals, educators, and school personnel.* Washington, DC: American Psychological Association. Retrieved from http://www.apa.org/pi/lgbc/publications/justthefacts.html

Kennedy, K. G., & Fisher, E. S. (2010). Bisexual students in secondary schools: Understanding unique experience and developing responsive practices. *Journal of Bisexuality, 10*(4), 472–485. doi:10.1080/15299716.2010.521061

King, M., Semlyen, J., Tai, S. S., Killaspy, H., Osborn, D., Popelyuk, D., & Nazareth, I. (2008). A systematic review of mental disorder, suicide, and deliberate self-harm in lesbian, gay, and bisexual people. *BMC Psychiatry, 8*(70). doi:10.1186/1471-244X-8-70

Kocarek, C. E., & Pelling, N. J. (2003). Beyond knowledge and awareness: Enhancing counselor skills for work with gay, lesbian, and bisexual clients. *Journal of Multicultural Counseling and Development, 31*, 99–112. doi:10.1002/j.2161-1912.2003.tb00536.x

Langdridge, D. (2007). Gay affirmative therapy: A theoretical framework and defence. *Journal of Gay and Lesbian Psychotherapy, 11*(1/2), 27–43. doi:10.1300/J236v11no1_03

Leslie, L. A. (1995). Psychotherapy: The evolving treatment of gender, ethnicity, and sexual orientation in marital and family therapy. *Family Relations, 44*, 359–378. doi:10.2307/584991

Lucassen, M. F. G., Merry, S. N., Robinson, E. M., Denny, S., Clark, T., Ameratunga, S., . . . Rossen, F. V. (2011). Sexual attraction, depression, self-harm, suicidality & help-seeking behavior in New Zealand secondary school students. *Australian and New Zealand Journal of Psychiatry, 45*, 376–383. doi:10.3109/00048674.2011.559635

Mann, J. J., Apter, A., Bertolote, J., Beautrais, A., Currier, D., Haas, A., . . . Hendin, H. (2005). Suicide prevention strategies: A systematic review. *Journal of the American Medical Association, 294*(16), 2064–2074. doi:10.1001/jama.294.16.2064

McCabe, P. C., & Rubinson, F. (2008). Committing to social justice the behavioral intention of school psychology and education trainees to advocate for lesbian, gay, bisexual, and transgendered youth [Special topic]. *School Psychology Review, 37*, 469–486. Retrieved from http://www.nasponline.org

McGeorge, C., & Carlson, T. S. (2011). Deconstructing heterosexism: Becoming an LGB affirmative heterosexual couple and family therapist. *Journal of Marital and Family Therapy, 37*, 14–26. doi:10.1111/j.1752-0606.2009.00149.x

Meyer-Bahlburg, H. F. L. (2009). Variants of gender differentiation in somatic disorders of sex development: Recommendations for Version 7 of the World Professional Association for Transgendered Health's Standards of Care. *International Journal of Transgenderism, 11*, 226–237. doi:10.1080/15532730903439476

Mustanski, B. S., Garofalo, R., & Emerson, E. M. (2010). Mental health disorders, psychological distress, and suicidality in a diverse sample of lesbian, gay, bisexual, and transgender youths. *American Journal of Public Health, 100*(12), 2426–2432. doi:10.2105/AJPH.2009.178319

National Association of School Psychologists (NASP, 2006). *Gay, lesbian, bisexual, transgender, and questioning (GLBTQ) youth* (Position Statement). Bethesda, MD: Author. Retrieved from http://www.nasponline.org/about_nasp/positionpapers/GLBQYouth.pdf

National Association of Social Workers. (2008). *Code of Ethics of the National Association of Social Workers.* Washington, DC: National Association of Social Workers. Retrieved from http://www.socialworkers.org/pubs/code/code.asp

Nicolosi, J. (1991). *Reparative therapy of male homosexuality: A new clinical approach.* Northvale, NJ: Jason Aronson.

Oswald, R. F., Blume, L. B., & Marks, S. R. (2005). Decentering heteronormativity: A model for family studies. In V. L. Bengtson, A. C. Acock, K. R. Allen, P. Dilworth-Anderson, & D. M. Klein (Eds.), *Sourcebook of family theory & research* (pp. 143–165). Thousand Oaks, CA: Sage.

Pachankis, J. E., & Goldfried, M. R. (2004). Clinical issues in working with lesbian, gay, and bisexual clients. *Psychotherapy: Theory, Research, Practice, Training, 41*(3), 227–246. doi:10.1037/0033-3204.41.3.227

Pearson, Q. M. (2003). Breaking the silence in the counselor education classroom: A training seminar on counseling sexual minority clients. *Journal of Counseling and Development, 81*(2), 292–300. doi:10.1002/j.1556-6678.2003.tb00256.x

Perez, R. M., DeBord, K. A., & Bieschke, K. J. (Eds.). (2000). *Handbook of counseling and psychotherapy with lesbian, gay, and bisexual clients.* Washington, DC: American Psychological Association.

Phillips, J. C., & Fisher, A. R. (1998). Graduate students' training experiences with lesbian, gay, and bisexual issues. *The Counseling Psychologist, 2,* 712–734. doi:10.1177/0011000098265002

Poteat, V. P., Aragon, S. R., Espelage, D. L., & Koenig, B. W. (2009). Psychosocial concerns of sexual minority youth: Complexity and caution in group differences. *Journal of Consulting & Clinical Psychology, 77,* 196–201. doi:10.1037/a0014158

Remafedi, G. (1999). Suicide and sexual orientation: Nearing the end of controversy? *Archives of General Psychiatry, 56,* 885–886. doi:10.1001/archpsyc.56.10.885

Richardson, M. A., Myers, H. F., Bing, E. G., & Satz, P. (1997). Substance use and psychopathology in African American men at risk for HIV infection. *Journal of Community Psychology, 25,* 353–370. doi:10.1002/(SICI)1520-6629(199707)25:4<353::AID-JCOP4>3.0.CO;2-V

Robinson, B. A. (2006). *Reparative & similar therapies.* Retrieved from http://www.religioustolerance.org/homexod.htm

Rowson, R. (2001). Ethical principles. In F. P. Barnes & L. Murdin (Eds.), *Values and ethics in the practice of psychotherapy and counseling* (pp. 6–22). Philadelphia, PA: Open University Press.

Russell, S. T. (2003). Sexual minority youth and suicide risk. *American Behavioral Scientist, 46*(9), 1241–1257. doi:10.1177/0002764202250667

Russell, S. T., & Joyner, K. (2001). Adolescent sexual orientation and suicide risk: Evidence from a national study. *American Journal of Public Health, 91*(8), 1276–1281. doi:10.2105/AJPH.91.8.1276

Russell, S. T., Kosciw, J., Horn, S., & Saewyc, E. (2010). Safe schools policy for LGBTQ students. *Social Policy Report, 24*(4), 1–24. Retrieved from http://www.srcd.org/index.php?option=com_docman&task=doc_download&gid=1164

Saewyc, E. M., Skay, C. L., Hynds, P., Petingell, S., Bearinger, L. H., Resnick, M. D., & Reis, E. (2007). Suicidal ideation and attempts in North American school-based surveys: Are bisexual youth at increasing risk? *Journal of LGBT Health Research, 3*(2), 25–36. doi:10.1300/J463v03n02_04

Safren, S., & Rogers, T. (2001). Cognitive behavior therapy with lesbian, gay, and bisexual clients. *In Session: Journal of Clinical Psychology, 57,* 629–643. doi:10.1002/jclp.1033

Sanchez, H. G. (2001). Risk factor model for suicide assessment and intervention. *Professional Psychology: Research and Practice, 32*(4), 351–358. doi:10.1037//0735-7028.32.4.351.

Savage, D., & Miller, T. (2011). *It gets better: Coming out, overcoming bullying, and creating a life worth living.* New York, NY: Penguin Group.

Savage, T. A., Prout, H. T., & Chard, K. M. (2004). School psychology and issues of sexual orientation: Attitudes, beliefs, and knowledge. *Psychology in the Schools, 4,* 201–210. doi:10.1002/pits.10122

Savin-Williams, R. C. (2001). *"Mom, Dad. I'm gay": How families negotiate coming out.* Washington, DC: American Psychological Association.

Savin-Williams, R. C., & Ream, G. L. (2003). Suicide attempts among sexual-minority male youth. *Journal of Clinical Child and Adolescent Psychology, 32,* 509–522. doi:10.1207/S15374424JCCP3204_3

Sherry, A., Whiled, M. R., & Patton, J. (2005). Gay, lesbian, and bisexual training competencies in American Psychological Association accredited graduate programs. *Psychotherapy: Theory, Research, Practice & Training, 42*(1), 116–120. doi:10.1037/0033-3204.42.1.116

Shidlo, A. & Schroeder, M. (2002). Changing sexual orientation: A consumer's report. *Professional Psychology: Research and Practice, 33,* 249–259. doi:10.1037/0735-7028.33.3.249

Simon, R. I. (2004). *Assessing and managing suicide risk: Guidelines for clinically based risk management.* Washington, DC: American Psychiatric Publishing, Inc.

Smith, I. P., Oades, L, & McCarthy, G. (2012). Homophobia to heterosexism: Constructs in need in re-visitation. *Gay & Lesbian Issues and Psychology Review, 8*(1), 34–44. Retrieved from http://aipa.groups.psychology.org.au/Assets/Files/GLIP%20Review%20Vol%208%20No%201.pdf#page=38

Swann, S., & Herbert, S. E. (1999). Ethical issues in the mental health treatment of gender dysphoric adolescents [Special issue]. *Journal of Gay & Lesbian Social Services: Issues in Practice, Policy & Research, 10*(3/4), 19–34. doi:10.1300/J041v10n03_02

Suicide Prevention Resource Center. (2008). *Suicide risk and prevention for lesbian, gay, bisexual, and transgender youth*. Newton, MA: Education Development Center, Inc. Retrieved from http://www.sprc.org/library/SPRC_LGBT_Youth.pdf

The Trevor Project. (2012). Retrieved from http://www.thetrevorproject.org/Programs

Troiden, R. R. (1979). Becoming homosexual: A model of gay identity acquisition. *Psychiatry, 42*, 362–373. Retrieved from http://www.bibliopolis.com

Udry, R. J., & Chantala, K. (2005). Risk factors differ according to same-sex and opposite-sex interest. *Journal of Biosocial Science, 37*, 481–497. doi:10.1017/S0021932004006765

Vera, E. M., & Speight, S. L. (2003). Multicultural competence, social justice, and counseling psychology: Expanding our roles. *The Counseling Psychologist, 31*, 253–272. doi:10.1177/0011000003031003001

Walker, J. A., & Prince, T. (2010). Training considerations and suggested counseling interventions for LGBT individuals. *Journal of LGBT Issues in Counseling, 4*, 2–17. doi:10.1080/15538600903552756

White, T. (2011). *Working with suicidal individuals: A guide to providing understanding, assessment, and support*. London, England and Philadelphia, PA: Jessica Kingsley.

Whitman, J. S., Horn, S. S., & Boyd, C. J. (2007). Activism in the schools: Providing LGBTQ affirmative training to school counselors. *Journal of Gay & Lesbian Psychotherapy,11*(3/4), 143–154. doi:10.1300/J236v11n03_08

Worthington, R. L., Savoy, H. B., Dillon, F. R., & Vernaglia, E. R. (2002). Heterosexual identity development: A multidimensional model of individual and social identity. *The Counseling Psychologist, 30*(4), 496–531. doi:10.1177/00100002030004002

13 Educating and Empowering Families of Lesbian, Gay, Bisexual, Transgender, and Questioning Students

Caitlin Ryan and Stuart F. Chen-Hayes

Although schools have remained the focus of challenges and opportunities to meet the needs of lesbian, gay, bisexual, transgender, and questioning (LGBTQ) youth for more than two decades, schools and school professionals should also recognize the need to empower and promote the well-being of LGBTQ youth by supporting their families (Toomey, Ryan, Diaz, Card, & Russell, 2010; Toomey, Ryan, Diaz, & Russell, 2011).

Faced with many pressing needs including budget challenges, academic success expectations, and career and college readiness, school professionals, including school counselors, psychologists, and social workers, also need to understand the critical role that families play in contributing to LGBTQ children's risk and well-being; to serve LGBTQ students in the context of their families; and to view parents, families and caregivers as a critical support for students' academic, career/college, and personal/social success (American School Counselor Association [ASCA], 2010; Chen-Hayes, 2001; National Association of School Psychologists [NASP], 2010; National Association of Social Workers [NASW], 2008a, 2008b; Singh & Burnes, 2009; Smith & Chen-Hayes, 2004). However, many school and community professionals are reluctant and uncomfortable asking adolescents about their sexual orientation and gender identity. Moreover, school professionals routinely serve LGBTQ youth without asking about experiences with their families. This chapter examines experiences encountered by diverse families of LGBTQ children and adolescents, how family reactions affect LGBTQ youth, and ways school professionals can support families of LGBTQ students to promote well-being.

A Note About Language

Although community members have used the term "questioning" for a number of years and the practice literature has increasingly included "questioning" as a category related to lesbian, gay, bisexual, and transgender (LGBT) populations, predominantly youth, little is known about youth (or adults) who are questioning their sexual orientation or gender identity/expression, and this category has not been validated empirically (Hollander, 2000). The first specific discussion of *questioning* youth in the practice literature provides information on language and meanings associated with youth who may be questioning their sexual orientation and notes that:

> questioning youths are often referred to in school and community programs as part
> of the increasingly long abbreviation used to include all sexual minority youths

(i.e., lesbian, gay, bisexual, transgender, and questioning youths), [but] little has
been done to define to whom specifically the term questioning youths refers.

(Hollander, 2000, p. 173)

This point is relevant to the following discussion of emerging research related to LGBT
youth and families, which has focused on established identities and parental and
caregiver behaviors that can be measured, rather than unexpressed feelings or self-
perceptions that have not been empirically defined. Because this chapter is based on
specific findings and research-based practice with LGBT youth, the terminology used
here includes youth who may be questioning their sexual orientation or gender identity/
expression when pertinent but will not otherwise use acronyms in the same way as they
are uniformly used throughout this book.[1]

Psychosexual Milestones

Although professional associations in school counseling, social work, and psychology
call for affirmative work with families and LGBT youth, professional training for
education and mental health professionals does not require either family counseling or
sexuality counseling coursework in graduate programs in these disciplines (Council on
the Accreditation of Counseling and Related Educational Programs [CACREP], 2009,
Council on Social Work Education [CSWE], 2008; NASP, 2010). These gaps in training
occur despite an increase in LGBT young people coming out during childhood and
adolescence, unlike prior generations of LGBT individuals who came out as adults.
For example, researchers have observed for some time that the average age of sexual
attraction is around age 10 for heterosexual and gay-identified youth (McClintock &
Herdt, 1996), and this finding has been reported in subsequent studies of lesbian, gay,
and bisexual (LGB) young people (e.g., D'Augelli & Hershberger, 1993; Herdt & Boxer,
1993; Rosario, Meyer-Bahlburg, Hunter, Exner, Gwadz, & Keller, 1996; Ryan, Huebner,
Diaz, & Sanchez, 2009).

In an unpublished qualitative study conducted by the Family Acceptance Project
(FAP), LGB adolescents self-identified as LGB, on average, at age 13.4, and their parent(s)
found out, on average, about a year later (as cited in Wilber, Ryan & Marksamer, 2006).
A number of youth in this study reported self-identifying as LGB between ages 5 and 10.
By contrast, in a follow up study, LGB young adults self-identified as LGB, on average, at
14.2 and came out to their parents at nearly age 16 (Ryan et al., 2009). Understanding
these milestones is especially important for education and mental health professionals
who work with youth and families. In briefing sessions conducted with ethnically and
religiously diverse families, professionals, and LGBT youth that documented reactions
and responses to research findings from the Family Acceptance Project's young adult
survey and in follow up family intervention work, FAP researchers found that most
parents and caregivers—and many providers—were not aware that young people could
self-identify as LGB during childhood and early adolescence (Ryan, 2012; Ryan & Diaz,
2006). In fact, many parents and professionals believe that LGB identity is not formed
until adulthood. These perceptions are more likely among parents, caregivers, and
professionals with limited information about sexual orientation and gender identity/
expression, including persons with limited or no formal education; persons who

are monolingual or non-English speaking; immigrant families; and persons from conservative religious backgrounds.

In general, parents and practitioners are confused by issues related to gender identity and expression and do not know where to turn for information on how to help gender non-conforming and gender-variant youth (Ryan, 2012; Ryan & Diaz, 2006). Often, parents and caregivers conflate sexual orientation and gender non-conformity, assuming that children and youth who are gender variant are LGB (Ryan, 2012; Ryan & Diaz, 2006). Helping parents, foster parents, and caregivers understand normative identity development among LGBT youth is a critical component in educating families about how to support their LGBT children (Ryan, 2012).[2] Although research and information on gender identity is more limited and has only recently started to emerge relative to transgender adolescents, research on gay and lesbian youth has been conducted since the 1970s, so findings on LGB adolescents as a separate social and cultural cohort have been published over several decades (e.g., Herdt & Boxer, 1993).

At the same time, however, a critical aspect of LGBT identity development is the dynamic and evolving nature of these identities. As social stigma has decreased, the opportunities for children and adolescents to self-identify and disclose their identity to others at younger ages have increased. As a result, the experiences of LGB adolescents in the 1980s and 1990s differ from LGB and gender-variant adolescents in subsequent decades in the 2000s. This awareness is important for parents and professionals who seek information to support LGBT youth who may find dated materials that differ from the experiences of contemporary LGBT youth, especially youth of color, immigrant youth, and bilingual youth, who were rarely included in earlier research and publications.

Established Approaches to Services with and Care of LGBT Youth

Although connections to family and relationships with parents and caregivers provide a primary foundation for child and adolescent development, unlike their heterosexual peers, services and support for LGBT youth have primarily been delivered outside of the family context (Ryan & Diaz, 2006; Ryan, Russell, Huebner, Diaz, & Sanchez, 2010). The early focus on serving lesbian and gay youth, who became increasingly visible in the 1980s, was to protect them from harm (Ryan, 2011, 2012). Starting in the late 1970s, support programs for LGB, and increasingly transgender, youth emerged to provide a separate space for peer support and access to the broader LGBT community (e.g., Herdt & Boxer, 1993). Research on family experiences typically focused on disclosing LGB identity to others and close-ended questions about family relationships from the perspective of LGB youth (Ryan et al., 2010; Ryan, 2011; Ryan & Diaz, 2006). Concerns with protecting LGB youth from negative reactions and victimization related to high levels of stigma led to services and care that were provided either to the adolescent alone or through peer support services in emerging LGBT youth programs. The characteriz-ation of LGBT youth as a population that is served alone (Boxer, Cook & Herdt, 1999) across disciplines or through peer support has persisted despite significant social changes that have occurred over the past 30 years (Ryan & Diaz, 2006). These social changes include greater awareness and widespread access to more accurate information about sexual orientation and gender identity/expression among the general public, including parents, families, caregivers, and educators of LGBT youth (Ryan 2012; Ryan & Diaz, 2006).

Limited Research on LGBT Youth and Families

Although these broad social changes have occurred over more than three decades, little research has examined the family experiences of LGBT youth. In the late 1980s and 1990s, two studies asked LGB youth about their family experiences. In a large qualitative study of identity and psychosocial development of ethnically diverse LGB youth, researchers found that about half of parents (more often mothers than fathers) knew about their adolescent's sexual orientation, but few talked about it (Boxer & Cohler, 1989; Herdt & Boxer, 1993). Moreover, even youth with positive family relationships reported difficulty disclosing their sexual orientation to their parents. Using survey research, D'Augelli, Hershberger, and Pilkington (1998) found that LGB youth who came out to a parent or family member reported higher levels of verbal and physical abuse by family members and higher levels of suicidality than LGB youth who had not disclosed their sexual orientation to their families.

A few studies focused on parents whose children came out as adults, who generally reported substantial periods of adjustment following disclosure and learning about an adult child's LGB identity (e.g., Boxer, Cook, & Herdt, 1999; Robinson, Walters & Skeen, 1989). Boxer, Cook, and Herdt (1999) further observed differences in response based on age, where younger adolescents reported that parents were more likely to deny their LGB identity, while older youth and young adults reported more positive relationships with parents.

Since this small cluster of research was conducted more than two decades ago, little follow-up research has been done on LGB or transgender youth and families to guide practice, policy, and services for families with LGBT children across settings, including homes, schools, custodial care, homeless programs, mental health services and clinical care. Instead, services were based on anecdotal information and perceptions of how families might respond to LGB or gender-variant youth (Ryan, 2011; Ryan & Diaz, 2006). At that time (and today), perceptions were widespread that disclosure would precipitate conflict and potential homelessness, even though researchers had not historically studied family experiences or parental and caregiver reactions to an adolescent's LGBT identity from the perspective of both adolescents and their families (Ryan et al., 2010).

More recently, three studies have been published on issues related to LGB youth, young adults, and families. These include: a qualitative study of 30 gay male youth and young adults and parents on issues related to HIV risk (LaSala, 2007); a survey of the relationship between an LGB youth's identity and perceptions of reactions from a range of people (including family members, coaches, teachers, therapists, neighbors, and friends) and substance use (Rosario, Schrimshaw, & Hunter, 2009); and an analysis of the National Longitudinal Study of Adolescent Health to assess the relationship between LGB young adults' perceived family support (defined as general closeness, warmth, and enjoying time together) and depression, substance use, and suicidality (Needham & Austin, 2010). In other related studies, researchers reported on victimization of LGBT adolescents and provided reports on the experiences of LGBT youth, their parents, and their siblings (e.g., D'Augelli, Grossman, Starks, & Sinclair, 2010; Grossman, D'Augelli, & Howell, 2006).

Family Acceptance Project

This awareness of the significant gap between the lived experiences of contemporary, diverse LGBT youth and their families and actual practice, available services, and policy guidelines prompted researchers and clinicians to plan the Family Acceptance Project (FAP) in 2000. Affiliated with San Francisco State University, FAP was launched as a research, education, intervention, and policy project to study LGBT youth and families to develop a new family model of prevention, wellness, and care to help diverse families support their LGBT children. FAP included the first comprehensive study of LGBT youth and families from the perspectives of LGBT youth, parents, foster parents, caregivers, and other key family members using a mixed methods approach and a series of linked studies.

Realizing that research was needed to inform policy and practice that reflected the lived experiences of diverse LGBT youth and families, FAP designed an initiative to: (a) strengthen and help ethnically, linguistically, and religiously diverse families to support their LGBT children; (b) improve the health, mental health, and well-being of LGBT children and adolescents; (c) help LGBT youth stay in their homes to foster permanency and to prevent homelessness and the need for custodial care in the foster care and juvenile justice systems; (d) inform public policy and family policy; and (e) develop a new evidence-based family model of wellness, prevention, and care to promote well-being and positive youth development and decrease the high levels of risk for LGBT youth that restrict life chances. The Family Acceptance Project model offers an innovative evidence-based approach for practitioners to use across disciplines and systems of care and for school professionals to apply in K-12 settings to support the academic, career, college readiness, health, mental health, and personal/social competencies of LGBTQ youth and their families.

Family Acceptance Project Overview

Family Acceptance Project (FAP) research includes a series of linked qualitative and quantitative studies. FAP research (e.g., Ryan et al., 2009; Ryan et al., 2010) used a participatory approach that included families, LGBT adolescents, pediatricians, nurses, social workers, teachers, community advocates, and school professionals to inform the process and application of findings.

Phase 1. Initial research focused on experiences related to:

- child and adolescent development;
- LGBT identity development and gender expression;
- cultural values, religious beliefs, experiences and practices;
- family and caregiver reactions related to the youth's LGBT identity and gender expression;
- coping behaviors;
- peer and school experiences including victimization and school supports;

- related social experiences that affect the youth and family including immigration experiences, displacement, social status, homelessness, and placement in foster care and juvenile justice programs;
- social support; and
- family adjustment or disruption after learning about the adolescent's LGBT identity.

Research identified specific parental and caregiver behaviors that families exhibit in reaction to the adolescent's LGBT identity (accepting and rejecting behaviors) and studied their relationship to health, mental health, and well-being in young adulthood. Additional research includes case studies of the impact of school victimization on LGBT youth and families and school supports.

Phase 2. Findings were used to guide the development of research-derived educational materials, intervention videos, and assessment tools to educate families about how their reactions affect their LGBT children and to educate practitioners on helping families support their LGBT children. An important aspect of FAP educational materials is the use of lived experiences and stories of diverse families with LGBT children to provide role models to show how families from similar backgrounds learned to support their LGBT children; to humanize the experiences of LGBT youth and families to dispel myths and misconcep-tions; to teach about family accepting and rejecting behaviors and related health status (identified and measured in our research); and to give LGBT youth and families hope for greater connectedness and more positive relationships.

Materials and intervention development included briefing sessions with more than 100 ethnically, socioeconomically and religiously diverse families with LGBT children, as well as diverse LGBT youth and providers to document reactions. These briefing sessions informed the development of family intervention strategies and educational materials and were followed by an interview three months later to document changes in family dynamics as a result of learning about key research findings. The briefing sessions were conducted in English, Spanish, Cantonese, and Mandarin. Families who participated were evenly divided among African Americans, European Americans, Asian Americans, and Latinos, with a smaller number of Native American families. These interactions helped FAP learn how to present the findings to families from diverse backgrounds including those at diverse literacy and educational levels. Families, youth, and pro-viders guided FAP in developing family education materials and framing family interventions to decrease rejection and increase support for LGBT young people in culturally appropriate ways.

Phase 3. The final phase involved the development of a family intervention model for use with LGBT youth and families in multiple settings, including K-12 schools, mental health care, primary care, social services, pastoral counseling, and out-of-home settings.

Key Findings

Family Reactions to Disclosure. A key outcome of all aspects of the research regardless of participants (parent, family member, or caregiver; LGBT youth or young adult; or provider) was that talking about family dynamics (including discussing the behavioral research findings) and interactions within and related to families was an intervention in and of itself since few families and youth had ever discussed these issues (Ryan, 2009c, 2012; Ryan & Diaz, 2006). In addition, professionals other than family therapists had limited experiences talking about family issues. In fact, most professionals had not initiated these discussions with LGBT youth (Ryan, 2009a, 2012; Ryan & Diaz, 2006).

Through interactions with parents, caregivers, and other family members in the initial qualitative study and in subsequent family sessions, FAP learned that families whose behaviors were experienced as rejecting by their children and adolescents (e.g., trying to change their LGBT identity or preventing them from participating in LGBT events) were instead motivated by parental care and concern to help their children "fit in," be respected by others, and have a good life (Ryan, 2009b, 2012; Ryan & Diaz, 2006). The FAP research team saw many missed opportunities where an informed professional could have made a critical difference in providing accurate information and support to prevent adolescents from being forced out of their homes or placed in custodial care and to decrease family conflict and alienation (Ryan, 2012; Ryan & Diaz, 2006; Ryan et al., 2010). A dearth of family systems research related to LGBT youth contributed to the widespread lack of awareness of (a) families as a potential source of support for their LGBT children by providers and by youth support programs and (b) the critical need to engage families and help them learn how to support their LGBT children (Ryan, 2012; Ryan & Diaz, 2006, 2011). As noted, prior to FAP's initial research with LGBT youth and families, researchers had only examined the experiences of adolescents themselves and not the family system.

FAP's early research with LGBT youth, parents, key caregivers, and family members revealed that family reactions were more diverse than the perceptions commonly held by LGBT youth, their peers, and providers and advocates who worked with them including school professionals. FAP's qualitative research with culturally, economically, education-ally, and linguistically diverse LGBT youth and families found that family reactions ranged from highly rejecting to celebratory of their adolescent's LGBT identity (Ryan, 2009b, 2012; Ryan & Diaz, 2006). About a third of families were rejecting when they first learned about their adolescent's LGBT identity, and they expressed a range of reactions from physically hurting the youth to religious condemnation and shame related to the adolescent's identity. Slightly more than half were ambivalent, and while they did not want to encourage their child by supporting his/her sexual orientation or gender identity/expression, they also did not want to push their child away. Ambivalent families expressed both rejecting and supportive reactions to their child's LGBT identity, which gave youth mixed messages about their parent/caregiver's ability to support them. Nearly one in five parents and caregivers accepted their youth's LGBT identity when first learning about his or her sexual orientation or gender identity. Parents and caregivers who were accepting expressed affection, openly discussed LGBT issues, welcomed the youth's LGBT friends and partners into their home and to family events and activities, and advocated for their adolescent when he or she was discriminated against or mistreated by others.

In addition to obtaining extensive knowledge on adolescent development, family life, and related experiences of LGBT youth, this research identified more than 100 accepting and rejecting behaviors expressed by parents, foster parents, and caregivers that were retrospectively measured for occurrence and frequency in a survey of LGBT young adults with the same characteristics as the LGBT youth in the adolescent quali-tative study (see Table 13.1). This approach was designed to assess if a specific experience of family acceptance or rejection related to the adolescent's LGBT identity had occurred (e.g., Did your parent or caregiver prevent you from having an LGBT friend? Did your parent or caregiver support your gender expression?) and the frequency of occurrence. By qualitatively identifying specific, objective family reactions of acceptance and rejection related to LGBT adolescents' identity and then measuring these reactions in a follow-up survey, FAP sought to minimize the potential for adolescents to inaccurately recall or characterize their relationship with their parents or caregivers when using more diffuse measures. This behavioral framework was intentional since the Family Acceptance Project was initiated to develop family interventions.

Impact of Family Reactions on LGBT Youth. Quantitative findings from the FAP young adult survey indicated that families and caregivers have a compelling impact on an LGBT young person's health, mental health, and well-being (Ryan et al., 2009; Ryan et al., 2010). Providers who have worked with LGBT populations have known this intuitively for years, but these studies provide key empirical evidence demonstrating that LGBT young adults whose parents and caregivers reject them during adolescence are at higher risk for depression, illegal drug use, suicide, and unsafe sex (Ryan et al., 2009). Conversely, LGBT youth whose parents support them show greater well-being, higher self-esteem and social support, better general health, and decreased risk for suicidal behavior, depression, and substance abuse (Ryan et al., 2010).

More specifically, those who reported high levels of family rejection during adole-scence were 8.4 times more likely to report having attempted suicide, 5.9 times more likely to report high levels of depression, 3.4 times more likely to use illegal drugs, and 3.4 times more likely to report having engaged in unprotected sexual intercourse, compared with peers from families that reported no or low levels of family rejection (Ryan et al., 2009). Similarly, LGBT young adults who reported high levels of family acceptance showed significantly higher levels of self-esteem, social support, and better overall health compared to peers with low levels of family acceptance (Ryan et al., 2010).

In addition, LGBT young adults with low levels of family acceptance were over three times more likely to report suicidal thoughts and suicide attempts compared to peers with high levels of family acceptance (Ryan et al., 2010). These findings are consistent with other studies that have shown families play an important role in adolescent health. For example, Resnick and colleagues (1997) found that connections to family are protective against major health risk behaviors including alcohol and other drug use, emotional distress, suicidality, and unsafe sex.

Forthcoming FAP research publications will focus on:

* coping styles of LGBT youth,
* parental and caregiver attempts to change an adolescent's sexual orientation,
* the impact of religious condemnation and support on an adolescent's LGBT identity, and
* health benefits of coming out during adolescence.

The Intersection of Schools and Families

Several published FAP school-related studies provide direction to help school-based professionals, parents, foster parents, and caregivers understand the impact of school victimization and the importance of family and school support (e.g., Russell, Ryan, Toomey, Diaz, & Sanchez, 2011; Toomey et al., 2010; Toomey et al., 2011). For example, in a FAP-related study of school victimization of LGBT youth, those who experienced high levels of LGBT school victimization in middle and high school reported impaired health and mental health in young adulthood (Russell et al., 2011). Specifically, those who reported high levels of LGBT school victimization during adolescence were 5.6 times more likely to report having attempted suicide, 5.6 times more likely to report a suicide attempt that required medical care, 2.6 times more likely to report clinical levels of depression, and more than twice as likely to have been diagnosed with a sexually transmitted disease and/or to report risk for HIV infection compared with peers who reported low levels of school victimization (Russell et al., 2011).

School experiences reported in these studies (e.g., victimization and school supports) provide important information to help families understand the costs of school victimization and the importance of school-related support for LGBT youth, particularly when these findings are considered in relation to other FAP findings concerning family accepting and rejecting behaviors (e.g., Ryan, 2009b; Ryan et al., 2009; Ryan et al., 2010). Family accepting and rejecting behaviors—as empirically defined in FAP's qualitative research—provide a framework to help parents, foster parents, and caregivers support LGBT children and youth without having to choose between their LGBT child and deeply held religious and cultural values. These behaviors are discussed in family education materials (Ryan, 2009b; Ryan & Rees, 2012) and are embedded in FAP family intervention and education videos—short documentaries that address a range of experiences of LGBT youth related to family, schools, and faith and provide direction to help diverse families, foster families, and caregivers support their LGBT children. For example, FAP research has found that parental attempts to change their child's gender expression is a high-risk rejecting behavior while supporting their child's gender expression is one of the most wellness-promoting family reactions (Ryan, 2009b, 2012). It is important for parents and caregivers to understand that other FAP research shows that gender-related victimization at school—a common experience for gender non-conforming young people—is related to higher levels of depression and decreased life satisfaction, affecting both the young person's quality of life and capacity to enjoy life (Toomey et al., 2010). Thus, family actions to support gender variant children and youth at home and school protect the child, help build their child's self-worth, and teach self-care and conflict management skills.

FAP researchers have found that families, in general, do not know how to support their LGBT children, especially in school and community settings (Ryan, 2012; Ryan & Diaz, 2006). Yet, family and caregiver reactions to stand up for LGBT youth when they are mistreated by others, including school victimization, is an important protective behavior that is related to decreased health risks and increased well-being (Ryan, 2009b; Ryan et al., 2010). Similarly, blaming an LGBT youth when he or she is mistreated, discriminated against, or victimized by others—at school and in other settings—is a rejecting behavior that is related to high levels of risk for LGBT youth (Ryan, 2009b;

Ryan & Monasterio, 2011). Helping parents, families, and caregivers understand that their capacity to protect and advocate for their LGBT children extends to school, community, and religious institutions is an important part of helping parents learn how to reduce their LGBT child's risk and promote his/her well-being.

Similarly, a common rejecting behavior, especially among families who have limited information about sexual orientation (and who may believe that being LGB is learned from others or from reading or hearing about homosexuality), is to prevent adolescents from having an LGBT friend, from learning about their LGBT identity, or from participating in LGBT-related activities, such as a Gay-Straight Alliance (GSA) or school diversity club (see Ryan, 2009b and Ryan et al., 2010 for common family rejecting and accepting behaviors). Although FAP research indicates that such rejecting behaviors are motivated by trying to protect an adolescent from harm, these specific family rejecting behaviors are among those related to the highest risk for serious health outcomes for LGBT youth, including suicide attempts (Ryan, 2009b; Ryan & Monasterio, 2011). In relation to increasing school-based support, a FAP study of the impact of school diversity clubs or GSAs on adjustment and educational attainment found that LGBT youth who attend middle or high schools with GSAs have better mental health as young adults, are less likely to drop out of high school, and are more likely to attend college (Toomey et al., 2011). Understanding that participating in LGBT-related activities can increase their child's well-being and help foster educational attainment helps families recognize the importance of these core sources of support for their LGBT children and can decrease resistance to allowing their children to participate.

The lack of focus on the needs and role of families with LGBT youth across settings and systems of care, including educator and clinician training, has inhibited the development of practitioner skills including knowledge of how to engage, educate, and support families, particularly ethnically, religiously, and linguistically diverse families (Ryan, 2011; Ryan & Diaz, 2006). In addition, services for parents and families with LGBT family members were developed for parents whose children came out as adults, and few specific services have been available for contemporary families with LGBT children, particularly those who are ethnically, religiously, and linguistically diverse (Ryan, 2011; Ryan & Diaz, 2006).

Schools offer a largely untapped educational, support, and referral resource for families with LGBT and gender-variant children and adolescents. Some school professionals also may provide family intervention services that (a) can help educate parents, caregivers, and family members; (b) provide family counseling to increase communication, build empathy, and help families decrease rejecting behaviors; and (c) make a range of referrals to service providers who are knowledgeable and sensitive to the needs of LGBT youth and their families. However, with increasing school counselor to student ratios across the United States (U.S.), the use of workshops with families and classroom guidance lessons with students are equally important strategies that can be used to empower LGBT students, allies, and their families to help improve academic achievement, career/college access, and personal/social competencies of all students (ASCA, 2010; Goodrich & Luke, 2009; Smith & Chen-Hayes, 2004).

Part of the challenge in starting to address an unmet and emerging need—in this case providing assessment, education, and in some cases, counseling or support services for families with LGBT children and adolescents—is the need to change established practices.

Learning new information and talking about issues that educators, school-based professionals, and families may experience as uncomfortable (yet must be done to address LGBT student needs) requires educators and practitioners to understand and affirm the family's critical role in providing support for their child. In particular, findings on the role of families in contributing to both risk (Ryan, 2009b; Ryan et al., 2009) and well-being (Ryan, 2009b; Ryan et al., 2010) in their LGBT children call on school professionals to follow practice guidelines and ethical standards to develop competencies and to "acquire educational, consultation and training experiences to improve awareness, knowledge, skills and effectiveness in working with diverse populations," including issues related to sexual orientation and gender identity and expression (ACSA, 2010, p. 5).

FAP research and intervention work has found that families want to learn how to help their LGBT children, how to help their family, and how to help themselves (Ryan, 2009a). Many school professionals believe that parents who are struggling with having an LGBT child will not be open to discussing these issues and will resist efforts to engage them in these discussions. However, the FAP intervention team has found that parents and caregivers are often distraught because they lack information about how to help their LGBT children (Ryan & Diaz, 2011). Families with little information about sexual orientation and gender identity/expression issues, immigrant families, and socially and religiously conservative families often perceive and fear that they are losing their child to a world they know little about (Ryan & Diaz, 2011). This makes families more fearful and less receptive to learning about LGBT issues, which is why it is critical for schools to establish and maintain strong school–family–community partnerships.

Recommended Practices for School Professionals

School professionals often are unsure how to talk with families, especially ethnically, religiously, and linguistically diverse families, about sexual orientation and gender identity/expression. Asking parents and caregivers to talk about their concerns for their child, including their hopes, dreams, and aspirations for their child, is a helpful way to engage them, to understand their priorities, and to start to build an alliance. In scores of interactions with parents of LGBT children, FAP found that parents and caregivers had few opportunities to talk about these issues in a setting where they felt respected and validated (Ryan, 2009c). Talking with a knowledgeable, sensitive school professional who can answer parents' questions and concerns about sexual orientation and gender identity/expression is reassuring and is a critical aspect of empowering families to learn to support their LGBT children.

Many families, especially immigrant and non-English speaking families, have limited information about contemporary LGBT identities. Parents and family members who emigrated to the U.S. more than 10 years ago typically carry impressions of being gay or transgender that are out of sync with current representations of gay and transgender people in their countries of origin and in the U.S. For immigrant parents, struggles with acculturation of their children to a new culture are exacerbated when they learn that their child or adolescent is LGBT. Negative perceptions of LGBT persons and how LGBT persons were treated by others in their culture of origin inform parental reactions and fears (Ryan & Diaz, 2011). Asking parents to talk about their perceptions and experiences of LGBT people in their cultures helps school practitioners understand how these perceptions shape the family response to having an LGBT child or adolescent, which will inform appropriate responses (both prevention and intervention). Educating parents and families about sexual orientation and explaining gender identity/expression in simple, non-clinical terms is important since most families have varying levels of misconceptions about LGBT identity, and their perceptions are usually negative. Straightforward descriptions of LGBT identity are included in English, Spanish, and Chinese in FAP's family education booklets (Ryan, 2009b; Ryan & Rees, 2012).

The Family Acceptance Project's model uses a strengths-based approach that views families and caregivers as potential allies in reducing risk, promoting well-being, and creating a healthy future for their LGBT children (Ryan & Diaz, 2011). FAP's approach to working with parents, families, and caregivers includes several core assumptions that help school professionals build an alliance with parents, foster parents, families, and caregivers with LGBT children and adolescents (see Appendix).

Recommended Strategies

Understanding the critical role of families and caregivers in nurturing and supporting their LGBTQ children is essential to enable educators and mental health professionals to empower parents, foster parents, caregivers, guardians, and other family members in affirming LGBTQ youth. But, professionals need the support, time, and skills to do so. The following strategies can direct school professionals' work to help families support LGBTQ students' academic, career, and personal/social development to promote positive development and well-being (Smith & Chen-Hayes, 2004; Stone, 2003). School practitioners are urged to incorporate the following strategies into their practice.

School–Family–Community Partnerships. School professionals are encouraged to use the research-based School–Family–Community Partnership model developed by Epstein and associates (2009). This model of parent engagement in schools was originally developed to work with poor and working class families and families of color to help close achievement gaps, but is equally viable for supporting LGBTQ youth through engaging and empowering their families. Evidence-based interventions for successful school–family–community partnerships with implications for LGBTQ students include the following six key areas.

Parenting. School-based practitioners need to share FAP research findings and resources with parents and guardians of LGBTQ youth to engage and empower families to increase knowledge and self-awareness of how their reactions contribute to their LGBTQ children's risk and well-being. Families are a critical support for LGBTQ students but they need information and specific suggestions and skills in how to support them.

Communicating. Families and school-based practitioners need to work as allies to foster success of LGBTQ students. This involves ongoing communication about the LGBTQ student's success and struggles in academics, career and college access and readiness, and personal/social competencies as well as information on how families can best support students as partners in academic and social success. This area also includes educating parents and families about the importance of communicating with their LGBTQ child about his or her school experiences and peer relationships, discussing the school climate and support for LGBTQ students and overall diversity, identifying and intervening early when victimization occurs, and advocating for their LGBTQ child if he or she is victimized or harassed by peers or adults.

Volunteering. FAP research shows that parental and family support for LGBT activities helps protect their LGBTQ child from risk and promotes the young person's well-being (Ryan, 2009b; Ryan et al., 2010). School professionals play an important role in encouraging the parents of LGBTQ students to volunteer at school or in the community to support LGBTQ students and families. This can include assisting with a GSA or helping with a wide range of events that support and affirm LGBTQ youth such as *Ally Week, Day of Silence, No Name Calling Week, National Coming Out Day*, and inclusion of *Safe Schools* curriculum to support LGBTQ students and the *Welcoming Schools* curriculum to support students with LGBT family members.

Learning at home. Fostering an LGBTQ student's academic success and career and college readiness includes helping parents and guardians support the student's learning at home—this is a key role for school professionals. Supportive home environments increase the likelihood of academic, career, college, and personal/social success for students. They also help protect an LGBT student from health and mental health risks and promote their well-being (Ryan, 2009b).

Decision making. Supporting LGBTQ students is an on-going role for school professionals, and helping families to make appropriate decisions to affirm an LBGTQ youth promotes the adolescent's self-worth. It also affects his or her ability to plan for future dreams and rigorous academics that lead to the widest array of college and career pathways, planning, and decision making.

Collaborating with the community. Connecting LGBTQ youth and families with community resources is more important than ever given multiple cutbacks to school services and programs. To ensure that all LGBTQ youth and families have access to a wide range of supports and educational opportunities, a variety of venues need to be explored outside of school, both online and in person, such as GSAs, support groups, mentoring, and social venues for LGBT youth and allies. Chapter 15 of this volume provides a wide range of information related to community resources.

Education of Key Stakeholders. School professionals can sponsor annual training in schools that includes school staff and welcomes family members to reduce risk and promote the well-being of LGBTQ students with information on increasing supportive parenting, decreasing risky behaviors, identifying critical referral sources, and promoting supportive school environments (Whitman, Horn, & Boyd, 2007). See Chapter 8 of this volume and contact FAP for how to train school professionals to work with LGBTQ students and families.

Support for diversity. School professionals can support and sponsor GSAs and other school diversity clubs that affirm and provide support for students throughout the school year. Clubs should be encouraged to welcome and engage parents and families as volunteers, speakers, and activity resources. School professionals also may play an active role in celebrating diversity by creating inclusive and responsive classroom environments as discussed in Chapter 10 of this volume.

Supportive school climates. School professionals can help create supportive school climates by educating parents and families on how their participation as allies and advocates for LGBTQ students helps ensure academic success, promotes career and college access, and fosters personal/social competencies (Chen-Hayes, 2001; Smith &

Chen-Hayes, 2004). Such actions by parents and families also promote an LGBT student's well-being and protect against further risk or poor outcomes in adulthood (Ryan, 2009b; Ryan & Rees, 2012; Ryan et al., 2010).

Coordinated health services and sexuality education. Professional development is especially critical for school nurses and health educators who are often on the front lines in identifying and responding to LGBTQ students who are experiencing suboptimal family support. Educators and school mental health professionals are encouraged to collaborate with other key health providers (e.g. school nurses, health educators, etc.) to ensure inclusion of LGBT health issues in health fairs and other events. Moreover, education and mental health professionals are urged to promote comprehensive sexuality education models that focus on both healthy families and healthy sexuality development for all students including sexual orientation and gender identity/expression, such as the evidence-based Sexuality Information and Education Council of the United States' (SIECUS) K-12 comprehensive sexuality education guidelines (SIECUS, 2012).

Outreach to affirm multiple cultural identities. Supportive school professionals should find ways to affirm and advocate for LGBTQ students of multiple cultural identities who are often marginalized due to multiple oppressions (Holcomb-McCoy & Chen-Hayes, 2011). For instance, bilingual students, students of color, students from low income families, religious students, and students with diverse abilities may not participate in GSAs or other such clubs as they are sometimes perceived as not affirming for students of multiple non-dominant identities. Thus, it is important for professionals to create a safe space so that all students can more readily find support for all of their identities in schools.

Advocacy. School professionals are urged to model inclusive language and to advocate for affirming policies and procedures to support LGBTQ students in school and community settings (Chen-Hayes, 2001; Smith & Chen-Hayes, 2004). Chapter 14 of this volume discusses how to be an advocate and ally for LGBTQ students and families.

Access for diverse families. School professionals should use inclusive language and multiple languages whenever possible to communicate with families that are bilingual, fluent in a language other than English, or who have limited educational backgrounds. Culturally responsive professionals ensure that families have access to key information in languages and reading levels they can understand about LGBTQ issues, including educational brochures, policies and procedures, and websites for supportive organizations for families and LGBT youth.

Community referral network. School professionals are encouraged to develop an appropriate referral network of knowledgeable clinicians and advocates outside of schools who can affirm and support LBGTQ youth and their families, particularly in ethnically, linguistically, and religiously diverse communities. School professionals will need to routinely update school websites with the latest online resources for affirming and supporting LBGTQ youth and their parents, guardians, and family members. Chapter 15 of this volume provides a range of community resources and helpful tips for accessing such resources.

Unproven and risky practices. In discussing counseling and clinical needs and making referrals, school professionals should educate and inform parents, guardians, and family members on the unscientific basis of reparative therapy and the risk of requiring young people to participate in these experiences. There is currently no evidence to support the use of reparative therapies or attempts to change a person's lesbian, gay, or bisexual orientation (APA Task Force, 2009; Arana, 2012). FAP research on the health impact of attempts to change an adolescent's sexual orientation is forthcoming.

Career development and college access and readiness. School professionals should involve family members in the college and career access, planning, and readiness process starting in elementary school; ensure that LGBT role models for students are available in diverse professions; and include information on LGBT-affirmative colleges during the search and selection process (Chen-Hayes, 2012; Rankin, Blumenfeld, Weber, & Frazer, 2010; Windemeyer, 2006).

Partner with universities. School professionals can work with school counseling, social work, and psychology practicum/internship candidates to ensure that LGBTQ-affirmative practices are implemented while collaborating with university faculty and supervisors to ensure that LGBTQ-affirmative curriculum is incorporated into graduate counselor education, social work, and psychology programs (Goodrich & Luke, 2009, 2010; Luke, Goodrich, & Scarborough, 2011).

Family Education, Assessment, and Practice Resources

In addition to these recommended practices, research-based educational materials are available to help school professionals educate and support the families of LGBTQ youth. The Family Acceptance Project's family education materials have been designated as "Best Practice" resources to prevent suicide in LGBT young people by the national Best Practices Registry for Suicide Prevention and are the first resources of this kind. The peer-reviewed Best Practices Registry is maintained by the Suicide Prevention Resource Center and the American Foundation for Suicide Prevention. FAP education and intervention resources include the following.

Family Education Materials

Based on findings from FAP research, the FAP family intervention team developed multilingual family education materials with direction from diverse families with LGBT youth, LGBT young people, and their providers. *Supportive Families, Healthy Children: Helping Families with Lesbian, Gay, Bisexual and Transgender Children* (in English, Spanish, and Chinese) is available at http://familyproject.sfsu.edu/publications and also available for purchase (Ryan, 2009b). Lower literacy level versions are being developed at fifth- and third-grade reading levels. Faith-based versions are in development for families from diverse religious backgrounds, including a recently published version for Latter-Day Saint (Mormon) families with LGBT children (see Ryan & Rees, 2012).

FAPrisk Screener

The *FAP*risk Screener is an evidence-based screening tool to help providers quickly identify LGBT youth at risk for family rejection and related health and mental health risks. This screening tool helps providers determine youth in need of intervention to decrease family conflict, risk for suicide, depression, illegal drug use, and sexually transmitted infections. It engages families in a brief intervention to help maintain LGBTQ youth in their homes to prevent homelessness or removal from their homes. Information on training is available at http://familyproject.sfsu.edu/assessment.

Family Video Stories

FAP is producing a series of family video stories—short documentaries that show the journey of ethnically, religiously, and linguistically diverse families from struggle to support of LGBT children and adolescents. These videos are used in work with LGBTQ youth and their families, to train providers, and to educate the public on how diverse families learn to support their LGBT children and adolescents. The videos educate about family behaviors that put youth at risk and family behaviors that promote well-being. Information on these videos is available at http://familyproject.sfsu.edu/family-videos.

Conclusion

K-12 schools represent a major untapped resource to identify LGBTQ students who are in need of family support, to educate and inform families on how to support their LGBTQ children in order to reduce their children's risk, promote their well-being, and help keep families together. Families respond to information and direction that is based on research, respects cultural and religious values and beliefs, and helps support the child or adolescent in the context of families, faith, and culture. The information included in this chapter provides a framework for helping educators and school mental health professionals understand that biological families, foster families, and caregivers are critical allies in reducing risk and promoting well-being for LGBTQ students and how to make schools more responsive to the needs of LGBTQ students in the context of their families.

Notes

1 Readers should note that some practice publications and literature reviews in research studies and professional journals incorrectly add "questioning" and/or "transgender" to research conducted with lesbian, gay, and bisexual (LGB) youth or adults to support the use of a uniform acronym such as "LGBTQ." In addition, research literature may incorrectly define "questioning" as a sexual orientation rather than as an undefined category that likely includes people with very diverse experiences. This further confuses terminology that describes LGBT populations with colloquial use and with established definitions of sexual orientation or identity. Clarity is especially important when dealing with groups from very diverse cultures that may have multiple and often pejorative meanings related to homosexuality, bisexuality and gender diversity. As research discussed in this chapter has shown, denial, silence, and minimizing LGBT identities are risk factors for LGBT young people (see Ryan, 2009c). For the most recent and scientifically rigorous discussion of sexual orientation and gender identity, see Institute of Medicine (2011).
2 For basic descriptions of sexual orientation and gender identity, see Ryan (2009b), and Ryan & Rees (2012).

References

American School Counselor Association (ASCA). (2010). *ASCA Ethical Standards.* Alexandria, VA: American School Counselor Association. Retrieved from http://www.schoolcounselor.org/files/EthicalStandards2010.pdf

APA Task Force on Appropriate Therapeutic Responses to Sexual Orientation. (2009). *Report of the Task Force on Appropriate Therapeutic Responses to Sexual Orientation.* Washington, DC: American Psychological Association. Retrieved from http://www.apa.org/pi/lgbt/resources/therapeutic-respsonse.pdf

Arana, G. (2012). My so-called ex-gay life. *The American Prospect.* Retrieved from http://prospect. org/article/my-so-called-ex-gay-life/

Boxer, A. M., & Cohler, B. J. (1989). The life course of gay and lesbian youth: An immodest proposal for the study of lives. *Journal of Homosexuality, 17*(3–4), 315–355.

Boxer, A. M., Cook, J. A., & Herdt, G. (1999). Experiences of coming out among gay and lesbian youth: Adolescents alone. In J. Blustein & C. Levine (Eds.), *The adolescent alone: Decisionmaking in health care in the United States* (pp. 121–138). London: Cambridge University Press.

Chen-Hayes, S. F. (2001). Counseling and advocacy with transgendered and gender-variant persons in schools and families. *Journal of Humanistic Counseling, Education, and Development, 40*(1), 34–48. doi:10.1002/j.2164-490x.2001.tb00100.x

Chen-Hayes, S. F. (2012). Empowering multiple cultural identities in college readiness counseling. In National Association for College Admission Counseling (Ed.), *Fundamentals of college admission counseling* (3rd ed., pp. 149–170). Arlington, VA: Author.

Council on the Accreditation of Counseling and Related Educational Programs (CACREP). (2009). *2009 Standards.* Alexandria, VA: Council on the Accreditation of Counseling and Related Educational Programs (CACREP). Retrieved from http://www.cacrep. org/doc/2009%20Standards%20with%20cover.pdf

Council on Social Work Education (CSWE) (2008). *2008 Educational policy and accreditation standards.* Alexandria, VA: Council on Social Work Education (CSWE). Retrieved from http:// www.cswe.org/Accreditation/2008EPASDecription/aspx

D'Augelli, A. R., Grossman, A. H., Starks, M. T., & Sinclair, K. O. (2010). Factors associated with parents' knowledge of gay, lesbian, and bisexual youths' sexual orientation. *Journal of GLBT Family Studies, 6*(2), 178–198. doi:10.1080/15504281003705410

D'Augelli, A. R., & Hershberger, S. L. (1993). Lesbian, gay, and bisexual youth in community settings: Personal challenges and mental health problems. *American Journal of Community Psychology, 21*(4), 421–448. doi:10.1007/BF00942151

D'Augelli, A. R., Hershberger, S. L., & Pilkington, N. W. (1998). Lesbian, gay, and bisexual youth and their families: Disclosure of sexual orientation and its consequences. *American Journal of Orthopsychiatry, 68*(3), 361–371. doi:10.1037/h0080345

Epstein, J. L., & Associates. (2009). *School, family, and community partnerships: Your handbook for action* (3rd ed.). Thousand Oaks, CA: Corwin.

Goodrich, K. M., & Luke, M. (2009). LGBTQ responsive school counseling. *Journal of LGBT Issues in Counseling, 3*(2), 113–127. doi:10.1080/15538600903005284

Goodrich, K. M., & Luke, M. (2010). The experiences of school counselors-in-training in group work with LGBTQ adolescents. *Journal for Specialists in Group Work, 35*(2), 143–159.

Grossman, A. H., D'Augelli, A. R., & Howell, T. J. (2006). Parent's reactions to transgender youth's gender nonconforming expression and identity. *Journal of Gay & Lesbian Social Services, 18*(1), 3–16. doi:10.1300/J041v18n01_02

Herdt, G. H. & Boxer, A. (1993). *Children of horizons: How gay and lesbian teens are leading a new way out of the closet.* Boston, MA: Beacon Press.

Holcomb-McCoy, C., & Chen-Hayes, S. F. (2011). Culturally competent school counselors: Affirming diversity by challenging oppression. In B. T. Erford, (Ed). *Transforming the school counseling profession* (3rd ed., pp. 90–109). Boston, MA: Pearson.

Hollander, G. (2000). Questioning youth: Challenges to working with youths forming identities. *School Psychology Review, 29*(2), 173–179.

Institute of Medicine. (2011). *The health of lesbian, gay, bisexual, and transgender people: Building a foundation for better understanding.* Washington, DC: The National Academies Press. Retrieved from http://www.iom.edu/Reports/2011/The-Health-of-Lesbian-Gay-Bisexual-and-Transgender-People.aspx

LaSala, M. C. (2007). Parental influence, gay youths, and safer sex. *Health & Social Work, 32*(1), 49–55. doi:10.1093/hsw/32.1.49

McClintock, M. K., & Herdt, G. (1996). Rethinking puberty: The development of sexual attraction. *Current Directions in Psychological Science, 5*(6), 178–183.

National Association for School Psychologists (NASP). (2010). *Standards for Graduate Preparation of School Psychologists.* Bethesda, MD: National Association for School Psychologists (NASP). Retrieved from http://www.nasponline.org/standards/2010standards.aspx

National Association of Social Workers (NASW). (2008a). *Code of Ethics of the National Association of Social Workers.* Washington, DC: National Association of Social Workers (NASW). Retrieved from http://www.socialworkers.org/pubs/code/code.asp

National Association of Social Workers (NASW). (2008b). Lesbian, gay and bisexual issues, policy statement. *Social Work Speaks.* Washington, DC: NASW.

Needham, B. L., & Austin, E. L. (2010). Sexual orientation, parental support, and health during the transition to young adulthood. *Journal of Youth and Adolescence, 39*(10), 1189–1198. doi:10.1007/s10964-010-9533-6

Rankin, S., Weber, G. N., Blumenfeld, W. J., & Frazer S. J. (2010). *State of higher education for lesbian, bisexual, gay, and transgender people.* Charlotte, NC: Campus Pride. Retrieved from http://www.campuspride.org/campus pride 2010 LGBT Report Summary.pdf

Resnick, M. D., Bearman, P. S., Blum, R. W., Bauman, K. E., Harris, K. M., Jones, J., & Udry, J. R. (1997). Protecting adolescents from harm: Findings from the National Longitudinal Study on Adolescent Health. *Journal of the American Medical Association, 278*(10), 823–832. doi:10.1001/jama.1997.03550100049038

Robinson, B. E., Walters, L. H., & Skeen, P. (1989). Response of parents to learning that their child is homosexual and concern over AIDS: A national study. *Journal of Homosexuality, 18*(1/2), 59–80.

Rosario, M., Meyer-Bahlburg, H. F. L., Hunter, J., Exner, T. M., Gwadz, M., & Keller, A.M. (1996). The psychosexual development of urban lesbian, gay, and bisexual youths. *Journal of Sex Research, 33,* 113–126. doi:10.1080/00224499609551823

Rosario, M., Schrimshaw, E. W., & Hunter, J. (2009). Disclosure of sexual orientation and subsequent substance use and abuse among lesbian, gay, and bisexual youths: Critical role of disclosure reactions. *Psychology of Addictive Behaviors, 23*(1), 175–184.

Russell, S. T., Ryan, C., Toomey, R., Diaz, R., & Sanchez, J. (2011). Lesbian, gay, bisexual, and transgender adolescent school victimization: Implications for young adult health and adjustment. *Journal of School Health, 81*(5), 223–230. doi:10.1111/j.1746-1561.2011.00583.x

Ryan, C. (2009a). *Helping families support their lesbian, gay, bisexual, and transgender (LGBT) children.* Washington, DC: National Center for Cultural Competence, Georgetown University Center for Child and Human Development. Retrieved from http://nccc.georgetown.edu/documents/LGBT_Brief.pdf

Ryan, C. (2009b). *Supportive families, healthy children: Helping families with lesbian, gay, bisexual and transgender children / Niños saludables con el apoyo familiar: Ayuda para familias con hijos e hijas lesbianas, gays, bisexuales y transgranener o / 家庭接受和支持，培養健康孩子：幫助家裡有同志（女同性戀、男同性戀、雙性戀、跨性別）成員的家庭.* San Francisco, CA: Marian Wright Edelman Institute, San Francisco State University. Retrieved from http://familyproject.sfsu.edu/publications

Ryan, C. (2009c). The Family Acceptance Project: Understanding the experiences of LGBT youth. *Focal Point—Research, Policy, and Practice in Children's Mental Health, 23*(1), 19–20.

Ryan, C. (2011, October). *Changing the future for LGBT youth & families: Returning to our roots.* Plenary session presented at Council on Social Work Education, Atlanta, GA.

Ryan, C. (2012). *Raising happy, healthy LGBT children and adolescents: A guide for parents, foster parents and caregivers.* Unpublished manuscript.

Ryan, C., & Diaz, R. (2006, November). Family responses as a source of risk & resiliency for LGBT youth. Paper presented at Finding Better Ways Conference, Child Welfare League of America, Nashville, TN.

Ryan, C., & Diaz, R. (2011). *Family acceptance project: Intervention guidelines and strategies.* Unpublished manuscript.

Ryan, C., Huebner, D., Diaz, R. M., & Sanchez, J. (2009). Family rejection as a predictor of negative health outcomes in white and Latino lesbian, gay and bisexual young adults. *Pediatrics, 123*(1), 346–352. doi:10.1542/peds.2007-3524

Ryan, C., & Monasterio, E. (2011). *Provider's guide for using the FAPrisk screener for family rejection & related health risks in LGBT youth.* San Francisco, CA: Marian Wright Edelman Institute, San Francisco State University.

Ryan, C., & Rees, R. A. (2012). *Supportive families, healthy children: Helping Latter-day Saint families with lesbian, gay, bisexual & transgender children.* San Francisco, CA: Family Acceptance Project, Marian Wright Edelman Institute, San Francisco State University.

Ryan, C., Russell, S. T., Huebner, D. M., Diaz, R., & Sanchez, J. (2010). Family acceptance in adolescence and the health of LGBT young adults. *Journal of Child and Adolescent Psychiatric Nursing, 23*(4), 205–213. doi:10.1111/j.1744-6171.2010.00246.x

Sexuality Information and Education Council of the United States (SIECUS). (2004). *Guidelines for comprehensive sexuality education: Kindergarten through 12th grade* (3rd ed.). New York: Author. Retrieved from http://www.siecus.org/index.cfm?fuseaction=Page.viewPage&pageId=516&grandparentID=477&parentID=514

Singh, A. A., & Burnes, T. R. (2009). Creating developmentally appropriate, safe counseling environments for transgender youth: The critical role of the school counselor. *Journal of LGBT Issues in Counseling, 3*(3–4), 315–334. doi:10.1080/15538600903379457

Smith, S. D., & Chen-Hayes, S. F. (2004). Leadership and advocacy strategies for lesbian, bisexual, gay, transgendered, and questioning (LBGTQ) students: Academic, career, and interpersonal success. In R. Perusse and G. E. Goodnough (Eds.), *Leadership, advocacy, and direct service strategies for professional school counselors* (pp. 187–221). Belmont, CA: Brooks/Cole.

Stone, C. B. (2003). Counselors as advocates for gay, lesbian, and bisexual youth: A call for equity and action. *Journal of Multicultural Counseling and Development, 31*(2), 143–155. doi:10.1002/j.2161-1912.2003.tb00539.x

Toomey, R. B., Ryan, C., Diaz, R., Card, N. A., & Russell, S. T. (2010). Gender-nonconforming lesbian, gay, bisexual, and transgender youth: School victimization and young adult psychosocial adjustment. *Developmental Psychology, 46,* 1580–1589. doi: 10.1037/a0020705

Toomey, R., Ryan, C., Diaz, R., & Russell, S. T. (2011). High School Gay-Straight Alliances (GSAs) and young adult well-being: An examination of GSA presence, participation, and perceived effectiveness. *Applied Developmental Science, 15*(4), 175–185. doi:10.1080/10888691.2011.607378

Whitman, J. S., Horn, S. S., & Boyd, C. J. (2007). Activism in the schools: Providing LGBTQ affirmative training to school counselors. *Journal of Gay & Lesbian Psychotherapy, 11*(3–4), 143–154. doi:10.1300/J236v11n03_08

Wilber, S., Ryan, C., & Marksamer, J. (2006). *Serving LGBT Youth in Out-of-Home Care: Best Practices Guidelines.* Washington, DC: Child Welfare League of America (CWLA).

Windemeyer, S. (2006). *The advocate college guide for LGBT students.* New York: Alyson Publications.

APPENDIX

Family Acceptance Project—Core Assumptions

(Ryan & Diaz, 2011)

1. Assumes that families love their children and want the best for them. At the same time, these aspirations and dreams for their children's future are shaped by cultural and religious beliefs that may be at odds with a child or adolescent's sexual orientation as lesbian, gay or bisexual and with their gender identity/expression.
2. Supports the need for families to be heard. Families need to feel they are being listened to and understood. Providers build an alliance with diverse parents and caregivers by hearing and understanding their expressions of care and concern for their children's well-being that are rooted in culture, values, and specific beliefs such as faith traditions.
3. Uses FAP research findings to link family reactions to their child's LGB sexual orientation and gender identity with health, mental health and well-being. Beyond building a strong alliance between families and providers, family awareness of the consequences of their behavioral reactions is the most important mechanism of change. Once families learn and understand that specific behavior they perceive as supportive and caring is instead experienced as rejecting and harmful by their LGBT child or adolescent, and can contribute to serious health and mental health problems, they are motivated to decrease rejecting behavior to help and support their LGBT child.
4. Understands that family behaviors are not isolated incidents, but occur in a cultural context aimed at socializing their children and adolescents to adapt and be successful in a heteronormative society, and to protect them from harm, including victimization by others because of their LGBT identity and/or gender expression. Many parental behaviors perceived as rejecting are attempts to protect children and adolescents from discrimination and harm. However, once families become aware that behaviors they deem protective are actually perceived as rejecting by their children and adolescents, they are more open and willing to change them.

Table 13.1 Family Acceptance Project: Examples of Some Family Accepting and Rejecting Behaviors Identified and Measured in Studies with LGBT Youth, Young Adults, and Families

Some Family Behaviors that Increase LGBT Youth's Risk for Health & Mental Health Problems	Some Family Behaviors that Reduce LGBT Youth's Risk for Health & Mental Health Problems & Help Promote Their Well-Being
• Hit, slap or physically hurt youth because of their LGBT identity • Verbally harass or call youth hurtful names because of LGBT identity • Exclude LGBT youth from family events and family activities • Block access to LGBT friends, events & LGBT resources, including GSAs, school diversity clubs, and support groups • Blame youth when they are mistreated because of their LGBT identity • Pressure youth to be more (or less) masculine or feminine • Tell youth that God will punish them because they are gay • Tell youth they are ashamed of them or that how they look or act will shame the family • Make youth keep their LGBT identity a secret and not let them talk about it © 2009, Caitlin Ryan, PhD, Family Acceptance Project	• Talk with youth/foster youth about their LGBT identity • Support youth's LGBT identity even though the parent/caregiver may feel uncomfortable • Require that other family members respect LGBT youth • Welcome youth's LGBT friends & partners to their home, to family events & activities • Advocate for youth when they are mistreated because of their LGBT identity • Support youth's gender expression • Talk with clergy and help their congregation or faith community support LGBT people • Connect youth with an LGBT adult role model to show them options for the future • Bring youth to LGBT organizations or events • Believe youth can have a happy future as an LGBT adult © 2009, Caitlin Ryan, PhD, Family Acceptance Project

Source: *Supportive Families, Healthy Children: Helping Families with Lesbian, Gay, Bisexual & Transgender Children* by Caitlin Ryan, 2009, Family Acceptance Project, San Francisco State University. Copyright © Caitlin Ryan, PhD. Reprinted with permission.

14 Educators as Allies in Support of Lesbian, Gay, Bisexual, Transgender, and Questioning Students and Parents

Robert A. McGarry

It is a widely held belief that all children "have the right to be physically and emotionally safe at school" (Wessler & Prebble, 2003, p. 4). Yet, research consistently tells us that a majority of lesbian, gay, bisexual, transgender and questioning (LGBTQ) students as well as students with lesbian, gay, bisexual, and transgender (LGBT) parents/caregivers do not feel safe in their own schools. As a result, these students are more likely than their peers to skip class or even full days of school to avoid the non-inclusive, non-affirming, and hostile spaces they face on a daily basis (Kosciw, Greytak, Diaz, & Bartkiewicz, 2010). Not only are these students often targeted with verbal attacks and violence, but also they and their peers are rarely exposed to positive depictions of LGBTQ people or families or LGBTQ-relevant historical events in the school curriculum (Kosciw et al., 2010).

When such externally imposed oppression goes unchallenged, students can begin to buy into stereotypes and develop a deeper sense of internalized oppression that can compel them to engage in a range of risky behaviors (Biddulph, 2006; Bochenek & Brown, 2001; Lewis & Arnold, 1998; Rutter & Leech, 2006). In terms of unaddressed issues of homophobia/transphobia in classrooms and schools, the possible outcomes that have been suggested are many and include further verbal harassment or physical abuse, drug and alcohol abuse, premature sexual involvement, and suicide attempts (Russell & Joyner, 2001). Sears (1991) and Fontaine (1997) suggested that LGBTQ students were those least likely to have their needs (academic, social, physical, and emotional) met by schools. Clearly, the belief that students should be safe at school does not always prompt appropriate actions by schools on behalf of LGBTQ students or students with LGBT family members.

Among the responsibilities held by educators is the development of positive learning environments for students. An overwhelming majority of educators believe this includes making their classrooms safe and welcoming spaces for all. The juxtaposition of two specific findings from a recent research study illustrates the troubling disconnect between educator beliefs and actual practice. In examining teachers' beliefs about safety for gender non-conforming elementary school students, the majority of teachers (69%) strongly believe they have an obligation to ensure a safe and supportive learning environment for such students yet only a third (34%) of them engage in any efforts to create a safe/supportive environment for those students (GLSEN & Harris Interactive, 2012). The enacted decisions that teachers make and how they position themselves in relation to their students greatly influences the climate that they and their students co-construct. Once again, the outcomes for LGBTQ students in this regard have been well documented, as suggested above (Lipkin, 1999).

While school may not always be a safe place for LGBTQ students, supportive adults in a school can make a difference in both fostering affirming environments (Espelage, Aragon, Birkett, & Koenig, 2008) and providing support to individual students. For many students (both those who identify as LGBTQ and others), school success can be dependent upon interactions with or awareness of supportive educators within the school community (Kosciw et al., 2010). Those with teaching assignments do much more than teach specific subjects or perform other duties in the school, and often can have an impact that extends well beyond the delivery of course content. For many students, the presence of these individuals, or "allies," as they will be referred to here—or even the simple knowledge that they exist in the school—can help create a welcoming and safe environment in which LGBTQ students can learn, achieve, and develop healthy aspirations for post-secondary education (Kosciw et al., 2010).

Unfortunately, as has already been suggested, research renders a very unfavorable picture of school staff, especially when related to issues of safety and inclusion for LGBTQ students or students with LGBT family members. For example, in terms of intervening in incidents of bullying or harassment, one study indicates that 41.4% of staff members never intervened while another 43.4% only sometimes did so (Kosciw et al., 2010). That only 16% of students report that staff members always intervened is certainly a distressing statistic (Kosciw et al., 2010). In efforts to explain this, some have suggested that educators lack the background knowledge they need to deal effectively with such issues (Herek, 1988; Macgillivray, 2004). Sears' (1991) assertion is that educators' failure to address issues of safety and inclusion may be based upon feelings of self-doubt in terms of their abilities to perform effectively. This chapter, as with the rest of this book, is intended to assist educators endeavoring to gain relevant knowledge and develop the skills that may help them become allies for LGBTQ students and children from LGBT-headed families in their schools.

Research Perspective

Overall, there is a paucity of literature related to allies of LGBTQ people, how individuals come to take on such roles, and how they locate and manage themselves as allies within their profession. Furthermore, literature related specifically to ally behavior directed to support those with LGBT parents or caregivers is lacking as well. Even research pertaining to the more broadly defined topic of "social justice allies" is limited (Broido, 2000; DiStefano, Croteu, Anderson, Kampa-Kokesch & Bullard, 2000). It stands to reason that literature which speaks to K-12 school professionals engaged in such work or positioning themselves as such would be even more limited. Because researchers struggle to gain the necessary qualitative access to practicing educators, the literature that focuses on such controversial topics tends to remain within "the academy" and exclusive to higher education professionals.

Even the literature on teacher preparation and issues of diversity is limited in terms of issues of sexual orientation and gender identity/expression (Akiba, Sunday Cockrell, Cleaver Simmons & Agarwal, 2010). This may help to explain the assertion that a void exists in educators' knowledge and skills (Herek, 1988; Macgillivray, 2004). As the following section of this chapter suggests, knowledge and skills around LGBTQ issues are critical in the process of becoming an ally.

Given the developmental differences between K-12 students and those in post-secondary pursuits, there are inherent limitations in applying the existing literature to the context in which such school professionals work. Being an ally in a university or other post-secondary institution is different for myriad environmental and developmental reasons. Psychosocial development during the college years is markedly different than for students in K-12 schools. Among developing several other competencies, post-secondary students typically engage in the often reciprocally related development of self-sufficiency, mature interpersonal relationships, and identity (Chickering & Reisser, 1993). That K-12 students remain developmentally in a stage that is at best a direct antecedent of this phase must be considered in espousing a developmental model for K-12 allies.

Even though the research about allies in K-12 settings is limited, we know through other research that having supportive school staff has a positive effect on a student's educational experience (Kosciw et al., 2010). For example, LGBTQ students with supportive educators are less likely to miss school because of safety concerns and have higher grade point averages than LGBTQ students with no supportive educators (Kosciw et al., 2010). Adult allies help students to feel safer and more included in school, resulting in a more positive and successful school experience (Espelage et al., 2008).

Ally Development

As with any social justice issue, there are undoubtedly an unlimited number of pathways leading one to take on an activist, advocate, or ally role. For the sake of this discussion, an *"ally"* will be defined as an individual (sometimes a member of the majority or dominant group) who speaks out and stands up for a person or group that is targeted. An ally works to end oppression by supporting and advocating for people who are stigmatized, discriminated against, or treated unfairly. For LGBTQ students and students with LGBT parents/caregivers or family members, an ally is any person who supports and stands up for the rights of LGBTQ people and their families and friends.

Washington and Evans (1991) explicate a sequence of levels through which educators progress in the process of positioning themselves as allies to LGBTQ students. These levels, or steps, provide a developmental framework for consideration of ally strategies. They include (1) developing awareness, (2) gaining knowledge, (3) practicing relevant communication skills, and (4) taking action. The three initial levels are somewhat iterative in nature, and as Athanases and Larrabee (2003) suggested, they provide for the interchange between knowledge and disposition that prepares novice allies for the fourth level. A closer examination of these levels as well as strategies drawn from more recent research (e.g., Graybill, Varjas, Meyers & Watson, 2009) can provide insight into the behaviors that supportive school personnel develop and use on behalf of LGBTQ students in their schools.

Developing Awareness and Acquiring Knowledge

The first level, awareness, may be the most personally intense step in the process of becoming an ally. According to Dillon et al. (2004), even those in the counseling profession or pursuing a career in the counseling profession suggest that they lack adequate self-awareness and knowledge about LGBTQ issues. Awareness involves not only knowing the issues that affect LGBTQ students and those with LGBT family members, but also giving thoughtful consideration to one's own identity, experiences, and heterosexist biases. Beyond this, it also means endeavoring to become familiar with the actual experiences of LGBTQ students or students with LGBT family members in one's specific setting. Several chapters in this volume provide insights into the issues faced by LGBTQ students and family members and can help to develop a global understanding of these complexities. Of course, each school climate bears its own nuances and each student experiences school in very different way. It is important to consider how and to what extent the issues discussed here impact the LGBTQ students or students with LGBT family members in a given school.

Teachers' life experiences and beliefs, values, and attitudes can influence their capacity for being an ally. Educators endeavoring to become allies to LGBTQ students and families need to begin by assessing their personal beliefs in order to develop the awareness that permits one to be an authentic ally. Cranton and Carusetta (2004) suggest that authenticity allows educators to connect with students in ways that are meaningful. It is important to recognize that students are often connoisseurs of authenticity in adults and respond best when an adult is authentic.

The relational benefits of such self-reflective work are clear, but this work also simply clears the way for taking on other ally behaviors. In qualitative studies of ally development, participants identified the self-clarification of beliefs and values related to social justice issues as one of several key factors in their development as allies (Broido, 2000; Dillon et al., 2004). The identification and honest critique of these is crucial, especially given that some research has suggested that in general, educators may find it difficult to separate personal beliefs from professional responsibility (Blumenfeld & Lindop, 1996).

Examination of one's own experiences with anti-LGBTQ name-calling, bullying, or harassment and determination of its effects upon oneself and others (including students) is another critical step in this process. This involves forming and understanding the narrative of one's personal and professional life and reflecting on these lived experiences.

People are not born prejudiced, but from the moment they are born, they are bombarded with messages, spoken and unspoken, about different types of people that may impact their potential to take on an ally role. Stereotypes and prejudices often are learned devoid of consciousness, and all people, LGBTQ and non-LGBTQ identified, have learned messages about those who are LGBTQ. Understanding these messages can help one to identify held beliefs and biases that then can be challenged in a process that helps to make one a stronger ally.

Anti-LGBTQ bias is all around, especially the more subtle bias-based behaviors such as anti-LGBTQ jokes, the exclusion of LGBTQ related-themes in curricula, and even anti-LGBTQ name-calling. Subtle or not, bias has the power to hurt and isolate people. An ally's work includes recognizing and challenging the anti-LGBTQ bias they may possess. Once the biases that may affect actions and thoughts are identified, an ally can work towards eliminating them through further reading and conversations with other allies who may serve as mentors through this process.

Duhigg, Rostosky, Gray, and Wimsatt (2010) suggest that for some people, becoming an ally is dependent upon the individual's acquaintance with LGBT people. Broido

(2000) cited this as a critical part of becoming an ally around such issues. In a study of pre-service teachers, Butler (1999) found that those who possessed more factual, first-hand knowledge relevant to LGBTQ issues held and exhibited more positive attitudes and behaviors. This, too, is an important part of building awareness. Gaining the most emic perspective of the experiences of LGBTQ students or students with LGBT family members, especially one's own students, can help an ally develop a level of empathy that is, once again, authentic.

Learning How to Communicate

Developing awareness and gaining knowledge provide the opportunity to engage in the practice of relevant communication skills and use of words. Gaining facility with vocabulary is a necessary step in the process of becoming an ally. Language has a huge impact on the way we see others and ourselves. Whether it is in developing supportive relationships with LGBTQ students or those with LGBT parents or family members, or in confronting homophobia/transphobia or heterosexism, utilizing LGBTQ-related terminology accurately and respectfully is one simple yet important way to be an ally.

Unfortunately, many people do not have the experience or knowledge to use LGBTQ terminology in an accurate or appropriate manner. It is important, for example, to understand the differences between sexual orientation (our inner feelings of who we are attracted to) and gender identity (our inner feelings of maleness or femaleness). Far too often these terms are confused, and the result can be harmful to a student. To make matters more complicated, language is constantly evolving, and, in some circumstances, varies upon one's context. Familiarizing oneself and keeping up-to-date with LGBTQ-related terms and concepts is a key component of being an ally. Conducting an Internet search of respected sites for such information is a good starting point for this process. Of course, the best way to ensure that you are using the proper terminology when referring to individuals is to find out the terminology they themselves prefer.

It is critical that an ally use appropriate and respectful terminology at all times, in casual conversation as well as during class time. Using words like "partner" instead of "boyfriend/girlfriend" or "husband/wife" and avoiding gendered pronouns and using "they" instead of "he/she" help LGBTQ students feel more comfortable being themselves and seeking the support that an ally can provide. Endeavoring to learn and use an individual's preferred gender pronoun, for example, sends an important message of respect and inclusion to that individual.

Taking Action

The final level, as described by Washington and Evans (1991), is the one in which the ally acts and therefore establishes his or her position as an ally in his or her setting. The notion of "taking action" can mean different things depending upon the individual involved and the context in which one works. For some, it is a simple act of asserting themselves as an ally while for others it is also a mechanism for social change. There is a spectrum of actions one can take from simply being a visible ally to LGBTQ students to more complicated advocacy efforts described in the next section of this chapter.

Graybill et al. (2009) found that school-based allies implement strategies that are responsive to contextual variables.

One of the simplest yet most important parts of being an ally to LGBTQ students or students with LGBT family members is being visible. The act of visibility signifies affirmation (DiStefano et al., 2000). In order to come to someone for help, students need to be able to recognize who their allies are. Even if students do not come to an ally directly, research has shown that just knowing there is a supportive educator at school can help LGBTQ students feel safe and included (Kosciw et al., 2010).

There are many ways for one to be visible as an ally. Being visible can be as simple as posting a sticker or as direct as modeling supportive behavior. DiStefano et al. (2000) identified visibly displaying relevant symbols, such as a safe space sticker or a rainbow flag as a frequently cited ally activity. Making a classroom or office identifiable as a safe space for LGBTQ students or students with LGBT family members helps them identify that the person responsible for that space in the school is someone to whom they can go for support and that the space is one where they will be safe. Posting supportive materials such as quotes from famous LGBTQ icons, information about the LGBTQ community, or materials from LGBTQ organizations in that space will more deeply affirm that the person responsible for creating the learning or office environment is an ally. Seizing special opportunities for public display of LGBTQ-relevant information such as *LGBT History Month* in October, *LGBTQ Pride Month* in June or the *National Day of Silence* in April are simple acts that help LGBTQ students feel validated and creates visibility by letting them and their heterosexual peers know that there are and have been LGBTQ people who have achieved great success and are working to improve society.

Beyond the classroom or office, making oneself physically visible as an ally in spaces throughout the school allows students to easily identify the most supportive educators within their school. Wearing a supportive button or wristband, such as those available from various LGBTQ rights organizations, lets students know who supportive allies are without them having to say a word. It also lets other educators know that you are an ally and someone to whom they can refer students for support or guidance. Visibility also can inspire others to become allies themselves. Participating in or providing professional development to colleagues reinforces one's position as an ally and is an often-cited ally activity (DiStefano et al., 2000).

Enacting responses to anti-LGBTQ behavior (and words) and challenging discrimination whenever and wherever it occurs are critical ally behaviors. In an assessment of various ally preparation programs at the university level, Draughn, Elkins, and Roy (2002) cited the preparation of allies to confront homophobia and heterosexism in group settings as particularly challenging and an area in which allies need continued training and development. Anti-LGBTQ behavior comes in all shapes and sizes: biased language, name-calling, harassment, and even physical assault. Kosciw et al. (2010) found that nearly three-quarters of LGBTQ students hear homophobic slurs, such as "faggot" or "dyke," often or frequently at school, and nearly 9 in 10 LGBTQ students had been verbally or physically harassed in school. Consistent response to such behaviors lets everyone in the school know that there are allies present.

Lastly, it is important that when engaging with students, staff, and parents, allies do not assume their sexual orientation or gender identity. Similarly, allies should not assume that everyone is heterosexual or fits into a prescribed gender role. Instead, allies need to be open to a great variety of identities and expressions. In this heterosexist society, students and their families constantly receive the message that everyone is supposed to be heterosexual or conform to gender expression stereotypes. An ally needs to reinforce the notion that there is no one way a person "should" be.

Allies and Advocacy

A key role of allies is to use their power and influence as educators to advocate for the rights of LGBTQ students and those with LGBT family members and ensure safe schools for all. In the typical school district, allies are provided multiple venues for engaging in advocacy efforts. Chen-Hayes (2000) describes three distinct types of advocacy efforts. He suggests that one can engage in advocacy on the individual level by the kinds of ally actions identified in previous sections of this chapter or in cultural or systemic ways described below.

The first step in advocating for changes in a school is to assess the current climate in the school by engaging in strategies drawn from the burgeoning practice of practitioner or action research. Such site-based activity "has the potential for empowerment and the inclusion of a greater diversity of voices in educational policy and social change" (Anderson, Herr, & Nihlen, 1994, p. 6). Climate assessment helps focus efforts by identifying areas for improvement and uncovering the experiences of those in the school and is also a good precursor to looking more deeply at a school's existing policies, practices, and resources.

Principals, district administrators, and school board members are good partners or targets in advocacy efforts. Engaging such individuals in an assessment of a school's climate as well as policies and practices can lead to the development of an effective action plan for a school or school district. This is an effective way to begin to implement comprehensive anti-bullying/harassment policies and embrace non-discriminatory policies and practices.

Conducting a survey of members of the school community, including students, staff, and parents, is an effective strategy for two reasons. It can provide rich, descriptive data about the school to use when advocating for changes. Conducting a survey in a setting in which there may already be some anecdotal evidence of problems can also serve as a low-level intervention. Such a survey might include questions that ask about the frequency of biased language, harassment, and assault, as well as the level of intervention by educators.

Understanding how inclusive a school is of LGBTQ students, families, and issues is key to creating a plan of action to ensure that a school is safe and welcoming for all students. To assess a school's policies and practices, advocates should take into account and closely examine the school's policies and procedures, course content, school events and celebrations, extracurricular activities, and athletics.

Once a school's policies and practices have been assessed, a decision can be made regarding which areas of the school need the most work. Framing the work in terms of what failing to meet the needs of LGBTQ youth and families could mean in terms of academic achievement and healthy functioning of youth is a good message and motivation-building strategy (Graybill et al., 2009). Collaboration with colleagues, students, and parents/caregivers is critical in the process of implementing realistic changes within the school. The strategies described below can assist those advocating for specific changes. By making realistic goals and documenting them, schools are more likely to make the necessary changes to make a school safer and more respectful for LGBTQ students and students with LGBT family members. Using a well defined strategic plan can assist in maintaining focus and keeping the end goal in view.

Advocacy: Supporting Student Clubs

For many LGBTQ students, student clubs that address LGBTQ student issues (commonly called Gay-Straight Alliances or GSAs) offer critical support. These clubs are student led, usually at the high school or middle school level, and work to address anti-LGBTQ name-calling, bullying, and harassment in schools and to promote respect for all students. The existence of these clubs can make schools safer and more welcoming for LGBTQ students and students from LGBT-headed households.

Allies sometimes need to advocate for the rights of students to establish a GSA. Although some opponents of GSAs have attempted to restrict the existence of or access to these clubs, the federal Equal Access Act of 1984 requires public schools to allow GSAs to exist alongside other non-curricular student clubs. GSAs, like all student clubs, must have a faculty advisor. Serving as the advisor for a school's GSA is one of the most effective ways to be an ally to LGBTQ students and advocate on their behalf. Not only does being an advisor provide support for the efforts of the GSA, it enhances the ally's visibility, making it easier for LGBTQ students to identify a supportive school staff member. It also gives other staff the knowledge of a resource person to whom they can ask questions, seek advice, and refer students. See Chapter 15 of this volume for more information on GSA development.

Advocacy: Inclusive Curriculum

LGBTQ-inclusive curricula that provides positive representations of LGBTQ people, history, and events helps to create a tone of acceptance of LGBTQ people and increased awareness of LGBTQ-related issues, resulting in a more supportive environment for LGBTQ students and students with LGBT family members. Compared to students in other schools, students in schools with an inclusive curriculum heard fewer homophobic remarks, were less likely to be victimized or feel unsafe at school because of their sexual orientation or gender identity/expression, and had a greater sense of belonging to their school community (Kosciw et al., 2010). Chapter 10 of this volume is devoted to the discussion of LGBTQ-inclusive curriculum with tips and ideas for educators wishing to engage in this important work.

Advocacy: Promoting Non-Discriminatory Policies and Practices

One major step that educators can take to affirm their support for all students' safety is the implementation and enforcement of comprehensive anti-bullying or harassment policies, sometimes known as safe school policies. These policies can promote a better school climate for LGBTQ students when sexual orientation, gender identity, and gender expression are explicitly addressed. School officials may not recognize that anti-LGBTQ harassment and discrimination are unacceptable behaviors, or may not respond to the problem due to prejudice or community pressure without the cover of a specific policy. Comprehensive policies that specifically enumerate sexual orientation, gender identity, and gender expression as protected characteristics remove all doubt that LGBTQ students, and all students, are protected from anti-LGBTQ bullying and harassment in school. Information related to policy development is covered in Chapter 7 of this volume, and bullying prevention is covered in Chapter 9 of this volume.

Some argue that generic anti-bullying/harassment policies without enumerated categories are just as effective as comprehensive ones. Students' experiences indicate otherwise. LGBTQ students from schools with a generic policy experienced similar harassment levels as students from schools with no policies at all; whereas students from schools with a comprehensive policy that included sexual orientation, gender identity, and gender expression reported a less hostile and more supportive school climate (Kosciw et al., 2010). LGBTQ students in schools with comprehensive safe school policies heard fewer homophobic remarks, experienced lower levels of victimization, were more likely to report that school staff intervened when hearing homophobic language, and were more likely to report incidents of harassment and assault to school staff (Kosciw et al., 2010).

Allies should find out whether their school or school district has a comprehensive anti-bullying/harassment policy that includes protections based on sexual orientation, gender identity, and gender expression. If not, an advocacy plan to adopt one must be devised. If one exists, an ally can ensure that all members of the school community are regularly notified of the policy. Often times a policy may exist but students are not aware of it and thus, do not know that they are protected. If students are not aware of the policy or how to make a report of bullying or harassment, then the policy will not be effective.

Dress code. Homophobia, transphobia, and heterosexism can manifest in school practices, creating an unwelcoming, unsafe, and hostile environment for LGBTQ students. Practices that exclude LGBTQ students, or force them to conform to what is considered by others as "normal," can alienate such students from the school community. School uniforms and dress codes, for example, can be quite problematic. Dress codes that require students to wear clothing deemed appropriate for one gender can restrict students' gender identity and expression, resulting in students feeling unwelcome in their own school community. Uniform or dress codes should be gender-neutral, with the same set of rules and expectations for all students, regardless of gender.

School events. School events, such as proms or other such activities that limit a student's guest/date choices to those of another gender or specify gender-specific attire also can make students feel excluded and unwelcome. This is particularly true in cases when LGBTQ students are explicitly told that they cannot bring their same-gender guest or are refused entry because of their guest's gender. By ensuring that school events are inclusive of same-gender and gender-non-conforming couples, students can attend with anyone they wish, or alone, regardless of gender.

Athletics. Homophobia/transphobia and heterosexism are often heavily present on athletic fields, in the gym, in locker rooms, and at sporting events (Morrow & Gill, 2003). As such, sports activities can be one of the most unwelcoming school programs for LGBTQ students. Some LGBTQ students, facing ridicule, harassment, or assault, may choose to avoid the athletics program altogether. Those LGBTQ athletes that do participate may learn to feel shame and self-hatred and hide their identities, at great psychological cost. Engaging school coaches and physical education teachers in combating anti-LGBTQ language among students and staff, responding when anti-LGBTQ behavior occurs, and creating a safe environment within school athletics for LGBTQ students makes these activities and spaces more welcoming.

Libraries. When resourced in a thoughtful way, school libraries can provide students with literature and resources on many topics, including literature about sexual orientation and gender identity/expression, historical books about LGBTQ people or events, and LGBTQ-inclusive fiction. Far too often school library literature collections exclude LGBTQ people, history, and struggles. A lack of LGBTQ people, history, and events in the library can contribute to LGBTQ students or students with LGBT family members feeling excluded from their school. Including LGBTQ-themed literature in the school library collection can remedy this.

Internet access. Finally, Internet filters are often used in schools to block materials harmful to students, such as violent or pornographic sites. Internet filters also can block useful and necessary information. Too often, websites providing people with positive and important information about the LGBTQ community are blocked on school computers. Students may be denied access to websites that have LGBTQ-related information such as research, historical facts, or support services for LGBTQ youth. Yet, in some cases, these students who are blocked from positive LGBTQ sites may still have access to sites condemning LGBTQ people. Ensuring that Internet filters are not blocking students from finding positive and helpful information about the LGBTQ community is an important part of implementing inclusive policies and practices.

The "Dos and Don'ts" of Being an Ally

Educators are in a unique position to impact the school experience of LGBTQ students and students with LGBT family members and must make concerted efforts so that all students feel physically and emotionally safe at school regardless of sexual orientation, gender identity/expression, or family structure. The next two sections include helpful tips and reminders to assist those actively engaging in the process of becoming a true ally to LGBTQ students and students with LGBT family members. These recommendations should be recalled and reflected upon on a regular basis as one learns and grows in this process.

What Allies Should Do

One of the simplest, yet most important ways to be an ally is to listen to students. Like all other students, LGBTQ students need to feel comfortable to be able to express themselves. When students come to an ally to talk about being harassed, feeling excluded, or just about their life in general, it is important to keep in mind that the ally may be the only person with whom the student feels safe speaking about him/herself. It is important to actively listen, remain free of judgment, and respect students' privacy. Someone who is coming out may not want everyone to know. Allies should assume that the student expects confidentiality, unless indicated otherwise. Informing others can create an unsafe environment for the student and lead to additional problems. An effective ally is one who knows when and how to refer students to outside help and has up-to-date referral information available. There are times, such as when a student may be in danger, when allies may need to break confidentiality, especially if school policy and protocols require them to do so. However, in such a circumstance the ally should always let a student know confidence cannot be maintained and explain that it is out of concern for the student.

Finally, effective allies acknowledge how homophobia, transphobia, and heterosexism have played out in their lives and consistently challenge this within themselves. Allies return to prior levels of preparation as needed and acknowledge that they may need to gain additional knowledge, understandings, or expertise in meeting the needs of LGBTQ students or students with LGBT family members. Allies may need to brush up on LGBTQ-related language and current issues facing the LGBTQ community or they may simply need to reaffirm their commitment to working against the oppression of the individuals for whom they became allies in the first place. Allies should always share their new understandings as appropriate with those LGBTQ students and others to whom they are allies. Doing so sends a strong message to such students about their commitment and models appropriate ally behavior.

What Allies Should Avoid

As discussed in this chapter, it is vital that allies avoid making assumptions and perpetuating stereotypes. These can be extremely offensive and may turn a student away from a potential ally. Allies must also avoid feeling as if they need to have all of the answers. This is complicated work, and allies do not always have the answer nor can they always fulfill every student's needs. When faced with a problem for which no solution is evident, looking into the subject to try to find an answer is often best. Many times the best thing for an ally to do is to refer the student to an outside source that may be able to help. Allies must be careful not to promise something they may not be able to deliver. This can damage the relationship between student and ally.

Allies as Works in Progress

Becoming an ally to LGBTQ students or students with LGBT family members in schools is not something to be accomplished by reading a book, completing an on-line tutorial, or even listening to a speaker or trainer. Certainly all of these are good steps to take; but becoming an ally is an ongoing and complex process that involves knowing the issues, knowing oneself, and examining one's beliefs, words, and actions while imagining, planning, and seizing the anti-oppressive educative possibilities that exist in the teachable and support-providing moments that present themselves in classrooms and schools. It is then that educators can enact the belief that all students, regardless of sexual orientation, gender identity, or gender expression, have the right to be physically and emotionally safe and respected at school.

References

Akiba, M., Sunday Cockrell, J., Cleaver Simmons, S., & Agarwal, G. (2010). Preparing teachers for diversity: Examination of teacher certification and program accreditation standards in the

50 states and Washington, DC. *Equity & Excellence in Education, 43*(4), 443–462. doi:10.1080/10665684.2010.510048

Anderson, G., Herr, K., & Nihlen, A. (1994). *Studying your own school: An educator's guide to qualitative practitioner research.* Thousand Oaks, CA: Sage Publications.

Athanases, S., & Larrabee, T. (2003). Toward a consistent stance in teaching for equity: Learning to advocate for lesbian- and gay-identified youth. *Teaching and Teacher Education: An International Journal of Research and Studies, 19*(2), 237–261. doi:10.1016/S0742-051X(02)00098-7

Biddulph, M. (2006). Sexualities equality in schools: Why every lesbian, gay, bisexual or transgender (LGBT) child matters. *Pastoral Care, 24*(2), 15–21.

Blumenfeld, W., & Lindop, L. (1996). Road blocks and responses: Responding to resistance from teachers, administrators, students, and the community. New York, NY: Gay, Lesbian and Straight Teachers' Network.

Bochenek, M., & Brown, A. W. (2001). *Hatred in the hallways: Violence and discrimination against lesbian, gay, bisexual, and transgender students in U.S. schools.* New York, NY: Human Rights Watch.

Broido, E. (2000). The development of social justice allies during college: A phenomenological investigation. *Journal of College Student Development, 41*(1), 3–18.

Butler, K. L. (1999). Preservice teachers' knowledge and attitudes regarding gay men and lesbians. *Journal of Health Education, 30*(2), 125–129.

Chen-Hayes, S. F. (2000). Social justice advocacy with lesbian, bisexual, gay, and transgendered persons. In J. Lewis & L. Bradley (Eds.), *Advocacy in counseling: Counselors, clients, & community* (pp. 89–98). Greensboro, NC: Caps publications (ERIC/CASS).

Chickering, A. W., & Reisser, L. (1993). *Education and identity* (2nd ed.) San Francisco, CA: Jossey-Bass.

Cranton, P., & Carusetta, E. (2004). Perspectives on authenticity in teaching. *Adult Education Quarterly, 55*(1), 5–22. doi: 10.1177/0741713604268894

Dillon, F. R., Worthington, R. L., Bielstein Savoy, H., Rooney, S. C., Becker-Schutte, A., & Guerra, R. M. (2004). On becoming allies: A qualitative study of LGB-affirmative counselor training. *Counselor Education and Supervision, 43*, 162–178.

DiStefano, T., Croteu, J., Anderson, M., Kampa-Kokesch, S., & Bullard, M. (2000). Experiences of being heterosexual allies to lesbian, gay, and bisexual people: A qualitative exploration. *Journal of College Counseling, 3*(2), 131–141. doi: 10.1002/j.2161-1882.2000.tb00173.x

Draughn, T., Elkins, B., & Roy, R. (2002). Allies in the struggle. *Journal of Lesbian Studies, 6*(3–4), 9–20. doi:10.1300/J155v06n03_02

Duhigg, J., Rostosky, S., Gray, B., & Wimsatt, M. (2010). Development of heterosexuals into sexual minority allies: A qualitative exploration. *Sexuality Research and Social Policy Journal of NSRC, 67*(2), 225–241. doi:10.1007/s13178-010-0005-2

Espelage, D. L., Aragon, S. R., Birkett, M., & Koenig, B. W. (2008). Homophobic teasing, psychological outcomes, and sexual orientation among high school students: What influence do parents and schools have? *School Psychology Review, 37*(2), 202–216. Retrieved from http://www.nasponline.org/publications/spr/pdf/spr372espelage.pdf

Fontaine, J. (1997). The sound of silence: Public school response to the needs of gay and lesbian youth. In M. B. Harris (Ed.), *School Experiences of gay and lesbian youth: The invisible minority* (pp. 101–109). New York, NY: Haworth Press.

GLSEN & Harris Interactive (2012). *Playgrounds and prejudice: Elementary school climate in the United States, a survey of students and teachers.* New York, NY: GLSEN. doi: http://www.glsen.org/binary-data/GLSEN_ATTACHMENTS/file/000/002/2027-1.pdf

Graybill, E. C., Varjas, K., Meyers, J., & Watson, L. B. (2009). Content-specific strategies to advocate for lesbian, gay, bisexual, and transgender youth: An exploratory study. *School Psychology*

Review, 38(4), 570–584. Retrieved from http://www.nasponline.org/publications/spr/pdf/spr384graybill.pdf

Herek, G. (1988). Heterosexuals' attitudes toward lesbians and gay men: Correlates and gender differences. *The Journal of Sex Research, 25*, 451–477. doi:10.1080/00224498809551476

Kosciw, J. G., Greytak, E. A., Diaz, E. M., & Bartkiewicz, M. J. (2010) *The 2009 National School Climate Survey: The experiences of lesbian, gay, bisexual and transgender youth in our nation's schools.* New York, NY: GLSEN.

Lave, J., & Wenger, E. (1989). *Situated learning: Legitimate peripheral participation.* Cambridge, England: Cambridge University Press.

Lewis, J., & Arnold, M. (1998). From multiculturalism to social action. In C. C. Lee & G. R. Walz (Eds.), *Social action: A mandate for counselors* (pp. 51–56). Alexandria, VA: American Counseling Association.

Lipkin, A. (1999). *Understanding homosexuality, changing schools: A text for teachers, counselors, and administrators.* Boulder, CO: Westview Press.

Macgillivray, I. K. (2004). *Sexual orientation and school policy: A practical guide for teachers, administrators, and community activists.* Lanham, MD: Rowman & Littlefield.

Morrow, R. G., & Gill, D. L. (2003). Perceptions of homophobia and heterosexism in physical education. *Research Quarterly for Exercise and Sport, 74*(2), 205–214.

Russell, S. T., & Joyner, K. (2001). Adolescent sexual orientation and suicide risk: Evidence from a national study. *American Journal of Public Health, 91*(8), 1276–1281. doi:10.2105/AJPH.91.8.1276

Rutter, P., & Leech, N. (2006). Sexual minority youth perspectives on the school environment and suicide risk interventions: A qualitative study. *Journal of Gay and Lesbian Issues in Education, 4*(1), 77–91. doi:10.1300/J367v04n01_06

Sears, J. T. (1991). Educators, homosexuality, and homosexual students: Are personal feelings related to professional beliefs? *Journal of Homosexuality, 22*, 29–79.

Washington, J., & Evans, N. (1991). Becoming an ally. In N. Evans & V. Wall (Eds.), *Beyond tolerance: Gays, lesbians and bisexuals on campus* (pp. 195–205). Alexandria, VA: American College Personnel Association.

Wessler, S. L., & Prebble, W. (2003). *The respectful school: How educators and students can conquer hate and harassment.* Alexandria, VA: Association for Supervision and Curriculum Development.

15 Accessing Community Resources
Providing Support for All

Kelly S. Kennedy

Students who are lesbian, gay, bisexual, transgender, and questioning (LGBTQ), their parents, and students with parents who are LGBTQ may benefit from resources that are beyond the scope of what can be provided by school professionals or within a school setting. Fortunately, schools do not exist in isolation, and professionals have an increasingly rich array of community resources they can access. In many regions, local agencies offer a variety of services to which students or families may be referred or with which schools can collaborate. In regions with fewer tangible sources of support, the internet provides a wealth of quality resources that school professionals can use and can assist students and family members in accessing.

In a typical referral paradigm, school professionals provide a recommendation for a student or family to make a connection with a particular agency by providing contact information or making a formal introduction. However, the use of community resources to help support LGBTQ students and families should not be limited to this format. Instead, practitioners are urged to consider the ways in which community resources can be utilized within the school community. This chapter will explore the traditional referral process as well as the potential for more collaborative school–community partnerships. Additionally, this chapter will also describe the use of Gay-Straight Alliances (GSAs) as broad supports for LGBTQ students and as channels to connect students with community resources within the school setting.

Identifying Local Resources

Uses for Community Resources

Traditionally, school professionals may have viewed community agencies as independent entities to which students or families can be referred. Although this is certainly an important venue through which services can be identified and accessed for LGBTQ youth and families, school professionals should also consider the possibility for true collaborative partnerships. Paradigms for the development of school–community partnerships have been identified as valuable and economical ways to provide services for complex social issues such as delinquency, mental health support, academic achievement, and school dropout prevention (e.g., Adelman & Taylor, 2006; Sheridan, Napolitano, & Swearer, 2008). Clearly, the presence of LGBTQ youth or youth from families with LGBTQ family members on a school campus does not present a "problem" along these lines, but the complexity of the needs of this population may constitute a parallel scenario in which these paradigms may be useful.

When discussing school–community collaborations, it is important for school professionals to remember that the possibilities are nearly endless. Arrangements for collaborative relationships between schools and community agencies may differ in terms of initiation (e.g., approached by school or approached by agency), nature (e.g., formal or informal), target recipients (e.g., students or staff), focus (e.g., creation of new service options or transformation of existing services), and location of services (e.g., on campus, at agency, or at a new location) (Adelman & Taylor, 2006). In a true collaborative relationship, all agencies involved are responsible for every stage of the collaboration, from the assessment of needs, selection of target population, evaluation of extant and needed resources or services, creation of new or enhanced services, to the ongoing evaluation of the collaboration (Sheridan et al., 2008).

If school professionals seek a collaborative relationship with a community agency, there may be benefits for both parties even if a long-term collaborative effort is not initiated or maintained. For example, if school employees meet with leaders of a local LGBTQ community center, an initial conversation aimed at identifying potential areas for collaboration may not result in the creation of a school-based program staffed by the community center. However, in working together, school professionals may learn new ideas or perspectives regarding LGBTQ youth and families, new approaches to help, and new insights into the needs of the local community. Additionally, school professionals will learn about the workings of the community center, the individuals working there, the resources available, and other information that will be invaluable when providing referrals to this resource.

Types of Resources and Needs

LGBTQ students and families may benefit from a wide array of the community resources and supports. Given the potential risks faced by LGBTQ youth and youth with LGBTQ family members, school professionals should be cognizant of the potential need for community resources such as substance abuse treatment, family counseling, legal support, or crisis shelters. The type of service provided to the referred student or parent may vary from formal appointments (e.g., counseling sessions, legal consultation, or doctor appointments) to informal social or peer-based supports (e.g., support group for parents of LGBTQ youth or lists of individuals in the local community that would provide emergency shelter to an LGBTQ student). Another type of resource may be simply an agency, library, or other place in which youth and/or family members may peruse information about what it means to be LGBTQ, find facts about sexual orientation or gender expression, or learn about the LGBTQ community.

However, school professionals should be careful not to assume that all referrals made for LGBTQ youth or families need to be LGBTQ-specific. In other words, these students and families share needs with all students and families for resources such as assistance with housing, medical care, faith or spiritual needs, and counseling. In many cases, referrals to community resources that are made for LGBTQ youth and families are the same resources that would be provided for any other student or family. Therefore, when compiling a list of community resources that a school professional may utilize when referring LGBTQ students or families, one can include broad community agencies that would provide assistance with issues not specific to this population. Agencies and individuals that are listed in such, regardless of the type of service they provide, should be sensitive to and have expertise in working with LGBTQ youth and families.

The Internet can be a rich source of information, especially for LGBTQ youth and families. Due to the ease of access and anonymous nature of the online community, the Internet may be a key method through which LGBTQ youth search out answers to questions regarding sexuality, gender expression, and sexual orientation. Online chat rooms and social networking sites may provide social opportunities and identity exploration in ways that are simply not available in the physical community surrounding many schools (Macintosh & Bryson, 2008). Unfortunately, the Internet also may be a source for inaccurate, misleading, or explicitly anti-LGBTQ information. With this in mind, it may be prudent for educators to create a list of reputable websites where youth or families may seek accurate and affirming information on LGBTQ issues. The websites provided later in this chapter are a good start, but educators are also encouraged to conduct their own searches for websites that they judge to be accurate and useful. In addition to the ability to provide a recommended list of web-based resources, this search will help school professionals to stay current regarding the types of information and misinformation about the LGBTQ community that is available online.

Lists of Resources

Many schools, counties, and districts have compiled lists of resources available to students and families in their community. Some may have been created and provided by local social services or mental health agencies, and others may have been generated by school employees. Typically, a list of this type is divided by resource type (e.g., crisis shelter, family counseling, suicide hotline), and provides names, brief descriptions of each agency, and contact information. Depending upon the purpose of a given list, as well as who created it, these lists of resources may or may not include agencies that provide services specifically designed to assist LGBTQ individuals. Including a category in this list with specific agencies that specialize in helping unique populations, including LGBTQ individuals, would be useful. Additionally, it may be helpful to designate which broad agencies (e.g., counseling clinic, medical clinic) provide services tailored to the needs of LGBTQ individuals. In other words, if a particular counseling clinic has a therapist who specializes in working with LGBTQ youth, it should be noted on the list.

When creating this type of resource list, it is important to ensure that each agency or resource is described in enough detail that an appropriate, well-informed referral can be made. Therefore, notes for all listed resources should include information regarding:

- the scope of services provided (e.g., family counseling, medical exams, emergency overnight shelter, youth support groups);
- any requirements for who may utilize these services (e.g., social security card needed, parental consent issues, eligibility for State or Federal assistant needed);
- hours of operation and location of agency;
- approximate costs associated with services;

- approximate timelines for accessing services (e.g., applications processed within 30 days, walk-in appointments available); and
- up-to-date contact information (e.g., website, phone number of agency, phone number of intake coordinator).

In order to have current information, lists of community resources must be updated frequently. To do so, at least once a year, a school professional can contact each agency listed to ensure contact information is accurate and to review services offered, cost, availability, and other information that would be necessary when making a referral. When refreshing contacts in this way, keep in mind that some agencies may have particular individuals that are the "point people" for referrals from schools, and therefore getting the names and contact information of those individuals may be critical.

When speaking with community agencies to update contact information, school professionals should take time to make personal and professional connections. The more that is known about who will answer the call of a referred student, how he or she will respond, and the process that will ensue, the better the school professional can be in making a clear and accurate referral. Additionally, it is via personal connections and relationships with individuals in community agencies and groups that school employees can discuss how the dynamic in-service provision between the school and an agency is functioning. For example, if a school psychologist often refers students to a particular counseling clinic, it will be beneficial to have an annual discussion with a person at that clinic regarding the nature of the referrals made over the past year (e.g., appropriateness, percentage of students that follow through with making and keeping appointments) in order to identify areas of improvement.

Finally, when updating resource lists, school professionals can ask for any new resources available within the community. As many agencies work in collaboration with others (e.g., social services and mental health providers), this may be an excellent way to discover new resources. Additionally, local community directories and the Internet should be reviewed annually for new resources.

Making a Referral

School professionals should be as familiar as possible with all agencies and resources to which they refer students and families. As the referral process may greatly impact a student's or family's impression of the referred agency, as well as the likelihood of follow-through, it is important that referrals are handled with care. Depending on the type of assistance needed, the referral process may be very different.

Informal referrals. In many cases, school professionals may lead youth or parents to appropriate community-based resources without a formal referral ever taking place. For example, a school counselor may have a list of available resources accessible for students and parents to browse through in a counseling center or office. This might be especially appropriate for information about support groups and organizations for LGBTQ youth, as it would provide access to these organizations even to youth who may not be comfortable discussing these interests with a school professional. Similarly, displaying lists of appropriate websites where youth or parents could seek information regarding being LGBTQ and have questions answered privately or discretely or posting flyers from national or regional agencies are ways in which a counselor or psychologist can lead youth or parents to resources in an indirect way.

There is some evidence to suggest that clients are more likely to follow through with intake appointments at outside agencies if they are self-referred, rather than referred by a counselor or psychologist (Sparks, Daniels, & Johnson, 2003). In light of this, the compilation of potential resources as well as the task of making this information accessible to youth and families to explore on their own terms may be especially important.

Formal referrals. In other scenarios, referrals may be made because a student or family needs a level of care unavailable in the school setting or requires expertise outside of the training or experience of available school personnel. In these cases, a direct discussion with the student (and potentially the student's parents or guardians as appropriate or required) regarding the reasons for referral, as well as the school professional's selection of potential community resources, is vital. Depending upon the situation, it may be helpful for the school professional to assist a student or family member in making initial contact with the community agency. The process of making a referral, in addition to other factors such as the wait time of the outside agency, will impact the likelihood that a student will follow through and attend an appointment at an outside agency (Sparks et al., 2003). Thus, school professionals are cautioned to handle referrals with care.

Once a referral has been made, it is important for school professionals to remain in communication with students and families to ensure continuity of support. For example, if a student is referred for individual counseling at a community agency because his or her needs are deemed too significant to be met on campus, it is important for the school counselor or psychologist to maintain contact with the student as his or her on-campus support system. If appropriate, school professionals can obtain consent to share information with community-based counselors, therapists, and other support systems in order to best meet the needs of their students in the school setting.

Gay-Straight Alliances

GSAs are non-academic student groups that include LGBTQ and supportive non-LGBTQ students. The number of GSAs nationwide has risen dramatically in recent years, from about 1,000 in 2001 to 4,000 by 2008 (http://www.glsen.org). According to the GSA Network, there were over 800 GSAs (in about 53% of all high schools) in California in 2012 (http://www.gsanetwork.org). GSAs support the students in a school's community in a number of direct (e.g., social support for members, member advocacy to school administration for revision of school anti-harassment policies) and indirect (e.g., recognition by school that LGBTQ persons are a part of the school community) ways, and the positive impact of a GSA on a safe and supportive campus climate for LGBTQ students is well documented (e.g., Cooper-Nichols & Bowleg, 2010; Szalacha, 2003; Watson, Varjas, Meyers, & Graybill, 2010).

Students or faculty who wish to start a GSA on a school campus can find a great deal of helpful information online. Organizations such as the GSA Network (http://www.gsanetwork.org), ACLU (http://www.aclu.org), and GLSEN (http:///www.glsen.org) each provide guidelines for creating GSAs that include checklists, legal information, and samples of letters to principals or other administrators. These and other groups also provide ideas for discussion topics and activities.

GSA Advisor as a Resource

In many instances, the advisor of a GSA is a rich resource for the entire school community. First, many advisors are members of the LGBTQ community or have close connections to the LGBTQ community (although this is not a requirement or necessary qualification for being an advisor). As such, advisors are often resources for students, parents, and teachers wishing to connect with someone who has experience with issues such as coming out, having loved ones disclose LGBTQ identities, and self-advocacy. Many GSA advisors report being utilized as a resource for information about LGBTQ issues by students, teachers, parents, and even administrators (Graybill, Varjas, Meyers, & Watson, 2009). Advisors may function or be viewed as role models of successful LGBTQ adults in the school community. GSA advisors (LGBTQ and non-LGBTQ) also may serve as role models via their efforts in advocacy for LGBTQ students (Valenti, 2010). For example, GSA advisors may be the school employees who are most active in reviewing school policies for LGBTQ-inclusive language or may serve as role-models as they intervene on campus when they hear anti-gay slurs or remarks made by students. Chapter 14 of this volume provides more information on being an ally and advocate.

GSA as a Resource for Non-Members

A common function for GSAs is to be the on-campus organization that leads the school campus in LGBTQ awareness. Members frequently engage in various forms of on- and off-campus advocacy for LGBTQ persons. The impact of this advocacy is two-fold: the school and broader community contexts receive information about the LGBTQ community, and members receive personal benefits from engaging in advocacy (e.g., a feeling that they can make a difference to better society and a more positive view of the future; Mayberry, 2006; Savin-Williams, 2005).

Through activities such as *No Name Calling Week* or the *National Day of Silence* (http://www.glsen.org), GSA members serve as on-campus resources by educating peers and staff about the LGBTQ community and the impact of discrimination against this population. In combination with these events, GSA members may facilitate a number of activities designed to raise awareness and teach school members about the LGBTQ community, including:

- inviting a leader or member of the local Parents, Families, and Friends of Lesbians and Gays (PFLAG) chapter to speak to students and parents;
- inviting a leader or member of the local LGBTQ Community Center to discuss regional resources for LGBTQ youth;
- inviting an attorney knowledgeable in LGBTQ rights and advocacy to discuss a legal issue such as the Equal Protection clause of the Fourteenth Amendment;
- inviting a leader or member of the local LGBTQ Community Center to lead a discussion about his or her experiences when in school and recommendations for improving campus climates for LGBTQ youth; and

- hosting a screening of the film *Bullied: A Student, A School, and A Case that Made History* (Brummel, 2010) followed by a discussion of bullying and harassment occurring on campus.

Community Resources as Support for GSA Members

Just as school professionals and GSA advisors can assist in bringing in community resources as supports for GSA-sponsored activities, these resources can be utilized by members of the GSA. Guest speakers can present at GSA meetings or be presented as potential personal resources for GSA members via an introduction from the GSA advisor. Similarly, lists of community-based resources for LGBTQ youth and families compiled by other school staff should be made available to GSA members and advisors. GSA members may require the assistance of community-based resources and also may be approached by other students on campus who view GSA members as personal resources.

Community Resources

The number and type of community-based resources available to support LGBTQ youth, their parents, and students with parents who are LGBTQ varies widely by region. The resources listed here are nationally recognized agencies that include extensive web-based presences, many with site-based supports in multiple states. Many of these resources are appropriate for use by students, parents, and educators. School professionals are encouraged to explore the information and local supports provided by these agencies, as well as to search for regionally based supports that may be important in their communities.

CenterLink

CenterLink (http://www.lgbtcenters.org) is an organization that connects over 2000 LGBTQ Community Centers nationwide. The CenterLink website includes a search engine to help individuals identify the closest LGBTQ Community Center to their address. LGBTQ Community Centers are a diverse group of non-profit community-based programs, and many offer direct services such as counseling, support groups, and assistance for homeless youth. As there is much variation, school professionals are encouraged to explore the resources available at the community centers in their area.

Gay, Lesbian, and Straight Education Network (GLSEN)

GLSEN (http://www.glsen.org) is a national organization committed to creating safe and supportive educational experiences for LGBTQ youth. In addition to GLSEN's extensive research efforts, it is also dedicated to providing information to educators and students. GLSEN's website includes extensive information for students regarding establishing and leading GSAs, as well as activities to increase awareness of and safety for LGBTQ individuals on school campuses (e.g., *Day of Silence, No Name Calling Week*). Additionally, GLSEN's website provides links to other agencies that provide suicide crisis support, legal resources, and general support for LGBTQ youth.

Gay-Straight Alliance Network (GSA Network)

The GSA Network (http://www.gsanetwork.org) is an organization that assists students and school staff in planning for, creating, and maintaining GSAs. Its website provides a wealth of information for students and advisors seeking to form a GSA, as well as resources and ideas for planning events and activities. Through the website, GSA members and leaders can connect with those in similar positions at other schools to share ideas and network. The website provides links to several state-specific GSA Network sites as well.

American Civil Liberties Union (ACLU)

The ACLU (http://www.aclu.org) is an organization dedicated to promoting the civil liberties of all individuals. This organization provides information for LGBTQ students regarding their legal rights with regard to issues such as forming a GSA, protection from bullying and harassment, and attending events such as prom with the date of their choice. The ACLU supports legal actions that advocate for the rights of LGBTQ individuals, and the status of numerous court cases regarding LGBTQ issues is updated regularly on the website. The website includes a link for students to contact the ACLU if they need legal assistance due to discrimination or harassment.

Human Rights Campaign (HRC)

The HRC (http://www.hrc.org) is an organization dedicated to the achievement of equal rights for all individuals, and the website provides resources for students, parents, and educational professionals. The student/youth section hosts a weekly video newsletter (*Queerly Speaking*), and provides in-depth information regarding issues such as the coming out and disclosure process. The website also provides links to a variety of additional supports, such as suicide hotlines. The section for adults provides information regarding all aspects of life for LGBTQ individuals, including issues such as marriage, adoption, and issues of equality regarding employment and health care. HRC's main website includes links to several state and regional chapters.

The Trevor Project

The Trevor Project (http://www.thetrevorproject.org) aims to eliminate suicide in the LGBTQ population. The website provides general information for LGBTQ youth, as well as a social networking platform for youth to connect with others for social support. Additionally, the website refers youth to a 24-hour crisis call center (1-866-488-7386).

Parents, Families, and Friends of Lesbians and Gays (PFLAG)

PFLAG (http://www.pflag.org) is an organization that embraces all aspects of diversity and strives to support equal rights for all persons. PFLAG is primarily a community-based program, with local chapters in all 50 states. Although there is variation among local chapters in terms of types of resources, number of meetings, and so on, many

PFLAG chapters provide support groups for parents, youth, and siblings of LGBTQ youth, with the goal of providing a sense of community and a network of personal resources and supports for LGBTQ individuals and their families. PFLAG's web-based resources are predominately designed to support parents and provide information about being LGBTQ (including addressing myths and stereotypes), as well as information on how to advocate for equal rights and fair treatment for LGBTQ students. The website includes a search engine to assist in locating the nearest chapter.

Bisexual Resource Center (BRC)

The BRC (http://www.biresource.org) was founded in 1985 and is the oldest national support organization for bisexual individuals. Its goals include decreasing marginalization and increasing awareness of bisexuality in both the LGBTQ and heterosexual communities. BRC's website includes links to Boston-based bisexuality groups for all ages, as well as other regional and international bisexual groups and organizations. In addition, information is available in downloadable formats on topics including: facts about bisexuality, starting and running a support group for bisexual individuals, and being an ally. A page focused on youth includes general information about bisexuality (including an extensive review of terminology), information about coming out, and information for parents. In addition, BRC has an online store selling bi-supportive clothing, stickers, and books.

Children of Lesbians and Gays Everywhere (COLAGE)

COLAGE (http://www.colage.org) is an organization dedicated to achieving recognition of and ending discrimination against children with LGBTQ parents. There are regional chapters of COLAGE, which organize activities for children and are typically led and organized by adults who have LGBTQ parents. COLAGE also hosts a number of e-communities and closed e-groups (available only to children with LGBTQ parents) for youth based on age/grade level. The COLAGE website provides information for children and parents, with some information also available in Spanish. There is also an interactive media section, including several student-developed films and an art page that encourages children to draw their families.

Gay and Lesbian Alliance Against Defamation (GLAAD)

GLAAD (http://www.glaad.org) aims to promote social justice by bringing attention to media issues involving the LGBTQ community. GLAAD posts personal accounts, news events, and all forms of media, highlighting celebrations, contributions, and holding media outlets accountable for their portrayal of LGBTQ issues. Among other topics, GLADD has focus groups monitoring national news, sports, entertainment, and advertising media. GLAAD's website includes newsletters, blogs, and answers to frequently asked questions regarding a variety of topics related to advocacy and current events (e.g., Frequently Asked Questions about the Defense of Marriage Act). In addition to their website, GLADD communicates with subscribers with a variety of social media platforms, including Facebook, Twitter, and Instagram.

Immigration Equality

Immigration Equality (http://www.immigrationequality.org) is dedicated to the establishment of equal rights for immigrants who are LGBT or HIV-positive. The efforts of this organization are divided between two primary purposes: to provide free legal support to LGBT and HIV-positive immigrants and to lobby and advocate for legal reform to increase and protect the rights of this unique group. Its website provides a wealth of legal information on immigration law, asylum, and details for binational couples and families, transgender persons, and HIV-positive individuals. In addition, there is a law library containing articles, briefs, and links to other resources.

Lambda Legal

Lambda Legal (http://www.lambdalegal.org) was founded in 1973 as an organization committed to advancing the civil rights of LGBT persons of all ages. Lambda Legal selects and supports cases with outcomes impacting the protection of individuals' rights based on sexual orientation, gender identity, gender expression, or HIV status. Lambda Legal has offices in New York, Atlanta, Chicago, Dallas, and Los Angeles. The website contains general information about laws and cases, as well as an interactive page that provides detailed legal information for each state. In addition, Lambda Legal supports two online publications: *In Brief*, a monthly newsletter reviewing litigation and other efforts made by Lambda Legal and *Of Counsel*, a bimonthly newsletter providing reflections, information, and strategies for legal professionals working to advocate for the LGBT community.

National Gay and Lesbian Task Force (NGLTF)

The NGLTF (http://www.thetaskforce.org) is a grassroots organization that aims to create equality for the LGBT community. It supports broad campaigns to create and lobby for pro-LGBT legislation, as well as organizes opposition to anti-LGBT efforts. The issues addressed by this organization are broad and cover the lifespan of the LGBT community (e.g., youth and education, aging, parenting and adoption). The website includes reports on NGLTF initiatives, as well as fact sheets on key topics. The NGLTF hosts a national organizing and skill-building conference annually, which includes workshops, training sessions, and networking opportunities.

Straight Spouse Network (SSN)

SSN (http://www.straightspouse.org) is an organization that aims to provide support to adults whose current or former spouses or partners are LGBT. Available supports include online groups and traditional support groups in 30 States and Canada, Europe, and Australia. SSN's website includes answers to many questions that may be posed by straight spouses or family members. In addition, SSN lists recommended resource materials for adults and children.

Family Equality Council

The Family Equality Council (http://www.familyequality.org) works to celebrate and enhance the rights and recognition of families with parents who are LGBT. Information provided on the Family Equality Council's website includes resources for advocacy for diverse families, resources for parents who are LGBT (e.g., guides for starting parent groups, lists of books about LGBTQ families, and ideas for talking to children about their unique family), and *Opening Doors*, a publication aimed to help parents and educators create safe and welcoming educational environments for all children. The website also provides a searchable map to help families locate support groups in their area.

Gay and Lesbian National Help Center

The Gay and Lesbian National Help Center (http://www.glnh.org) provides phone and internet-based support services for LGBT persons of all ages. All services provided by the Gay and Lesbian National Help Center (including the Gay, Lesbian, Bisexual and Transgender National Hotline, 1-888-843-4564, and the GLBT National Youth Talkline, 1-800-246-7743) are confidential and free. The website also includes a list of answers to frequently asked questions for LGBTQ youth and adults.

National Center for Lesbian Rights

The National Center for Lesbian Rights (http://www.nclrights.org) was founded in 1979 and is a non-profit legal organization that provides community-based education on legal issues impacting the LGBT community, as well as free legal services for LGBT persons. The website provides detailed legal information about a variety of issues impacting the LGBT community (e.g., healthcare, immigration, transgender law), including issue overviews, position statements, news releases, and relevant case summaries.

Gay Asian Pacific Support Network (GASPN)

The GAPSN (http://www.gapsn.org) is a Los-Angeles based support network for gay and bisexual men of Asian and Pacific Islander (API) descent. It organizes networking events in the Los Angeles area. In addition, the GAPSN website includes answers to questions about being gay and bisexual and the coming out process.

National Black Justice Coalition (NBJC)

The NBJC (http://www.nbjc.org) advocates for the unique needs and challenges faced by African American and Black LGBT persons. The NBJC focuses on wide-reaching topics such as nondiscrimination in employment, marriage equality, military service, and safe and inclusive schools. The website provides in-depth information about these and related issues, as well as annual reports on NBJC efforts and progress toward equality.

Latino Equality Alliance (LEA)

LEA (http://www.latinoequalityalliance.com) is a coalition of organizations aimed at serving Latino/Latina LGBT individuals and communities. Based in California and providing information in both English and Spanish, LEA focuses on three advocacy areas: marriage equality, immigration reform, and family acceptance.

National Center for Transgender Equality

The National Center for Transgender Equality (http://www.transequality.org) focuses on eliminating violence and discrimination against transgender people by educating legislators and the public about transgender issues. The website includes information about suggested policy steps and links to related information for a broad variety of topics that impact the transgender community, including immigration, hate crimes, discrimination, and homelessness. In addition, the website provides resources for advocacy efforts, reports on the experiences of the transgender community, as well as detailed information regarding transgender rights.

Religious and Spiritual Organizations

Many religious and spiritual organizations are supportive of members of the LGBTQ community. Educators may use web-searches (using keywords such as church, LGBTQ, affirmative, etc.), local directories, and personal communications to discover which local organizations are welcoming of LGBTQ individuals. The types of supports available vary widely, with some churches simply acknowledging that LGBTQ persons are welcome members of their community and others having designated LGBTQ youth pastors and special support groups for LGBTQ persons and families. The following are some Internet sites related to specific religions:

- www.affirmation.org (Mormon)
- www.umaffirm.org (United Methodist)
- www.wabaptists.org (Baptist)
- www.rainbowbaptists.org (Baptist)
- www.dignityusa.org (Catholic)
- www.emergence-international.org (Christian Scientist)
- www.ecwr.org (Evangelical Christian)
- www.gaybuddhist.org (Buddhist)
- www.integrityusa.org (Episcopalian)
- www.lcna.org (Lutheran)
- www.mlp.org (Presbyterian)
- www.sdakinship.org (Seventh-Day Adventist)
- www.ucccoalition.org (United Church of Christ)
- www.glbtjews.org (Jewish).

Conclusion

School professionals are experts on many topics and are capable of providing a wide array of services. However, it is impossible for any given practitioner to be able to meet every need of every student and family at his or her school. Fortunately, our local and online communities offer a wealth of expertise and service options to which school practitioners can refer clients. Although outside agencies may provide support services with little or no involvement on the part of the school professional, the process of identifying appropriate resources and matching students and families with the agencies that are best able to meet their needs is a task that requires time and attention. In the end, time spent searching for appropriate agencies, updating referral lists, making contact with agencies to gather information about their services and requirements, and guiding students and families through the contact process with outside agencies is time well spent!

References

Adelman, H., & Taylor, L. (2006). *The implementation guide to student learning supports in the classroom and schoolwide: New directions for addressing barriers to learning.* Thousand Oaks, CA: Corwin Press.

Brummel, B. (Producer), Rhode, J. (Director), & Newfield, J. (Director). (2010). *Bullied: A student, a school, and a case that made history* [Motion Picture]. United States: Teaching Tolerance.

Cooper-Nicols, M., & Bowleg, L. (2010). "My voice is being heard": Exploring the experiences of gay, lesbian, and bisexual youth in schools. In C. Bertram, M. Crowley, & S. Massey (Eds.), *Beyond progress and marginalization: LGBTQ youth in educational contexts* (pp. 15–51). New York, NY: Peter Lang Publishing, Inc.

Graybill, E., Varjas, K., Meyers, J., & Watson, L. (2009). Content-specific strategies to advocate for lesbian, gay, bisexual, and transgender youth: An exploratory study. *School Psychology Review, 38*(4), 570–584. Retrieved from http://www.nasponline.org/publications/spr/sprissues.aspx

Macintosh, L., & Bryson, M. (2008). Youth, MySpace, and the interstitial spaces of becoming and belonging. *Journal of LGBT Youth, 5*(1), 133–142. doi:10.1300/J524v05n01_11

Mayberry, M. (2006). The story of a Salt Lake City Gay-Straight Alliance: Identity work and LGBT youth. *Journal of Gay & Lesbian Issues in Education, 4*(1), 13–31. doi:10.1300/J367v04n01_03

Savin-Williams, R. (2005). *The new gay teenager.* Cambridge, MA: Harvard University Press.

Sheridan, S. M., Napolitano, S., & Swearer, S. M. (2008). Best practices in school–community partnerships. In A. Thomas & J. Grimes (Eds.), *Best practices in school psychology – V* (pp. 321–336). Bethesda, MD: National Association of School Psychologists.

Sparks, W., Daniels, J., & Johnson, E. (2003). Relationship of referral source, race, and wait time on preintake attrition. *Professional Psychology: Research and Practice, 34*(5), 514–518.

Szalacha, L. (2003). Safer sexual diversity climates: Lessons learned from an evaluation of Massachusetts safe schools program for gay and lesbian students. *American Journal of Education, 110*, 58–88. Retrieved from http://www.jstor.org/action/showPublication?journal Code=amerjeduc

Valenti, M. (2010). The roles of Gay-Straight Alliance (GSA) advisors in public high schools. In C. Bertram, M. Crowley & S. Massey (Eds.), *Beyond progress and marginalization: LGBTQ youth in educational contexts* (pp. 52–88). New York, NY: Peter Lang Publishing, Inc.

Watson, L., Varjas, K., Meyers, J., & Graybill, E. (2010). Gay-Straight Alliance advisors: Negotiating multiple ecological systems when advocating for LGBTQ youth. *Journal of LGBT Youth, 7*(2), 100–128. doi:10.1080/19361651003799700

Index

hate crimes 17–18
Hawaii 14–15, 61
Hazelwood v. Kuhlmeier (1988) 101
health 42, 48, 156, 216, 222; *see also* mental
    health problems
healthcare 222; transgender and intersex
    individuals 66
Henkle v. Gregory (2001) 95, 101–2
heteronormative assumptions 195–6,
    197–8
heterosexism 24, 37, 44, 45, 61, 74, 76, 156,
    195, 235, 238, 240; internalized 195
heterosexual orientation 7, 58, 198–199
heterosexual privilege 73–4, 76, 195, 198
Hill v. National Collegiate Athletic Association
    (1994) 113
Hindu beliefs 80
Hispanic youth *see* Latino(a)/Hispanic youth
historical influences 11–13
HIV/AIDS 33, 78, 162, 212, 217, 252
homelessness 42, 46, 80, 129, 223
homophobia 24, 37, 47, 141, 142, 156, 161,
    176, 230, 235, 238, 240; as ambiguous term
    195; internalized 31, 36, 44, 46; origins of
    term 12–13; reduction workshops (Speakers
    Bureau) 21; rural communities 81
homosexuality: criminalization of 11, 12;
    depathologization of 13; divergent views of
    11–12; as a term 7, 11
housing 17
Human Rights Campaign (HRC) 17, 182–3,
    250
Human Rights Watch 21–2

identity 73; commitment to 30; conflict of
    29–30; crisis/exploration 30, 34–5, 57;
    foreclosure 30; gender 6, 7, 16, 17, 32–3, 57,
    58, 59, 67; group 10–11; in-group 10;
    moratorium 30; out-group 10; racial 33;
    social 10, 74
identity-achievement 30
identity development 29–40, 128; ego 29–30;
    ethnic 33, 34; multiple 33–4, 74–87, 128,
    222; sexual orientation 30–2 (acceptance
    35–6; disclosure *see* disclosure; exploration
    30, 34–5, 131); stage theory of 29–30;
    transgender 32–3
identity diffusion 30
Illinois Safe Schools Alliance (ISSA) 134,
    149–50

Immigration Equality 252
in-group identity 10
*In My Shoes: Stories of Youth with LGBT
    Parents* (documentary) 180
inclusiveness 6, 23, 157–8, 165–70, 236, 237
indigenous peoples 61, 78–9
individual domain, risks and protections 43,
    44–5
Ingraham v. Wright (1977) 93
Institute for Sexual Science (Berlin) 11
inter-spirit identity 61
interactive model 74
internet 68, 82, 103, 108, 239, 243, 245;
    and sexual orientation development
    34–5, 37
interracial marriage 14
intersectionality model 74–5
intersex individuals 6, 57, 58, 63–5; advocacy
    strategies 66–8, 69; competencies for
    working with 64–5; diagnosis and treatment
    64; empowerment and resilience 65–6;
    family environment 65–6; feminist
    perspective 60; healthcare access 66;
    multicultural perspective 60; social justice
    perspective 60–1, 66–8, 69; social support
    66; statistics 59
Intersex Initiative 59
Intersex Society of America 64
intervention/intervention programs 5, 6, 37–8,
    42, 50–2, 144–51, 161, 178–80; *see also*
    Family Acceptance Project
Islamic sects 79
It Gets Better Campaign 201, 202
*It's Elementary: Talking About Gay Issues in
    School* (documentary) 149, 179–80

J.C. v. Beverly Hills Unified School District
    (2010) 103
J.S. v. Bethlehem Area School District (2002)
    103
Jacksonville Area Sexual Minority Youth
    Network (JASMYN) 21
Jenny Lives with Eric and Martin 184
Jewish sects 79
Johns Committee 18–19
Just the Facts Coalition 169, 193

Keyishian v. Board of Regents (1967) 100
King v. State (2000) 113
knowledge construction 160

264   *Index*

social identity 10, 74
social isolation 44, 141, 142
social justice perspective 126, 132, 176, 233;
    transgender and intersex individuals 60–1,
    66–8, 69
social networking 68
social support 48–50, 81, 82, 143–4, 191, 216;
    transgender and intersex individuals 66
social trends 13–18
social work 124
Society for Adolescent Medicine 164
socioeconomic status 80
Speakers Bureau 21
spiritual organizations 79, 80, 254; *see also*
    churches
sports activities 99, 238–39
state anti-discrimination protections 92–9
State Education Agency 95
statistics, transgender and intersex 59
Steps to Respect: A Bullying Prevention Program
    (STR) 145
stereotyping 10, 36, 130, 166, 233
Sterling v. Borough of Minersville (2000) 113,
    114
stigmatization 44, 74, 76, 79, 80, 163
Stonewall Rebellion 12
Straight Spouse Network (SSN) 252
*Straightlaced—How Gender's Got Us All Tied
    Up* (film) 149
Straights & Gays for Equality v. Osseo Area Sch.
    (2006) 112
stress 44
stress resistance 45
student groups 110–12, 162, 184–5, 218, 222,
    237; *see also* Gay-Straight Alliances (GSAs)
Style, E. 157, 158
substance use/abuse 44–5, 46, 48, 49, 79, 129,
    143, 190–1, 200, 212, 216; *see also* alcohol
    use; drug use
"substantial disruption" test 101, 102
suicidality 37, 44, 46, 48, 49, 79, 129, 143, 190,
    193–4, 202, 212, 216, 217, 223, 230; risk
    assessment 201–2
Suicide Prevention Resource Center (SPRC)
    201, 223
Swedish National Council for Crime
    Prevention 146
Syracuse University, School of Education 126,
    135

T.L.S. v. Montana Advocacy Program (2006)
    113
teachers 5, 18–20; as allies and advocates 6,
    131–2, 230–42; coming out 106–7; First
    Amendment rights 105–7; gender/sexuality
    exploration 57; homophobic comments
    176; professional development 126, 131–2;
    training 57, 123, 126, 127, 128, 176–80
    (pre-service 6, 123, 125–6, 128)
teaching assistants 5
Tehachapi Unified School District 95
terminology 6–8, 127–8, 234
Thailand 61
Theno v. Tonganoxie Unified (2005) 94, 96
Thomas v. Board of Education (1979) 103
*Tinker v. Des Moines Independent School
    District* (1969) 18, 101, 103
Title IX mandates 92, 94, 95, 97
training: online 136; parent-centered 181;
    pre-service 6, 123, 125–6, 168; school
    professionals 57, 123–39, 167–8, 176–80,
    210, 221; student-centered 180–1
transgender individuals 6, 17, 22, 57, 75, 162,
    200, 201; advocacy strategies 66–8, 69;
    competencies for working with 63;
    counseling 63; and culture 61; and
    curriculum 159, 163–4, 165–6; definitions 7,
    58; diagnosis and treatment of 62;
    empowerment and resilience 65–6;
    feminist perspective 60; healthcare access
    66; in history 61; identity development
    32–3; legal/ethical standards regarding
    97–9; mental health problems 191;
    multicultural perspective 60; social justice
    perspective 60–1, 66–8, 69; social support
    66; Standards of Care 63; statistics 59;
    substance abuse 44–5; victimization of
    141, 142
Transgender Youth Family Allies 71
transphobia 12, 44, 156, 161, 230,
    238, 240
Trevor Project 201, 250
triple jeopardy 74
truancy 42, 44, 50, 143, 190
two-spiritedness 61, 79

*U.S. Dep't of Justice v. Reporters Comm. for
    Freedom of the Press* (1989) 113
universities 223
urban density 81–2

Made in the USA
Coppell, TX
23 April 2021

54256746R00154